Censorship and Civic Order in Reformation Germany, 1517–1648

For my parents,
Arlene Oblak Creasman
and
Joseph F. Creasman, Jr.

Censorship and Civic Order in Reformation Germany, 1517–1648

'Printed Poison & Evil Talk'

ALLYSON F. CREASMAN
Carnegie Mellon University, USA

ASHGATE

© Allyson F. Creasman 2012

All rights reserved. No part of this publication may be reproduced, stored in a retrieval system or transmitted in any form or by any means, electronic, mechanical, photocopying, recording or otherwise without the prior permission of the publisher.

Allyson F. Creasman has asserted her moral right under the Copyright, Designs and Patents Act, 1988, to be identified as the author of this work.

Published by
Ashgate Publishing Limited
Wey Court East
Union Road
Farnham
Surrey, GU9 7PT
England

Ashgate Publishing Company
Suite 420
101 Cherry Street
Burlington
VT 05401-4405
USA

www.ashgate.com

British Library Cataloguing in Publication Data
Creasman, Allyson F.
  Censorship and civic order in Reformation Germany, 1517-1648 : 'printed poison & evil talk'. -- (St Andrews studies in Reformation history)
  1. Reformation--Germany. 2. Religious literature--Censorship--Germany--History--16th century. 3. Religious literature--Censorship--Germany--History--17th century. 4. Freedom of information--Germany--History--16th century. 5. Freedom of information--Germany--History--17th century. 6. Germany--Church history--16th century. 7. Germany--Church history--17th century.
  I. Title II. Series
  323.4'4'0943'09031-dc23

Library of Congress Cataloging-in-Publication Data
Creasman, Allyson F.
  Censorship and civic order in Reformation Germany, 1517-1648 : 'printed poison & evil talk' / Allyson F. Creasman.
     pages cm. -- (St. Andrews studies in Reformation history)
  Includes bibliographical references and index.
  ISBN 978-1-4094-1001-0
  1. Censorship--Germany--History--16th century. 2. Censorship--Germany--History--17th century. 3. Reformation--Germany. I. Title.

Z658.G3C74 2012
363.31--dc23

2012006244

ISBN 9781409410010 (hbk)
ISBN 9781409451020 (ebk)

Printed and bound in Great Britain by the MPG Books Group, UK

Contents

List of Illustrations		vii
Acknowledgments		ix
List of Abbreviations		xi
Introduction		1
1	"Words, Works, or Writings:" Communication and the Law of Censorship	23
2	Policing the Word: Censorship and Reformation	63
3	Keeping the Peace: Censorship and Confessional Relations under the Peace of Augsburg	109
4	"A Fire Started:" Sedition, Censorship, and the Calendar Conflict	147
5	"The Times, They are so Troubled:" Censorship in Wartime, 1618–1648	185
Conclusion		227
Bibliography		231
Index		275

List of Illustrations

1.1 "The Pope Calls on His Protectors." SStBA, Rar 78, [Martin Schrot], *Von der Erschrocklichen Zurstörung unnd Niderlag deß gantzen Bapstumbs...* ([Augsburg: David Danecker, 1558]), fol. 9. © Staats- und Stadtbibliothek Augsburg. Used by permission.   39

3.1 Christof Lecherer's drawing of Pastor Simon Haderdey (StAA, Strafamt Urgichten, Christof Lecherer, 3–14 Feb. 1605). © Stadtarchiv Augsburg. Used by permission.   135

4.1 Broadsheet depicting the rescue of Georg Müller and ensuing riot in Augsburg, April 1584 (SStBA, Graphik 22/12, *Wahrhaffte fürstellung der begebenheit so sich A 1584 d. 25 Mai mit Herrn D. Georg Müller gewesenen Pfarrer beÿ St. Anna, auch Superintendens und Rector des Evangelische Collegii zugetragen...*[np: np, nd]). © Staats-und Stadt Bibliothek Augsburg. Used by permission.   156

5.1 Christof Glatz's song, *A Sad Song About the Abolished Ministry in Augsburg*, showing his marginal notes and the Latin words written by "Johann." (StAA, Strafamt Urgichten, Christof Glatz, 7–11 March 1630). © Stadtarchiv Augsburg. Used by permission.   207

Acknowledgments

In the writing of this book, I have benefitted from the help and generosity of a great many people. Above all, I am grateful to H. C. Erik Midelfort, my doctoral advisor at the University of Virginia, who guided me in this project from its earliest stages. I am also indebted to Anne J. Schutte and Duane Osheim for their invaluable comments, critiques, and questions at the outset of this project. While in Augsburg, I was tremendously fortunate to find myself working among an extremely supportive circle of scholars. For their encouragement, advice, and ready friendship, I am deeply grateful to Duane Corpis, Susanne Eser, Georg Feuerer, Alexander Fisher, Helmut Graser, Emily and Austin Gray, Mitch Hammond, Michele Zelinsky Hanson, Bridget Heal, Carl Hoffman, Christine Johnson, Hans-Jörg Künast, Benedikt Mauer, Wolfgang Mayer, Beth Plummer, Kathy Stuart, Ann Tlusty, and Helmut Zäh. I am particularly indebted to Hans-Jörg Künast who, in addition to being a friend and neighbor, shared with me his (seemingly limitless) knowledge of all things related to printing in early modern Augsburg. My fellow Virginian, Mitch Hammond, helped me learn how to read early modern script, and my fellow laborers in the *Urgichten*, Ann Tlusty, Michele Zelinsky Hanson, and Kathy Stuart, schooled me in the workings of the "criminal element" in early modern Germany.

The research for this study would not have been possible without the financial support of the German-American Fulbright Commission. I am also grateful for support from the University of Virginia Society of Fellows, Davidson College, Sewanee: The University of the South, and Carnegie Mellon University. For their assistance with my research, I wish to express my thanks to the staff at the Augsburg Staats- und Stadtbibliothek and the Augsburg Stadtarchiv, the Nürnberg Staatsarchiv, the Stadtarchiv Ulm, the Frankfurt Institut für Stadtgeschichte, the Bayerisches Hauptstaatsarchiv, the British Library, and the Herzog August Bibliothek in Wölfenbüttel. I owe special thanks to Alois Senser at the Augsburg Stadtarchiv for his help with my research. At the Universität Augsburg, I wish to thank Professors Johannes Burkhardt and Rolf Kießling for assisting with my project.

At Ashgate, I owe particular thanks to Andrew Pettegree, series editor of the St Andrews Studies in Reformation History, for his support of my project. I also wish to thank the readers and editors who helped turn this into a better book.

I am deeply indebted to the many friends I made in Germany for their support during my research. Above all, I wish to thank Gerburg and Lothar Wolf, who essentially adopted me in Augsburg. They took me in, improved my German, showed me around, took care of me when I was in the hospital, kept me entertained, and saw to it that I ate very well. Their help to me has been invaluable, and I cannot express my thanks enough. For their friendship and support in Germany, I am also deeply grateful to Barbara Hunter and her family, Alena Schäfer, and Ursula Hell. I also owe special thanks to the Augsburg Fulbright representatives, Eleanor and Joachim Hermann, and to their son David, for all their help during my stay there.

For their friendship, encouragement, and good humor through the early stages of this project, I thank my friends and colleagues at Virginia, particularly Taylor Fain, Robert Ingram, Krister Johnson, Susan Maxwell, James Owens, and Scott Taylor. I also owe thanks to Eric and Tania Mings, Madeline Gutierrez, Dan Lewbel, and Mary Doty Solik for their help stateside while I was abroad. At Carnegie Mellon, I'm grateful to my colleagues Kate Lynch, Donna Harsch, and Wendy Goldman for their help and advice on turning this into a book. Lisa Tetrault was great company as we were stuck in the library revising our respective manuscripts on many a summer's day.

Portions of this book have been published previously in 'Side-Stepping the Censor: the Clandestine Trade in Prohibited Texts in Early Modern Augsburg,' in *Shell Games: Studies in Scams, Frauds and Deceits (1300–1650)*, eds Mark Crane, Richard Raiswell, and Margaret Reeves (Toronto: Centre for Reformation and Renaissance Studies, 2004), 211–37, and in 'Lies as Truth: Policing Print and Oral Culture in the Early Modern City,' in *Ideas and Cultural Margins in Early Modern Germany*, eds Marjorie E. Plummer and Robin Barnes (Aldershot: Ashgate, 2009). I am grateful to those presses for their kind permission to re-publish this material.

List of Abbreviations

BHStA	Bayerisches Hauptstaatsarchiv
BL	British Library
BSB	Bayerische Staatsbibliothek
FaM ISG	Frankfurt am Main Institut für Stadtgeschichte
Freytag	*Flugschriften-Sammlung Gustav Freytag*, ed. Paul Hohenemser. Hildesheim: Georg Olms Verlagsbuchhandlung, 1966. With item number.
HAAB	Herzogin Anna Amalia Bibliothek Weimar
HAB	Herzog August Bibliothek Wolfenbüttel
LKAN	Landeskirchliches Archiv Nürnberg
QNR	*Quellen zur Nürnberger Reformationsgeschichte von der Duldung liturgischer Änderungen bis zur Ausübung des Kirchenregisments durch den Rat (Juni 1524–Juni 1525)*, ed. Gerhard Pfeiffer (Nuremberg: Selbstverlag des Vereins für bayerische Kirchengeschichte, 1968)
RV	*Ratsverlass*
SStBA	Staats- und Stadtbibliothek Augsburg
StAA	Stadtarchiv Augsburg
StAN	Staatsarchiv Nürnberg
StAU	Stadtarchiv Ulm
StBB	Staatsbibliothek Berlin
StBU	Stadtbibliothek Ulm
Urg.	*Urgicht*

Introduction

In the summer of 1563, the Lutheran pastor of Augsburg's Holy Cross church received an anonymous note. "Dear Sir," it began, "you have long wanted to know where Casper Schwenckfeld's books are being printed; now I will tell you."[1] The informant revealed that a tailor named Sixt Schilling and a furrier's apprentice named Jorg distributed Schwenckfeld's books all over town. He asked the pastor to alert the *Bürgermeister*, for "I believe that print should be for the learned, and not for tailors and furriers."[2] Schilling lived in a stone house by the Red Gate; if the *Bürgermeister* sent for him, the informant said, he would likely reveal all.

Indeed he did. Schilling told the *Bürgermeister* that a man from Trier had sent him a manuscript, purportedly by Schwenckfeld, and requested that he engage local printer Philip Ulhart to print it. He was then to ship the tracts to Frankfurt.[3] Ulhart admitted he printed the texts; he also confessed that he had deliberately withheld them from Augsburg's censors. Schilling had warned him "to keep the matter a great secret, so that the books wouldn't come to light."[4] Ulhart claimed he had no real alternative, as he hadn't had any business in the past six months and had nothing else to live on.[5]

Schilling told the *Bürgermeister* that he had first learned about Schwenckfeld from a fellow tailor, Bernhart Unsinn. Ten years previously, Augsburg magistrates had jailed Unsinn on suspicion that he was organizing secret conventicles to teach and practice Schwenckfeldian "errors." Unsinn had insisted that this was no "sect," only loosely knit reading circles which exchanged Schwenckfeld's books.[6] Unsinn himself loaned out "all kinds of books" by Schwenckfeld; he also borrowed books from contacts in other cities.[7]

---

[1] Note, filed in StAA, Strafamt, Urg. Sixt Schilling, 11–13 Aug. 1563.
[2] Ibid.
[3] StAA, Strafamt, Urg. Sixt Schilling, 11 Aug. 1563
[4] Note, filed in ibid.
[5] StAA, Strafamt, Urg. Philip Ulhart, 11 Aug. 1563.
[6] StAA., Literalian, 'Schwenkfeldiana & Reformations-acten,' Urg. Bernhart Unsinn, 19 Sept. 1553.
[7] Ibid., Urg. 26 Sept. 1553.

Unsinn and his friend, Leonhart Hieber, told the magistrates of an extensive circle of readers reaching into the highest levels of Augsburg society. Hieber alone named more than 50 people to whom he had either given or sold Schwenckfeld's books. In addition to humble tradesmen like themselves, the list of names included members of some of the most illustrious patrician families in the city; especially prominent in the group were several patrician widows, one of whom ferried letters to Schwenckfeld through a contact in Ulm.[8]

Both men had insisted that their books were neither objectionable nor illegal. Hieber declared, "these books have had a free pass for more than 25 years and have never been prohibited by any Imperial Diet, unlike so many other two-bit scandal sheets on religious matters."[9] Unsinn agreed; as far as he knew, their books had never been prohibited by anyone.[10] The Augsburg city council, however, did not agree, and ordered their books confiscated and burned. It also ordered local pastors to try to persuade the men to recant their "errors."[11] Hieber recanted and was released; Unsinn refused, and was banished.[12]

Hieber and Unsinn were entirely correct that Schwenckfeld's books had never been expressly banned by either imperial or local law.[13] The city council nonetheless prosecuted both of them for attacking the local clergy in "abusive, threatening writings."[14] Essentially, the Augsburg magistrates were interpreting long-standing imperial and local prohibitions of *Schmähschriften*, or libels, to include works of religious controversy. These proscriptions usually applied to defamatory attacks targeting specific individuals or groups.[15] Here, however, Augsburg officials extended them

---

[8] StAA, Literalian, 'Schwenkfeldiana & Reformations-acten,' Urg. Leonhart Hieber, 19 Sept. 1553. On Schwenckfeld's contacts in Augsburg, see K. Wolfhart, 'Casper Schwenckfeld und Bonifacius Wolfhart in Augsburg,' *Beiträge zur bayerischen Kirchengeschichte* 7 (1901): pp. 145–61.

[9] StAA, Literalian, 'Schwenckfeldiana & Reformation-acten,' Urg. Leonhart Hieber, 19 Sept. 1553.

[10] Ibid., Urg. Bernhart. Unsinn, 26 Sept. 1553.

[11] StAA, Ratsbuch, Nr. 27, 1553, Part II, fol. 17r.

[12] StAA, Strafbuch Nr. 96.1, 1543–1553, fol. 64v.

[13] By the 1560s, imperial law had long outlawed Anabaptists and their writings; Schwenckfeld, however, was no Anabaptist. StAA, Wiedertäufer und Religionsacten, 23 April 1529. On his theology, see David C. Steinmetz, *Reformers in the Wings: From Geiler von Kayserberg to Theodore Beza*, 2nd ed. (Oxford: Oxford University Press, 2001) pp. 131–7; on his conflicts with Anabaptists, see George Huntston Williams, *The Radical Reformation*, 3rd ed. (Kirksville, MO: Truman State University Press, 2000) pp. 681–721; 1213–18; 1270–73.

[14] StAA, Strafbuch, Nr. 96.1. 1543–1553, fol, 64v.

[15] See Günther Schmidt, *Libelli Famosi. Zur Bedeutung der Schmähschriften, Scheltbriefe, Schandgemälde und Pasquille in der deutschen Rechtsgeschichte* (Diss.,

to include generalized critiques of an entire theology. What Unsinn and Hieber discovered was that the law of censorship was a slippery thing—although it never explicitly banned their books, that itself offered them no safe harbor. The vagueness of the law gave magistrates the license to apply it as they deemed appropriate in any given case. Its meaning and application easily shifted with the council's religious and political priorities.

What happened to Sixt Schilling, Philip Ulhart, and Bernhardt Unsinn highlights how ideas flowed through early modern communities—and how magistrates tried to police them. Like the pastor's anonymous informant, civic and religious authorities believed that "print should be for the learned," and they feared its effects upon the common man. The simple folk, they reasoned, could not be trusted to discern truth from error, making it imperative that their leaders police what the printers placed before them. The fact was, however, that the written culture of authors and printers like Schwenckfeld and Ulhart was already deeply enmeshed in the oral culture of the streets. While books like Schwenckfeld's circulated through far-flung interregional networks of authors, printers, and distributors, they were dissected through local word of mouth. In the workshops and streets, ordinary folk like Schilling and his friends talked together, read together, and exchanged books and opinions. Neighbors gossiped about each other and, sometimes—as Schilling learned—they informed on each other. As ideas cycled through print and the "common talk," magistrates erected an elaborate complex of laws seeking to control their spread and limit their impact. These controls were sometimes frustrated by the economic pressures driving the book trade and the political and religious instability of the early modern era.

This book examines these themes, focusing on censorship in the imperial cities of the German southwest during the Empire's tumultuous "long Reformation," from the first impulses toward religious reform in the 1520s through the end of the Thirty Years' War. It aims to reassess the Reformation's spread by examining how censorship impacted public understanding of reform. It reveals the networks through which ideas circulated and examines how legal controls and social pressures combined to shape religious consciousness and precipitate change. Drawing primarily on criminal court records, trial transcripts, and journals of the period, it reveals the lively mix of rumor, gossip, cheap print, and popular song circulating in the city streets, and in the process, explores how ordinary Germans appropriated and adapted the printed message to their own purposes. In analyzing how print and oral culture intersected to fuel popular protest and frustrate official control, the book highlights the limits of both the reformers' influence and the magistrates' authority. In this, it challenges our traditional understandings of the urban Reformation.

Universität Köln, 1985).

"A Media Event?"—Communication and Reformation

In the first decades of the sixteenth century, Europe was swept by unprecedented religious change. Within the span of a single generation, it seemed, the Reformation reordered societies, divided communities, and precipitated more than a century of religious conflict. In accounting for these developments, historians have long assigned central importance to the printing press—"no printing, no Reformation," as Bernd Moeller once remarked.[16] Indeed, in the Holy Roman Empire, as elsewhere in Europe, the coming of the Reformation witnessed an unprecedented flood of books, pamphlets, and news-sheets broadcasting the message of reform. Even in a still largely unlettered age, reformers harnessed the power of print to transmit their message though simple images and texts, as well as through songs and sermons. But while Reformation Europe was awash in prints and pamphlets, the disorder they generated also prompted authorities at every level of society to establish mechanisms to suppress them.

The free and imperial cities of southwestern Germany were among the most prominent centers of the Reformation movement and were of central importance to the European book trade. The Reformation found some its earliest and most vocal support in these communities, and they were among the first in the Empire to confront the problems of managing religious dissent and institutionalizing reform. The imperial cities of Upper Germany were also the hubs of a major regional network for the circulation of books and ideas. This book traces the distribution of prohibited texts and ideas across these networks, exploring how information flowed between these communities and, ultimately, to the rest of the Holy Roman Empire. The regional focus of this study also aims to shed light on the complex jurisdictional battles that often frustrated the enforcement of law across the Empire. By examining the political and religious calculations driving censorship in this area, the book addresses, in particular, how religiously mixed areas of the Empire, such as Augsburg, compared in their regulatory policies with their more uniformly Protestant or Catholic neighbors, such as the Lutheran city of Nuremberg or the Catholic duchy of Bavaria. Such comparisons will reveal the extent to which censorship influenced the spread of reform among the Protestant and Catholic estates of the Empire, and how religious politics impacted regional conflicts over censorship and the book trade.

---

[16] Bernd Moeller, 'Stadt und Buch: Bemerkungen zur Struktur der Reformatorischen Bewegung in Deutschland,' in *The Urban Classes, the Nobility, and the Reformation: Studies on the Social History of the Reformation in England and Germany*, ed. Wolfgang J. Mommsen (Stuttgart: Klett-Cotta, 1979) p. 30.

Each of the communities examined here erected a formal censorship apparatus to oversee the local book trade, but city magistrates were also careful to control troublesome ideas in whatever form they arose, be it in print, preaching, speech, song, or symbol. For even in Germany's greatest imperial cities, the majority could not read.[17] They lived in a predominantly oral and visual culture, albeit one that increasingly felt the influence of the printed word. Indeed, as Adam Fox has observed, it would be false to posit a sharp divide between print and oral culture in this era.[18] Rather, as we will see, the printed word readily filtered into the talk on the streets, and local gossip worked its way into print.

In order to fully understand censorship's role in early modern societies, we must recognize that communication in the era occurred largely outside the four corners of the printed page. While this point would seem to be obvious, it has generally not been addressed in most historical studies of censorship to date. Most historians examining "censorship" in the pre-modern era have focused exclusively on the censorship of print; indeed, those examining the control of oral and symbolic communication often do not even recognize the term "censorship" in that context.[19] But books are not censored—*ideas* are censored, and in a largely illiterate society, ideas could not be communicated by print alone.[20] Early modern magistrates fully

---

[17] Mark U. Edwards, *Printing, Propaganda, and Martin Luther* (Berkeley: University of California Press, 1994) pp. 37–8; Hans-Jörg Künast, *'Getruckt zu Augspurg:' Buchdruck und Buchhandel in Augsburg zwischen 1468 und 1555* (Tübingen: Max Niemeyer Verlag, 1997) pp. 11–13.

[18] Adam Fox, *Oral and Literate Culture in England, 1500–1700* (Oxford: Oxford University Press, 2000) pp. 5–50.

[19] One important exception is Dagmar Freist's 1997 study on popular opinion in mid-seventeenth-century London, *Governed by Opinion: Politics, Religion and the Dynamics of Communication in Stuart London, 1637–1645*. (London: Tauris Academic Studies, 1997). On policing oral culture, see Franciska Loetz, *Mit Gott handeln. Von den Zürcher Gotteslästerern der Frühen Neuzeit zu einer Kulturgeschichte des Religiösen* (Göttingen: Vandenhoeck & Ruprecht, 2002); Elizabeth Horodowich, *Language and Statecraft in Early Modern Venice* (Cambridge: Cambridge University Press, 2008); David Cressy, *Dangerous Talk: Scandalous, Seditious, and Treasonable Speech in Pre-Modern England* (Oxford: Oxford University Press, 2010); Arlette Farge, *Subversive Words: Public Opinion in Eighteenth-Century France*, trans. Rosemary Morris (University Park: The Pennsylvania State University Press, 1994). On the censorship of song, see Robert Darnton, *Poetry and the Police: Communication Networks in Eighteenth-Century Paris* (Cambridge, MA: Belknap Presss, 2010); Alexander J. Fisher, *Music and Religious Identity in Counter-Reformation Augsburg* (Aldershot: Ashgate, 2004) pp. 24–70. On the censorship of images, see Christiane Andersson, 'The Censorship of Images in Nuremberg, 1521–1527: Art and Politics in the Reformation,' in *Dürer and his Culture*, eds Dagmar Eichberger and Charles Zika (Cambridge: Cambridge University Press, 1998).

[20] For a cogent analysis of the media's role in the European Reformation, see Andrew Pettegree, *Reformation and the Culture of Persuasion* (Cambridge: Cambridge University Press, 2005).

understood this fact and sought to control not only the book trade, but all means of conveying unwanted messages. It is this broader understanding of "censorship" that prevails throughout this book.

In examining censorship in these major centers of the German Reformation, this study seeks to engage two historiographical models that have, to date, seldom intersected. Historians seeking to understand the unprecedented spread of Reformation ideas have long focused on the role of print in transmitting the reformers' message among the "common man." The "social disciplining" and "confessionalization" models, however, have highlighted the role of governmental and social institutions in defining and enforcing religious identity. Despite the merits of these approaches, there remains a gap between the assumption that change occurred in response to the ideas that people encountered, and the reality that states were urgently trying to control what people knew. This book seeks to bridge this divide, demonstrating both how governments used censorship to impede or channel the flow of ideas, and how the governed steered it to their purposes. It looks beyond the magistrates' decrees to assess the practical consequences of censorship in daily life, revealing both the effective limits of official control and the influence of public opinion on official policy.

Communication has long been considered central to an understanding of the religious changes that swept Europe in the early sixteenth century, and a number of important studies have explored the role of print in the spread of the Reformation message.[21] Much of this work has focused on the production and reception of Reformation texts and images. While undeniably important, the study of book production has tended to devote comparably little attention to the means by which texts found their way into the hands of their readers. Indeed, we have tended to assume that texts and ideas enjoyed a relatively free circulation during the period. This premise therefore presupposes that patterns of book production may serve as largely transparent measures of interest and demand, allowing us to speculate confidently about the relative "appeal" of various ideas as

---

[21] See, for example, Hans-Joachim Köhler, ed. *Flugschriften als Massenmedium der Reformationszeit* (Stuttgart: Klett-Cotta, 1981); Edwards, *Printing, Propaganda*; Miriam Usher Chrisman, *Conflicting Visions of Reform: German Lay Propaganda Pamphlets, 1519–1530* (Atlantic Highlands, New Jersey: Humanities Press, 1996); Josef Schmidt, *Lestern, lesen und lesen hören. Kommunikationsstudien zur deutschen Prosasatire der Reformationszeit* (Bern: Peter Lang, 1977); Bernd Balzar, *Bürgerliche Reformationspropaganda: Die Flugschriften des Hans Sachs in den Jahren 1523–1525* (Stuttgart: J. B. Metzlersche Verlagsbuchhandlung, 1973); Peter Matheson, *The Rhetoric of the Reformation* (London: T & T Clark International, 1998); Paul A. Russell, *Lay Theology in the Reformation: Popular Pamphleteers in Southwest Germany, 1521–1525* (Cambridge: Cambridge University Press, 1986); Tessa Watt, *Cheap Print and Popular Piety, 1550–1640* (Cambridge: Cambridge University Press, 1991).

revealed in the books produced and presumably read within the period. These assumptions require further examination, for virtually nowhere in early modern Europe were ideas likely to flow unregulated through some critical discursive field.

This "print-driven" explanation of the Reformation also tends to overlook other forces influencing the understanding of the message, and thereby overstates the importance of the book. Elizabeth Eisenstein has famously stressed the power to print, as a touchstone of authority, to change the way readers think and analyze information.[22] She is by no means alone in centering the new technology at the heart of the intellectual changes of the early modern era in general, and the Reformation in particular.[23] But as Andrew Pettegree has cautioned,

> ... by elevating the book in this way as a primary instrument of change, we are promoting a view of reading that is essentially modern (and academic). We conceive a world of private reading and private, largely individual decision making. But this essentially modernistic reconstruction of the process of religious choice goes very much against the grain of sixteenth-century society. In the early modern world most information was conveyed in public, communal settings: the market place, the church, a proclamation from the town hall steps. And it was conveyed by word of mouth, sometimes subsequently reinforced in print.[24]

This is not to say that books and pamphlets were not important to the Reformation; Martin Luther famously described printing as "God's highest and extremest act of grace, by which the business of the Gospel is driven forward."[25] But readers did not simply absorb the ideas of the reformers and translate them into action. Literary scholars have stressed the reader's active role in creating meaning from a text.[26] In Reformation

---

[22] Elizabeth L. Eisenstein, *The Printing Press as an Agent of Change: Communications and Cultural Transformations in Early Modern Europe* (Cambridge: Cambridge University Press, 1979). On the impact of writing more generally, see Walter J. Ong, *Orality and Literacy: The Technologizing of the Word* (NY: Routledge; 1982).

[23] See, for example, Michael Giesecke, *Der Buchdruck in der frühen Neuzeit: eine historische Fallstudie über die Durchsetzung neuer Informations-und Kommunikationstechnologien* (Frankfurt am Main: Suhrkamp, 1991); Johannes Burkhardt, *Das Reformationsjahrhundert. Deutsche Geschichte zwischen Medienrevolution und Institutionenbildung, 1517–1617* (Stuttgart: W. Kohlhammer, 2002) pp. 16–77.

[24] Pettegree, *Reformation and the Culture of Persuasion* p. 8.

[25] Quoted in Eisenstein, *The Printing Press as an Agent of Change*, p. 304.

[26] See, for example, Wolfgang Iser, 'Interaction Between Text and Reader,' in *The Reader in the Text: Essays on Audience and Interpretation*, eds Susan K. Suleiman and Inge Crossman (Princeton, NJ: Princeton University Press, 1980) pp. 106–19.

studies, historians Mark Edwards and Carlo Ginzburg have shown that readers' understanding of a text could be quite different from the author's own understanding of his or her work.[27] Adrian Johns has also drawn attention to the frequent corruption and adaptation of texts through the widespread reprinting of pirated editions. Given these changes, Johns stresses the difficulty of identifying anything like a definitive, "authorized" text in the early modern period.[28] Historians must be cautious, therefore, in evaluating the influence of texts, or any media, within a given community. Readers might encounter a text quite different from the author's original, and might construe it in entirely different ways.

One arena in which these varying interpretations might come to the fore was within the social and legal institutions that regulated public life. Historians of social disciplining[29] and confessionalization[30] in the early modern era have stressed the role of these institutions in shaping public opinion and private belief. Indeed, these historiographical models see the religious reform movements of the sixteenth century—both Protestant and Catholic—as devices allowing emerging states to extend their control over people's lives. Much of this work shows how early modern political and religious institutions used their regulatory powers to inculcate approved concepts of piety, thrift, and obedience to consolidate their authority and create obedient subjects. Critics have argued, however, that the confessionalization thesis tends to disregard countervailing trends toward religious tolerance and irenicism in the early modern era.[31] Other historians contend that these models overstate the role of governmental

---

[27] Edwards, *Printing, Propaganda*; Carlo Ginzburg, *The Cheese and the Worms: the Cosmos of a Sixteenth-Century Miller*, trans. John Tedeschi and Anne C. Tedeschi (Baltimore: The Johns Hopkins University Press, 1992).

[28] Adrian Johns, *The Nature of the Book: Print and Knowledge in the Making* (Chicago: University of Chicago Press, 1998).

[29] On social disciplining, see Gerhard Oestreich, *Strukturprobleme der frühen Neuzeit: Ausgewählte Aufsätze* (Berlin: Duncker & Humbolt, 1980); Winfried Schulze, 'Gerhard Oestreich's Begriff Sozialdisciplinierung in der frühen Neuzeit,' *Zeitschrift für historische Forschung* 14 (1987): pp. 265–302; R. Po-chia Hsia, *Social Discipline in the Reformation: Central Europe, 1550–1750* (London: Routledge, 1989).

[30] On the confessionalization thesis, see Heinz Schilling, *Konfessionskonflikt und Staatsbildung: eine Fallstudie über das Verhältnis von religiösem und sozialem Wandel in der Frühneuzeit am Beispiel der Grafschaft Lippe* (Gütersloh: Gütersloher Verlaghaus Mohn, 1981); Wolfgang Reinhard, 'Zwang zur Konfessionalisierung? Prolegomena zu einer Theorie des konfessionellen Zeitalters,' *Zeitschrift für Historische Forschung* 10 (1983): pp. 257–77.

[31] Winfried Schulze, 'Konfessionalisierung als Paradigma zur Erforschung des konfessionellen Zeitalters,' in *Drei Konfessionen in einer Region. Beiträge zur Geschichte im Herzogtum Berg vom 16. bis zum 18. Jahrhundert*, eds Burkhard Dietz and Stefan Ehrenpreis (Cologne: Rheinland-Verlag, 1999) pp. 15–30; Martin Heckel, *Deutschland im konfessionellen Zeitalter* (Göttingen: Vandenhoeck & Ruprecht, 1983).

and ecclesiastical authority, while ignoring the influence of popular and communal values in regulating public life.[32]

To the extent that the social disciplining model has recognized censorship, it has typically seen it as a vehicle for the extension of state or church authority over the molding of public opinion and private belief. In this book, however, I aim to assess the practical consequences of censorship, looking not simply at the formulation of normative policy at magisterial levels, but at the actual enforcement of these measures on a practical level. While the legislative pronouncements and policies of city magistrates are critical to an understanding of censorship's purpose in these communities, the focus here is on how these controls were implemented and how they impacted daily life. This approach reveals both the effective limits of official control and the influence of public opinion on official policy. Censorship in the early modern German city was not merely an instrument of state control, but a product of negotiation between governmental expectations and communal demands at multiple levels.

The Study of Censorship

Despite the importance early modern magistrates attached to censorship, there has been essentially no comprehensive treatment in English of censorship in Germany during the confessional era. Moreover, much of the German scholarship in this area tends to focus entirely on the censorship of print. Within this context, most studies concentrate on the formulation of policy at a legislative and administrative level, with virtually no attention given to the actual enforcement of these measures on a practical level. The influence of these controls on German political and religious expression—particularly within the oral culture—are therefore almost impossible to gauge from the current historiography.

Much of the scholarly attention devoted to censorship in the confessional age has been focused on censorship in Catholic lands, particularly in Italy and Spain, where censorship fell under the jurisdiction of inquisitorial tribunals. The Spanish inquisition published the first official Spanish Index of Prohibited Books in 1551, and the papacy followed with the first of

---

[32] See Heinrich Richard Schmidt, 'Sozialdisziplinierung? Ein Plädoyer für das Ende des Etatismus in der Konfessionalisierungsforschung,' in *Historische Zeitschrift* 265 (1997): pp. 639–82, and *Dorf and Religion. Reformierte Sittenzucht in Berner Landgemeinden der Frühen Neuzeit* (Stuttgart: Fischer, 1995) pp. 377–400; Marc R. Foyster, *The Counter-Reformation in the Villages: Religion and Reform in the Bishopric of Speyer, 1560–1720* (Ithaca: Cornell University Press, 1992).

a series of papal indexes in 1559.[33] Scholars have debated the cultural impact of these controls for centuries. Some of the earliest historians of the inquisition blamed censorship for Italy and Spain's supposed cultural backwardness in the seventeenth century.[34] Much of the modern historiography has been devoted to testing this theory in light of more recent work evidencing significant gaps in censorial controls and the existence of a thriving clandestine book trade in these regions.[35] Closely associated with this inquiry is the effort to evaluate the psychological consequences of censorship. Censorship, it has been argued, cast a web of suspicion around the book, imbuing it with the threat of punishment. This "pedagogy of fear" not only suppressed the transmission of heterodox thought, but also inculcated in the reader a sense of doubt as to his or her own ability to evaluate truth.[36] In this sense, governmental controls produced a form of self-censorship governing not only what was written, but what the reader was willing to read and how she or he was prepared to understand it.

Censorship, however, was by no means the exclusive province of the Roman Catholic Church in the early modern period. Protestant authorities, no less than their Catholic counterparts, accepted the importance of censorship in preserving doctrinal uniformity and the communal order.[37] Throughout Protestant Europe, acceptance of the evangelical cause was often closely followed by the introduction of censorship to enforce the

---

[33] Virgilio Pinto Crespo, 'Thought Control in Spain,' in *Inquisition and Society in Early Modern Europe*, ed. Stephen Haliczer (Totowa: Barnes & Noble Books, 1987) pp. 175–9; Paul F. Grendler, *The Roman Inquisition and the Venetian Press, 1540–1605* (Princeton: Princeton University Press, 1977).

[34] See Shifra Armon, 'Ungilding Spain's Golden Age,' in *Tainted Greatness: Anti-Semitism and Cultural Heroes*, ed. Nancy Harrowitz (Philadelphia: Temple University Press, 1994) p. 80; Angel Alcalá, 'Inquisitorial Control of Humanists and Writers,' in *The Spanish Inquisition and the Inquisitorial Mind*, ed. Angel Alcalá (Boulder: Social Science Monographs, 1987) pp. 322–3; C. M. Arroyo, 'The Inquisition and the Possibility of Great Baroque Literature,' in *The Spanish Inquisition and the Inquisitorial Mind*, p. 363.

[35] For Spain, see Henry Kamen, *The Spanish Inquisition: A Historical Reassessment* (New Haven: Yale University Press, 1999) and *Inquisition and Society in Spain in the Sixteenth and Seventeenth Centuries* (London: Weidenfeld & Nicholson, 1985); Clive Griffin, *Journeymen-Printers, Heresy, and the Inquisition in Sixteenth-Century Spain* (Oxford: Oxford University Press, 2005). With regard to Italy, see Grendler, *The Roman Inquisition and the Venetian Press*; John Tedeschi, *The Prosecution of Heresy: Collected Studies on the Inquisition in Early Modern Italy* (Binghampton: Medieval and Renaissance Texts and Studies, 1991).

[36] Virgilio Pinto Crespo, 'Censorship: A System of Control and an Instrument of Action,' in *The Spanish Inquisition and the Inquisitorial Mind* p. 306.

[37] Joan Hemels, 'Pressezensur in Reformationszeitalter (1475–1648),' in *Deutsche Kommunikations-kontrolle des 15. bis. 20. Jahrhunderts*, ed. Heinz-Dietrich Fischer (Munich: K.G. Saur, 1982) p. 18.

new orthodoxy.[38] Indeed, Luther and Melanchthon both served as censors in their official capacities at the University of Wittenberg, and censorship played a prominent role in policing theological dissent within the Lutheran and Reformed churches.[39] There are, nonetheless, comparatively few studies of censorship in Protestant communities. The roots of this may lie in long-held assumptions about the nature of Catholicism and Protestantism themselves.

In the older historiography, it has often been assumed that notwithstanding Protestants' efforts to regulate expression, censorship must have had little impact among them. Franz Heinrich Reusch, for example, contended in his 1883 study, *Der Index der verbotenen Bücher*,[40] that, while Protestant censorship in sixteenth-century Germany shared roughly the same goals as the Roman Congregation of the Index, it was less effective in operation. Protestant censorship differed from Catholic censorship, according to Reusch, in that it lacked a central organizational structure to administer a uniform censorship policy. Moreover, the very nature of the faith made the Protestant states' efforts less effective. Protestants, unlike Catholics, could disobey their religious superiors without falling into mortal sin. Without the threat of excommunication to enforce compliance, Reusch argued, Protestant controls could be more readily ignored.[41]

George Haven Putnam, in his 1906 book, *The Censorship of the Church of Rome and its Influence Upon the Production and Distribution of Literature*,[42] likewise argued that the inability of the Protestant censors to wield the ultimate spiritual penalty of excommunication rendered their controls largely unenforceable. Protestant religious leaders, Putnam correctly noted, were largely dependent on civil authorities for the enforcement of doctrinal orthodoxy. He argued that in Catholic Germany, however, officials could enforce censorship through moral coercion.[43]

---

[38] Paul F. Grendler, 'Printing and Censorship,' in *The Cambridge History of Renaissance Philosophy*, ed. Charles B. Schmitt and Quentin Skinner (Cambridge: Cambridge University Press, 1988) p. 44.

[39] See Hans-Peter Hasse, *Zensur theologischer Bücher in Kursachsen im Konfessionellen Zeitalter. Studien zur kursächsischen Literatur-und Religionspolitik in den Jahren 1569 bis 1575* (Leipzig: Evangelische Verlagsanstalt, 2000).

[40] Franz Heinrich Reusch, *Der Index der verbotenen Bücher* (1883) (Aalen: Scientia Verlag, 1967).

[41] Ibid., pp. 595–8.

[42] George Haven Putnam, *The Censorship of the Church of Rome and Its Influence Upon the Production and Distribution of Literature: A Study of the History of the Prohibitory & Expurgatory Indexes, Together With Some Consideration of the Effects of Protestant Censorship and of Censorship by the State* (New York: Benjamin Bloom, 1906).

[43] Ibid., pp. 206–7.

Catholics also had recourse to a highly centralized administration in Rome organized for the purpose of ensuring uniformity and orthodoxy in belief. Protestants, however, were divided on basic theological principles and could not articulate a unified response to the problem of heterodoxy.

More fundamentally, however, Putnam seemed to see Protestantism as incompatible with the suppression of free theological and intellectual inquiry. Protestantism, for Putnam, represented the casting off of the intellectual shackles of the "Church of Rome." Catholic censors might easily impose their will on subjects accustomed to subordinating their consciences to the dictates of their church, but Protestants had "the right to think and to speak, to print and to read for themselves, free from decisions to be arrived at by the Dominican Congregation of Italy or the Jesuit censors of Vienna."[44] This vision of Protestantism celebrated Luther as the champion of individual Christians' right to ascertain the truth for themselves. Protestant readers, therefore, were bound to follow their consciences, regardless of what their censors told them. This view of the Protestant Reformation—certainly of the Lutheran Reformation—has long been countered by better-informed studies, but the willingness to assume that we know how censorship must have played out remains.

Joseph Hilgers, a Jesuit scholar, presented a very different picture of Luther and Protestant censorship in his 1904 book, *Der Index der verbotenen Bücher*.[45] Luther, Hilgers correctly noted, quickly distanced himself from his early advocacy of the individual Christian's right to interpret scripture unaided by learned guidance, and, in fact, urged civil authorities to adopt censorship controls not only against Catholic writings, but against other Protestants.[46] Hilgers contended that, compared to Catholic censorship, Protestant censorship was far more arbitrary and irrational in its scope. To a greater degree than their Roman Catholic counterparts, Protestant censors suppressed works of purely literary or intellectual concern having no direct relation to religion or politics. This approach, Hilgers suggested, reflected an anti-intellectual orientation fundamental to Protestantism itself.[47]

Fundamental assumptions about the place of intellectual inquiry and received authority in Catholicism and Protestantism, therefore, seem to have colored the historical approach to early modern German censorship.

---

[44] Ibid, p. 358.

[45] Joseph Hilgers, *Der Index der Verbotenen Bücher* (Freiburg im Breisgau: Herdersche Verlagshandlung, 1904).

[46] Ibid., pp. 18–20. On the evolution of Luther's thinking on religious instruction, see Gerald Strauss, *Luther's House of Learning: Indoctrination of the Young in the German Reformation* (Baltimore: The Johns Hopkins University Press, 1978).

[47] Hilgers, *Der Index der Verbotenen Bücher*, p. 93.

Modern understandings of freedom of expression have also shaped our views about the subject. In evaluating censorship in the pre-modern era, we confront a culture that did not place the same moral value on individual expression that post-Enlightenment thought has enshrined.[48] In contemporary Western political and legal theory, freedom of expression has emerged as a fundamental value: it is "one of the most precious of the rights of man;" the "bulwark of liberty."[49] Indeed, it is thought to be the most basic of individual liberties; if freedom of thought or speech were sacrificed, the United States Supreme Court has held, "neither liberty nor justice would exist ... one may say it is the matrix, the indispensable condition, of nearly every other form of freedom."[50] But, in the sixteenth century, very different values prevailed. The magistrates' authority to regulate expression was rooted in long-standing concepts of good government and social order. Ideally, all members of society were to be integrated into a sacral community, united in Christian faith for the common good.[51] In this "moralised universe," the tolerance of deviance and moral error could call down divine wrath on the community as a whole.[52] As the spiritual and moral integrity of the community was the foundation upon which all civic order rested, the public good demanded that the magistracy protect society from the potentially disruptive influence of political dissent and unorthodox doctrine.[53] While the religious conflicts of the Reformation era would generate significant debate as to the limits of the magistrate's power to compel private conscience, the public expression of belief was widely seen as a legitimate sphere of magisterial control.[54] Indeed, a broad consensus held that Christian authorities had not only the

---

[48] On debates concerning censorship and the limits of free expression in the Enlightenment and in revolutionary France, see Charles Walton, *Policing Public Opinion in the French Revolution: The Culture of Calumny and the Problem of Free Speech* (Oxford: Oxford University Press, 2009).

[49] French Declaration of the Rights of Man and of the Citizen (1789), Art. 11; Virginia Bill of Rights (1776), Art. 12.

[50] *Palko v. Connecticut*, 302 U.S. 319, 326–7 (1937).

[51] Benjamin J. Kaplan, *Divided By Faith: Religious Conflict and the Practice of Toleration in Early Modern Europe* (Cambridge, MA: Harvard University Press, 2007) pp. 60–72; Bob Scribner, 'Preconditions of Tolerance and Intolerance in Sixteenth-Century Germany,' in *Tolerance and Intolerance in the European Reformation*, eds Ole Peter Grell and Bob Scribner (Cambridge: Cambridge University Press, 1996) p. 40.

[52] Scribner, 'Preconditions of Tolerance,' p. 43.

[53] Brad S. Gregory, *Salvation at Stake: Christian Martyrdom in Early Modern Europe* (Cambridge: Cambridge University Press, 1999) pp. 78–90; Grendler, 'Printing and Censorship,' pp. 41–2.

[54] Lorna Jane Abray, 'Confession, Conscience and Honour: The Limits of Magisterial Tolerance in Sixteenth-Century Strassburg,' in *Tolerance and Intolerance*, pp. 97–9; Hasse, *Zensur theologischer Bücher in Kursachsen*, pp. 375–6; Debora Shuger, *Censorship and*

right, but the duty to police opinion and belief. Lazarus Spengler, secretary to the Nuremberg city council, took this to be self-evident:

> It is without doubt clear to everyone that the duty and highest office of every Christian authority is to have the greatest concern, not only for those things which are useful to the general civic order, universal peace, and ordinary bodily nourishment, but even more so for the things which are useful for the spiritual salvation of the subjects under its command ... because the Almighty will demand the blood of subjects from their rulers, as the godly script demonstrates.[55]

Martin Luther, undoubtedly the most prominent target of imperial censorship in this era, agreed that censorship served the public good and was a legitimate governmental concern. As noted, he himself censored texts in his official capacities at the University of Wittenberg, and he freely acknowledged that secular authorities had the right to censor his work, with one important exception: "it seems entirely appropriate to me that I publish nothing without [the censors'] prior review—except the pure and clear word of God, which must and should be unfettered."[56] Luther's thinking on this subject reflected his understanding of the "two kingdoms" of secular and spiritual authority. While Luther insisted that all Christians owed a duty to obey the secular authorities God had placed over them, the temporal government

> has laws which extend no farther than to life and property and what is external on earth. For over the soul God can and will let no one rule but Himself. Therefore, where temporal power presumes to prescribe laws for the soul, it encroaches upon God's government and only misleads and destroys the souls.[57]

On this basis, he counseled Christian readers in 1523 to defy their rulers' efforts to confiscate their Bibles.[58] In the 1560s, some of his followers extended this rationale to oppose secular efforts to censor

---

Cultural Sensibility: The Regulation of Language in Tudor-Stuart England (Philadelphia: The University of Pennsylvania Press, 2006) pp. 138–71.

[55] Günther Vogler, 'Imperial City Nuremberg, 1524–1525: The Reform Movement in Transition,' in *The German People and the Reformation*, ed. R. Po-Chia Hsia (Ithaca: Cornell University Press, 1988) p. 46.

[56] Hasse, *Zensur theologischer Bücher in Kursachsen*, p. 63.

[57] Martin Luther, 'Secular Authority: To What Extent It Should Be Obeyed,' in *Martin Luther: Selections From His Writings*, ed. John Dillenberger (New York: Doubleday, 1962) pp. 382–3.

[58] Ibid., p. 388.

Lutheran theological texts.⁵⁹ But while Lutheran thought carved out some limited sphere for free expression in religious matters, it stopped far short of advocating freedom of expression in its modern sense.

The historical treatment of censorship in Germany also reflects certain underlying assumptions about the nature of the Holy Roman Empire. Friederich Kapp, in his *Geschichte des deutschen Buchhandels bis in das siebzehnte Jahrhundert*,⁶⁰ argued that the political fragmentation of the Holy Roman Empire prevented the implementation of any effective censorship campaign at either the imperial or state level. According to Kapp, printers or booksellers under pressure from censors in one territory could easily move their operations to a more hospitable area. Because there was little cooperation between the various jurisdictions of the Empire, little effort was made to prevent printers and booksellers from exporting their goods to territories where they were not welcome. Although the emperor sought to enforce censorship controls, Kapp argued that his efforts were largely ignored at the territorial level. The religious debates of the sixteenth and seventeenth centuries, Kapp noted, had produced a veritable flood of controversial literature, and neither Catholic nor Protestant rulers showed any particular interest in stemming their subjects' attacks against the other side.⁶¹

Kapp's analysis seems entirely plausible. The map of the Holy Roman Empire in the Reformation era was a bewildering crazy quilt of territories— it is difficult to imagine how any comprehensive policy of restraint could be implemented across so many borders and through so many religiously and politically divided jurisdictions. Any study of German book production in the sixteenth and seventeenth centuries would also reveal no shortage of controversial and potentially illegal material coming from all over the Empire.⁶² While Kapp's observations may indeed be accurate, there has been little historical scholarship directed towards testing their validity. Many historians seem to have proceeded on the assumption that the states of the Empire could not have been anything *but* uncooperative towards each other and that the emperor's policies could not have been anything *but* ineffective. These conclusions reflect the deeply negative assessments of the

---

⁵⁹ Robert Kolb, 'Mattheaus Judex's Condemnation of Princely Censorship of Theologians' Publications,' in *Luther's Heirs Define His Legacy: Studies on Lutheran Confessionalization* (Aldershot: Variorum, 1996) pp. 401–14.

⁶⁰ Friedrich Kapp, *Geschichte des deutschen Buchhandels bis in das siebzehnte Jahrhundert*, in Geschichte des deutschen Buchhandels, Bd. 1. Leipzig, 1886 (Leipzig: Reprogr. Nachdruck, 1970).

⁶¹ Ibid., pp. 539–53.

⁶² See Stephan Fitos, *Zensur als Mißerfolg: die Verbreitung indizierter deutscher Druckschriften in der zweiten Hälfte des 16. Jahrhunderts* (Frankfurt am Main: Peter Lang, 2000).

Empire and its institutions that, until recently, have tended to dominate the historiography on the Holy Roman Empire. In the age of absolutism, the Empire's decentralized structure prompted critics like Samuel von Pufendorf to dismiss it as an impotent political "monstrosity." For later historians, it remained an aberration, an obstacle on Germany's path to the creation of a centralized, unified nation. This line of thinking deeply colored historical approaches to the Empire at least through the 1960s.[63] It is hardly surprising, therefore, that most of the earlier historiography assumed imperial censorship to have been ineffectual; but to what extent is that picture true?

Perhaps the most extensive consideration of imperial censorship policy in the confessional era published to date is Ulrich Eisenhardt's 1970 book, *Die kaiserliche Aufsicht* über *Buchhandel und Presse in Heiligen Römischen Reich Deutscher Nation (1496–1806)*.[64] Eisenhardt focuses primarily upon the formulation of imperial censorship law within the Diets and the imperial courts and commissions charged with its administration. He regards imperial censorship as an effective instrument of control, able to command respect within the states of the Empire despite their confessional differences and often conflicting political ambitions. The evidence of widespread confessional polemic and political posturing among the states suggests that Eisenhardt may, in some respects, be overstating the case for the effectiveness of imperial control; it is difficult to evaluate his conclusions, however, because he devotes little attention to how the imperial law was actually carried out.

Communication controls within the German states in the early modern era have been the subject of a handful of local studies. Helmut Neumann has surveyed the history of Bavarian book censorship in the Reformation era in his 1977 book, *Staatliche Bücherzensur und Aufsicht in Bayern von der Reformation bis zum Ausgang des 17. Jahrhunderts*,[65] while Hilger Freund has examined early modern censorship in Electoral Mainz.[66] For Protestant states, Thomas Sirges and Ingeborg Müller have outlined the history of censorial controls in the landgraviate of Hesse in *Zensur in*

---

[63] On historical assessments of the Holy Roman Empire, see Peter H. Wilson, 'Still a Monstrosity? Some Reflections on Early Modern German Statehood,' in *The Historical Journal* 49 (2006): pp. 565–76; Thomas A. Brady, *German Histories in the Age of the Reformations, 1400–1650* (Cambridge: Cambridge University Press, 2009) pp. 6–8.

[64] Ulrich Eisenhardt, *Die kaiserliche Aufsicht über Buchdruck, Buchhandel und Presse in Heiligen Römischen Reich Deutscher Nation (1496–1806)* (Karlsruhe: Verlag C.F. Müller, 1970).

[65] Helmut Neumann, *Staatliche Bücherzensur und Aufsicht in Bayern von der Reformation bis zum Ausgang des 17. Jahrhunderts.* (Heidelberg: G.F. Müller Juristischer Verlag, 1977).

[66] Hilger Freund, *Die Bücher- und Pressezensur im Kurfürstentum Mainz von 1486–1797* (Karlsruhe: Verlag C.F. Müller, 1971).

Marburg, 1538–1832: Eine lokalgeschichtliche Studie zum Bücher- und Pressewesen.[67] Likewise, Hans-Peter Hasse's study, *Zensur theologischer Bücher in Kursachsen im Konfessionellen Zeitalter*,[68] examines the censorship of theological writings in Electoral Saxony as an element of Lutheran confessionalization. Wolfgang Wüst's 1998 essay, *Censur als Stütze von Staat und Kirche in der Frühmoderne: Augsburg, Bayern, Kurmainz und Württemberg in Vergleich* is a welcome examination of censorship in an interregional perspective, comparing the use of censorship for political and religious ends in Augsburg, Bavaria, Württemberg and electoral Mainz.[69] However, the study treats the sixteenth and seventeenth centuries only briefly, focusing primarily on censorship in the eighteenth century. Moreover, virtually all of the studies of print censorship in confessional-era Germany, whether at the imperial, state, or urban level, examine the control of communication from a normative perspective, focusing on how these communication controls were *supposed* to work. Given the relative dearth of information regarding how censorship *actually* worked, any attempt to describe its administration or gauge its impact remains largely a matter of speculation.

Some of the most significant recent scholarship on censorship has focused on the eighteenth-century European print trade. For scholars interested in the spread of Enlightenment culture, censorship has always been a central concern. Indeed, even in 1784, Kant conditioned the progress of Enlightenment on the unfettered "public exercise of reason."[70] Echoing Kant, much of the scholarship in this area has posited a fundamental tension between the free critical debate nourished within the "Republic of Letters" and the efforts of governmental authorities to regulate discussion. This perceived opposition informs Jürgen Habermas's highly influential 1962 study, *The Structural Transformation of the Public Sphere*. Habermas links the emergence of a recognized arena for public comment and debate to the relaxation of censorship controls in the eighteenth century.[71] Thus,

---

[67] Thomas Sirges and Ingeborg Müller. *Zensur in Marburg, 1538–1832: Eine lokalgeschichtliche Studie zum Bücher- und Pressewesen* (Marburg: Presseamt der Stadt, 1984).

[68] Hasse, *Zensur theologischer Bücher in Kursachsen*.

[69] Wolfgang Wüst, *Censur als Stütze von Staat und Kirche in der Frühmoderne: Augsburg, Bayern, Kurmainz und Württemberg in Vergleich*. (Munich: Verlag Ernst Vögel, 1998).

[70] Immanuel Kant, 'An Answer to the Question: "What is Enlightenment?"'(1784) in *Kant: Political Writings*, 2nd ed., ed. Hans Reiss (Cambridge: Cambridge University Press, 1991) pp. 54–61.

[71] Jürgen Habermas, *The Structural Transformation of the Public Sphere: An Inquiry Into a Category of Bourgeois Society* (1962), trans. Thomas Berger and Frederick Lawrence (Cambridge, Mass.: The MIT Press, 1995), p. 58.

he suggests, the creation of a discursive space open to public commentary and criticism necessarily requires the elimination of governmental controls that would otherwise impede the circulation of ideas.

Habermas maintains that the early modern public sphere, once freed of government control, became open to free communication of pure "public opinion." Such a model presupposes not only an opposition between criticism and censorship, but also between governmentally imposed controls and internalized self-regulation. However, censorship is often internalized, and may influence public expression even in the absence of recognizable governmental control. Pierre Bourdieu, for example, has argued that there are two distinct kinds of censorship: a "manifest censorship" and deeper, "secondary" or structural censorship that it masks:

> The manifest censorship imposed by orthodox discourse, the official way of speaking and thinking about the world, conceals another, more radical censorship: the overt opposition between "right" opinion and ... "wrong" opinion, which delimits the universe of possible discourse, be it legitimate or illegitimate, euphemistic or blasphemous, masks in its turn the fundamental opposition between the universe of things that can be stated and hence thought, and the universe of that which is taken for granted.[72]

Recent investigations of censorship in eighteenth-century France and Britain have attempted to examine the connection between this "manifest" and "secondary" censorship and its relationship to the "Republic of Letters." Robert Darnton has questioned the assumed opposition between Enlightenment and censorship, showing that the denizens of the Republic of Letters were often participants in, and beneficiaries of, the censorship apparatus. Moreover, the early modern public sphere is presented as less an arena for free public commentary and criticism than as both a censored and censoring discursive space. While Darnton's work has uncovered a promiscuous mixing of Enlightenment values within eighteenth-century French popular culture, his studies of the careers of the French *philosophes* finds evidence of extensive networks of patronage and support linking the Republic of Letters to the institutional culture of the Old Regime. Far from positing an inherent opposition between the "philosophic spirit" and the governing institutions of pre-revolutionary France, Darnton finds that they were populated by men who shared the same ethos and frequently worked together in furtherance of similar interests.[73]

---

[72] Pierre Bourdieu, *Outline of a Theory of Practice*, trans. Richard Nice (Cambridge: Cambridge University Press, 1977), pp. 169–70.

[73] See Robert Darnton, *The Forbidden Best Sellers of Prerevolutionary France* (New York: W. W. Norton & Co., Inc., 1995); 'The High Enlightenment and the Low Life of

Other scholars have drawn attention to the commonalities between the literary and intellectual values of the world of letters and the standards imposed by government censors. It seems that scholars and censors often internalized and self-enforced similar criteria of taste, accuracy, and quality. Indeed, in many cases authors and journalists were also censors.[74] In Britain, the economic interests of the book trade reinforced this identity of interest. Economic protectionism, John Feather argues, ensured the trade's continued cooperation with governmental overseers, not necessarily because such participation was legally mandated, but because the trade sought legislative recognition of copyright. The book trade's efforts to secure governmental recompense for its efforts represented, according to Feather, a form of self-censorship. Moreover, the conservatism of the press was more or less assured by the mounting expense associated with publication.[75] The interests of authors and publishers, therefore, necessarily required the imposition of some form of self-censorship calculated to avoid prosecution. This internal control regulated the circulation of ideas in print nearly as effectively as the legal controls imposed by government censors.

Although Reformation-era Germany was preoccupied with issues and concerns seemingly far removed from the Enlightenment's "Republic of Letters," we will see many of the same dynamics at work within the cities' censorship systems. In their practical effects, policing and censorship in these communities were much more a process of accommodation to communal expectations than the simple imposition of state authority over a passive population. Most citizens, both within the book trade and in the community at large, shared the magistrates' view that regulation of expression was not only appropriate but essential to protect the public welfare. Within the book trade, economic interest combined with official oversight to encourage a degree of self-regulation independent of the

---

Literature,' and 'A Spy in Grub Street,' in *The Literary Underground of the Old Regime* (Cambridge, Mass.: Harvard University Press, 1982); 'A Police Inspector Sorts His Files: The Anatomy of the Republic of Letters,' in *The Great Cat Massacre and Other Episodes in French Cultural History* (New York: Basic Books, 1984).

[74] Ann Goldgar, 'The Absolutism of the Taste: Journalists as Censors in Eighteenth-Century Paris,' in *Censorship and the Control of Print in England and France, 1600–1910*, eds Robin Myers and Michael Harris (Winchester: St. Paul's Bibliographies, 1992) pp. 87–111; Edoardo Tortarolo, 'Censorship and the Conception of the Public in Late Eighteenth-Century Germany: Or, are Censorship and Public Opinion Mutually Exclusive?' in *Shifting the Boundaries: Transformation of the Languages of Public and Private in the Eighteenth Century*, eds Dario Castiglione and Lesley Sharpe (Exeter: University of Exeter Press, 1995) pp. 131–49.

[75] John P. Feather, 'From Censorship to Copyright: Aspects of the Government's Role in the English Book Trade, 1695 to 1775,' in *Books and Society in History*, ed. Kenneth E. Carpenter (New York: R.R. Bowker Co., 1983) pp. 187–9.

magistrates' official controls. In large measure, residents internalized similar standards of what was appropriate and reinforced the systems of control. They expected their government to reflect these values, and conflict arose when they perceived that it did not. This tension was nowhere more apparent than in the realm of confessional relations. Although few questioned the magistrates' right to regulate expression, conflict sometimes erupted over the purposes that regulation should serve, particularly regarding religious practice. In order to keep the peace, regulatory policy had to accommodate itself to civic expectations. In this sense, urban censorship became both a forum for negotiating competing demands and a vehicle for creating and enforcing new concepts of community.

This book will focus on how censorship operated in four critical episodes in the urban Reformation and in the so-called "confessional age" of the late sixteenth and seventeenth centuries. The first chapter will analyze censorship laws within the Empire and the dynamics of communication in the German cities. In these communities, uniformity of belief and opinion were considered essential to the maintenance of the social order and the common good, and the government's power to censor therefore found wide acceptance. The coming of the Reformation challenged these notions, as Chapter 2 will show. Forced to steer a "middle way" between the popular agitation for reform and the emperor's demands for allegiance to the Catholic faith, Protestant communities adjusted their censorship policies to accommodate the demand for religious change while working to maintain social order and political security.

The remaining chapters will examine the so-called "long Reformation" of the later sixteenth and seventeenth centuries, when the gains of the Reformation were consolidated and the religious divisions in the Empire became more pronounced. Chapter 3 examines how censorship could be used both to suppress unwanted ideas and foster new ideologies, looking specifically at imperial and local efforts under the Peace of Augsburg of 1555 to censor religious polemic and promote religious coexistence. Chapters 4 and 5 analyze the religiously divisive years leading up to the Thirty Years' War and focus more directly on the imperial city of Augsburg. This city had always played a major role in the German Reformation, but after 1555, Augsburg became the largest and most prominent of the officially bi-confessional cities created under the Religious Peace. Now obligated by imperial law to accommodate both the Lutheran and Catholic faiths, Augsburg's magistrates used censorship to try to keep the peace. Chapter 4 will examine the so-called "Calendar Conflict" of the 1580s, when protests over the Gregorian calendar reform nearly toppled the city government. Although the City Council clamped down on dissent, the songs, rumors, and pamphlets circulating in the city demonstrated how far Augsburgers had internalized the ideal of religious accommodation under the Peace of Augsburg, but how differently they had come to define it. Chapter 5 will analyze the Thirty Years' War, when political power in Augsburg repeatedly shifted between Catholics and Protestants. Although both groups tried to enforce religious conformity, each regime was ultimately forced to bow to the public's expectation of religious accommodation. Thus, censorship in Augsburg remained geared more toward the maintenance of peace between the religious factions than the promotion of an officially sanctioned religious orthodoxy. In this, the system both reflected and reinforced communal expectations of cooperation in the civic order, which ultimately took precedence over religious ideology. In this contested sphere, the control of expression became a means to debate and define acceptable communal standards in matters of faith and governance.

CHAPTER 1

"Words, Works, or Writings:" Communication and the Law of Censorship

The printing of books was a gift from God, designed to serve the welfare of humanity and honor His name—or so the Augsburg city council declared in 1541. This salutary gift, however, had been "misused to the point that one may wonder whether it is more harmful than constructive, for as much evil as good arises from it, without any distinction between them." What was more, the evils of print were "offered up indiscriminately to impudent, curious young people so that they may read and hear and learn many things to which they would doubtless otherwise not be exposed." As a result, the council concluded, "unchristian, blasphemous teachings are spread about, to the disgrace of the godly Truth."[1]

The council's decree reflects the deep ambivalence with which early modern authorities greeted the coming of the book. Print offered unprecedented opportunities for the exchange of knowledge and ideas, but these new opportunities also created new dangers. Truth and falsehood might be indiscriminately presented before a public unable to discern between them, leading many into error. Misguided opinion toppled governments, set neighbor against neighbor, and led simple souls to their damnation. God—and good government—required that rulers carefully monitor what their subjects were to read and hear.

Officials feared the destructive potential of the press, but the control of communication in Europe long pre-dated the advent of printing. For centuries, medieval authorities, both secular and clerical, had sought to limit the spread of potentially heretical and dangerous ideas, in whatever form they arose.[2] While print created its own unique problems and opportunities for early modern magistrates, its control may be understood as simply an outgrowth of an already well-defined policy of oversight of public expression.

---

[1] StAA, Schätze Nr. 16, 'Anschläge,' fol. 67v–68r.
[2] See R. I. Moore, *The Formation of a Persecuting Society* (Oxford; Basil Blackwell, 1987); Debora Shuger, *Censorship & Cultural Sensibility: The Regulation of Language in Tudor-Stuart England* (Philadelphia: University of Pennsylvania Press, 2006).

The impulse toward control intensified with the religious controversies that split the continent in the sixteenth and seventeenth centuries. It seemed to observers at the time, as it has to many historians ever afterwards, that the printed page was central to the spread of the reforming message.[3] The stream of religious polemic, and the tumult that accompanied it, demonstrated to authorities that the selective controls then in place would no longer suffice to keep order and uphold truth.[4] The 1520s thus marked the emergence of the first fully coordinated efforts by civil and ecclesiastical authorities to erect comprehensive controls over the dissemination of ideas, both locally and within the Holy Roman Empire as a whole.

In the Holy Roman Empire, a complex web of laws and institutions policed expression. Imperial decrees and the recesses of the Imperial Diets established censorship laws intended to apply throughout the Empire. Territorial princes and lords also regulated expression in their lands, often assigning the task of censoring texts to university faculties or religious authorities. In the free and imperial cities, censorship was entrusted to the governing city councils, which erected their own tribunals to control expression.

In their practical application, these measures often did not function as intended. The diverse laws, offices, and courts across the Empire were not generally coordinated in their missions, and although all were theoretically subject to imperial law, the estates' competing political and religious agendas often frustrated any attempts at comprehensive controls. At the local level, economic interests and political constraints moderated enforcement efforts. In the following chapters, we will examine the evolution and operation of censorship across the Empire. First, however, we must outline the various censorship systems operative in the Holy Roman Empire and their intended functions. We will begin where the Reformation message found some of its earliest support—in the German imperial cities.

---

[3] See Bernd Moeller, 'Stadt und Buch: Bemerkungen zur Struktur der reformatorischen Bewegung in Deutschland,' in *The Urban Classes, the Nobility, and the Reformation: Studies on the Social History of the Reformation in England and Germany*, ed. Wolfgang J. Mommsen. Stuttgart: Klett-Cotta, 1979) pp. 25–39; Mark U. Edwards, *Printing, Propaganda, and Martin Luther* (Berkeley: University of California Press, 1994); Holgar Flachmann, *Martin Luther und das Buch: Eine historische Studie zur Bedeutung des Buches im Handeln und Denken des Reformators* (Tübingen: Mohr, 1996).

[4] Joan Hemels, 'Pressezensur in Reformationszeitalter, (1475–1648),' in *Deutsche Kommunikations-kontrolle des 15. bis. 20. Jahrhunderts*, ed. Heinz-Dietrich Fischer (Munich: K.G. Saur, 1982) pp. 18–19.

Censoring the Civic Order

The free and imperial cities of the Holy Roman Empire were among Europe's most important hubs for the exchange of information and ideas. Since the advent of the European print trade in the 1450s, the German imperial cities had been dominant in the field. Nuremberg, Augsburg, Cologne, and Strasbourg counted among the most prolific printing centers in Europe, and their close trading connections to the Low Countries and the Italian ports assured their dominance. They were among the Empire's largest, most prosperous, and politically powerful cities.

In Germany's imperial cities, the control of public expression formed part of a broader governmental effort to regulate private, as well as public, spheres of conduct and belief in the name of the public good. Even before the Reformation had taken root, magistrates had been careful to regulate immodest and frivolous public behavior, such as public drunkenness and boisterous singing, dancing, and music-making.[5] Authorities also issued repeated decrees against the swearing of blasphemous oaths, as well as insults against another person's honor, whether in speech, song, or writing.[6]

Urban magistrates monitored public expression through a vague, and sometimes arbitrary, body of laws. Unlike the censorship systems operative in many Catholic lands, German cities did not typically publish indices of forbidden books, authors, or themes.[7] Rather, authorities issued decrees as circumstances warranted prohibiting broad categories of speech and writings that might be interpreted as "disgraceful" (*schmachvoll*) or "defamatory" (*schmählich*).[8] These taboo subjects typically included:

1. Insults or criticisms directed against the emperor, princes of the Empire, or other political dignitaries;

---

[5] See, for example, the ordinances collected in *Die gute Policey im Reichskreis*, Bd. 3: *Der Bayerische Reichskreis und die Oberpfalz: Zur frühmodernen Normensetzung in den Kernregionen des Alten Reiches*, ed. Wolfgang Wüst (Berlin: Akademie Verlag, 2004).

[6] See, for example, StAA, 'Anschläge und Dekrete, 1490–1649, Teil I,' Nr. 4; SStBA, 2 Aug. 10, 'Anschläge, 1522–1677,' fol. 23; 2°S. 14, Kapsel I, 'Anschläge 1524–1734,' Nr. 17; Gerd Schwerhoff, *Zungen wie Schwerter: Blasphemie in alteuropäischen Gesellschaften 1200–1650* (Konstanz: UVK Verlagsgesellschaft, 2005); Francisca Loetz, *Mit Gott handeln. Von den Zürcher Gotteslästerern der Frühen Neuzeit zu einer Kulturgeschichte des Religiösen* (Göttingen: Vandenhoeck & Ruprecht, 2002); Günther Schmidt, *Libelli Famosi. Zur Bedeutung der Schmähschriften, Scheltbriefe, Schandgemälde und Pasquille in der deutschen Rechtsgeschichte* (Diss., Universität Köln, 1985).

[7] Franz Heinrich Reusch, *Der Index der verbotenen Bücher* (1883) (Aalen: Scientia Verlag, 1967); Stephan Fitos, *Zensur als Mißerfolg. Die Verbreitung indizierter deutscher Druckschriften in der zweiten Hälfte des 16. Jahrhunderts* (Frankfurt am Main: Peter Lang, 2000).

[8] On the history of German laws on libel and defamation, see Schmidt, *Libelli Famosi*.

2. Insults or criticisms of the local government, or other local officials or magnates;
3. Words or writings considered contrary to the community's recognized religion;
4. Insults of local clerics or other religious authorities;
5. Slanderous remarks or libelous writings directly targeting a named person; or
6. Any speech, writing, or conduct that might tend to "stir up the common man," foment violence, incite unrest, promote disrespect of authority, or create enmity or disunity within the community.

Clearly, these standards were open to considerable interpretation. Complicating matters was the fact that interpretations of the laws shifted over time, in response to changing political and religious developments, as did the targets of enforcement. While prevailing policy might suspend enforcement in one area, a change of circumstances or government might immediately redirect enforcement against what had once been freely tolerated. As many printers were to discover, they could not interpret any temporary relaxation in enforcement as necessarily signaling any abeyance of the law.

The generality of the law fostered substantial confusion as to its application and created opportunities both for circumvention and political compromise. Because urban governments rarely definitively articulated the standards by which their officials were to judge expression, censorship laws could, in effect, be held to mean whatever magistrates considered expedient under the circumstances of each case. The arbitrary nature of the law made it virtually impossible for local residents to know with certainty what was safe to print or say. Indeed, magistrates relied upon the very vagueness of the system to encourage compliance. With the scope of the law uncertain, those operating at its margins would learn to exercise a measure of "self-censorship" for their own protection.

In the early modern city, officials monitored the public mood through constabulary forces, paid spies, and volunteer informants among the citizenry. Laws were enforced through tribunals of magistrates and censors drawn from the cities' political and intellectual elites. While the magistrates erected separate controls geared to the unique regulatory challenges of the print trade, censorship of both the spoken and the printed word shared a common concern to safeguard the public peace and the social order. In most communities, all forms of communication were judged according to essentially similar standards, as part of what was intended as a comprehensive system of control over expression. This was essential, for, in the early modern city, these various media referenced and influenced each other, creating sometimes a seemingly interlocking web of ideas and information. Opinion formed and spread along multiple channels, and the fluid boundaries between speech and text, word and deed made it exceedingly difficult for local authorities to trace the origins of ideas or to follow their spread. Given this dynamic, early modern magistrates understood censorship of the printed and the spoken word as a unified effort. In a 1546 decree against malicious gossip, Augsburg officials explicitly addressed the troublesome link between speech and text. Warning against the "dangerous and idle talk" circulating in the city, the city council observed that it arose "perhaps in part out of ignorance and indiscretion" but was also caused "in part by all the news sheets published abroad and sent into [the city]." To avert the "damage and destruction" such talk could bring upon the city, the council warned all residents to be moderate and discreet in their "speech, ... writings, ... and in all other ways."[9]

"A Bridle for the Tongue" – Policing Oral Culture

"Death and life are in the power of the tongue," the Bible warns, and "the wicked is snared by the transgression of his lips."[10] Early modern magistrates saw the danger; they assumed the link between word and deed to be immediate and potentially explosive. The threat was thought to be most acute in the cities, where neighbors clashed, rumors swirled, and crowds assembled. In the Empire's greatest free cities, neighbors lived in close proximity to one another, sharing many common living, work, and social spaces. Augsburg, for example, housed a population of over 30,000 in an area of approximately two square miles.[11] Of Nuremberg, one chronicler said it was "so populous that people live on top of each other, some under the steps because there is a terrible shortage of apartments."[12] The proximity in which people lived created ample opportunity for friction and required that neighbors find ways to smooth over their differences. Magisterial decrees from this era almost constantly appealed to citizens to work together for the "common good" (*der Gemeine Nutzen*) and the public order, but this was never hollow rhetoric—these were values that deeply resonated in the daily experience of city life. Despite all efforts, however, arguments did sometimes arise, frequently resulting in insults

---

[9] StAA, Ratserlasse, 1507–1599, 'Wider daß übel Nachreden, Aug. 26, 1546'.
[10] Proverbs 18: 21; 12:13.
[11] Herbert Immenkötter, 'Die katholische Kirche in Augsburg in der ersten Hälfte des 16. Jahrhunderts,' in *Die Augsburger Kirchenordnung von 1537 und ihr Umfeld*, ed. Reinhard Schwarz (Gütersloh: Gütersloher Verlagshaus-Gerd Mohn, 1988) p. 10.
[12] Russell, *Lay Theology in the Reformation*, p. 148.

and sometimes even violence. And as city dwellers lived much of their daily lives in public streets, courtyards, and rooms open to public view, careless talk was easily overheard and broadcast about, giving rise to gossip and rumors. This "common talk" profoundly shaped public notions of community and order, and for this reason, early modern authorities were especially careful to monitor it.

Gossip, a seemingly mundane and inescapable feature of civic life, fixed the bounds of social inclusion and exclusion and, in the process, defined the limits of community. Particularly in times of crisis, rumors articulated communal anxieties and could create powerful counter-narratives of public life at odds with official decrees. As James Scott has noted, gossip, rumor, and satire often functioned as screens behind which the weak could safely critique their superiors.[13] Without openly challenging the civic order, the word on the street could subvert its very foundations.[14]

Gossip, rumors, insults—all were a common feature of urban life. Singing, too, was a sound often heard in the city streets. Many communities allowed boys' choirs from the local schools to sing on the streets for money, while beggars and peddlers also sang for pay.[15] Nuremberg was famous for its *Meistersinger*—local men trained to sing traditional ballads and religious songs—but other communities also housed schools for this purpose.[16] The *Meistersinger* gave public performances and concerts, with official approval.

Of greater concern to authorities was unauthorized singing on unauthorized themes. Public singing presented a particularly effective means of protest for early modern Germans, as songs readily drew attention and were easily remembered, especially when set to a well-known popular

---

[13] J. C. Scott, *Domination and the Arts of Resistance. Hidden Transcripts* (New Haven: Yale University Press, 1990) pp. 142–8.

[14] On efforts to police seditious talk in early modern England, see David Cressy, *Dangerous Talk: Scandalous, Seditious, and Treasonable Speech in Pre-Modern England* (Oxford: Oxford University Press, 2010) pp. 1–235.

[15] SStBA, 2° Aug. Cod. 437, 'Acta Augustana d. i. Amtshandlung und Amtliche Correspondenz der Stadt Augsburg, 1566–1745,' fol. 83–4; Paul Hektor Mair, 'Das Diarium Paul Hektor Mairs von 1560–1563.' in *Die Chroniken der Schwäbischen Städte: Augsburg*, Bd. 8, *Die Chroniken der deutschen Städte vom 14. bis ins 16. Jahrhundert*, Bd. 33, ed. Historische Kommission bei der Bayerischen Kommission der Wissenschaften, 1928 (Göttingen: Vandenhoek & Ruprecht, 1966) pp. 57–8 fn. 2; Fisher, *Music and Religious Identity in Counter-Reformation Augsburg*, pp. 73–4.

[16] Christopher Brown Boyd, *Singing the Gospel: Lutheran Hymns and the Success of the Reformation* (Cambridge, MA: Harvard University Press, 2005) p. 46; Fritz Schnell, *Zur Geschichte der Augsburger Meistersingerschule* (Augsburg: Verlag Die Brigg, 1958) pp. 11–13.

tune.[17] Moreover, songs were relatively easy to create and spread. One did not need to be a *Meistersinger* to write a song—even an ordinary person with a bit of imagination could set a new rhyme to a well-worn tune. Such ditties could be taught to one's friends or committed to paper and passed around. If the new song was particularly catchy or clever, it might find its way into print, thanks to the efforts of an alert printer or bookseller looking for something new to please his customers.

The Augsburg plasterer Sebastian Hundertkass, for example, was a humble man, but a prolific songwriter. Following a dispute with a local baker, he wrote and distributed a song accusing the bakers of cheating the poor. The bakers, he sang, gave less bread to the poor than to the rich and stole from the common folk by selling underweight loaves at full price.[18] With bread an essential staple of the daily diet, allegations of unfair practices by the bakers were potentially explosive. Hundertkass implicitly accused the Augsburg authorities of failing to properly regulate the trade; indeed, the town council prosecuted him for attacking the city government as much as the bakers' guild.

Hundertkass wrote out several copies of his song and distributed them among his friends and acquaintances. He also admitted to writing several other songs, copies of which are included in his criminal file. The songs, all in the same labored handwriting and set to popular melodies, reveal Hundertkass to have been an eager, if not gifted, songwriter. He evidently found in his hobby a valuable means of self-expression, for his songs covered a wide range of subjects and experiences. Even as a lowly plasterer, Hundertkass did not shrink from the big issues, weighing in on heavenly portents, the death of Emperor Charles V, the birth of Christ, and in his words, "the course of the world."[19] Hundertkass also returned to his favored theme of airing his personal grievances with local tradesmen in another song, to the tune of *One Day I Went A-Walking* (*Ich Ging Einmal Spazieren*),[20] which recorded his punishment by the fishermen's guild for illegal ice fishing.[21]

The Augsburg magistrates concluded that Hundertkass had written and circulated a defamatory song directed against not only the bakers and bread-weighers, but also against the city government. They expelled him

---

[17] Rebecca Wagner Oettinger, *Music as Propaganda in the German Reformation* (Aldershot: Ashgate, 2001) pp. 33–4.

[18] StAA, Strafamt, Urg. Sebastian Hundertkass, 25 May 1579.

[19] Ibid., Answer Nr. 15.

[20] Otto Böckel, *Handbuch des Deutschen Volksliedes* (Hildesheim: Georg Olms Verlagsbuchhandlung, 1967) p. 229.

[21] "Dis lied Ist im thon Ich gieng ains mals Spaziern Eÿn weglin klaÿn," filed in StAA, Strafamt, Urg. Sebastian Hundertkass, 25 May 1579.

from the city and issued a decree outlawing the singing and distribution of such songs:

> It has come to the attention of the Honorable Council of this Holy Imperial City of Augsburg that several troublesome people have been composing all sorts of frivolous, disgraceful songs and writings and distributing them among the citizenry to be read and sung. The Honorable Council earnestly decrees that everyone in this city should refrain from such acts, for they are not only strictly proscribed in the Imperial Recesses and the common laws, but are wrongful in themselves, and the cause of all manner of disobedience and unrest ...[22]

The Council's decree reflected a common official view of public singing—that it was a frivolous pursuit encouraging disorder and disobedience. Of particular concern were the activities of itinerant singers who performed on the public streets.[23] As strangers with no fixed abode, such people were seen as a threat, as no responsible citizen could vouch for their honesty or answer for their behavior. Officials generally equated such people with beggars, who sometimes also sang for money, and often punished them under the laws against vagrancy. Given their poor earnings and constant traveling, itinerant singers and musicians were also generally assumed to be prone to thievery and in league with the robbers with whom they shared the highways.[24]

The very qualities of song that made it a popular mode of communication also made it particularly difficult for authorities to control. Song, like speech, was ephemeral: unless committed to paper, it left no physical trace from which authorities could establish its contents. Songs were easily created, copied out, and passed around from hand to hand. The censors' review was therefore impossible, for there were no essential links in the distribution chain upon which authorities could impose their supervision.[25]

"To Write is Very Dangerous"—Controlling the Written Word

Songs were part of a lively manuscript culture, wherein all manner of verses, ballads, cartoons, and satires circulated through the streets. The circulation

---

[22] StAA, Evangelisches Wesensarchiv Augsburg Nr. 1561, 'Öffentliche Anschläge und Verrufe, 1490–1599, Tom. 2.'

[23] StAN, B-Laden SIL 196, Nr. 12, Doc. Nr. 2, fol. 1v–2r.

[24] See Theodor Hampe, *Die fahrenden Leute in der deutschen Vergangenheit* (Jena: Eugen Diedrichs Verlag, 1924) pp. 22–31.

[25] On efforts to police the circulation of political songs in pre-revolutionary Paris, see Robert Darnton, *Poetry and Police: Communication Networks in Eighteenth-Century Paris* (Cambridge, MA: Harvard University Press, 2010).

of these manuscripts raises the important question of readership. Although assessment of literacy rates historically is problematic,[26] all indications suggest that very few early modern Germans could read the texts available to them.

Literacy rates varied substantially according to location, gender, social class and professional status. In the major German cities, some estimates suggest that perhaps about 30 percent of the male population in the early sixteenth century was able to read.[27] Wealthier and more highly skilled urban men were more likely to be able to read and write, although many middling merchants and artisans might also acquire some reading and writing skills to carry on their trades. Women at every social level were, on average, typically less literate than their male peers. Even those individuals who could read often could not write, as this skill was typically taught later, if at all.[28]

Substantially lower literacy rates existed in the countryside, where the majority of Germans lived. Here, perhaps only 4–5 percent of the rural population would have been able to read in the early sixteenth century.[29] Taking urban and rural literacy rates together, Robert Scribner has estimated that, with a total estimated population of 16 million, the reading population of the Holy Roman Empire during the Reformation era comprised only about 400,000 people; that is, perhaps only one person in 43 could have encountered the Reformation message in written form.[30]

For those who could read, the urban book market offered a wide assortment of texts in all price ranges. A complete, unbound copy of Luther's 1534 German Bible would have cost 2 gulden, 8 groschen, or roughly the equivalent of a month's wages for an unskilled worker.[31] Although only wealthier readers could have afforded such expensive

[26] R. A. Houston, *Literacy in Early Modern Europe: Culture and Education, 1500–1800* (Harlow: Pearson Education Limited, 2002) pp. 125–39.

[27] Hans-Jörg Künast, *'Getruckt zu Augspurg:' Buchdruck und Buchhandel in Augsburg zwischen 1468 und 1555*. (Tübingen: Max Niemeyer Verlag, 1997) pp. 11–13; Edwards, *Printing, Propaganda*, pp. 37–8.

[28] Houston, *Literacy*, pp. 68–9; Roger Chartier, 'The Practical Impact of Writing,' *A History of Private Life*, Vol. 3 (Cambridge, MA: Harvard University Press, 1989) pp. 111–59.

[29] Edwards, *Printing, Propaganda*, pp. 37–8; Oettinger, *Music as Propaganda*, pp. 23–4.

[30] R.W. Scribner and C. Scott Dixon, *The German Reformation*, 2nd ed. (Basingstoke: Palgrave Macmillan, 2003) pp. 19–20. For somewhat higher figures, see R. W. Scribner, 'Oral Culture and the Transmission of Reformation Ideas,' in *The Transmission of Ideas in the Lutheran Reformation*, ed. Helga Robinson-Hammerstein (Dublin: Irish Academic Press, 1989) p. 83.

[31] R. Gawthrop and Gerald Strauss, 'Protestantism and Literacy in Early Modern Germany,' in *Past and Present*, 104 (1984): p. 40.

editions, most cities also had many small-time printers and peddlers who made their living selling broadsheets and songs to "the common man." From the testimony of these tradesmen, we learn that they frequently earned very little from such sales; a four-page pamphlet might be had for a little as a single pfenning.[32] For urban workers in the 1520s, this was less than the price of a *Maß* of beer or a half-pound of beef—not a trifling investment, but not a great sacrifice for many.[33]

For the majority who could not read, the printed word might have been indecipherable to them, but it was not closed off. The written word filtered through the community through public readings and discussions, as well as through other media. Indeed, Hans-Joachim Köhler has described a "two-stage" communication process in which "opinion leaders" such as clergymen, teachers, and magistrates read and were influenced by pamphlets, then transmitted their message orally to wider audiences.[34] The urban sources establish that pamphlets and broadsheets were also topics of conversation in far humbler settings, wherever people might gather. In these communities, reading aloud was a common feature of family devotions and other intimate gatherings.[35] Andrew Pettegree has questioned the impact of public reading in spreading the Reformation message, but, as we will see, it was a commonly cited source of information in the interrogation records of the period.[36] As in the case of manuscript copies and adaptations, these modes of transmission both spread the printed message and transformed it. As a result, the printed word often took on new forms and meanings as it passed through the city streets.

The Problem of Print

The conspicuous wealth of Nuremberg, Augsburg, Strasbourg, and Cologne made them magnets for trade in both commodities and ideas. Their extensive trading networks brought them a constant stream of visitors,

---

[32] Prices, of course, were heavily dependent on press runs, production costs, and shipping charges. See Künast, *Getruckt zu Augspurg*, pp. 188–96.

[33] M. J. Elsas, *Umriss einer Geschichte der Preise und Löhne in Deutschland vom ausgehenden Mittelalter bis zum Beginn des neunzehnten Jahrhunderts*, Bd. I (Leiden: A.W. Sijthoff's Uitgeversmaatschappij, 1936) pp. 575, 609.

[34] Hans-Joachim Köhler, 'The *Flugschriften* and Their Importance in Religious Debate: A Quantitative Approach,' in '*Astrologi hallucinati*': *Stars and the End of the World in Luther's Time*, ed. Paola Zambelli (New York, 1986) pp. 153–75.

[35] Robert W. Scribner, 'Flugblatt und Analphabetentum. Wie kam der gemeine Mann zu reformatorischen Ideen?' in *Flugschriften als Massenmedium der Reformationszeit*, ed. Hans-Joachim Köhler (Stuttgart: Klett-Cotta, 1981) pp. 65–9; Chartier, *A History of Private Life*, pp. 111–59.

[36] Pettegree, *Reformation and the Culture of Persuasion*, pp. 117–18.

and their international links provided them with important contacts with learned communities across the continent. These cities became hubs for the circulation of ideas, and the texts produced by their printers circulated throughout Germany and beyond.[37]

Given the importance of the regional book trade, many of these cities had mechanisms to police the market even before the Reformation broke on the scene. In Cologne, the university faculty, acting under papal authorization and with the cooperation of the city council, had been authorized since 1479 to censor theological works submitted for publication in that city. This was a mere 13 years after the establishment of Cologne's first press, and is thought to be one of the earliest local censorship measures in the Empire.[38] Acting under its own authority, Nuremberg's city council issued in 1513 the first of a series of measures to control the new media. The council required that the city's printers appear before it and swear neither to print nor to distribute any material that might "cause harm, disgrace, or disadvantage" to the clergy, the city council, the imperial estates or other distinguished figures.[39] Similar measures were adopted in many other communities, but these early decrees depended almost entirely upon the voluntary compliance of the printers. To encourage compliance and increase accountability, many towns enacted systems of pre-publication censorship. Augsburg, for example, mandated in 1523 that all works were to be approved in advance by one of the city's *Bürgermeister*, and all texts were to bear the name of the author or the person who had given the material to be printed, as well as the name of the printer.[40] Bowing to complaints from the print trade, however, the council soon relaxed the rules requiring identifying imprints.[41] This exchange between the policy aims of the council, the economic concerns of the book trade, and the demands of public opinion would become a consistent feature of urban censorship systems in the years to come.

City censors were often drawn from local clergymen, scholars, and civic officials. Typically, a panel of censors was appointed to share the work and, when necessary, they consulted with experts with specialized

---

[37] Hans-Jörg Künast, 'Augsburg als Knotenpunkt des deutschen und europäischen Buchhandels (1480–1550),' in *Augsburg in der Frühen Neuzeit: Beiträge zu einem Forschungsprogramm*, eds Jochen Brüning and Friedrich Niewöhner (Berlin: Akademie Verlag, 1995), pp. 240–51.

[38] Viktor Muckel, *Die Entwicklung der Zensur in Köln* (Diss. Jur. Köln. Würzburg: 1932) 9; Schmidt, *Libelli Famosi*, pp. 208–09, 273.

[39] Arnd Müller, 'Zensurpolitik der Reichstadt Nürnberg,' *Mitteilungen des Vereins für Geschichte der Stadt Nürnberg*, 49 (1959): p. 73.

[40] StAA, Ratsbuch Nr. 15, 1520–1529, fol. 26r–v.

[41] Ibid., fol. 27r.

linguistic or theological training. For the most part, however, they were expected to personally oversee all the texts submitted for review.[42]

City censors, however, did more than just censor books. As printers were typically not organized into guilds, censors were often tasked with overseeing the regulation of the trade, setting commercial standards for the business and resolving disputes among the printers. Although complete records of the office-holders are often lacking, there was typically no requirement, either by law or practice, that the censors be themselves active in the printing trade. In those few instances where we can identify individual censors, they were typically well-educated, well-connected members of the urban social, intellectual, and political elite.

The role of censor was typically an honorary, unpaid appointment.[43] This had several consequences for the book trade. First, those who took on the job would of necessity require sufficient income from other sources to support themselves. Not surprisingly, those censors known to us in this period were often drawn from the professional elites and wealthier strata of urban society. Presumably, these men shared the concerns and prejudices common to their station and identified most closely with the priorities of the government that they served. This institutional identification is significant, for the lack of clear guidelines left urban censorship laws to be filtered through the subjective understandings of its enforcers. With no specific titles or authors prohibited, it was left to the censors to apply their own judgment as to how a given text might be understood within the community, and whether it might generate the type of response that the city council wished to proscribe. Thus, the censors' inquiry was far more concerned with predicting a text's effect within the mind of its reader than in reviewing the contents of text itself. This evaluation was supremely subjective, and doubtless reflected the values and priorities of the reviewer.

Forced to look to their own affairs, urban censors also could not afford to give their duties their undivided time and attention. In Strasbourg, officials complained that it would take years for them to read all the theological texts they were asked to censor—they opted instead to simply read the titles.[44] Frankfurt censors, who were often clergymen, were apparently more diligent, sometimes affirming in their reports that they had read their assigned texts "from beginning to end."[45] This was time-consuming,

---

[42] Künast, *Getruckt zu Augspurg*, p. 207.

[43] Wolfgang Wüst, *Censur als Stütze von Staat und Kirche in der Frühmoderne: Augsburg, Bayern, Kurmainz und Württemberg in Vergleich*. (Munich: Verlag Ernst Vögel, 1998) pp. 18; 38–9.

[44] Lorna Jane Abray, *The People's Reformation: Magistrates, Clergy, and Commons in Strasbourg 1500–1598* (Oxford: Basil Blackwell, 1985) p. 63.

[45] FaM ISG, Buchdruck und Zensur Nr. 55: Sammlung von Zensurzetteln (1609–1615), Nr. 41.

however, and with a review process that functioned only part-time, delays were inevitable, creating a lag in the market for competing printers to exploit. In the competitive, time-driven economy of the book trade, this delay could be profoundly costly to printers and booksellers. As a result, the censorial review process could pose a genuine financial disadvantage to some printers. By their very structure, then, urban censorship systems held within them certain disincentives to full compliance.

Although the censors may have had no personal stake in the book trade, they regulated its activities and reported to the city council on the printers' and booksellers' concerns. Their immersion in the commercial concerns of the printers meant that they could not fully ignore the financial interests of the trade as they executed their duties. Indeed, it seems that the censors understood the economic consequences of censorship on the book trade and attempted at some level to balance the magistrates' requirements against the commercial needs of the tradesmen. Above all, however, the censors were expected to be loyal to the city council's priorities.

The World of the Printers

While printers and booksellers were typically not organized into officially recognized guilds, they nevertheless operated in a tight-knit business and social network, often united by ties of marriage and family.[46] Urban printers and booksellers were by no mean a homogenous group, however. In the major imperial cities, the book trade typically supported tradesmen and merchants serving several markets, offering everything from highly crafted, expensive treatises for humanists and scholars to crude cartoons and broadsheets priced for the humblest day laborer. Some printers and book merchants were quite well educated, being trained in Latin and other languages. Others, however, knew only German, although they sometimes dealt in texts printed in other languages.[47] Some booksellers claimed not to be able to read at all, a not altogether surprising fact, given that many were merely peddlers selling whatever might bring them a bit of money.

With the coming of the Reformation, most of the imperial cities embraced the evangelical cause; of the 69 imperial cities in 1521, all but 14 of them had adopted some form of Protestantism by mid-century.[48] Cologne, one of the Empire's largest free cities and most important printing

---

[46] Künast, *Getruckt zu Augspurg*, p. 102.

[47] Ibid., p. 72–8.

[48] Thomas A. Brady, Jr., *Ruling Class, Regime, and Reformation at Strasbourg, 1520–1555* (Leiden: Brill, 1978) p. 10; Bernd Moeller, 'Imperial Cities and the Reformation,' in *Imperial Cities and the Reformation: Three Essays*, ed. & trans. H. C. Erik Midelfort and Mark U. Edwards, Jr. (Durham, N.C.: Labyrinth Press, 1982) pp. 41–2.

centers, was the most notable exception to this trend. Robert Scribner has pointed to the close cooperation between Cologne's city government, ecclesiastical administration, and university faculty as an important factor in its opposition to Protestant reform.[49] This early coordination between civic, clerical, and university interests checked evangelical support and turned Cologne's printing industry firmly to the service of the Catholic cause.[50] But in most of the Empire's major print centers, local magistrates were slow to respond to the new reform movement, sending their printers decidedly mixed signals on their religious priorities.

Many urban booksellers and printers helped spread the reform message, but in many cases their work seems to have been motivated more by market forces than the printers' religious affiliations. Indeed, the printers' own religious sympathies did not necessarily dictate what they printed.[51] Analysis of the prints produced in Augsburg in the first half of the sixteenth century reveals that Protestant printers sometimes produced Catholic texts, while some Catholic printers produced Protestant ones.[52] While Natalie Zemon Davis found strong religious identification and activism among the printers of Lyon,[53] for many German printers, economics—not religion—dictated the work they were willing to undertake and the risks they were prepared to assume. Catholic printers in Leipzig, where Duke Georg had explicitly banned Lutheran texts, protested that such works offered the only money to be made in the business. In a 1524 supplication to the Duke on their behalf, the Leipzig town council noted that "what they have in overabundance [that is, Catholic texts] is desired by no one and cannot even be given away," but what the public wanted—Luther's works—they were not allowed to even possess, let alone sell.[54]

The Leipzig council's petition highlights the printers' often precarious economic existence. The intensive capital requirements of the business and the vagaries of market demand exposed printers to considerable financial risk. In an effort to generate needed capital, printers often sought credit from the wholesale book dealers and publishers who sold their product, incurring substantial debts in the bargain.[55] The printers' need to bring

---

[49] R. W. Scribner, 'Why Was There No Reformation in Cologne?,' in *Popular Culture and Popular Movements in Reformation Germany* (London: Hambledon Press, 1987) pp. 217–41.

[50] Muckel, *Zensur in Köln* pp. 8–26.

[51] Künast, *Getruckt zu Augspurg*, p. 80.

[52] Ibid, pp. 82–3.

[53] Natalie Zemon Davis, 'Strikes and Salvation in Lyon,' in *Society and Culture in Early Modern France* (London: Duckworth, 1975) pp. 1–16.

[54] Edwards, *Printing, Propaganda*, p. 14.

[55] Künast, *Getruckt zu Augspurg*, pp. 32–78.

their goods quickly to market to discharge their debts sometimes brought them into direct conflict with the censors.

The censors and the local book trade also came into conflict because the very texts that the censors found most objectionable were often the most popular with the public.[56] Numerous studies of book production and readership in early modern Germany have documented the popularity of controversial religious polemic and political satire—topics that authorities were particularly keen to censor. The financial gains such texts could bring were particularly tantalizing to often cash-strapped printers and booksellers. In the financially risky book business, it was vital that dealers be able to gauge public interest and respond to market demand as quickly as possible.[57] Securing the censors' approval, however, could significantly delay the bringing of a text to market, resulting sometimes in a competitive disadvantage to printers and booksellers eager to exploit the public demand for timely and topical writing.[58] The reward for non-compliance could also be substantial: illicit texts could reasonably command a 100 percent mark-up over their usual retail price.[59]

The forbidden book market was not without its own economic risks, however. As most printers operated under a heavy load of debt, even a temporary shutdown by the magistrates could prove financially catastrophic.[60] The more marginal operators, however, had little to lose and often much to gain in the clandestine book trade. Indeed, the printers most often implicated in the illegal book trade in Augsburg were among some of the poorest citizens on the city's tax rolls.[61] Economic pressures encouraged printers and booksellers to try to dodge the censors in hopes of realizing the financial pay-offs forbidden books could bring.

The 1559 arrests of the Augsburg wood block cutter (*Formschneider*) David Danecker and his associates illustrate the risks printers were prepared to take to meet their obligations. Danecker had been arrested for printing an apocalyptic text foretelling the imminent destruction of the papacy, *The Terrible Destruction and Fall of the Entire Papacy* (*Von der Erschrocklichen*

---

[56] Hildegard Schnabel, 'Zur historischen Beurteilung der Flugschriftenhändler in der Zeit der frühen Reformation und des Bauernkrieges,' *Wissenschaftliche Zeitschrift der Humboldt-Universität zu Berlin, Gesellschafts-und Sprachwissenschaftliche Reihe* 14 (1965): p. 879.

[57] Künast, *Getruckt zu Augspurg*, pp. 58–72.

[58] StAA, Censuramt, 'Die Buchdrucker betreffend, Tom I, 1550–1729,' Petition of Printers dated 19 March 1551; Petition of Printers dated 12 June 1561.

[59] Pettegree, *Reformation and the Culture of Persuasion*, p. 160.

[60] Künast, *Getruckt zu Augspurg*, p. 62.

[61] Ibid., pp. 48–52.

Zurstorung unnd Niderlag deß gantzen Bapstumbs).⁶² Danecker made the woodcuts for it himself, "with the hope of accomplishing something big."⁶³ The printing cost him a fortune—400 gulden—and when it was finished, he intended to present the first exemplars, bound in gold, to the Protestant electors and other notables. Danecker had staked a lot on *The Destruction of the Papacy* and had great hopes for it, but he denied any religious motive for his efforts. His objective was purely financial: the book was to be such a "work" that would pay his debts and, hopefully, turn a profit.⁶⁴

Before the magistrates, Danecker made no attempt to excuse his crime. He had made a calculated financial decision, and his confession made clear he was unwilling to risk his investment by seeking the censors' pre-approval:

> He has fretted over this project and dedicated a lot of trouble, work, and cost to it: if he made a big fuss [and] asked for permission to print it and this was denied, he would be left in great distress. So he went ahead and printed it and hoped that no harm would come of it because it is a laughable thing. He asks, for God's sake, that this Honorable Council not place him in jeopardy, but rather be merciful … He will never do such a thing again, for he must make 2,200 coats of arms for the memorial mass of His Imperial Majesty [Emperor Charles V]; his apprentices cannot do this work without him and he would suffer great disadvantage [if he were imprisoned and unable to complete the project].⁶⁵

In three further interrogations, Danecker was asked about several other anti-Catholic texts circulating in the city. Danecker denied any knowledge of them, whereupon he was bound in the *strappado* to be tortured. Crying and swearing by his salvation, he protested his innocence, begging again to be released in time to finish his work for the late Emperor's memorial mass. Without that income, he said, he would be "in great trouble and debt." Moreover, he needed especially to attend the upcoming Frankfurt book fair and retain "trust and credit" there.⁶⁶

---

⁶² SStBA, Rar 78, [Martin Schrot], *Von der Erschrocklichen Zurstörung unnd Niderlag deß gantzen Bapstumbs/geproheceyet und geweissagt/durch die propheten/Christum/und seine Apostoln/und auß Johannis Apocalypsi Figürlich und sichtlich gesehen. Durch ain hochgelehrten/dise gegen würtige ding/vor sehr vil Jaren beschriben/und der wellt trewlich/ auffs kürtzest hiermit fürgehallten/zü Nutz unnd güt/der Seelen/zum Ewigen Leben. Mathei am 7. Weicht ab ir ubeltheter all behendt Dan ich hab euch noch nie kain mal erkent.* [Augsburg: Danecker, 1558].

⁶³ StAA, Strafamt, Urg. David Danecker, 24 Jan. 1559.

⁶⁴ Ibid.

⁶⁵ Ibid., Answer Nr. 11.

⁶⁶ Ibid, Urg. 30 Jan. 1559.

Figure 1.1 "The Pope Calls on His Protectors." SStBA, Rar 78, [Martin Schrot], *Von der Erschrocklichen Zurstörung unnd Niderlag deß gantzen Bapstumbs...* ([Augsburg: David Danecker, 1558]), fol. 9.

Danecker's stated hope that the authorities would find his book, as he did, merely a "laughable thing" seems grossly naive, given that the text and images of *The Destruction of the Papacy* contained precisely the sort of virulent anti-Catholic, anti-imperial polemic the Augsburg authorities were most eager to suppress after 1555. The tone of the book is well captured in one of Danecker's full-page woodcuts early in the text: under the heading, "The Pope Calls on His Protectors," a figure resembling Charles V is shown dutifully kneeling and drinking from a chalice offered him by the Whore of Babylon, who wears the papal tiara and is seated on the Seven-Headed Beast of the Apocalypse (see Figure 1.1). Danecker's confession indicates that he understood very well that the censors would not approve his book, for he chose not to show it to them rather than risk its suppression. Indeed, he admitted that the Augsburg bookseller Georg Willer had secretly warned him not to print the book, as it would "bring him misfortune," but he was already too financially invested in the work to halt the project. Danecker stated that he had no option but to bring the book to market.[67] Rather than risk the book's seizure, he gambled that the Augsburg authorities would never catch up with him.

Also caught up in Danecker's prosecution was Georg Willer, perhaps the most important book distributor in southern Germany. In a petition to the city council on his behalf, Willer's wife and relatives stressed the economic consequences of his arrest. They noted that he had suffered great hardship from the confiscation of books he had purchased at the Frankfurt book fair, many of which were merely calendars, sermons, and other uncontroversial texts. If the books were not soon returned to him, other foreign booksellers would beat him to market with such books, to his considerable disadvantage. Moreover, many booksellers in other locales were waiting for Willer to send them inventory. The delay was causing them hardship and jeopardizing Willer's ability to keep his customers.[68] In response, the council released Willer with merely a "serious warning" to refrain from such activities in the future.[69]

Danecker's attempt to settle his debts with a banned book illustrates the financial pressures that drove printers into the clandestine book trade. It also suggests the laxity of enforcement of local censorship laws within the period. Although the printers understood that violation of such laws could have a devastating impact upon their livelihoods, they did not regard the threat of enforcement as sufficiently real to offset the economic rewards of dealing in prohibited books.

---

[67] Ibid., Urg. 20 Jan. 1559, Answer Nr. 12.
[68] Petition to Council, filed ibid.
[69] StAA, Strafbuch Nr. 98, 1554–1562, fol. 119r.

In Willer's case, the Augsburg council appears to have been hesitant to jeopardize Willer's trade. As Danecker and other printers testified, they were dependent on Willer both for material to print and for bringing their works to market. According to printer Valentin Ottmar, Willer's understanding of the market was so profound, he could always be trusted to spot a crowd-pleaser; Ottmar noted that he always printed extra copies of anything Willer gave him and sold them for his own account.[70] As a main conduit for books throughout the region, Willer's business was a vital link that sustained Augsburg's book trade—one that the city could ill afford to disrupt. While Augsburg had many printers able to pick up the work of a middling tradesman like David Danecker, few were equipped to step into the shoes of Georg Willer. His treatment by the Augsburg authorities reflects the economic concerns that frequently tempered the enforcement of local censorship laws within the period.

These prosecutions also illustrate some of the endemic weaknesses of local censorship efforts. The printers and booksellers were clearly not consistently observing the city council's order that they secure the review and approval of the censors before printing or selling texts in the city. Rather, many appeared to believe that only potentially controversial texts required pre-authorization and that they were otherwise free to deal in materials on other themes. The printers and booksellers often had far different views of what might be objectionable than did the censors. Their decisions as to which texts to submit for review and which to withhold deprived the censors of the very control the magistrates had sought to give them. Moreover, these arrests revealed the limits of the enforcement methods then in place. The printers and booksellers were clearly willing to deal in illegal materials in the hope of a big profit. The illegal operators were gambling that the local officials would never apprehend them, and they would continue to do so until the threat of enforcement became more real.

The region's book dealers and printers also exploited the laxity of interterritorial enforcement to shelter a long-distance trade in prohibited texts. As some of the Empire's most important printing centers, the southwestern cities served both the legitimate and the clandestine markets for books. Controversial authors engaged couriers to smuggle manuscripts to local printers, finance their production, and ferry the exemplars back for distribution in other locales.[71] Such arrangements were safer for both parties: engaging a foreign printer made it less likely that an illegal text could be traced back to its author, and reliance on a middle-man shielded both parties from access to too much incriminating information.[72]

---

[70] StAA, Strafamt, Urg. Valentin Ottmar, 6 Oct. 1559, Answer Nr. 4.
[71] StAA, Censuramt XVI, Nr. 6.
[72] Schnabel, 'Flugschriftenhändler,' p. 875.

Itinerant booksellers also engaged local printers to print or reprint prohibited texts, which they then sold throughout their journeys.[73] Such merchants were often impossible to trace, as they were constantly on the move. The local printers and booksellers they dealt with purported not even to know their full names, identifying them to local officials only by first names or more often, simply as "a foreigner."[74] Indeed, the unnamed "foreigner" soliciting these illicit transactions appeared so often in printers' testimony as to become something of a stock figure in the cities' criminal files. Usually poor, and often illiterate, these itinerant booksellers typically sold whatever they could to earn a bit of money. A printer or bookdealer looking to unload prohibited texts on the market could expect that these peddlers might be willing to take on items that a more savvy or scrupulous merchant might consider simply too risky. Indeed, many peddlers caught with prohibited texts testified that they were illiterate and entirely ignorant of what they were actually selling.[75]

If illiterate peddlers did not know what they were selling, they would also not know enough to avoid the censors, as Georg Willer discovered in 1566. Willer had allowed an itinerant bookseller named Hans Nideraur to sell a number of his books and pamphlets on consignment. The books included over 100 separate titles, mostly stolid Lutheran devotional works, some moralistic treatises, and a few anti-Catholic broadsides. Nideraur took the books into the Tyrol region, in Catholic Austria, where all such texts had been expressly banned. Nideraur likely went where he hoped he could find a market, but given the fact that he could not read, he may not have even been aware of the contents of his books, let alone that they were prohibited in Tyrol. He did know, however, where he had procured the books, and when apprehended, he readily led the Austrian authorities back to Willer. Nideraur, and Willer's books, were sent back to Augsburg, along with a stern letter to the city council from Archduke Ferdinand II demanding that Augsburg stop the export of sectarian books into his territories.[76]

In addition to exporting prohibited texts, local book dealers also relied on their contacts in other cities to tap into the forbidden book market.

---

[73] See, for example, StAA, Strafamt, Urg. Josias Wöhrle, 1 Aug. 1584; Hans Schultes d. Ä, 3 Aug. 1584; Bartolme Keppeler, 10 April 1592; Georg Kress, 15 March 1595; Christosmus Dapertshofer, 6 Feb. 1613.

[74] See StAN, B-Laden SIL 296, Nr. 12, Doc. Nr. 1, fol. 1r; StAA, Strafamt, Urg. Bartolme Keppeler, 10 April 1592; Georg Kress, 15 March 1595; Christosmus Dapertshofer, 6 Feb. 1613.

[75] StAA, Strafamt, Urg. Stoffel Plattner, 18 March 1555; Barbara Mollin, 29 Dec. 1572.

[76] StAA, Censuramt, 'Die Buchdrucker betreffend, Tom I, 1550–1729;' John L. Flood, 'Umstürzler in den Alpen: Bücher und Leser in Österreich im Zeitalter der Gegenreformation,' Daphnis 20(2) (1991): pp. 241–2.

Material deemed too dangerous to print in one city could be printed in neighboring cities and imported back for sale. If locals had any difficulty finding forbidden books in their own communities, they could arrange with private couriers to smuggle them in when they next visited the city.

While magistrates relied on small contingents of city watchmen and market inspectors to police the goods sold in the city streets, their numbers were typically inadequate to regularly patrol a city of any great size. To make the inspectors' jobs harder, dealers in prohibited texts generally kept on the move throughout the city, making the rounds of taverns, churches, or even selling door-to-door.[77] Nuremberg booksellers complained repeatedly to the city council that foreign peddlers were selling locally forbidden tracts in "every corner." Indeed, they were to be found "by almost every church, inn, market, next to the City Hall itself, even in front of our shops."[78] To better their chances still more, booksellers sometimes hired fleet-footed boys to peddle their most dangerous items, hoping that they could out-run the inspectors. Booksellers also relied on simple camouflage to conceal the true nature of their books from the inspectors. Illegal texts might be sold under innocuous titles calculated to mislead the casual reader as to their contents, with the true message buried well within the body of the text. Faced with such ruses, effective control over the sale of imported texts depended upon sharp-eyed inspectors and tips from well-placed informants, but the evidence suggests that a substantial corpus of such literature was nevertheless circulating beyond their reach.

One important technique used to maintain secrecy and confuse the censors was the publication of texts anonymously or with false names, dates, or places of printing. By law, all texts produced or sold in the Empire were required to list the names of the author and the printer and the date and place of printing.[79] Printers and authors hoping to prevent the censors from tracing prohibited works back to them, however, routinely omitted or altered such identifying information. Frequently, printers who reprinted a text originally produced elsewhere simply restated the original printer's imprint, making it appear to the censors as if the text were an original imported from an outside press. Sometimes, however, printers and booksellers deliberately appropriated the names of other printers or locations to help cover their tracks. As the Augsburg Printer's Ordinance noted, an unscrupulous printer might deceptively place "Printed in

---

[77] StAA, Censuramt, 'Die Buchtrucker betreffend, Tom I, 1550–1729.'

[78] StAN, B-Laden SIL 196, Nr. 6, fol. 4r–v; B-Laden SIL 196, Nr. 12, Doc. 1, fol. 1r.

[79] Reichsabschied Augsburg 1530, § 58, in *Neue vollständige Sammlung der Reichs-Abschiede, welche von den Zeiten Kayser Conrads des II. bis jetzo auf den Teutschen Reichs-Tagen abgefasset worden*, 1747 (Osnabrück: Otto Zeller, 1967), p. 314.

Hamburg, Magdeburg, Frankfurt, or Leipzig" on his works, and "no one will be able to turn in such books or authors."[80]

Magistrates sometimes attempted to trace books with falsified or missing imprints by the materials they used. Regensburg officials wrote to Nuremberg in 1626 asking the city council to investigate the origins of a news-sheet circulating in that area under a false Regensburg imprint. The Regensburgers established that the text could not have come from their city as claimed because "the type is wrong and no such paper is to be found here."[81] Although Nuremberg officials questioned the local printers and booksellers, they found no one who recognized the typeface.[82] Printers were evidently aware of this tactic; the printer of an anonymous 1526 treatise by the Anabaptist leader Eitelhans Langenmantel,[83] for example, took pains to set the entire text in lower-case letters, avoiding any of the decorative initials or distinctively-styled upper-case letters that might identify his shop.[84]

While the clandestine book market developed devices to skirt local censorship efforts, some texts were simply too dangerous to circulate in any market. The most sensitive religious and political writings, therefore, were often not put into print at all, but were copied out and circulated hand-to-hand. Indeed, the sources attest to the widespread copying and distribution of manuscripts. Some of the manuscripts circulated were copies of incendiary protests against political or religious authorities. Quite often, the shared manuscripts were adaptations of printed texts, frequently songs, that had been modified to comment upon concerns specific to the local community. Thus, forbidden prints often formed the basis for the creation of even more punishable manuscripts.

The networks through which these manuscripts circulated were *ad hoc* and informal, consisting of little more than the passing around of letters or songs among friends and neighbors. Other networks, however, were highly coordinated, relying on members to act as copyists and couriers. Through these networks, the forbidden book trade became not simply a market for controversial prints, but a forum in which the printed word was absorbed and adapted into new formats. Thus, illegal prints worked their way into an even more shadowy world of prohibited songs, punishable

---

[80] StAA, Censuramt XVI, Nr. 9, ¶ 5.

[81] StAN, B-Laden SIL 196, Nr. 7, fol. 4r.

[82] Ibid, fol. 6–10.

[83] The text was entitled *Ein kurzer Begriff von dem alten und neuen Papisten, auch von den rechten und wahren Christen*. Karl Schottenloher has identified the printer as Philip Ulhart of Ausgburg. See Karl Schottenloher, *Philip Ulhart, ein Augsburger Winkeldrucker und Helfershelfer der Schwärmer und Wiedertäufer, 1523–1529* (Nieuwkoop: B. De Graaf, 1967) p. 126.

[84] Ibid.

writings, and subversive rumor. Ephemeral as they were, these adaptations rarely come to the attention of historians, and it is precisely this transitory element that made them so vital in the dissemination of messages that magistrates did not want their subjects to hear. Although such texts could not have the widespread impact afforded by the printed word, the very limited circulation they allowed also offered the secrecy necessary to ensure the circulation of the message beyond the oversight of the city and its censors.

Policing the City

In addition to installing censors over the print trade, urban magistrates monitored public expression and behavior through the reports of city militia and the guards posted at the city gates. Except in times of war or civic unrest, town councils generally did not keep large numbers of troops within the city; they did, however, organize an armed watch from among the adult male citizenry to patrol the city's neighborhoods. Organized under the command of a designated "quarter captain," adult male citizens took turns patrolling quarters of the city at night; in times of public emergency, they were to report to their captain ready to defend the city. Men were expected to keep weapons and equipment at home for this purpose.[85] For local magistrates, the presence of arms among the citizenry provided all the more reason to carefully manage the expression of dissent, lest intemperate talk lead to open violence.

Given the cities' small constabulary forces, urban censorship systems were, by necessity, dependent upon citizen reporting and voluntary compliance. The cooperation of the citizenry was secured, in part, by a general acceptance of the magistrates' asserted right to regulate expression for the protection of communal values and the public peace. All citizens were required to swear an oath pledging obedience to the city's governmental authority and its mandates, and the town councils repeatedly drew upon this obligation in seeking to suppress dissent and civic unrest. Citizens were reminded in repeated decrees of their duty to report individuals who spoke or wrote against the council, imperial authority, or the prevailing religious settlement within the city. As we will see, that neighbors frequently turned informants is reflected in the sworn statements of countless such people in local criminal files.

---

[85] B. Ann Tlusty, *The Martial Ethic in Early Modern Germany: Civic Duty and the Right of Arms* (NY: Palgrave Macmillan, 2011) p. 11–45; Jürgen Kraus, *Das Militärwesen der Reichsstadt Augsburg, 1548–1806* (Augsburg: Verlag Hieronymus Mühlberger, 1980) pp. 74–94.

City officials also offered substantial rewards for information. Magistrates frequently used rewards to combat the nighttime posting of anonymous placards or pasquinades in public places—a popular means of protest in the period. These pasquinades—often merely satirical and mocking, but sometimes darkly menacing—provided a forum for political, religious, and social comment, as well as the airing of purely private disputes. They were, in all cases, highly forbidden.[86]

In addition to tips from the community, authorities monitored dissent through a network of paid informants. In Augsburg, ordinances governing the duties of the *Bürgermeister* set forth a payment schedule for informants, based upon the penalties imposed against the accused:

> When someone is reported by an informant, arrested, and put in irons, and also found to be guilty and punished, one pays the informant for that: 2 gulden.
>
> Also, when the accused is whipped out of the city, [pay] no more than ordinarily: 2 gulden.
>
> Otherwise, [pay] according to the circumstances.[87]

For urban magistrates, surveillance was not simply a local, but a regional, operation. Although some imperial cities, such as Nuremberg, had a sizable *contado* subject to their rule, most did not. This had several consequences. First, the city could not provision itself without cooperation from its neighbors. In times of war, the town could be easily cut off from needed supplies, making it highly vulnerable to siege. In times of peace, the city's efforts to enforce its laws were often frustrated by its magistrates' limited jurisdiction. Outside the city walls, where the magistrates' writ did not run, fugitives from local justice could find a safe haven. As a practical matter, these territorial constraints limited the city council's ability to impose its policies on an unwilling population.

Already in 1479, Pope Sixtus IV's grant of censorship authority to the University of Cologne had recognized the problem: "since it may be that printers, fearing your measures, will move to other areas, we desire that you communicate our wishes to the officials of these places so that [these rules] will be observed everywhere."[88] In censorship, as in all other forms of policing, the cities relied heavily upon their contacts with neighboring jurisdictions and imperial authorities to share intelligence and enforce their laws in the region. For the most part, local governments expressed

---

[86] See Schmidt, *Libelli Famosi*.
[87] StAA, Bürgermeisteramt, 'Instruction die Herren Bürgermeister betreffend,' fol. 132.
[88] Muckel, *Die Entwicklung der Zensur in Köln*, p. 9.

willingness to cooperate, for every jurisdiction was faced with comparable problems in policing its territory, and all had to call on assistance from their neighbors from time to time.[89] However, religious or political differences might disincline a neighbor to offer aid, especially ideological disputes over censorship. Despite these differences, government officials were generally united in their suspicion of disorderly persons or subversive ideas, and were often willing to assist in their control. In the densely packed, politically fractured environment of early modern Germany, one territory's problems might quickly spill over into its neighbors' jurisdictions, either by accident or design.

With expulsion and exile a primary means of punishment in the era, early modern authorities assumed that a sizable and highly mobile criminal underclass was abroad on the region's highways.[90] To combat this menace, local officials exercised careful watch over persons entering and leaving their city and frequently corresponded with neighboring states regarding the movements of suspected criminals and troublemakers through their territories. For example, the city council of Frankfurt am Main, home to the great semi-annual book fair, devoted considerable attention to investigating its neighbors' complaints about books likely to appear at the fair.[91] Other cities followed suit. Suspicion was particularly great surrounding the traveling booksellers and singers who eked out their meager living on the region's byways. Itinerant peddlers and singers did not have to travel far before they were beyond the reach of a city's magistrates, and officials generally assumed they left trouble in their wake.

Even if such activities were not deemed punishable locally, city councils generally sought to accommodate requests for information and assistance from foreign and imperial officials, for each city relied on such cooperation in policing its own citizens. Acting upon tips received from neighboring territories, local officials apprehended dealers in prohibited texts or members of outlawed religious sects known to be active in the area. In enforcing their laws, as in all other matters, local officials had to be mindful of keeping the goodwill of their neighbors, for their city could not stand long without them.

---

[89] On the significance of such contacts in the urban Reformation, see Christopher W. Close, *The Negotiated Reformation: Imperial Cities and the Politics of Urban Reform, 1525–1550* (New York: Cambridge University Press, 2009).

[90] On banishment, see Jason P. Coy, *Strangers and Misfits: Banishment, Social Control, and Authority in Early Modern Germany* (Leiden: Brill, 2008).

[91] See, for example, FaM ISG , Buchdruck und Zensur Nr. 11, fol. 15; Buchdruck und Zensur, Nr. 91; Buchdruck und Zensur, Nr. 105; Bürgermeisterbuch 1621, fol. 53v; Ratsprotokolle 1621, fol. 15r.

Trial and Sentencing

Once an individual was taken into custody for suspicious speech or writings, the prisoner was typically referred for interrogation. Interrogators were authorized to summon and interview witnesses, question the accused, and apply torture, if warranted. Under imperial law, conviction in most criminal cases required either the testimony of two eyewitnesses or the confession of the accused.[92] Where full proof was lacking but compelling circumstantial evidence of guilt existed, torture might be applied to secure the requisite confession.[93] By the seventeenth century, evidentiary standards for non-capital offenses were often lower, with circumstantial evidence sometimes serving as a basis for conviction. Indeed, individuals could in some cases be punished for merely appearing "suspicious" (*Verdachtsstrafe*).[94]

Torture, when used, was typically administered by the city executioner, whose very touch was thought to be defiling by virtue of his unclean office. Thus, torture was not simply a method of interrogation, but was itself a punishment with potentially significant long-term consequences for the prisoner's status and social relationships.[95] Often, prisoners thought to be lying were merely threatened with torture, with the threat made more real by interrogating the prisoner in the presence of the executioner and the torture instruments.

Depending upon the nature of the offense, punishments in censorship cases typically ranged from the imposition of fines to imprisonment and banishment. Given that urban jails lacked the resources to house prisoners for long periods of time, lengthy incarceration was not generally used as a punishment. Rather, the city's jails were reserved for the holding of prisoners pending interrogation and sentencing. Most prisoners facing sentencing would have already spent some time in jail awaiting resolution of their case, an imprisonment that could stretch from days to months. Perhaps because of this pre-trial confinement, when imprisonment was used as a punishment, it typically limited the term to a brief confinement, sometimes with the proviso that the prisoner subsist on rations of only bread and water.[96]

---

[92] *Constitutio Criminalis Carolina*, Art. 22, 62, 67, in *Die Peinliche Gerichtsordnung Kaiser Karl V. von 1532*, ed. Gustav Radbruch (Stuttgart: Philipp Reclam, 1996) pp. 41, 60–61.

[93] See John H. Langbein, *Torture and the Law of Proof: Europe and England in the Ancien* Régime (Chicago: University of Chicago Press, 1977) pp. 3–64.

[94] Ibid., p. 47.

[95] Kathy Stuart, *Defiled Trades and Social Outcasts: Honor and Ritual Pollution in Early Modern Germany* (Cambridge: Cambridge University Press, 1999) pp. 140–42.

[96] See, for example, SStBA, 2°Cod. S. 65, 'Anon: Cath: Diar: Aug. ab anno 1633,' entry dated 22 June 1638 re: Tobias Widenmann.

Printers and booksellers charged with violations of local censorship laws could generally expect to suffer a brief term of imprisonment and the confiscation of the offending texts. In more serious cases, printers might be expelled from the city for a time or denied the right to continue in the trade. Given the economic pressures of the trade, such punishments could have potentially devastating financial consequences for the prisoner.[97]

The few individuals executed for dealing in prohibited texts were typically prosecuted under laws outlawing Anabaptist or other radical teachings. The Nuremberg printer and bookseller, Hans Hergot, for example, met his death in Leipzig in 1527 for allegedly authoring the Anabaptist tract, *On the New Transformation of the Christian Life*.[98] In that same year, the city council of Nuremberg ordered the execution of the Eltersdorf pastor Wolfgang Vogel, a follower of Hans Hut, for publishing an open letter evidencing a number of "unchristian errors" regarding baptism, the Eucharist, and other articles of faith.[99]

Although local laws often authorized capital punishment for seditious speech, executions typically occurred only in times of political instability or riot, against individuals judged guilty of inciting insurrection. Magistrates sometimes ordered that blasphemers and slanderers have their tongues ripped out, but such extreme corporal punishments were exceedingly rare. More typical in cases of disorderly speech was public shaming in the pillory. In more serious cases, offenders might be banished from the city, sometimes with the added humiliation of a public whipping. In many cases, magistrates subsequently allowed offenders to re-enter the city after a suitable period of time, particularly where the prisoner left behind dependents requiring support. However, some individuals were expelled for life. Given that banishment severed the economic and social links upon which the prisoner depended, expulsion could have irrevocable long-term consequences for the accused and his family.[100] For many offenders, expulsion marked the beginning of a life of poverty and wandering, for individuals expelled from their city could expect that word of their crime would follow them and complicate their efforts to find acceptance in another town.

---

[97] Künast, *Getruckt zu Augspurg*, p. 62.

[98] Carola Schelle-Wolff, *Zwischen Erwartung und Aufruhr: Die Flugschrift „Von der newen wandlung eynes Christlichen lebens" und der Nürnberger Drucker Hans Hergot* (Frankfurt am Main: Peter Lang, 1996), pp. 108–28.

[99] Hans-Dieter Schmid, *Täufertum und Obrigkeit in Nürnberg* (Nürnberg: Stadtarchiv Nürnberg, 1972) pp. 18–24; Werner O. Packull, *Mysticism and the Early South German-Austrian Anabaptist Movement 1525-1531*. (Scottsdale, PA: Herald Press, 1977; reprint, Eugene, OR: Wipf and Stock Publishers, 2008.)

[100] Coy, *Strangers and Misfits*, pp. 79–112; Abray, 'Limits of Magisterial Tolerance,' p. 105.

Within the cities, the magistrates' authority to regulate expression was not exclusive. Imperial and ecclesiastical officials from time to time asserted jurisdiction over local book trades or public comment in the cities. While the free cities jealously guarded their legal prerogatives, political necessity sometimes required that they enforce the demands of competing authorities within their community. Even in Protestant-leaning communities, political considerations could go a long way toward ensuring cooperation with imperial censorship policy.

Imperial Censorship Law

Germany's free and imperial cities, like all other estates of the Empire, were constitutionally bound to enforce imperial law in their communities. As a practical matter, however, the cities' compliance could not always be assured, as the following chapters will show. The cities' political and economic interests, however, meant that city magistrates always had to reckon with imperial power in the enforcement of their own policies.

The right to regulate expression within the Empire was assumed to be one of the highest regalian rights of the emperor, which he could, theoretically, legislate solely on his own authority. As a practical matter, however, imperial censorship laws were generally enacted through the Imperial Diets and implemented by territorial and civic officials at the local level. Although the states bore the primary responsibility for the enforcement of imperial censorship laws, the emperor retained oversight over their administration. After 1530, the Imperial Cameral Court (*Reichskammergericht*) was charged with investigating and punishing states judged to be negligent in the enforcement of imperial censorship laws, and the Imperial Aulic Council (*Reichshofrat*) was likewise authorized to direct local officials in the handling of censorship matters. The emperor also retained the ability to appoint commissions to oversee local censorship proceedings judged to be of particular significance to the Empire and could transfer jurisdiction of such cases from local magistrates to imperial officials.[101]

Until the Reformation era, imperial censorship measures were imposed largely on a case-by-case basis, perhaps most famously illustrated in the proceedings against the humanist Johannes Reuchlin in 1512. The first systematic controls implemented under imperial authority were codified in the 1521 Edict of Worms, which prohibited the works of Martin Luther

---

[101] Ulrich Eisenhardt, *Die kaiserliche Aufsicht über Buchdruck, Buchhandel und Presse in Heiligen Römischen Reich Deutscher Nation (1496–1806)* (Karlsruhe: Verlag C.F. Müller, 1970) pp. 6–9; 93–5.

and all other texts attacking the papacy or the Roman Catholic Church. Further provisions called for a system of pre-publication censorship (*Vorzensur*) requiring all religious texts to be approved by the theological faculty of the nearest university; non-religious texts were to be reviewed by secular authorities.[102] Thereafter followed a series of censorship measures enacted through the recesses of the Imperial Diets. The Diet of Nuremberg in 1524 reaffirmed the Edict of Worms and called on the estates to enforce its censorship provisions.[103] The recess of the Second Diet of Speyer in 1529 institutionalized pre-publication censorship, requiring that all state and local authorities designate officials to approve all texts to be printed or sold within their jurisdictions.[104] The 1530 Diet of Augsburg extended these provisions, requiring the name of the printer and the place of printing to be published on the title page of every book published in the Empire. Moreover, the Imperial Cameral Court was authorized to proceed against territorial officials who failed to carry out their duties, suggesting, perhaps, that prior enforcement efforts were perceived as ineffective.[105] Further legislation in the 1530s included the passage in 1532, of Section 110 of the *Constitutio Criminalis Carolina* reiterating the prohibition of libelous texts, and the prohibition of Anabaptist writings at the Diet of Worms of 1535.[106]

The most significant imperial censorship legislation of the 1540s was the Imperial Police Ordinance (*Reichspolizeiordnung*) of 1548. Acknowledging that prior censorship efforts had not been successful, the Ordinance set forth more comprehensive guidelines. The Ordinance reiterated earlier prohibitions of libelous works, but also specifically banned texts deemed "*auffrührisch*"—that is, likely to incite riot or rebellion.[107] Also specifically prohibited were all works contrary to "common Catholic doctrine and the holy Christian church," as well as texts inconsistent with the pronouncements of prior Imperial Diets.[108]

---

[102] Holgar Flachmann, *Martin Luther und das Buch: Eine historische Studie zur Bedeutung des Buches im Handeln und Denken des Reformators* (Tübingen: Mohr, 1996) p. 212.

[103] Reichsabschied Nürnberg 1524, § 28, in *Neue vollständige Sammlung der Reichs-Abschiede, welche von den Zeiten Kayser Conrads des II. bis jetzo auf den Teutschen Reichs-Tagen abgefasset worden*, 1747 (Osnabrück: Otto Zeller, 1967) p. 258.

[104] Reichsabschied Speyer 1529, § 9, ibid., pp. 294–295.

[105] Reichsabschied Augsburg 1530, § 58, ibid., p. 314.

[106] *Constitutio Criminalis Carolina*, § 110, in *Peinliche Gerichtordnung*, p. 79; Reichsabschied Worms 1535, § 45 in *Sammlung der Reichs-Abschiede*, p. 416.

[107] Reichs Policey Ordnung 1548, Art. XXXIV, § 1, in *Sammlung der Reichs-Abschiede*, p. 604.

[108] Ibid., Art. XXXIV, § 2.

The Ordinance required censors to pre-approve all texts to be printed or sold, and all texts were to bear the name of the author, printer, and city of publication. Printers who violated the laws were to be banned from the trade and punished with a "heavy" fine.[109] Officials were instructed to interrogate, under torture if necessary, anyone found selling or buying forbidden texts and to investigate until the offending author was found. The various estates were to share information and cooperate in investigating and punishing the guilty.[110] If officials were lax in their duty, the Imperial Cameral Court could proceed against the negligent officials, as well as against the offending printers, authors, or book sellers.[111]

Throughout this period, the emperor presented himself largely in his traditional role as the defender of the Roman Catholic church. Imperial censorship policy was therefore directed towards the suppression of Protestant attacks on the Catholic church and the office and person of the pope. These efforts met with a singular lack of success in much of the Empire, given the hostility of the Protestant states. The censorship provisions of the Edict of Worms, for example, found little support in much of the Empire, given resistance to its enforcement among the Protestant states and legal uncertainty concerning the validity of its enactment.[112]

The emperor's legal role in censorship fundamentally shifted with the Religious Peace of Augsburg of 1555. Although the Peace of Augsburg contained no express provisions addressing censorship, its pronouncements regarding the preservation of peace between the confessions were interpreted as a general prohibition of religious polemic by either side.[113] Moreover, as a constitutional matter, the Peace of Augsburg ensured that imperial law could no longer simply prohibit Lutheran works. Imperial law could, however, suppress any religious controversial writing deemed to be disruptive of the public peace. The role of emperor thus changed from protector of the Roman Catholic Church to guardian of the religious peace of the Empire.[114]

Consistent with these changes, the Diet of Speyer in 1570 banned writings that "incite nothing but quarrels, rebellion, mistrust, and breaches

---

[109] Ibid, Art. XXXIV § 1.
[110] Ibid., Art. XXXIV, § 2.
[111] Ibid., Art. XXXIV, § 3.
[112] On the enforcement of the Edict of Worms, see Paul Kalkoff, *Das Wormser Edikt und die Erlass des Reichsregiments und einzelner Reichsfürsten* (München: R. Oldenbourg, 1517); Martin Brecht, 'Das Wormser Edikt in Süddeutschland,' in *Der Reichstag zu Worms von 1521*, ed. Fritz Reuter (Worms: Stadtarchiv, 1971) pp. 475–89.
[113] On censorship under the Peace of Augsburg, see Chapter 3.
[114] Eisenhardt, *Die kaiserliche Aufsicht über Buchdruck*, pp. 22–3; 32.

of the peace."[115] To ensure enforcement of the laws regarding *Vorzensur*, printing was authorized only at imperial cities, university towns, or princely capitals where censorial oversight could be most effectively exercised.[116] Printers were required to obtain licenses and swear oaths to abide by the imperial laws, and the states were required to conduct unannounced inspections of book sellers, printers, printshops and private libraries to intercept works printed in violation of the law (*Nachzensur*).[117]

The preservation of the public and religious peace remained the central goal of imperial censorship in subsequent legislation. The Imperial Police Ordinance of 1577 prohibited writings that violated "common Christian doctrine and the Peace of Augsburg," or otherwise promoted unrest and breaches of the peace.[118] These restrictions were reaffirmed in the Peace of Westphalia of 1648, which expressly prohibited works which violated or in any way called into question the Peace of Passau, the Peace of Augsburg, or the Peace of Westphalia.[119]

Although the Peace of Augsburg required the emperor to exercise his censorship authority to preserve the peace between the confessions, both Catholics and Lutherans questioned the impartiality of the imperial administration. Ulrich Eisenhardt notes that the Frankfurt Book Commission became especially noted for pro-Catholic bias in the execution of its duties. First established in 1569, the Commission was to oversee the semi-annual book fairs at Frankfurt am Main.[120] Booksellers were required to submit catalogs of their inventory to the Commission, which would survey the catalogs for the presence of banned titles. Prohibited materials were to be confiscated with the cooperation of the Frankfurt city council.[121]

Almost from its inception, the Commission demonstrated a pronounced pro-Catholic bias. According to Eisenhardt, there are no known cases in which the Commission acted on its own instance against Catholic,

---

[115] Reichsabschied Speyer 1570, § 154, in *Sammlung der Reichs-Abschiede*, Bd. III, p. 308.

[116] Ibid., § 156.

[117] Ibid., §§ 154, 159.

[118] Reichs Policey Ordnung 1577, XXXV, § 3, in *Sammlung der Reichs-Abschiede*, Bd. III, p. 396.

[119] *Instrumentum Pacis Osnabrugense* (1648), Art. V, § 50 in *Kaiser und Reich: Verfassungsgeschichte des Heiligen Römischen Reiches Deutscher Nation vom Beginn des 12. Jahrhunderts bis zum Jahre 1806 in Dokumenten*, Teil II, ed. Arno Buschmann, 2nd ed. (Baden-Baden: Nomos Verlagsgesellschaft, 1994).

[120] It did not become a permanent body until 1597.

[121] Wolfgang Brückner, 'Die Gegenreformation im politischen Kampf um die Frankfurter Buchmessen. Die kaiserliche Zensur zwischen 1567 und 1619,' *Archiv für Frankfurts Geschichte und Kunst* 48 (1962) pp. 68–70.

anti-Protestant works. This may be attributable to the fact that the Frankfurt Book Commission was staffed in this period almost entirely by Roman Catholic clerics; moreover, the office of commissioner also carried with it the simultaneous appointment as the papacy's "apostolic book commissioner" in the Empire. The union of these offices appears to have been initially suggested from within the Book Commission itself, and was apparently kept secret both from the Protestant states and, until the 1680s, from the imperial court at Vienna.[122] Protestants complained frequently of the way the Commission carried out its work. Indeed, the Elector Palatine complained in 1597 that the fair catalog was so biased that Protestant religious texts bearing his electoral privilege were often classified with "the fables of Aesop."[123]

The Book Commission's efforts to safeguard Catholic doctrine frequently brought it into conflict with Frankfurt's Lutheran city council, on which it relied for enforcement of its orders.[124] To counter the "papists and Jesuits" on the Commission, the Frankfurt city council established its own fair catalog in 1598, policed by its own officials.[125] The council's catalog was no less religiously partisan, however, and drew complaints from Catholic printers and officials. Indeed, the reports from the council's censors in this period establish that confessional interests played a major role in their decisions. Frankfurt's censors, often Lutheran clerics, judged works with an eye toward whether they contained material that "is against our Christian Confession or belittles high potentates."[126] Anti-Catholic and anti-Calvinist texts, even if sharply polemical, got a pass in the Lutheran city. In evaluating Philipp Nicolai's *Short Report on the Calvinist God and Religion* (*Kurtzer Bericht von der caluinisten Gott vnd jrer Religion*),[127] for example, pastor Nicodemus Ulmer judged it "somewhat harsh, but it is,

---

[122] Beginning in 1653, Protestant opposition to the perceived bias of the Frankfurt Book Commission led to the inclusion of provisions in the emperors' electoral capitulations (*Wahlkapitulation*) obligating them to ensure the Commission's impartiality between the confessions. See Eisenhardt, *Die kaiserliche Aufsicht über Buchdruck*, pp. 35–6; 113–14; 135–6.

[123] Brückner, 'Frankfurter Buchmessen,' p. 81.

[124] Ibid., pp. 81–3. See the correspondence between the Commission and council collected at FaM ISG, Buchdruck und Zensur, Nr. 11, 'Tom. II: Schreiben und Handlungen Inspectionen der Bücher betreffend (1617–1655).'

[125] Brückner, 'Frankfurter Buchmessen,' pp. 81–2.

[126] FaM ISG, Buchdruck und Zensur, Nr. 20: Sammlung von Zensurzetteln (1591–98), fol. 11.

[127] Philipp Nicolai, *Kurtzer Bericht von der caluinisten Gott vnd jrer Religion ... sampt angehengter kurtzer Form, wie ein christlicher einfältiger Haussvatter sein Kindt vnnd Haussgesind für demselbigen vnseligen Caluinismo trewlich warnen vnd davon abhalten soll* (Frankfurt am Main: Johann Spiess, 1597).

of course, the bitter truth."[128] Ulmer also condemned the Jesuit Francisco Suarez's *Commentary on Aristotle's Metaphysics*.[129] In his report, Ulmer stressed the book's hidden dangers:

> This book appears as if it deals only with philosophy and Aristotle's metaphysics, but [the author] himself confesses that he understands this in terms of Thomistic theology ... and thus he advances the false teaching of the Roman papacy. It is to be especially considered whether the books of these enemies of Jesus Christ—call themselves what they may—should be printed in a Lutheran city. We pastors know not what to do to prevent this, other than to earnestly beg the Honorable Council to drive these and other such Jesuit writings from the place.[130]

Ulmer's appeal to the council's Lutheran sensibilities worked: a note appended to Ulmer's letter, in another hand, declares: "the printing of this book in Frankfurt is, for the above-stated reason, forbidden."[131]

While the Book Commission's work sparked retaliation, at the higher levels of imperial oversight, the Imperial Aulic Council and the Imperial Cameral Court were generally perceived as impartial in matters of religious censorship. After 1555, judicial panels hearing religious cases in the Imperial Cameral Court were composed of equal numbers of Catholic and Lutheran judges.[132] Although Catholic jurists predominated in the Imperial Aulic Council, Protestant estates continued to turn to it, and both courts were known to enforce laws and issue privileges on behalf of both Protestants and Catholics.[133] At least until the 1580s, the narrow political constraints under which the emperor operated required that he not appear to tolerate an overtly one-sided institution at the higher levels of imperial administration.[134]

---

[128] FaM ISG, Buchdruck und Zensur, Nr. 20: Sammlung von Zensurzetteln (1591–98), fol. 105.

[129] Francisco Suarez, *Metaphysicarum disputationum: in quibus et universa naturalis theologia ordinate traditur, et questiones omnes ad duodecim Aristotelis libros pertinentes, accuratè disputantur* (Venice: Baretium, 1599).

[130] FaM ISG, Buchdruck und Zensur, Nr. 20: Sammlung von Zensurzetteln (1591–98), fol. 208.

[131] Ibid.

[132] Martin Heckel, 'Die Religionsprozesse der Reichskammergerichts im konfessionell gespaltenen Reichskirchenrecht,' in *Zeitschrift der Savigny-Stiftung für Rechtsgeschichte, Kanonistische Abteilung* 77 (1991): 283–350.

[133] Eisenhardt, *Die kaiserliche Aufsicht über Buchdruck*, p. 113. On the Imperial Aulic Council, see Stefan Ehrenpreis, *Kaiserliche Gerichtsbarkeit und Konfessionskonflikt. Der Reichshofrat unter Rudolf II, 1576–1612* (Göttingen: Vandenhoeck & Ruprecht, 2006).

[134] Brady, *German Histories*, pp. 237–56; On irenicism, and its limits, at the imperial court, see Howard Louthan, *The Quest for Compromise: Peacemakers in Counter-Reformation Vienna* (Cambridge: Cambridge University Press, 1997).

Because imperial censorship laws relied on the states for their enforcement, these measures often evolved into political and confessional battles between the estates and the imperial administration. The vagueness of the law created frequent opportunities for evasion and political jockeying. Questions of interpretation gave recalcitrant local officials an excuse to suspend enforcement of imperial decrees without overtly denying the emperor's authority. The enforcement of the censorship provisions under the 1548 Imperial Police Ordinance is a case in point. In 1549, Elector Moritz of Saxony, as required under the law, issued a mandate implementing the Ordinance throughout his territories. Although the Imperial Police Ordinance expressly prohibited writings "against common Catholic teaching and the holy Christian church or the holy Imperial Recesses," the Elector's decree made no mention of such provisions. In Lutheran electoral Saxony, the Ordinance was interpreted merely as a general prohibition of *Schmähbücher*—or libels—with the explicitly pro-Catholic provisions of the legislation entirely read out of the text.[135] Throughout the Reformation era, strategies such as these often enabled Protestant states and cities to check imperial efforts to quash the evangelical movement.

The estates also checked imperial censorship policy by encroaching on the emperor's authority over the book trade. In the late medieval period, the emperors had held exclusive authority to issue privileges granting the holder the exclusive right to print a given work throughout the Empire. Over time, territorial lords undertook to issue their own privileges. Privileges from Saxony and Brandenburg were especially coveted and were recognized throughout the Empire, reflecting the importance of the book trade in those regions. The recognition of these rights within the Empire at large undermined imperial regulation of the book trade across the estates.[136]

Because imperial law depended almost entirely upon the territorial princes and local magistrates for its enforcement, the system of control that emerged was unsystematic and inconsistent. Its efficacy depended, in almost all cases, upon the competence and cooperation of local officials. As we will see, religious and political calculations often frustrated these efforts. Nonetheless, princes and magistrates had to reckon with imperial power, and few dared question the emperor's fundamental authority over matters of censorship.[137] Ultimately, however, the emperor's ability to

---

[135] Hasse, *Zensur theologischer Bücher in Kursachsen*, p. 26.

[136] Eisenhardt, *Die kaiserliche Aufsicht über Buchdruck*, pp. 135–9.

[137] Controversies over the implementation of the Augsburg Interim of 1548 gave rise to challenges over the right of secular authorities to censor religious texts, as discussed in Chapter 2. See also Robert Kolb, 'Matthaeus Judex's Condemnation of Princely Censorship

enforce compliance was a political, and often a religious, question. In states where the emperor had relatively little political leverage, local officials could generally pursue their own policy without imperial intervention. Nevertheless, imperial censorship law, grounded in the Peace of Augsburg, emerged as an important means of policing interconfessional dialogue and debate in the latter sixteenth century.

Territorial Jurisdiction

Below the emperor and the imperial courts ranked the many territorial princes and estates of the Holy Roman Empire. They varied widely in terms of their power, wealth, and religious policies. In enforcing censorship, however, the imperial princes, both Catholic and Protestant, tended to pursue similar strategies. All closely regulated the regional print trade and relied heavily on clerics and university faculty as censors.

Consistent with imperial mandate, territorial lords typically restricted the printing trade to princely residences and university towns, thus facilitating the censors' oversight. In both Catholic and Protestant states, university faculties were heavily involved in the censorship process. In Catholic Bavaria, the University of Ingolstadt censored texts published by its faculty and in the city at large.[138] In Cologne, the university and the city council shared oversight of the local book trade. Judging Luther's works to be heretical, the theological faculty of the University of Cologne oversaw the first public burning of his books in the Empire in 1519.[139] As has been noted, electoral Saxony charged the faculty of the University of Wittenberg with censoring theological texts; both Luther and Melanchthon acted as censors in this capacity.[140] In Marburg, Philip of Hesse made the university faculty responsible for overseeing censorship in the territory beginning in 1538.[141] Deans of the faculty were required to review all manuscripts submitted for printing in Marburg, as well as books imported

---

of Theologians' Publications,' in *Luther's Heirs Define His Legacy: Studies on Lutheran Confessionalization* (Aldershot: Variorum, 1996) pp. 401–14.

[138] Helmut Neumann, *Staatliche Bücherzensur und Aufsicht in Bayern von der Reformation bis zum Ausgang des 17. Jahrhunderts* (Heidelberg: G.F. Müller Juristischer Verlag, 1977) pp. 29–31.

[139] Muckel, *Zensur in Köln*, pp. 14–15.

[140] Hans-Peter Hasse, 'Bücherzensur an der Universität Wittenberg im 16. Jahrhundert,' in *700 Jahre Wittenberg. Stadt, Universität, Reformation* (Weimar: Hermann Böhlaus Nachfolger, 1995) pp. 194–5.

[141] Thomas Sirges and Ingeborg Müller, *Zensur in Marburg, 1538–1832: Eine lokalgeschichtliche Studie zum Bücher- und Pressewesen* (Marburg: Presseamt der Stadt, 1984) p. 7.

into Hesse.[142] Although censorship was directed primarily against religious and theological subjects, the censors also prohibited works disruptive of public order and public decency, as well as works they deemed to be of questionable academic value.[143]

In both Protestant and Catholic territories, censorship served the religious agenda of the state. The dukes of Bavaria erected a system of territorial controls fundamentally designed to protect Roman Catholic doctrine, the Church as an institution, and the Roman Catholic clergy and religious orders.[144] Bavaria cooperated early with the imperial decrees banning the writings of Luther and other evangelical reformers and entered into further pacts with Roman Catholic princes and bishops to censor Protestant materials in their territories.[145] Since 1524, all books published in the duchy were to be pre-approved by appointed censors.[146] In addition to passing Bavarian censors, works printed in the duchy were also required to display both imperial and Bavarian privileges on their title pages. In 1565, Duke Albrecht V restricted Bavarian privileges to only those books printed in Catholic cities such as Munich, Ingolstadt, Dillingen, Mainz, Cologne, Paris, Venice, or Rome; theological works published elsewhere were banned.[147] The following year, Bavaria prohibited book sellers from carrying any theological texts not included in an official catalog of permitted books. The permitted titles included only reliably Catholic authors such as Johann Eck, Peter Canisius, Friedrich Nausea, and Johann Wild; all other religious works were forbidden.[148]

Implementation of Bavaria's censorship laws was carried out with the assistance of the Roman Catholic clergy. Clerics assisted civil authorities in carrying out visitations of book shops and printing houses, and Jesuits censored manuscripts submitted for publication.[149] The Tridentine Index of Prohibited Books was enforced in Bavaria, and after 1582, was supplemented with a new Munich Index.[150] According to historian Helmut Neumann, very few conflicts arose between the church and state over the administration of the duchy's censorship laws, largely because the state's interpretation of its laws so closely incorporated the church's standards.[151]

---

[142] Ibid., pp. 9–11.
[143] Ibid, pp. 38–43.
[144] Neumann, *Staatliche Bücherzensur und Aufsicht in Bayern*, p. 13.
[145] Ibid., pp. 7–8.
[146] BHStA, Staatsverwaltung 2778, fol. 73.
[147] BHStA, Staatsverwaltung 2299, fol. 2.
[148] BHStA, Staatsverwaltung 3221, fol. 42.
[149] Neumann, *Staatliche Bücherzensur und Aufsicht*, pp. 25–7.
[150] Ibid., p. 9.
[151] Ibid., pp. 14–17; 65.

Between 1569 and 1571, ducal commissioners conducted searches of the private libraries of religiously suspect persons.[152] In a 1569 visitation in Munich, commissioners reported that only 20 people out of 150 were found with banned religious material in their possession.[153] Further visitations were conducted throughout the duchy, particularly in areas where market inspectors had found forbidden books for sale.[154]

To halt the import of Protestant texts, Bavaria erected tight controls to intercept suspect material coming across its borders with neighboring Protestant states. Customs officials were particularly on the lookout for Protestant literature coming into the duchy from Nuremberg and other evangelical imperial cities. The *Bürgermeister* and council of Munich complained in 1569 that "the imperial cities and other places are too near; anyone who wants to can get bad books [there] and bring them here."[155] Bavarian tradesmen were also unwittingly importing heretical prints from Augsburg and Nuremberg in the form of packing paper. In a 1644 decree, Elector Maximilian warned inspectors that booksellers in those cities sold their excess pages as packing material, and that they should keep a special lookout for such prints in their visitations.[156]

As the Bavarian example makes clear, the inter-regional book trade posed a significant obstacle to thorough enforcement. Although territorial censors exercised considerable oversight of books published or sold in their jurisdictions, the efficacy of these systems was substantially compromised by the censors' inability to stop the import of offending works from outside. The coordination of censorial efforts at the territorial level, therefore, was very much a political question to be resolved between the affected states.

Ecclesiastical Authority

Since the 1470s, the popes had designated the theological faculties of some of Germany's leading universities to censor religious texts.[157] During the Reformation era, numerous papal decrees attempted to outlaw the production and sale of Protestant texts. The first papal Index of Prohibited Books appeared in 1558. Unlike earlier, regional indices, the Roman Index was intended to apply throughout the church, including Catholic

---

[152] BHStA, Staatsverwaltung 2797, fol. 310.
[153] Neumann, *Staatliche Bücherzensur und Aufsicht*, pp. 44–5.
[154] Ibid, pp. 45–7.
[155] Ibid., p. 33, fn. 112.
[156] BHStA, Staatsverwaltung Nr. 3188, fol. 105v.
[157] Muckel, *Zensur in Köln*, p. 9; Schmidt, *Libelli Famosi*, pp. 207–10.

Germany.[158] In enforcing its censorship decrees, however, the Roman Catholic church was almost entirely dependent on the cooperation of local secular officials. Where there was close coordination between church officials and local lords or university faculties, ecclesiastical mandates could find support. But Germany's most important printing centers were in the free cities, which often had long histories of conflict with their local bishops. Well before the Reformation, the magistrates of many of Germany's largest cities had cast off ecclesiastic jurisdiction, wresting control over local church governance and vital civic functions. The diocesan capitals of Cologne and Strasbourg, for example, had won their freedom after long struggles with their archbishops, and their town councils vigilantly guarded their independence ever afterwards.[159] Augsburg, which had been the traditional seat of a storied line of bishops, had exiled its bishops since the mid-fifteenth century, as had a great many other medieval German communes.[160] With the episcopal hierarchy dislocated and its jurisdiction usurped, ecclesiastical authority in the imperial cities was severely circumscribed.

By the beginning of the sixteenth century, secular magistrates in many cities held exclusive legal jurisdiction over the laity, even in matters of blasphemy and moral crimes. In Augsburg, for example, there were no church courts or consistories having independent jurisdiction over the laity.[161] Even in Cologne, the "German Rome," episcopal or papal decrees governing the ownership or reading of forbidden books could only be enforced through the town council. The council worked closely with ecclesiastical authorities to suppress Protestant ideas, but even here the council was careful to assert its jurisdiction.[162] The practical limits of ecclesiastical censorship, however, were most apparent in the cities where support for reform was the strongest. In Augsburg, for example, the bishop

---

[158] Schmidt, *Libelli Famosi*, pp. 209–15.

[159] On Cologne, see L. Ennen, *Geschichte der Stadt Köln* (5 vols., Cologne and Neuss, 1863–80); for Strasbourg, see Thomas A. Brady, Jr., *Ruling Class, Regime, and Reformation at Strasbourg, 1520–1555* (Leiden: Brill, 1978).

[160] On these conflicts, see J. Jeffery Tyler, *Lord of the Sacred City: The Episcopus Exclusus in Late Medieval and Early Modern Germany* (Leiden: Brill, 1999).

[161] Carl A. Hoffman, 'Strukturen und Quellen des Augsburger reichsstädtischen Strafgerichtswesens in der ersten Hälfte des 16. Jahrhunderts,' *Zeitschrift des Historischen Vereins für Schwaben* 88 (1995): pp. 62–81; Walter Köhler, *Züricher Ehegericht und Genfer Konsistorium. Bd. II: Das Ehe- und Sittengericht in den süddeutschen Reichsstädten, dem Herzogtum Württemberg und in Genf* (Leipzig: Verlag von M. Heinsius Nachfolger, 1942) pp. 280–322; Wolfgang Wüst, 'Censur und Censurkollegien im frühmodernen Konfessionsstaat,' in *Augsburger Buchdruck und Verlagswesen von den Anfängen bis zur Gegenwart*, ed. Helmut Gier and Johannes Janota (Wiesbaden: Harrassowitz Verlag, 1997) p. 573.

[162] Muckel, *Zensur in Köln*, pp. 15–32.

ordered the laity to turn over Lutheran books and withheld absolution to those who refused, but he could not arrest offenders or confiscate books from local merchants without the council's cooperation.[163] Even his authority over the local clergy was limited by the rights of the local parish wardens and the superiors of the city's monastic houses.[164] As the efforts to publish the papal condemnation of Luther would show, these divisions would play a pivotal role in introducing Reformation ideas into the imperial cities and fostering their spread.

Conclusions

Throughout the Empire, the implementation of censorship policy varied in response to shifting political conditions. Cooperation with imperial censorship policies did not follow strictly religious lines, for both Catholic and Protestant states showed themselves ready to support and hinder imperial policy as it suited their interests. Although few states seriously challenged the emperor's authority over censorship within the Empire, territorial encroachments on the emperor's licensing authority and disputes over the proper interpretation of legal standards effectively blunted the force of much imperial legislation.

Across the Empire, in areas both Catholic and Protestant, censorship laws were overwhelmingly oriented toward the control of religious expression. The Protestant states, no less than the Catholic states, assumed that the civil authority had both the right and the duty to regulate religious writings to preserve both the spiritual welfare and the tranquility of the community. Their subjects, for the most part, shared in this consensus.

In the early modern city, censorship operated at many levels and encompassed all forms of communication. In addition to their efforts to oversee the production and sale of printed texts, local magistrates erected a wide spectrum of controls intended to detect and suppress public speech and conduct directed against the political, religious and social order of the city. The systems thus created were readily adaptable to the political and social constraints affecting the community, from both within and without. However, the flexibility and vagueness inherent in these systems

---

[163] Wilhem Rem, 'Cronica newer geschichten von Wilhelm Rem, 1512–1527,' in *Die Chroniken der Schwäbischen Städte: Augsburg*, Bd. 5, *Die Chroniken der deutschen Städte vom 14. bis ins 16. Jahrhundert*, Bd. 25, ed. Historische Kommission bei der Bayerischen Kommission der Wissenschaften, 1896, (Göttingen: Vandenhoek & Ruprecht, 1966) p. 139; Künast, *Getruckt zu Augspurg*, p. 201.

[164] Immenkötter, 'Die katholische Kirche in Augsburg,' pp. 12–13; Philip Broadhead, *Internal Politics and Civic Society in Augsburg During the Era of the Early Reformation, 1518–1537* (Diss. Univ. of Kent, 1981) pp. 53–65.

also made them potentially arbitrary, creating uncertainty as to the scope of the law and encouraging a degree of protective "self-censorship" in those operating at its margins.

Urban censorship was, by necessity, dependent upon citizen reporting and voluntary compliance. The cooperation of the citizenry was secured, in part, by a general acceptance of the magistrates' asserted right to regulate expression for the protection of communal values and the public peace. To encourage compliance, officials relied upon the very vagueness inherent within the system. Any assessment of censorship in the Empire must recognize not only the many opportunities for evasion the system created, but also the "chilling effect" and defensive self-regulation that the system's inconsistencies fostered within these communities.

The strategies individuals used to circulate their messages also provide some insight into the spectrum of opinion swirling within the early modern city. Both the legitimate and the illicit book markets served an urban readership and contributed to the mix of ideas discussed within the community. Locals read to each other from these books, discussed them, and frequently adapted them for their own purposes. To the extent that prohibited texts were able to side-step the censors, the community's absorption and appropriation of these messages allowed them to penetrate the city to a degree perhaps neither the authors nor the censors could have ever foreseen.

While the various administrative, investigatory, and enforcement arms of local censorship were often focused on discrete tasks, magistrates imbued each with the common purpose of creating and preserving an orderly and integrated society. The philosophical foundation of the system remained in place even as the targets of enforcement shifted with the cities' changing political and religious status over the course of the sixteenth and seventeenth centuries. While the Reformation years were focused upon efforts to enforce and instill changing conceptions of religious orthodoxy, the Empire was required to redirect its censorship policies after 1555 toward the preservation of peace between the Catholic and Lutheran faiths. Although uniformity of religious belief and expression no longer defined imperial censorship policies, the preservation of communal consensus and public order remained the goal. The evolution of urban censorship policies through this period of political and religious transformations forms the subject of the following chapters.

CHAPTER 2

Policing the Word: Censorship and Reformation

From his pulpit in Wittenberg in 1522, Martin Luther saw God's Word unfolding all around him. He assured his congregation that the religious awakening sweeping the Empire was the direct result of the power of the Word.[1] It needed only a voice to proclaim it, for before the Holy Spirit might quicken faith in believers' hearts, they must first hear the Word of God. "We must first hear the Word," Luther said, "and then afterwards the Holy Ghost works in our hearts; he works in the hearts of whom he will, and how he will, but never without the Word."[2]

Faith required, therefore, that the Word be spread. It must be preached, written, sung—proclaimed throughout the world so that all those God had called might hear his message. The centrality of the Word in Protestant thought dictated that the reformers harness the power of the press in its service.[3] The coming of the Reformation thus witnessed an unprecedented flood of books, pamphlets, and broadsheets proclaiming its message. And in a still largely unlettered age, reformers relied on sermons, songs, and simple images to reach the common folk.

The Word, however, did not merely build faith; it destroyed old patterns of belief. "Where the pure and plain Word of God goes," Luther declared, "it breaks into pieces all that is exalted of man, it makes valleys of their mountains, and all their hills it makes low … Every heart that hears this Word must lose faith in itself, else it will not come to Christ."[4] Where the Reformation's message went, therefore, it carried discord in its wake. It was precisely for this reason that clerics and magistrates alike sought to limit its spread.

---

[1] Martin Luther, 'The Second Sermon, March 10, 1522, Monday after Invocavit,' *Luther's Works*, Vol. 51, ed. and trans. John W. Doberstein (Muhlenberg Press, Philadelphia, 1959) pp. 77–8.

[2] Martin Luther, 'Of the Holy Ghost,' CCXLI, *Table Talk*, trans. William Hazlitt (London: G. Bell, 1902) pp. 106–7.

[3] Andrew Pettegree, *Reformation and the Culture of Persuasion* (Cambridge: Cambridge University Press, 2005) p. 128.

[4] Martin Luther, 'Sermon for Pentecost Wednesday; John 6:44–51,' *The Sermons of Martin Luther*, Vol. III, ed. John Nichols Lenker (Grand Rapids, MI: Baker Book House, 1992) p. 398.

Containing the disorderly power of the Word proved a challenge even for the reformers themselves. From decrying the suppression of Protestant texts in 1523, Luther was soon calling on secular authorities to suppress the "false teaching" arising from divisions within the very movement he had helped to found.[5] Policing the Word also bedeviled the governing councils of the imperial cities that had embraced the evangelical cause. As Bernd Moeller has observed, by the beginnings of the sixteenth century, the imperial city had come to see itself as a miniature *corpus christianum*, a community responsible before God for the salvation of its members.[6] But these communities were riven internally along multiple lines, making consensus—religious or otherwise—an often elusive ideal.[7] The evangelical imperial cities' political loyalties were also divided—they were among the earliest and most prominent centers of the German Reformation, yet were constitutionally bound to enforce imperial decrees banning the Protestant message. Confronted with popular agitation for reform and imperial demands for its suppression, urban magistrates struggled to balance their Christian duty to teach and uphold the word of God with their duty of loyalty to their emperor. In those cities that embraced the evangelical cause, censorship became an important tool in both the preservation of communal religious values and the maintenance of external political security. What emerged in Nuremberg, Augsburg, and in many other Protestant imperial cities was a deliberately vague body of law, whose interpretation and enforcement shifted as the religious and political objectives of the communities evolved.

The Coming of Reform: Defending the "Middle Way"

In 1518, Martin Luther visited Nuremberg on his way to Augsburg to meet with Thomas Cardinal Cajetan. He had already attracted a following in Nuremberg, particularly within the city's humanist circles

---

[5] Hans-Peter Hasse, 'Bücherzensur an der Universität Wittenberg im 16. Jahrhundert,' in *700 Jahre Wittenberg: Stadt. Universität. Reformation* (Weimar: Verlag Hermann Böhlaus Nachfolger, 1995) pp. 187–212; Holgar Flachmann, *Martin Luther und das Buch: Eine historische Studie zur Bedeutung des Buches im Handeln und Denken des Reformators.* Tübingen: Mohr, 1996) pp. 202–20.

[6] Bernd Moeller, 'Imperial Cities and the Reformation,' in *Imperial Cities and the Reformation: Three Essays*, ed. and trans. H. C. Erik Midelfort and Mark U. Edwards, Jr. (Durham, N.C.: Labyrinth Press, 1982) pp. 42–49.

[7] See, Thomas A. Brady, Jr., *Ruling Class, Regime, and Reformation at Strasbourg, 1520–1555* (Leiden: Brill, 1978) pp. 3–47; R. Po-Chia Hsia, 'The Myth of the Commune: Recent Historiography on City and Reformation in Germany,' *Central European History* 20 (3–4) (1987): pp. 203–15.

and professional elite.⁸ By the end of 1522, young clergymen appointed by the council were preaching reform in the city's most important churches: Andreas Osiander at St Lorenz's, Dominicus Schleupner at St Sebald's, Jakob Dolmann at St Jakob's, Thomas Venatorius at the Hospital of the Holy Ghost, and Martin Glaser in the Augustinian cloister church.⁹ While the Lutheran message was finding supporters among both the elite and humble elements of Nuremberg society, the city council had to proceed cautiously. Luther and his teachings had been outlawed by the emperor's 1521 Edict of Worms, and from 1522 to 1524, three Imperial Diets met in the city.¹⁰ With imperial officials demanding that the city council suppress the movement, reform in Nuremberg could proceed only haltingly.¹¹

The council sought to delay wide-ranging reforms pending the convocation of a hoped-for national church council at Speyer.¹² The council's cautious policy, however, was not met with universal enthusiasm—protests periodically flared against Catholic practices, and the council was repeatedly pressed to proceed more swiftly in the institution of reform. To discourage controversy, the council carefully oversaw public expression.

Even before the Reformation had reached Nuremberg, the city council had sought to suppress religious and political dissent. By 1513, the council was requiring printers and wood-block cutters (*Formschneider*) to swear an annual oath that they would not print anything "which may cause harm, disgrace, or disadvantage to the clergy, the estates of the Holy Empire, or any related or distinguished persons or groups, or from which errors, intentional or otherwise, may slander or disgrace the honorable

---

⁸ Gottfried Seebaß, 'The Importance of the Imperial City of Nuremberg in the Reformation,' in *Humanism and Reform: The Church in Europe, England, and Scotland, 1400–1643*, ed. James Kirk (Oxford: Blackwell Publishers, 1991) pp. 114–15.

⁹ Günther Vogler, 'Imperial City Nuremberg, 1524–1525: The Reform Movement in Transition,' in *The German People and the Reformation*, ed. R. Po-Chia Hsia (Ithaca: Cornell University Press, 1988) pp. 34–5. On the Reformation in Nuremberg generally, see Friedrich Roth, *Die Einführung der Reformation in* Nürnberg *1517-1528* (Würzburg: A Stuber, 1885); Günther Vogler, *Nürnberg, 1524/25. Studien zur Geschichte der reformatorischen und sozialen Bewegung in der Reichstadt* (Berlin: VEB Deutscher Verlag der Wissenschaften, 1982); Ronald Rittgers, *The Reformation of the Keys: Confession, Conscience, and Authority in Sixteenth-Century Germany* (Cambridge, MA: Harvard University Press, 2004).

¹⁰ On the enforcement of the Edict of Worms, see Martin Brecht, 'Das Wormser Edikt in Süddeutschland,' in *Der Reichsstag zu Worms von 1521: Reichspolitik und Luthersache*, ed. Fritz Reuter (Worms: Stadtarchiv, 1971) pp. 475–89; Paul Kalkoff, *Das Wormser Edikt und die Erlasse des Reichsregiments und einzelner Reichsfürsten* (München & Berlin: R. Oldenbourg, 1917).

¹¹ Vogler, *Nürnberg*, pp. 33–64; Seebaß, 'The Importance of the Imperial City of Nuremberg,' pp. 120–23.

¹² Vogler, 'Imperial City Nuremberg,' pp. 36–7. Seebaß, 'The Importance of the Imperial City of Nuremberg,' pp. 121–2.

Council."[13] After 1518, no new works could be printed in Nuremberg without prior authorization of the city's censors, and all Nuremberg booksellers were required to provide the censor with a list of texts they imported for sale in Nuremberg.[14]

The city council's censorship measures in these years were less concerned with stemming the tide of Lutheran support in Nuremberg than with intercepting material potentially damaging to the city's political interests. While the council issued vague prohibitions of "shameful" poems and woodcuts, its records reveal little systematic effort to intercept such material.[15] Instead, the council took aim against polemical writings and lampoons targeting politically powerful persons and institutions. In September 1524, for example, officials confiscated some Lutheran polemical pamphlets "in which the imperial mandates are published and the emperor and the princes are called 'fools'."[16] The magistrates arrested Johann Faust, a foreign bookseller, but released him with a warning in exchange for information about his suppliers. His associate, Lenhart Finck, a Nuremberg bookseller, was not so well treated, receiving four days' imprisonment in the tower for his part in the enterprise. Finck's sentence was mild, however, compared to the two months' imprisonment the council had meted out four years earlier against Sebolten Pusch for publishing an almanac containing woodcuts holding the papacy and the Catholic clergy up to "calumny, dishonor, and disgrace."[17] In the space of four years, the council had become considerably more indulgent of anti-Catholic propaganda, but politically damaging attacks against Catholic authorities were still subject to official sanction.

The council was also careful to scrutinize images that might cause offense. In 1521, the council prohibited the sale of woodcuts depicting Luther as a divinely inspired prophet.[18] Three years later, all images of

---

[13] Arnd Müller, 'Zensurpolitik der Reichsstadt Nürnberg,' *Mitteilungen des Vereins für Geschichte der Stadt Nürnberg*, 49 (1959): p. 73.

[14] August Jegel, 'Altnürnberger Zensur vor allem des 16. Jahrhunderts,' in *Festschrift für Eugen Stollreither*, ed. Fritz Redenbacher (Erlangen: Universitätsbibliothek, 1950) p. 57.

[15] RV Nr. 24, 11 June 1524 and RV Nr. 57, 4 July 1524 in *Quellen zur Nürnberger Reformationsgeschichte von der Duldung liturgischer Änderungen bis zur Ausübung des Kirchenregiments durch den Rat (Juni 1524–Juni 1525)*, ed. Gerhard Pfeiffer (Nürnberg: Selbstverlag des Vereins für bayerische Kirchengeschichte, 1968) ("*QNR*") pp. 6, 9.

[16] RV Nr. 154, 6 Sept. 1524, in *QNR*, p. 20.

[17] RV Nr. 1281, 27 Nov. 1520, in *Nürnberger Ratsverlässe über Kunst und Künstler*, ed. Theodor Hampe, Bd. 1 (Vienna: Karl Graeser, 1904) p. 196.

[18] Christiane Andersson, 'The Censorship of Images in Nuremberg, 1521–1527: Art and Politics in the Reformation,' in *Dürer and his Culture*, ed. Dagmar Eichberger and Charles Zika (Cambridge: Cambridge University Press, 1998) pp. 168–9. R.W. Scribner, *For the Sake of Simple Folk: Popular Propaganda for the German Reformation* (Oxford: Oxford University Press, 1981) pp. 36, 94.

Luther were banned, apparently in an effort to appease the emperor, although there is no evidence that the ban was consistently enforced.[19] Also in 1524, officials inspected a painting in the home of Endress Stengel which apparently contained anti-papal lampoons. Stengel was not punished, but was ordered to cover up a portion of the painting depicting a fox wearing the papal tiara.[20]

In its frequent protestations of loyalty to the emperor, the Nuremberg city council cited its efforts to suppress anti-Catholic and anti-imperial propaganda.[21] In imperial and papal circles, however, the council's efforts were seen as empty measures meant only to curry favor with the emperor, while Lutheran texts were still allowed to circulate.[22] When Nuremberg dispatched Christoph Schuerl in 1524 to assure the pope's legate, Lorenzo Cardinal Campeggio, of the city's continued loyalty to the old faith, the cardinal shot back: Nuremberg's city council had allowed common folk by the hundreds to write and read in German about controversial religious matters. "Every day," he complained, "some new shameful picture, along with some disgraceful song against the clergy, comes to me from Nuremberg; what are my lords [of the council] thinking?"[23]

The emperor's brother, Archduke Ferdinand, had voiced similar complaints. The council protested that it had forbidden its citizens to sell books that might encourage heresy, rebellion, or insults against the emperor. If such things were sold in Nuremberg, they said, it was not their fault—everyone knew that Nuremberg was a large and bustling market town, and there was only so much officials could do to police it.[24]

No matter how the council tried to play up its efforts, the fact was that, by 1524, it was not particularly interested in suppressing the spread of Lutheran ideas in Nuremberg. The council's tolerance of Lutheran texts may have been due, in part, to the fact that the city censor was council secretary Lazarus Spengler, himself a committed Lutheran. Spengler's close association with Luther was no secret; in fact, Pope Leo X had named him as one of Luther's supporters in *Exsurge Domine* and excommunicated

[19] Andersson, 'Censorship of Images,' pp. 169–70.

[20] RV Nr. 154, 6 Sept. 1524; RV Nr. 157, 7 Sept. 1524, in *QNR*, pp. 20–21.

[21] See the council's 'Instruktion für die Gesandtschaft zu Erzherzog Ferdinand,' dated 22 June 1524; 'Bericht Schuerls über die Aussprache bei Erzherzog Ferdinand,' dated 25 June 1524; and 'Bericht Christoph Schuerls über sein Gespräch mit Campeggi,' dated 29 June 1524, in *QNR*, pp. 261–7.

[22] Müller, 'Zensurpolitik der Reichstadt Nürnberg,' pp. 77–91; Seebaß, 'The Reformation in Nürnberg,' in *The Social History of the Reformation*, ed. Lawrence P. Buck and Jonathan W. Zophy (Columbus: Ohio State University Press, 1972) pp. 23–39.

[23] 'Bericht Christoph Scheurls über sein Gespräch mit Campeggi,' in *QNR*, p. 266.

[24] Harold J. Grimm, *Lazarus Spengler: A Lay Leader of the Reformation* (Columbus: Ohio State University Press, 1978) p. 67.

them both in 1521.²⁵ Moreover, Spengler was himself the author of pro-Lutheran pamphlets, which he took care to publish anonymously in neighboring cities.²⁶ As a censor, Spengler was not inclined to vigorously suppress works of the sort he himself was producing.²⁷

As in Nuremberg, calls for reform were growing in Augsburg. Luther's message had been winning support there since his 1518 interview with Cajetan. Numerous other reformers, particularly the Swiss reformer Ulrich Zwingli, also found an audience in Augsburg, as did many other writers associated with the emerging Anabaptist and Spiritualist movements.

Faced with these assaults on the city's religious order, the Augsburg city council proceeded cautiously. While the influential Fuggers aligned with the church and emperor, many members of the council were sympathetic to the reformers' cause. As in other imperial cities, the reform movement presented city magistrates with the opportunity to further extend civic control over ecclesiastical institutions and public worship.²⁸ Although the city council had long ago wrested legal control over public life from the city's bishop, he retained authority over most of Augsburg's churches and monastic houses.²⁹ But while Augsburg's political interests may have favored opposition to the bishop, its survival as an imperial city required allegiance to the Holy Roman Emperor.

As in Nuremberg, Augsburg's city council elected to steer a "middle way" between the popular clamor for religious reform and the emperor's demands for allegiance to the Catholic faith.³⁰ Seeking to quiet debate in the city, the council banned controversial religious texts in August 1520. The council's designees, Jacob Fugger and city secretary Conrad Peutinger, summoned the printers before them and instructed them that they should print nothing further concerning "the errors [*Irrungen*] debated by the clergy and the doctors of the Holy Writ" without the prior knowledge and approval of the council.³¹ According to the chronicler Wilhelm Rem,

---

²⁵ Ibid., pp. 52; 38–43.

²⁶ Ibid.; Miriam Usher Chrisman, *Conflicting Visions of Reform: German Lay Propaganda Pamphlets, 1519–1530* (Boston: Humanities Press, 1996) pp. 208–10, 214; Rittgers, *The Reformation of the Keys*, pp. 58–61.

²⁷ Müller, 'Zensurpolitik der Reichstadt Nürnberg,' p. 92.

²⁸ Rittgers, *The Reformation of the Keys*, pp. 63–5.

²⁹ J. Jeffery Tyler, *Lord of the Sacred City: The* Episcopus Exclusus *in Late Medieval and Early Modern Germany* (Leiden: Brill, 1999) pp. 85–102, 184.

³⁰ On the city council's policy in this regard, see Andreas Gößner, *Weltliche Kirchenhoheit und reichsstädtische Reformation: die Augsburger Ratspolitik des "milten und mitleren weges," 1520–1534* (Berlin: Akademie Verlag, 1999).

³¹ StAA, Ratsbuch Nr. 14, 1501–1520, fol. 272.

there was little doubt who was behind the measures. "People say Fugger brought it about," he noted.[32]

Despite the city council's decree, evangelical tracts found a ready market in Augsburg. It is a measure of Luther's popularity there that Bishop Christoph von Stadion could find no printer in the city willing to print Pope Leo X's 1520 bull, *Exsurge Domine*.[33] When he finally located a printer, the council blocked its publication, claiming that the printer was inexperienced and unqualified to print Latin texts. It vetoed the printing contract, noting that "ridicule and disadvantage may stem from it."[34] With the bull finally printed in Ingolstadt, the bishop ordered the clergy to announce that all Lutheran books were to be turned over to the vicars and deacons. "Of course, few books were brought to them," Rem commented, "people practically make fun of it now."[35]

Johann Eck, who had been charged with publicizing the bull in Germany, demanded that the city council confiscate Luther's writings in Augsburg. When it took no action, Eck seized the banned books from the local clergy.[36] In accordance with Bishop von Stadion's mandate, some Augsburg priests also refused to hear the confessions of parishioners who failed to turn over Luther's books. The decision was unpopular, particularly among the city's artisans, and according to Rem, some even threatened violence against the priests.

Relations between the Catholic clergy and the laity had become so strained by 1521 that Augsburg's cathedral chapter sent representatives to the council requesting protection. The council advised the priests that it was unable to guarantee their safety and instructed them not to antagonize the laity on account of Luther. The council also cautioned them to avoid areas in which Luther's books were sold.[37] The council's warning, of course, ignored the fact that under the pope's bull, there weren't *supposed* to be places in Augsburg were Luther's books were sold.

As in Nuremberg, the Augsburg city council's "middle way" anticipated that a religious settlement might be reached for the Empire, if not the church as a whole. With Luther's condemnation at the 1521 Diet of Worms, however, the prospect of reconciliation seemed remote. Augsburg's city

---

[32] Wilhem Rem, 'Cronica newer geschichten von Wilhelm Rem, 1512–1527,' in *Die Chroniken der Schwäbischen Städte: Augsburg*, Bd. 5, *Die Chroniken der deutschen Städte vom 14. bis ins 16. Jahrhundert*. Bd. 25, ed. Historische Kommission bei der Bayerischen Kommission der Wissenschaften (18 96) (Göttingen: Vandenhoek & Ruprecht, 1966) p. 137.

[33] Gößner, *Weltliche Kirchenhoheit*, p. 36.

[34] Hans-Jörg Künast, *'Getruckt zu Augspurg:' Buchdruck und Buchhandel in Augsburg zwischen 1468 und 1555*. (Tübingen: Max Niemeyer Verlag, 1997) p. 201.

[35] Rem, 'Chronica,' p. 139.

[36] Künast, *Getruckt zu Augspurg*, p. 201.

[37] Ibid., pp. 144–5.

council issued a decree announcing the Edict of Worms, but someone tore it from the door of the city hall in the middle of the night.[38] As in many other cities across the Empire, the council's unwillingness to antagonize Luther's many supporters in Augsburg complicated their enforcement of the Edict. "People place no stock in it," Wilhelm Rem reported, "and turn over no books."[39]

In October 1522, however, city officials arrested Silvan Othmar for reprinting one of Luther's works in violation of the Edict. Othmar, like most printers in Augsburg, was sympathetic to the evangelical cause. During his career, he produced numerous texts by Luther, Urban Rhegius, Johann Agricola, Justus Jonas, Matthäus Alber, and Johann Oecolampadius.[40] Although Othmar made a good living pirating Luther's works, neither he nor any other Augsburg printer had ever been punished for producing them. Lutheran texts, however, were forbidden in Augsburg not only under the Edict, but also under the council's 1520 decree against controversial religious writings.

Othmar was arrested for reprinting Luther's attack against the Roman Catholic clergy, *Against the Falsely So-Called Spiritual Estate of the Pope and the Bishops* (*Wider den falsch genannten geistliche Stand des Papsts und der Bischöfe*).[41] He admitted he knew that Luther's writings had been prohibited in Augsburg; this was a fact that he could hardly deny, as he had reprinted the Edict of Worms for the council a mere three months earlier.[42] In his defense, however, he explained that he had noted so many other people printing Luther's texts without penalty that he assumed the restrictions had been lifted.[43] For the last six months, Othmar said, he had observed others printing all manner of illegal books, while he took care to print only what was allowed. When he "saw and understood that no one punishes people and they weren't prosecuted," Othmar said, he "concluded nothing other than that it was no longer illegal."[44]

Othmar's claim that he had never before printed banned books was not strictly true; he had already printed several tracts by Luther contrary

---

[38] Rem, 'Chronica,' p. 147.

[39] Ibid., pp. 147, 166.

[40] Karl Schottenloher, 'Silvan Othmar in Augsburg, der Drucker des Schwäbischen Bundes, 1519–1535,' *Gutenberg-Jahrbuch* 15 (1940): p. 282.

[41] Martin Luther, *Wider den falsch genanten gaystlichen Stand des Bapsts und derBischofe. D. Martin. Luther Ecclesiasten zu Wittenberg. M.D. XXII* ([Augsburg: Silvan Othmar], 1522) [BSB, Res 4° Th. U. 103 XXX, 3].

[42] Künast, *Getruckt zu Augspurg*, p. 202, n. 22; Schottenloher, 'Othmar,' p. 284. Schottenloher gives the year as 1523.

[43] StAA, Strafamt, Urg. Silvan Othmar, 29 July 1522.

[44] Ibid.

to the council's 1520 prohibition.[45] However, Othmar was entirely correct that illegal Lutheran texts had become a staple of the Augsburg printing trade and that no one had yet been prosecuted there on that account. He had done nothing that he had not often done before and that others did not continue to do with impunity. Indeed by 1521, Augsburg had become, behind Leipzig, the largest producer of Lutheran texts in the Empire, with over 125 editions published.[46]

Given the flood of Lutheran texts pouring out of Augsburg's print shops, Othmar's prosecution was essentially a show trial meant to convince imperial observers of the council's good faith efforts to enforce the Edict of Worms. The council did not wish to antagonize Luther's supporters in the community by clamping down, but neither did it want conflict with imperial authorities. Othmar himself seems to have understood the council's squeamishness and took steps to soften the impact of Luther's words. He testified that when he reprinted the tract, he censored the text himself by altering the "coarse words and rancor" of Luther's original.[47] He urged his interrogators to compare his version with the original if they did not believe him.

In the context of a 30-page pamphlet, Othmar's changes did little to alter Luther's argument.[48] Nor were they sufficient to avoid the council's ire.[49] His revisions indicate, however, that printers were beginning to learn and internalize the standards the authorities were attempting to legislate. Despite the city's lax enforcement, Othmar's testimony suggests that he, at least, was sufficiently concerned about the risk of prosecution to censor his own work. Clearly, he did not believe that officials were serious in their blanket prohibition of Luther's writings; he knew from his own experience that those restrictions were not enforced. However, he testified that he did understand that certain restrictions were supposed to apply. From his perspective, the law's real aim was, in his words, to tone down "coarse words and rancor." He judged that the council's censorship laws, in practice, were not meant to stifle all discussion of reform, but to limit

---

[45] Schottenloher, 'Othmar,' p. 282.

[46] Mark U. Edwards, *Printing, Propaganda, and Martin Luther* (Berkeley: University of California Press, 1994) pp. 22–5.

[47] StAA, Strafamt, Urg. Silvan Othmar 29 July 1522.

[48] A comparison of Othmar's edition (BSB, Res 4° Th. U. 103 XXX, 3, Martin Luther, *Wider den falsch genanten gaystlichen Stand des Bapsts und der Bischofe* in *D. Martin. Luther Ecclesiasten zu Wittenberg. M.D. XXII.* [Augsburg: Silvan Othmar], 1522) with the Wittenberg original (BSB, Res 4° Th. U. 104 VII, 41, Martin Luther, *Widder den falsch genantten geistlichen Stand des Bapst und der Bischoffen. D. Martinus Luth. Ecclesiasten zu Wittemburg.* [Wittenberg: Lotter, 1522]) reveals only minor changes.

[49] The entry in the Punishment Book on Othmar's case does not record what type of punishment was meted out to him. StAA, Strafbuch Nr. 94, 1509–1526, fol. 128.

divisive and inflammatory rhetoric. He took it upon himself, therefore, to essentially bowdlerize Luther to meet these expectations. Othmar's changes may not have satisfied the council, but they establish that at least some printers in Augsburg were already policing their work through self-censorship.

What Othmar did to Luther's original highlights the changes that texts underwent during reprinting. In an era before effective enforcement of copyrights and licenses, printers freely pirated texts produced by others.[50] For short tracts, printers and booksellers found it more economical to simply reprint a text locally rather than pay to have it shipped from the original press. In addition to saving money, the unauthorized reprints saved considerable time, as texts could be reproduced much faster than they could be shipped. Ever eager to meet the public demand for timely writing, printers and booksellers were quick to rush the works of popular authors to market, even if it meant ignoring the rights of their fellow tradesmen in other cities.[51]

Although the flood of unauthorized reprints helped guarantee the rapid spread of reform ideas throughout the Empire, the pirated editions also created the potential for errors and unauthorized changes to creep into the text.[52] As a result, popular authors such as Martin Luther could not be certain that their words and meaning were being faithfully reported throughout the Empire. Although Luther himself complained of the adaptations, the economic realities of the book trade and the lack of adequate legal protections effectively guaranteed the spread of unauthorized reprints throughout the period.[53]

As Adrian Johns has rightly observed, the ease with which texts could be adapted complicates efforts to assess the influence of print in historical change.[54] Mark Edwards has also noted that the messages readers took from Luther's writings were often not consistent with Luther's own understanding of his work.[55] In part, these differences resulted from alterations and misinterpretations of his words as they were reprinted and discussed in each community. Rather than simply translating the words of the reformers into action, printers and readers adapted them to reflect local

---

[50] For further discussion of the broader implications of this practice, see Adrian Johns, *The Nature of the Book: Print and Knowledge in the Making* (Chicago: University of Chicago Press, 1998) pp. 1–58; 160–82; 343–79.

[51] Andrew Pettegree, 'Books, Pamphlets, and Polemic,' *The Reformation World*, ed. Andrew Pettegree (London: Routledge, 2000) p. 116.

[52] Ibid.

[53] Hans-Peter Hasse, *Zensur theologischer Bücher in Kursachsen im konfessionellen Zeitalter*, (Leipzig: Evangelische Verlagsanstalt, 2000) pp. 46–7.

[54] Johns, *The Nature of the Book*, pp. 1–58.

[55] See Edwards, *Printing, Propaganda*, pp. 5–6.

issues and concerns. As magistrates would find over the coming decades, the texts and ideas that circulated in the streets were often conglomerations of multiple adaptations and distortions. The swift transmutation of these ideas not only stymied official efforts to control them, but also provided burghers with a vehicle for expressing uniquely local concerns.

Despite Augsburg's prosecution of Silvan Othmar, papal officials continued to doubt the city's willingness to police its book trade. In a letter of December 1522, Pope Adrian VI demanded that the council step up efforts to suppress the printing of evangelical texts. The Pope stated that he had heard that Lutheran books were "diligently printed and read in Augsburg," and warned the city council that such books would only spread "poison and evil talk" if not controlled.[56]

Two months later, the council announced a new series of regulations governing the print trade. The printers were required to swear that they would not print any "disgraceful book, song, or rhyme in this city."[57] If they wished to print other materials, they were to first obtain permission from one of the *Bürgermeister*. Anything they printed was required to set forth the names of the author and the printer.[58]

Only a few weeks later, however, the council reversed itself, announcing that the printers would be allowed, upon request, to print their works without identifying either themselves or the authors.[59] Although the council did not explain its reasoning, the city's printers likely feared prosecution by church and secular authorities in other jurisdictions. Augsburg's printers and booksellers exported books across the Empire, and given the religious divisions throughout the region, would have had reason to fear that even shipments approved by local authorities might cause offense in other markets. The most effective precaution against this was to print anonymously, as did printers in other cities. By eliminating this protection, Augsburg's city council had not only exposed its printers to increased risks, it had placed them at a competitive disadvantage.

While the council's reversal shielded the city's printers and booksellers from prosecution in other cities, it also made it more difficult for its own inspectors to police the local book trade. In fact, there is little evidence that the council was even particularly interested in policing the market, at least as far as reform texts were concerned. These materials were popular with "the common man," and the council was loath to take a public stand against reform. Its policy of a "middle way" in religious matters translated

---

[56] StAA, Literalien, 1522, Letter dated 1 Dec. 1522 from Pope Adrian VI to Augsburg City Council.
[57] StAA, Ratsbuch Nr. 15, 1520–1529, fol. 26r-v.
[58] Ibid.
[59] StAA, Ratsbuch Nr. 15, 1520–1529, fol. 27r.

into a censorship policy of deliberate non-enforcement of public law. Although Augsburg was obligated to enforce the Edict of Worms, official policy essentially negated it in practice. As Silvan Othmar had surmised, the council's primary objective was not to silence Luther or any other reformer; it was to damp down divisive controversy. Despite the sweeping prohibitions of the council's public declarations, its deputies followed an unannounced policy of unofficial tolerance for religious debate, provided it did not undermine public order and the council's rule.

For Augsburg, the council's vacillating enforcement efforts must have confirmed to its critics that it had no real intention of enforcing the Edict of Worms. Indeed, Emperor Charles V himself complained to the council early the following year that Augsburg was not doing enough to enforce the Edict. The emperor demanded that the council intensify its control over the book trade.[60] By that time, the council itself had been forced to grapple with the consequences of the new ideas spreading in Augsburg.

The pope's fears about the "evil talk" spreading in Augsburg began to be realized in 1523. This year marked the first appearance of overt religious protests in Augsburg. In July of that year, a baker's assistant, Georg Fischer, was arrested for disrupting a sermon in the cloister church of St Margaret. According to Rem's chronicle, a Dominican friar had been preaching to the congregants about St Margaret's intercession on behalf of pregnant women. Fischer interrupted, challenging him to show where in the Bible he had found that story. He rebuked the friar for preaching such things, as they "seduced" the people. The friar angrily threatened to have him punished; Fischer retorted that he would gladly submit to whatever punishment was due if he could prove to him from the Bible that what he preached was true.[61]

The confrontation between Fischer and the friar soon degenerated into a shouting match among the nuns present.[62] According to Rem, many people believed that Fischer should have been punished for causing the disturbance, but the council "let it happen."[63] Although the council noted that it was "disconcerted and annoyed" by the episode, it ordered the *Bürgermeister* to release Fischer with merely a warning not to disrupt sermons in the future.[64] Not long thereafter, Fischer confronted another cleric about his preaching. The council again ordered Fischer not to harass the clergy, either in public or in private, for "such served only to [promote]

---

[60] Künast, *Getruckt zu Augspurg*, p. 204.
[61] Rem, 'Chronica,' p. 199.
[62] Ibid.
[63] Ibid.
[64] StAA, Ratsbuch Nr. 15, 1520–1529, fol. 39r–40r.

riot."[65] The council would permit him to privately consult with clergymen, provided he was polite, and allowed him to study the Bible if he wished.[66] When the cathedral chapter complained that the punishment was too mild, the council's secretary, Conrad Peutinger, explained the citizenry had petitioned on Fischer's behalf. He noted that the clergy could avoid such disputes in the future if they simply took care to preach only according to the Bible. The laity were now in a position to correct their preachers' errors, Peutinger reminded them, "for the Holy Bible and [other books] are much read by the laity—women and men, young and old—as has never happened before."[67]

The council's muted response to Fischer's protests establishes that it was far more concerned with avoiding public controversy than in policing private belief. Far from seeking to reconcile Fischer to the church, the council allowed him to continue studying the Bible and conversing with clergymen. Whether Fischer avowed the Catholic or evangelical faith was of little concern to the council, provided he expressed his views politely. The "middle way" did not demand orthodoxy; it required only that both sides in the religious debate smooth over their differences for the sake of the common peace.

In the month following the Fischer incident, the council ordered the clergy in the convents and parish churches to preach "nothing but the Holy Gospel and the Word of God."[68] At the council's request, the bishop also instructed the clergy to preach only from the Gospel and to avoid all subjects that might prompt a quarrel.[69] The council's restrictions acknowledged the pressure building within the community to reform public preaching. While the council would not go so far as to force the city's preachers to teach an evangelical message, it recognized that a vocal segment of the community expected it to do so. By restricting the themes on which clergy could preach, the council sought to limit public criticism of its policies.

Religious unrest was also stirring in Nuremberg. By 1525, the council resolved to finally decide the city's religious future. In March of that year, it sponsored a colloquy between Catholic theologians and the city's evangelical pastors to weigh the issue of reform. This move was prompted not only by popular agitation, but also by the discovery of texts and individuals in Nuremberg advocating the views of religious "radicals"

---

[65] Ibid.

[66] Ibid.

[67] Heinrich Lutz, *Conrad Peutinger. Beiträge zu einer Politischen Biographie* (Augsburg: Verlag die Brigg, 1958) p. 227.

[68] StAA, Ratsbuch Nr. 15, 1520–1529, fol. 45r.

[69] Lutz, *Peutinger*, p. 227.

such as Thomas Müntzer and Andreas Karlstadt.[70] The toleration of false teaching, the council declared, would not only lead its subjects to their damnation, but undermine the moral order on which society rested. Public order demanded a final resolution of the religious debate, the council declared:

> For a long time, many divisive teachings and discordant sermons have arisen, and yet both sides claim that theirs is the truth and grounded in Holy Scripture ... These offensive and extreme teachings not only contribute to unrest and ensnare the human conscience, but [they] also undermine the morals of the subjects, which in time give no little cause to uprisings, disobedience, adversity, and also the destruction of civic peace.[71]

Although the ultimate decision was little in doubt, the council officially adopted the evangelical faith, making Nuremberg the first of the imperial cities to institutionalize reform. The city's censorship laws were redirected toward promoting a Lutheran understanding of the faith and enforcing uniformity in doctrine and practice. Nonetheless, city magistrates remained careful not to offend powerful Catholic interests abroad. While Lutheranism enjoyed the council's protection within the city's walls, the export of anti-Catholic literature often attracted the censors' eye.[72]

One year after Nuremberg's adoption of reform, Andreas Osiander, pastor of St Lorenz, enlisted the shoemaker and *Meistersinger* Hans Sachs to help him bring an anti-papal tract to press.[73] Based on a collection of medieval prophecies, *A Miraculous Prophecy on the Future of the Papacy* (*Ein wunderliche Weyssagung von dem Babstumb, wie es yhm bis an das Endt der Welt gehen sol*) purported to relate the history of the papacy and foretell its ultimate demise. Osiander wrote an introduction, while Sachs provided rhymes expounding on illustrations crafted by the Nuremberg wood-block cutter and printer Hans Guldenmund. Printed by Guldenmund, the pamphlet hit the Nuremberg streets in early 1527. One copy found its way to Martin Luther, who hoped to have it re-printed in Wittenberg.[74] In Nuremberg's city hall, however, the pamphlet received a

---

[70] Volger, *Nürnberg*, pp. 194–250; Seebaß, 'The Reformation in Nuremberg,' pp. 28–9.

[71] Vogler, 'Imperial City Nuremberg,' p. 47.

[72] Reinhard Heinritz, 'Politisches Musengespräch. Hans Sachs und die "Zensur" in der Reichsstadt Nürnberg,' *Archiv für Kulturgeschichte* 85 (2003): pp. 493–507, 496.

[73] On Hans Sachs, see Bernd Balzer, *Bürgerliche Reformationspropaganda: Die Flugschriften des Hans Sachs in den Jahren 1523–1525* (Stuttgart: J. B. Metzlersche Verlagsbuchhandlung, 1973); Vogler, *Nürnberg*, pp. 151–76.

[74] Andersson, 'Censorship of Images,' p. 176; Paul A. Russell, *Lay Theology in the Reformation: Popular Pamphleteers in Southwest Germany, 1521–1525* (Cambridge: Cambridge University Press, 1986) p. 167.

chillier reception. Although the city had officially cut its ties to the papacy, magistrates feared antagonizing the emperor. They accordingly confiscated the pamphlet and summoned Osiander, Sachs, and Guldenmund before the council. It found that the book served more to "inflame and embitter the common man than anything else," and that all manner of discord and disadvantage could befall the council as a result.[75] The council was acutely conscious of the damage the book could do to its relations with the emperor. Citing the 1524 Imperial Diet's prohibition of anti-Catholic publications, the council stressed that the work had been published without its prior knowledge or consent. It also wrote to the Frankfurt city council, asking it to buy up all copies to be found at the book fair at Nuremberg's expense. The councilors scolded Osiander, informing him that they "had expected him to show more sense in this case" and warning him to desist from such activities in the future.[76] They rebuked Sachs for his literary exploits, for, as a shoemaker, "such is not his office, nor does it befit him."[77] They ordered him to stick to his last and never again publish any pamphlets or rhymes. The printer, Guldenmund, received a much more sympathetic hearing. Finding that he had not knowingly violated the law and had relied on Osiander's assurances, the council was lenient. On account of his "poverty and his many small children," the council compensated Guldenmund 12 gulden for the 600 confiscated pamphlets. They even permitted him to reprint the woodcuts without the offending text.[78]

It was not long before Guldenmund was back before the council for publishing anti-papal literature, but Sachs seems to have heeded the council's warning, at least in part. For three years he published nothing. When Sachs resumed publication, he steered clear of controversial themes, taking care to cloak any potentially dangerous ideas in allegorical language.[79] "To write is very dangerous," Sachs noted in a 1553 poem,

> For people hardly suffer the truth these days.
> Be it to write, to sing, or to speak

---

[75] StAN, Ratsbuch Nr. 13, 1525 IV 19–1527 V 22, fol. 256r–257r.

[76] Ibid., fol. 256v.

[77] Ibid., fol. 257r.

[78] Ibid.

[79] Eckhard Bernstein, '"Auch ist zw dichten gar geferlich…" Literarische Zensur und Selbstzensur bei Hans Sachs,' in *Akten des VIII. Internationalen Germanisten-Kongresses, Tokyo 1990: Begegnung mit dem "Fremden": Grenzen, Traditionen, Vergleiche*, 11 (1991) pp. 15–23, 19. He wrote numerous verses attacking Margrave Albrecht Alcibiades of Brandenburg-Kulmbach after his attack on Nuremberg in the 1550s, but withheld them from publication. Even this was not sufficient to calm the Nuremberg Council: the day after Sachs's death, it ordered its deputies to confiscate two particularly incendiary manuscripts from among his papers.

Of such evil knavery,
One must keep silent in print,
Or speak with hypocrisy and honeyed words ...[80]

As Sylvan Othmar had discovered before him, Sachs's encounter with the Nuremberg censors taught him that he could not safely predict how magistrates would apply the law. Sachs was a prolific publicist for the cause of reform but had never before run afoul of the city's censors. Even when Nuremberg was still nominally Catholic, authorities had ignored his songs praising Luther and his religious pamphlets.[81] Sachs and Osiander could have expected that if anti-Catholic texts did not merit punishment then, they were certainly unlikely to draw fire now that the city was officially Protestant. Instead, Sachs found himself not only punished for publishing an anti-Catholic text, but prosecuted under imperial legislation designed specifically to protect the Roman Catholic church. With Sachs, the Nuremberg city council demonstrated that it was entirely prepared to reverse course and apply imperial law against its subjects whenever its political interests seemed to dictate. Faced with such shifting standards, Sachs, like Othmar, seems to have learned that the safest course was to censor his own work.

The Word in the Streets: Religious Protest from Pulpit to Rumor

While Nuremberg took the lead in the urban Reformation, popular agitation continued in Augsburg, fed by fiery preaching and troubling rumors. Arising at the intersection of print and oral culture, the "common talk" in the streets created a filter through which the reform message was understood. Just as readers tended to understand texts through their own interpretive filters, rumor and gossip shaped how ideas would be understood within the oral culture of the streets.[82] In critiquing the council's religious policies, these stories underscored critical themes in the sermons and texts discussed within the community and helped shape the laity's understanding of its own role in the process of reform.

---

[80] Heinritz, 'Politisches Musengespräch,' p. 500.

[81] See Horst Brunner, 'Hans Sachs – Über die Schwierigkeiten literarischen Schaffens in der Reichsstadt Nürnberg,' in *Bedingungen und Probleme reichsstädtischer Literatur Hans Sachs zum 400. Todestag am 19. Januar 1976*, eds H. Brunner, G. Hirschmann and F. Schnelbögl (Nürnberg: Vereins für Geschichte der Stadt Nürnberg, 1976) pp. 4–13; Russell, *Lay Theology in the Reformation*, pp. 165–81.

[82] See, in this regard, Carlo Ginzburg, *The Cheese and The Worms: the Cosmos of a Sixteenth-Century Miller*, trans. John Tedeschi and Anne C. Tedeschi (Baltimore: The Johns Hopkins University Press, 1992) p. xii.

By 1524, the Benedictine chronicler Clemens Sender was reporting that "Lutheranism and heresy had practically taken over" in Augsburg and that all priestly rites were jeered at and disrupted.[83] Well into the mid-1530s, however, Augsburg's city council clung to its policy of finding a "middle way" between the emperor's dictates and the popular demand for reform. While the council hesitated, Augsburg's bishop worked for the arrest or removal of preachers thought to be teaching an evangelical message. He asked the council to arrest the reforming preachers Johann Frosch, prior of the Carmelite church of St Anna's, and Johann Speiser of St Moritz. The council, fearing a riot, declined his request.[84] On his own authority, the bishop ordered the arrest of Caspar Adler, a priest and supporter of Luther, who was snatched off the streets while visiting Augsburg in August 1523.[85] The bishop's very public effort to silence the preachers sparked rumors in Augsburg that he—and perhaps the city council—were conspiring to expel the reforming clergy. Fearing a crackdown, 400 men gathered at one of the city's churches to petition the council to protect the clergy from the bishop.[86]

With reform-minded preachers winning support in Augsburg, the bishop's efforts to silence them focused attention on who had legitimate authority to set policy for the city's churches: was it the bishop, the city council, or the community itself? These issues were a central theme of Reformation prints and preaching. While Luther stressed the role of the prince and magistrate in instituting reform, Augsburg's more radical preachers were suggesting that the community might take the lead. One of the most influential was Johannes Schilling, a Franciscan friar and lector at the city's Franciscan church, the *Barfüsser*. Heavily influenced by Zwingli, Schilling was extremely popular among the weavers and other poor artisans who lived within the *Barfüsser* parish. In addition to calling for preaching in the vernacular and the elimination of ritual not founded on scriptural authority, Schilling emphasized the establishment of a godly community.

---

[83] Clemens Sender, 'Die Chronik von Clemens Sender von ältesten Zeiten der Stadt bis zum Jahre 1536,' in *Die Chroniken der Schwäbischen Städte: Augsburg*, Bd. 4. *Die Chroniken der deutschen Städte vom 14. bis ins 16. Jahrhundert* Bd. 23, ed. Historische Kommission bei der Bayerischen Kommission der Wissenschaften (1894) (Göttingen: Vandenhoek & Ruprecht, 1966) p. 154.

[84] Wolfgang Zorn, *Augsburg: Geschichte einer deutschen Stadt* (Augsburg: Hieronymus Mühlberger Verlag, 1972) p. 170; Friedrich Roth, *Augsburgs Reformationsgeschichte*, Bd. I (Munich: Theodor Ackermann, 1907) pp. 120–22.

[85] Georg Preu der Ä., 'Die Chronik des Augsburger Malers Georg Preu des Älteren, 1512–1537,' in *Die Chroniken der Schwäbischen Städte: Augsburg*, Bd. 6, *Die Chroniken der deutschen Städte vom 14. bis ins 16. Jahrhundert*, Bd. 29, ed. Historische Kommission bei der Bayerischen Kommission der Wissenschaften (1906) (Göttingen: Vandenhoek & Ruprecht, 1966) p. 24; Roth, *Reformationsgeschichte*, Bd. I, p. 124.

[86] Roth, *Reformationsgeschichte*, Bd. I, p. 125.

If secular authorities would not countenance reform, Schilling suggested that the community seize the initiative.[87] "A community is greater than a council," he had supposedly said from the pulpit.[88]

In this atmosphere, news of the arrest of the reforming preacher struck a responsive chord. The depth of public concern became clear in a heated confrontation in the Carmelite church of St Anna's two months after Adler's arrest. Parishioners nearly rioted when they discovered that the bishop had sent his bailiff, Claus Hirschmann, to secretly report on what their priest, Johannes Frosch, was preaching to his congregation. Hirschmann did not like what he heard and complained loudly to the person next to him that Frosch encouraged disobedience to the pope, the emperor, and the bishop. He was overheard, however, and soon found himself surrounded by angry parishioners, all demanding to know what business he had there. Hirschmann replied that he had been sent by "his gracious lord, the bishop" to inform on the preachers—an explanation which enraged the crowd.[89]

Frosch had been one of the preachers that the bishop had sought to arrest only a few months before, and now, it seemed, he was renewing the campaign against him. The parishioners had clearly heard the gossip, and their reaction revealed the public anger this news had stirred. They hurled abuse at Hirschmann, calling him a traitor and a "Judas" for spying on the preachers. They also denounced him and the bishop for arranging Adler's arrest. Pointing at Hirschmann, one man shouted "there is the man who arrested the Truth!"[90] Another lectured him that, if he were a good Christian, he would never have tried to arrest the evangelical preachers, for one should be more obedient to God than to the bishop. "No," Hirschmann quipped, "I must be more obedient to the bishop because I get 100 gulden a year from him."[91] He also revealed that "there are still more [arrests] to come, according to my lord's orders!"[92] Hirschmann went on to tell the parishioners that the whole matter could have been settled if the city council simply took a harsher line against the preachers. It would have been better, he said, "if your lords here arrested some of these lying [preachers] and chopped their heads off."[93]

---

[87] Ibid., p. 157.
[88] Ibid.
[89] StAA, Strafamt, Urg. Claus Hirschmann, 8–15 Dec. 1523.
[90] Witnesses' Report dated 28 Oct. 1523, testimony of Caspar Herrich, filed ibid.
[91] Ibid, testimony of Jorg Rummel.
[92] Ibid, testimony of Isidore Rem.
[93] Ibid, testimony of Jorg Rummel.

Meanwhile, an increasingly large "mob" (*Zulauf*) of women gathered around Hirschmann, such that "he began to fear for himself."[94] He tried to soothe the women with "good words," addressing one woman as "my pretty lady." "The pretty ladies are all priests' whores," the woman shot back. Another noted that the bishop collected 1,500 gulden a year in fines from priests with concubines; that made him "the biggest whoremonger in the land," she said. The woman jeered at the bishop's spy: "go and tell him that, too—like you tell him everything else!"[95]

The *Bürgermeister* had to send soldiers to rescue Hirschmann from the church. In its investigation of the matter, however, the city council tellingly chose to align itself with the congregation, prosecuting Hirschmann for creating a public disturbance.[96] In particular, the council sought to distance itself from the bishop's efforts to silence the pastors. The council apparently feared that Hirschmann's remarks about the arrest and beheading of the reforming preachers would spark rumors that it had, in fact, done just that. He denied ever stating that the council had arrested or executed anybody, but he admitted that he "might have said" that more arrests were pending because he "had heard in the countryside that others had given such orders."[97]

The news and rumors of reprisals against the clergy intersected with reformed preaching to shape public debate. In their attacks on Hirschmann, the parishioners hurled a stream of abuse drawn from the sermons and writings of their pastors, attacking the church for being more loyal to its own interests and institutions than to the service of God. The congregation's reaction was also clearly informed by the rumors concerning the efforts to silence the preachers. The fact that the bishop had been able to pluck the most vocal supporters of reform off the streets and send his spies into their churches highlighted the vulnerability of the movement. These events drew attention to the council's uncertain support for reform and bred speculation that the government could not be trusted. It was in this environment that new rumors arose of a council-backed plot to silence the preachers. The stories, in turn, focused attention on the issue of the laity's right to direct communal worship. As these stories circulated, they repeatedly brought this issue to the fore, ensuring that the community's rights would increasingly dominate the reform debates.

How did these rumors arise, and how did they spread? Issues or events of great importance to a community tend to breed rumors, particularly when reliable information about those events is lacking or

---

[94] Ibid, testimony of Caspar Herrich.
[95] Ibid., testimony of Jorg Rummel.
[96] Roth, *Reformationsgeschichte*, Bd. 1, p. 125–6.
[97] StAA, Strafamt, Urg. Claus Hirschmann, 14 Dec. 1523.

poorly understood.⁹⁸ Although Augsburg's city council sought to justify its "middle way" in its public pronouncements, the basic deliberations behind its religious policy were known only within the inner circles of government—a world far removed from most of the humble artisans who most vocally agitated for reform. The efforts to silence the reforming pastors thus occurred in a political climate of doubt and mistrust, while the council's public temporizing did little to clear up public confusion. In such an environment, rumors of conspiracy and resistance satisfied the public's desire for information.

Rumor is relational; it requires a chain of social relationships through which it is spread.⁹⁹ In Augsburg, the artisan community formed the core of the reform movement's lay support, and it was here that these rumors found their most receptive audience. Within the city's artisan neighborhoods, people came together in the taverns, churches, and workshops to socialize and gossip. Here, news and speculation about the fate of the reform-minded preachers spread widely. These rumors also seem to have encouraged a more active lay involvement in reform, for it seems that it was within these social networks that plans were laid for public agitation in the Reformation cause. Throughout the early 1520s, Augsburg witnessed a series of lay protests for reform, most involving these same loose networks of artisans and their wives.

Shortly after Easter in 1524, Augsburgers awoke to find that someone had splattered blood on statues of the saints outside the cathedral of Our Lady.¹⁰⁰ Eventually, city officials arrested the shoemaker Georg Nass. He denied any involvement in the iconoclasm, but admitted that his servant Leonhart had often told him that he wished to paint the saints' images with blood to protest the Catholic veneration of "idols." Leonhart got these ideas, Nass said, from a priest who used to lodge with them. The priest often read to them from the Bible about idolatry. Images and "gods" were nothing, the priest said, and Leonhart was deeply affected. "Master, if I had blood," Leonhart frequently told Nass, "I would paint the saints with it."¹⁰¹ Nass warned him that he would be punished for this, but Leonhart said it mattered nothing to him; they must do away with the worship of idols. Without his knowledge, Leonhart sent a serving boy to the butcher to get him a pig's heart and a bucket of blood, which he hid in a

---

⁹⁸ Gordon W. Allport and Leo Postman, *The Psychology of Rumor* (New York: Henry Holt & Co., 1947) p. 2.

⁹⁹ Jörg R. Bergmann, *Discreet Indiscretions: The Social Organization of Gossip* (Hawthorne, NY: Aldine de Gruyter, 1993) pp. 45–8.

¹⁰⁰ StAA, Schätze, Nr. 31, 'Sammlung reichsstädtischer Verordnungen und geschichtlicher Notizen der Stadt Augsburg, 1575–1600,' fol. 170v.

¹⁰¹ StAA, Strafamt, Urg. Jorg Nass, 11 May 1524.

trunk. While Nass was sleeping, Leonhart and another apprentice smeared blood all over the saints' images outside the cathedral, then fled the city. When he discovered what had happened, Nass feared his own arrest and fled into the mountains.[102] Under torture, he swore he had nothing to do with Leonhart's protest and had not supported it. Despite his claims of innocence, the council expelled him from the city for a year. According to Sender, however, Nass was soon pardoned, and returned to Augsburg "even more Lutheran than he was before."[103]

According to Nass's testimony, Leonhart's iconoclasm sprang directly from what he had learned from the priest. Although he could not read himself, he heard the reforming message from the priest, who read to him and instructed him concerning the veneration of the saints. Acting on this teaching, Leonhart sought to spread the message further through the symbolic desecration of the holy images. His case thus provides a good example of the ways Reformation ideas flowed through the city streets: from print, through public reading and discussion, into ritual action. In this way, even an illiterate apprentice could adopt the message as his own and become a public spokesman for the cause.

The iconoclasm at the cathedral caused a sensation in Augsburg, but within a month, another, more provocative, confrontation in the local Franciscan church brought the issue of reform out into the open. In early May 1524, a crowd of angry parishioners confronted a friar who had come to bless the holy water at the Franciscan (*Barfüsser*) church. Word of the plan had evidently spread, for a crowd of people had gathered around the font expecting to witness a confrontation. When the friar appeared, the ringleaders seized a Latin prayer book from his hands, demanding that he pray with them in German, so that they could understand him. Witnesses reported that people were shouting that "a community is greater than an abbot!" and that "a community is greater than a *Bürgermeister*."[104]

The leaders of the protest testified that they acted so that "the preachers will not have preached in vain!"[105] One of the ringleaders, Bartolome Nussfelder, said that "they hear daily in the sermons how holy water does not take away sins and is of no use and that they should place their hope only in God and not in water."[106] Moved by these sermons, Nussfelder and several others hatched a plan in a local tavern to protest the next time the water was due to be consecrated. They did it all for the sake of the godly Word, Nussfelder said, just as the lector at the *Barfüsser*,

---

[102] Ibid, Urg. 8–11 May 1524.
[103] Sender, 'Chronik,' p. 155.
[104] StAA, Strafamt, Urg. Hans Beringer, 8 May 1524.
[105] StAA, Strafamt, Urg. Bartholme Nussfelder, 8 May 1524.
[106] Ibid.

Johannes Schilling, had taught them. Indeed, Schilling had been present at the planning meeting for the *Barfüsser* protest, and had given at least tacit approval to the idea.[107]

To the council, the assertion that the community held a superior right to decide its religious status was particularly subversive. But recognizing Schilling's popularity among the city's lower orders and ever wary of appearing to take a stand on reform, the council did not wish to move against him directly. Through secret negotiations, city officials induced Schilling to quietly leave in early August 1524.[108] Schilling's abrupt departure—and the council's alleged involvement in it—seemed to confirm the earlier rumors about its plots against the preachers. Concerns were also raised about the fact that the council had given the priests a guarded escort after the *Barfüsser* incident: were these guards to protect them, or jail them?[109] Rumors spread that the council had finally resolved to expel all the reform-minded preachers and that Schilling's removal was just the start of a general purge.[110] In protest, an estimated 1,800 people assembled before the city hall to demand Schilling's reinstatement.[111] Some were heard to shout "a community is greater than a council!" and called for the council's overthrow.[112]

When the council next met, it was with armed soldiers stationed around the city hall and Perlach Square. With a mercenary force of 600 men, the city council imposed martial law and banned all public and private assemblies. It also outlawed any speech "or other behavior" that might serve to promote disunity, disobedience, or resistance to the city council, "the lawful authority of this city of Augsburg."[113]

The *Barfüsser* protest and the near riot over Schilling's dismissal revealed the influence of the local preachers within some segments of the community. These episodes also highlight the power of rumor to fuel public protest and the social networks within which such rumors took shape. Many of Schilling's supporters had also been involved in the *Barfüsser* protest, the altercation in St Anna's, and in other public demonstrations.

---

[107] Ibid.; StAA, Strafamt, Urg. Ulrich Richsner, 9 May 1524; Peter Scheppach, 10 May 1524.

[108] Roth, *Reformationsgeschichte*, Bd. 1, p. 159.

[109] Georg Preu der Ä., 'Die Chronik des Augsburger Malers Georg Preu des Älteren, 1512–1537,' in *Die Chroniken der Schwäbischen Städte: Augsburg*, Bd. 6. *Die Chroniken der deutschen Städte vom 14. bis ins 16. Jahrhundert*. Bd. 29, ed. Historische Kommission bei der Bayerischen Kommission der Wissenschaften (1906) (Göttingen: Vandenhoek & Ruprecht, 1966), p. 25.

[110] Roth, *Reformationsgeschichte*, Bd. 1, p. 160.

[111] Ibid.

[112] StAA, Strafamt, Urg. Ambrose Miller and Melchior Schneider, et. al., 7 Aug. 1524.

[113] SStBA, 2° S. 14, Kapsel I, 'Anschläge 1524–1734,' Nr. 6.

Nussfelder, for example, had spearheaded the *Barfüsser* incident and had been at the head of the 1523 assembly that had lobbied the city council to protect the preachers from the bishop. Another of the protesters, Utz Richsner, had witnessed the *Barfüsser* showdown and was also involved in the altercation with the bishop's bailiff in St Anna's. His wife had been present at the meeting with Schilling and Nussfelder at which the plan to accost the priest in the *Barfüsser* had first been hatched. Another supporter of the reform movement was Haug Marschalck, who often attended sermons at the *Barfüsser* and had also participated in the confrontation with the bishop's bailiff in St Anna's.

In addition to supporting the pastors, both Richsner and Marschalck were also published pamphleteers, and their writings allow us to see how the concerns regarding the preachers helped shape their understanding of the laity's role in reform. In their writings, both men complained of the efforts to silence the evangelical clergy and their lay supporters. In defense of the pastors, they called for a lay apostolate that would show church and secular officials the path to reform.

Richsner, a weaver, was the author of four Reformation pamphlets, all published between January and November 1524. He seems to have been a careful and wide-ranging reader, drawing inspiration from saints' lives, medieval chronicles, as well as Scripture, published sermons, and the works of Luther, Zwingli, and Erasmus.[114] But Richsner's interpretation of his sources was informed by his own experience of the lay movement for reform in Augsburg. All Christians had the duty, he said, as brothers and sisters in Christ, to teach one another the word of God.[115] However, the Catholic clergy and the wealthy men who controlled the city council had neglected their obligations to their brethren. They persecuted clergy who sought to preach the word of God, threatening them with arrest, execution, or banishment.[116] And referring perhaps to his own arrest in the *Barfüsser* incident, Richsner complained that the laity were forbidden to correct their priests when they erred: "they [the clergy] have authority from God to correct us, but we can't correct them at all, as if they themselves are the Christian church."[117] Richsner emphasized the peoples' right to

---

[114] Russell, *Lay Theology*, pp. 120–27; Martin Arnold, *Handwerker als theologische Schriftsteller: Studien zu Flugschriften der frühen Reformation (1523–1525)* (Göttingen: Vandenhoeck & Ruprecht, 1990), pp. 217–50.

[115] Utz Richsner, *Ain Schöne Underweysung/wie und wir in Christo alle gebrüder und schwester seyen/dabey angezaigt nicht allain die weltlichen/wie sy es nennen/sonder auch die gaistlichen zustraffen/wa sy anders in den leybe dessen haubt Christus ist wöllen sein auff die geschrift gottes gegründt und darauß gezogen/zu nutz allen die das götlich wort leiben seindt.* [BL, 3906.c.98/14].

[116] Ibid., p. Bir–v.

[117] Ibid., p. Aiiiv.

institute the reform that their leaders would not, but he was careful to add that change must come by persuasion, and not by force.[118]

Haug Marschalck was likewise troubled by the authorities' failure to institute reform. As paymaster for the imperial troops in Augsburg, Marschalck condemned disobedience, but he shared the protesters' desire for religious change and protection of the reforming clergy.[119] In fact, the inspiration for his pamphlets, he said, came from the Augsburg preachers; listening to their sermons and with their guidance, he had been moved to his own private study of the Scriptures.[120] Like Richsner, he interpreted what he heard and read through the local controversies over reform. He condemned the higher clergy's efforts to expel those preachers who taught in accordance with the Scripture.[121] Church officials "scorned them," he said, "and drove them from place to place because they stood for evangelical truth."[122] Marschalck took this as a sign of the coming End Times. To prepare, he called for a lay apostolate, arguing, like Richsner, that lay Christians were God's instruments, with the duty to speak out in matters of faith.[123] Through their example, they might bring their leaders to recognize their duty to institute reform.

The rumors of the efforts to silence the reforming clergy offered a critique of the city council's temporizing religious policies. By highlighting official ambivalence to reform, the rumors encouraged an increasingly active role for the movement's lay supporters. In this, the rumors fed on the messages pouring from the city's pulpits and book stalls exhorting the laity to stand by God's word. By accentuating the peril posed by the authorities, the rumors helped ensure that these messages would be understood to demand that the laity come to the Gospel's defense. These stories, then, shaped the ways in which the Reformation message was interpreted in the city streets. As these ideas worked their way back into print in the writings of lay

---

[118] Ibid., p. Biv.

[119] On Marschalk, see Friedrich Roth, 'Wer war Haug Marschalck genannt Zoller von Augsburg?' in *Beiträge zur bayerischen Kirchengeschichte* 6 (1900) pp. 229–34; Miriam Usher Chrisman, *Conflicting Visions of Reform: German Lay Propaganda Pamphlets, 1519–1530* (Atlantic Highlands, New Jersey: Humanities Press, 1996) pp. 114–15, 123–4, 131–2; Russell, *Lay Theology*, pp. 127–47,

[120] Haug Marschalck, *Das Hailig ewyg wort gots/was dz in im kraft/strecke/tugendt/ frid/fred erleüchtung/unnd leben/in aym rechten Christen zu erwecken vermag, etc.* (Augsburg: Ramminger, 1523), p. Aiv. [BL, 3906.e.70].

[121] Haug Marschalck, *Ein Spiegel der Plinden/wan Christus der her hat geredt/Ich wird mein glory von den/hochweisen verberge/und/wird es den kleine/verkünden und offbaren./ Dann ee mein glory und eer solt undergon/es musten die steyn und holtz/reden lernen. Uff solichs ist uffgericht anzuschauwe dises Spiegel der Blinden.*

[122] Ibid.

[123] Ibid.

pamphleteers, they reflected this intensified focus on communal action. In rumor, oral and print culture formed a single circuit: the talk in the streets fed on the steady stream of reforming ideas flowing from the city's presses and pulpits, and fed back into the pamphlets hawked about town.

"The Devil's Work"—The Radical Challenge

Although the Augsburg city council tried to keep the peace on all sides, theological battles raged not only between Catholics and Protestants, but between Protestants themselves. Augsburg's presses churned out controversial works between adherents of Luther's teaching on the Real Presence and Zwingli's contention that the sacrament served as a merely symbolic representation of the body and blood of Christ. Much of the debate was local, with Keller, Rhegius, and other Augsburg clergymen publishing pamphlets outlining their positions.[124] Although it is unclear what ordinary Augsburgers knew or thought about the controversy, the council was concerned enough about the divisiveness to ban books and preaching regarding the sacrament in December 1526.[125]

Nuremberg had already confronted the challenge of policing Protestant dissent. By October 1524, magistrates were investigating reports that disciples of the "false prophet," Thomas Müntzer, were active in the area.[126] They soon arrested Müntzer's associate, Heinrich Pfeiffer, for preaching in the city. Both men had recently been banished from Mühlhausen for spearheading a campaign there for radical religious and social reform. Nuremberg authorities confiscated two manuscripts from Pfeiffer on his arrest.[127] Their author is unknown, but Andreas Osiander, asked to assess their orthodoxy, found them riddled with theological errors and political subversion. "In short, I found nothing good in them anywhere," he wrote.[128] The council expelled Pfeiffer, but not just for his religious views. As always, the council's religious policies weighed the political costs: Pfeiffer was both a known religious radical and a rebel exiled by another imperial city. To shelter such a man was bad in itself, but it would

---

[124] See Roth, *Reformationsgeschichte*, Bd. 1, pp. 197–210.
[125] StAA, Geheime Ratsbuch Nr. 2, 1527–1529, fol. 12r.
[126] RV Nr. 186, 26 Oct. 1524, in *QNR*, p. 25.
[127] Vogler, *Nürnberg*, pp. 201–05.
[128] T. Kolde, 'Hans Denck und die gottlosen Maler von Nürnberg,' in *Beiträge zur bayerischen Kirchengeschichte* 8 (1902), p. 28; Schelle-Wolff, *Zwischen Erwartung und Aufruhr: Die Flugschrift „Von der newen wandlung eynes Christlichen lebens" und der Nürnberger Drucker Hans Hergot*, pp. 39–40.

also give offense to Mühlhausen and could damage Nuremberg's standing among its sister cities.[129]

Around the same time, Nuremberg officials seized one of Müntzer's pamphlets from a "foreign bookseller" from "Mellerstat."[130] This was likely the bookseller Hans Hut from Bibra, not far from Mellrichstadt.[131] He had pledged himself to Müntzer's cause in Mühlhausen, and after their banishment, had sheltered Müntzer and Pfeiffer in Bibra. Müntzer asked Hut to use his connections in the Nuremberg book trade to get his work published there, and Pfeiffer and Hut may have traveled to Nuremberg together for this purpose, bringing several manuscripts with them.[132]

While Pfeiffer's manuscripts were confiscated, Hut managed to get Müntzer's *A Special Exposure of False Faith* (*Ausgedrückten Entblößung*) printed secretly in the shop of the Nuremberg printer Hans Hergot. Hergot's apprentices claimed that they had printed it without their master's knowledge while he was away.[133] They were imprisoned in the tower, and Hergot, perhaps hearing of their arrests, stayed away.[134] Officials learned that he had never taken the oath required of all Nuremberg printers; what they did not yet know was that he would soon emerge as a radical religious propagandist in his own right.[135] Three years later, he was executed at Leipzig for distributing the "seditious" pamphlet, *On the New Transformation of the Christian Life* (*Von der newen Wandlung eynes Christlichen Lebens*), outlining a peasant utopia of Christian communalism.[136]

With Hergot's apprentices jailed, the Nuremberg city council asked Dominicus Schleupner, the Lutheran preacher of St Sebald, to assess the orthodoxy of the Müntzer pamphlet. Although his report does not survive, the council recorded that he found many "errors and unchristian things" in the book, "which served more to promote rebellion than Christian

---

[129] RV Nr. 190, 29 Oct. 1524, in *QNR*, pp. 25–6; StAN, Ratsbuch 12, fol. 267.

[130] StAN, Ratsbuch 12, fol. 268.

[131] Karl Schottenloher, 'Beschlagnahmte Druckschriften aus der Frühzeit der Reformation,' *Zeitschrift für Bücherfreunde* N.F. 8 (1917), p. 313; Gottfried Seebaß, *Müntzers Erbe: Werk, Leben und Theologie des Hans Hut*, (Güthersloh: Gütersloher Verlaghaus, 2002), pp. 109–10

[132] Seebaß, *Müntzers Erbe*, pp. 110–111, 174–76; Vogler, *Nürnberg*, pp. 215–23.

[133] RV Nr. 192 29 Oct. 1524 and RV Nr. 196, 31 Oct. 1524, in *QNR*, p. 26.

[134] Vogler, *Nürnberg*, pp. 215–16.

[135] RV Nr. 196, 31 Oct. 1524, in *QNR*, p. 26. Little is known of how Hergot's religious ideas evolved during this time. On this point, see Schelle-Wolff, *Zwischen Erwartung und Aufruhr: Die Flugschrift „Von der newen wandlung eynes Christlichen lebens" und der Nürnberger Drucker Hans Hergot*, pp. 11–128.

[136] For an analysis of this text, see Schelle-Wolff, *Zwischen Erwartung und Aufruhr*, pp. 129–456.

and brotherly love."¹³⁷ The council fined the apprentices for the costs of their imprisonment and ordered them not to print any further works without prior review.¹³⁸ Officials seized the original manuscript and all of the remaining printed copies so that "no one may be seduced by them," but, by this time, 100 copies were already on their way to Augsburg.¹³⁹ Although Hans Hut, the "foreign bookseller," had lost his investment in the books, the council compensated him for his printing costs.¹⁴⁰

Two months later, in December 1524, the council received a tip that some of Andreas Karlstadt's works had been secretly printed in Nuremberg. They instituted a search, discovering in the print shop of Hieronymus Höltzel both Karlstadt's pamphlet, *On the Unchristian Misuse of the Lord's Bread and Chalice* (*Von dem widerchristlichen Missbrauch des Herrn Brot and Kelch*), and Müntzer's *A Highly Provoked Defense and Answer to the Spiritless, Soft-living Flesh at Wittenberg* (*Hoch verursachte Schutzrede und Antwort wider das Gaistloße Sanft lebende fleysche zu Wittenberg*).¹⁴¹ They jailed Höltzel, demanding to know where he'd gotten the manuscripts and what he had done with the printed copies. Like Hergot's apprentices, he testified that he, too, had received the manuscripts from "a foreign traveler."¹⁴² Although the "traveler's" identity is unknown, Höltzel's source for the Karlstadt materials may have been Martin Reinhardt, a former associate of Karlstadt's recently arrived in Nuremberg after his expulsion for radical activities in Allstedt. The council itself may have assumed some link between Reinhardt and Höltzel, for, on the same day it interrogated Höltzel, it expelled Reinhardt and his family.¹⁴³ Höltzel's source for the Müntzer pamphlet is likewise mysterious, but several scholars have speculated that it may have been Müntzer himself. The reformer stayed in Nuremberg sometime in late 1524, although it is unclear whether his visit could have coincided with the printing of his pamphlet.¹⁴⁴ In an undated letter, Müntzer spoke of his time in Nuremberg: "I could have played a

---

¹³⁷ StAN, Ratsbuch 12, fol. 268.
¹³⁸ RV 198, 2 Nov. 1524, in *QNR*, p. 26–7.
¹³⁹ StAN, Ratsbuch 12, fol. 268.
¹⁴⁰ RV Nr. 198, 2 Nov. 1524, in *QNR* pp. 26–7.
¹⁴¹ RV Nr. 228, 16 Dec. 1524, and RV Nr. 229, 17 Dec. 1524, in *QNR*, pp. 31–2; Vogel *Nürnberg*, pp. 224–5; Germanisches Nationalmuseum Nürnberg und die Evangelisch-Lutherische Kirche in Bayern, *Reformation in Nürnberg: Umbruch und Bewahrung* (Nürnberg: Verlag Medien & Kultur, 1979) pp. 148–50.
¹⁴² RV Nr. 231 and RV 232, 17 Dec. 1524, in *QNR*, p. 32.
¹⁴³ RV Nr. 233, 17 Dec. 1524, in *QNR*, p. 32.
¹⁴⁴ Schmid, *Täufertum und Obrigkeit in Nürnberg*, p. 11; Williams, *The Radical Reformation*, pp. 249–51; Vogler, *Nürnberg, 1524/25*, pp. 223–32. Gottfried Seebaß concludes that Müntzer likely could not have been in Nuremberg before December, 1524. Seebaß, *Müntzers Erbe*, p. 113.

pretty game with the people of Nuremberg had I cared to stir up sedition. Many people urged me to preach, but I ... was not there for that purpose, but rather to answer my enemies through the press."[145]

Müntzer's letter suggests that, despite the council's efforts to suppress his ideas, some Nurembergers were keen to hear more about them. Karlstadt likewise found an audience in Nuremberg. In late December, Nuremberg magistrates arrested a clerk, Erasmus Wisperger, for reading one of Karlstadt's books aloud in a public market.[146] The council dispatched five clergymen to question him on his views about the Eucharist and teach him "the godly truth."[147] They tracked down the man who had given him the book and demanded to know his motives.[148] A day later, magistrates interviewed a servant, a painter, and several others regarding "improper talk about the Sacrament."[149] The council's efforts to police Eucharistic errors were not new, however. The month before, magistrates had admonished the local painter Hans Greiffenberger for denying the Real Presence in a series of tracts dating back to 1523.[150] On the same day, they interrogated the innkeeper Marx von Wiblingen about the "shameful contempt of the body and blood of Christ" voiced in his tavern, and demanded to know the names of the guests who were present.[151] To the council, it seemed that dangerous ideas about the Sacrament had become a staple of conversation in the city's markets, workshops, and taverns.[152]

Although magistrates had acted quickly to suppress "radical" Protestant pamphlets, they had not severely punished the printers and booksellers who produced them. In the case of both Höltzel and Hergot's apprentices, the council appears to have been more interested in identifying the "foreign travelers" bringing radical texts into Nuremberg than in punishing local printers for violating its censorship laws. Even in the case of Hut, the "foreign bookseller" looking to publish Müntzer's work in Nuremberg, the council had been careful to compensate him for the tracts it seized from him. Its main concern was to get these books off the market, before they

---

[145] Thomas Müntzer, *Thomas Müntzers Schriften und Briefe. Kritische Gesamtausgabe*, ed. Günter Franz and Paul Kirn (Göttingen: Vandenhoeck & Ruprecht, 1968) pp. 449–50.

[146] RV Nr. 243, 28 Dec. 1524, in *QNR*, p. 34.

[147] RV Nr. 248, 29 Dec. 1524 and RV Nr. 249, 30 Dec. 1524, in *QNR*, p. 35.

[148] RV Nr. 254, 30 Dec. 1524, in *QNR*, p. 36.

[149] RV Nr. 255, 31 Dec. 1524, in *QNR*, p. 36.

[150] RV Nr. 196, 31 Oct. 1524 and RV 202, 10 Nov. 1524 in *QNR*, p. 26–7. On Greiffenberger, see Kolde, 'Hans Denck und die gottlosen Maler,' pp. 12–16; Vogler, *Nürnberg*, pp. 176–95.

[151] RV Nr. 203, 10 Nov. 1524, in *QNR*, p. 27.

[152] On Karlstadt's role in these debates, see Amy Nelson Burnett, *Karlstadt and the Origins of the Eucharistic Controversy: A Study in the Circulation of Ideas* (Oxford: Oxford University Press, 2011).

could "seduce" Nurembergers with their errors. The council's response in these cases suggests that, at this stage, it saw Protestant heterodoxy not as a local problem, but as a threat imported from without.

The council was forced to reassess the reality of internal dissent in early 1525 after uncovering a circle of "fanatics" deep within the city's artisanal and professional circles. In early January, Nuremberg prosecuted two brothers, Barthel and Sebald Beham, both painters in Albrecht Dürer's school, on charges of blasphemy and religious sectarianism. Under interrogation, they implicated another painter, Georg Pencz.

By this time, the painters Hans Greiffenberger and Hans Platner had already come before the Nuremberg magistrates for their heterodox views on the Eucharist, suggesting to some that religious radicalism had perhaps taken hold among the city's artists.[153] Indeed, Sebald and Barthel Beham both testified that they and their comrades frequently spoke of their doubts about baptism and the Real Presence, and none of them, it seemed, found this unusual.[154] They allegedly questioned baptism, the Eucharist, secular authority, the divinity of Christ, and even the existence of God. According to one witness, they also read the books of Karlstadt and Müntzer.[155]

Also implicated in the proceedings was the rector of St Sebald's school, Hans Denck.[156] Denck, like many in Nuremberg's humanist circles, had understood reform to mean a moral regeneration of individual devotional life, but he had increasingly come to believe that Luther's emphasis on justification by faith alone led to moral complacency.[157] He gravitated to the writings of Karlstadt and Müntzer, and Hut and Müntzer may have stayed with him during their visits to Nuremberg in late 1524.[158] Gradually, his ideas evolved in a more Spiritualist direction.[159]

---

[153] Kolde, Hans Denck und die gottlosen Maler," pp. 18–20. On the "three godless painters," see Herbert Zschelletzschky, *Die "drei gottlosen Maler" von Nürnberg. Sebald Beham, Barthel Beham und Georg Pencz: Historische Grundlagen und ikonologische Probleme ihrer Graphik zu Reformations- und Bauernkriegszeit* (Leipzig: Seemann, 1975).

[154] Theodor Kolde, 'Zum Prozeß des Johann Denck und der "drei gottlosen Maler" von Nürnberg,' in *Kirchengeschichtliche Studien* (Leipzig, 1888) p. 244–5; Vogler, *Nürnberg*, pp. 272–3.

[155] Kolde, 'Zum Prozeß,' p. 245.

[156] RV Nr. 276 and RV Nr. 279, 10 Jan. 1525; RV 280–281, 14 Jan. 1525, in *QNR*, pp. 38–9.

[157] Williams, *Radical Reformation*, pp. 248–51.

[158] Georg Baring, 'Hans Denck und Thomas Müntzer in Nürrnberg 1524,' in *Archiv für Reformationsgeschichte* 50 (1959) pp. 149–55; Schmid, *Täufertum in Nürnberg*, p. 11.

[159] Packull, *Mysticism and the Early South German-Austrian Anabaptist Movement*, pp. 35–61; Baring, "Hans Denck," pp. 155–80. Also on Denck's theology, see David C. Steinmetz, *Reformers in the Wings: From Geiler von Kayserberg to Theodore Beza*, 2nd ed. (Oxford: Oxford University Press, 2001) pp. 146–52.

The "three godless painters," as they came to be known, were held for further interrogation, while Denck was ordered to draft a confession of faith for examination by a committee of five of the city's Lutheran preachers.[160] Deeply mystical in tone, Denck's confession emphasized the presence of the divine within the human soul and outlined his differences with the local clergy, rejecting Lutheran teaching on *sola scriptura*, human sinfulness, justification, baptism, and the Eucharist.[161] Not surprisingly, the city's pastors condemned Denck's views, finding that he had not simply erred in fundamental matters of belief, but had refused proper instruction and attempted to win converts.[162] Denck and his kind were a threat to the faith and to the community and on 21 January 1525, the council banished him for life.[163] Five days later, it sent the "godless painters" into exile as well.[164] Denck settled in Augsburg for a time, where he continued to voice radical religious ideas.[165] He quickly emerged as one of the leading figures of the South German Anabaptist movement.[166]

Denck and the "three godless painters" proved to the council that religious error was not simply a threat posed from outside, but was, in fact, a "spiritual poison" spreading from within. Fearing the contagion, the council redoubled its efforts to defend Lutheran orthodoxy. In a 1526 decree, it ordered the city's printers and booksellers not to print or sell "any pamphlets on the Eucharist by Karlstadt, Oecolampadius, Zwingli, or their supporters" as well as any works commenting on "what was disputed at Baden in Aargau." The council declared that "nothing but temptation and the Devil's work" was to be found in such books.[167]

The council's 1526 decree suggests that it was primarily concerned with protecting Lutheran Eucharistic theology from the challenges to it posed

---

[160] See T. Kolde, 'Hans Denck und die gottlosen Maler von Nürnberg,' in *Beiträge zur bayerischen Kirchengeschichte* 8 (1902): 1–31.

[161] Packull, *Mysticism and the Early South German-Austrian Anabaptist Movement*, pp. 47–61.

[162] Ibid, p. 39; Williams, *Radical Reformation*, pp. 251–4.

[163] Ratsbücher 12, Nr. 282, 21 January 1525, in *QNR*, p. 42.

[164] RV Nr. 316, 26 Jan. 1525, in *QNR*; Russell, *Lay Theology*, pp. 157–65.

[165] In Augsburg, Denck allegedly taught a form of universalism. Challenged by Urban Rhegius on this point, Denck agreed to a public disputation, but fled Augsburg before it could take place. Packull, *Mysticism and the Early South German-Austrian Anabaptist Movement*, pp. 41–42.

[166] Ibid, pp. 40–61; Williams, *Radical Reformation*, pp. 254–69.

[167] Müller, 'Zensurpolitik der Reichsstadt Nürnberg,' p. 87. The 1526 Baden disputation between Johann Eck and several of the leading Swiss reformers debated Zwingli's positions on scriptural authority, the nature of the Mass, the Eucharist, and the doctrine of original sin. See Irena Backus, 'The Disputations of Baden, 1526 and Berne, 1528: Neutralizing the Early Church,' in *Studies in Reformed Theology and History* 1(1) (1993): 1–130.

by Zwingli and his followers, as well as Karlstadt and other "radicals." Early the following year, however, Nuremberg magistrates became aware of a "new unchristian league" in the area: the Anabaptists. Throughout the region, Hans Hut, Hans Denck, and their followers had helped lay the foundations for a small, but growing community of brethren.[168] In January 1527, Nuremberg magistrates arrested one of Hut's converts, Wolfgang Vogel, the pastor at Eltersdorf. He had published an open letter to the citizens of Bopfingen, where he had once been pastor, after the town council dismissed his successor in that post. He called on his former parishioners to bear their loss patiently, reminding them that true Christians must expect to suffer for God's Word. He criticized the authorities' religious agenda and called on citizens and magistrates alike to repent.[169] The magistrates of Bopfingen, however, did not repent—they sent the pamphlet to Nuremberg, in whose jurisdiction Vogel now resided, and asked them to investigate. Nuremberg officials did not initially suspect Vogel's orthodoxy, as there was little in his pamphlet that was explicitly Anabaptist. The city censor, Lazarus Spengler, released him with a warning.[170] Soon thereafter, however, the Nuremberg city council received word from Coburg of the arrests of several Anabaptists in Königsberg. They warned Nuremberg of the dangers of this sect and alerted them that Anabaptists were active in their own city; in fact, they had supposedly established a secret press in a house near St Clare's.[171] The council arrested Vogel and several others, and under interrogation, learned that they had been re-baptized. Although the interrogation records do not survive, the council concluded that the prisoners adhered to "a new, troublesome, unchristian league against all authorities,"[172] which adopted rebaptism as its rite of entrance, held the sacrament of Christ's body and blood to be nothing, denied the doctrine of the Atonement or the eternal damnation of the reprobate, and believed that even the Devil could be saved. They preached the imminent return of Christ and believed that he would entrust his followers with the sword of righteousness for the destruction of all civil authorities who stood in their way.[173] The scope of this heresy was unlike anything the Nuremberg authorities had yet encountered, but it was the threat of holy insurrection

---

[168] Schmid, *Täufertum und Obrigkeit in Nürnberg*, pp. 6–15; Packull, *Mysticism and the Early South German-Austrian Anabaptist Movement*, pp. 88–92.

[169] See Wolfgang Vogel *Ain trostlicher Sendbrieff und christliche Ermanung zum Evangelio an ain Erbarn Radt und gantze Gemain zu Bopfingen, und an alle die, so vom Evangelio und Wort Gotes abgefallen seind* ([Augsburg]: [M. Ramminger], 1526) [StAN, SIL 59, Nr. 21].

[170] Schmid, *Täufertum und Obrigkeit in Nürnberg*, p. 141.

[171] Ibid, pp. 18–20; 135–40.

[172] Ibid., p. 149.

[173] Ibid., p. 23.

that particularly alarmed the council. Even more disturbing, it seemed that Vogel and his comrades were actively seeking to spread their views. Coming in the wake of the Peasants' War, it seemed to authorities that secret conventicles of heretics and rebels were spreading fast across the Empire. The council resolved that harsher measures would now be needed, and on 26 March 1527, it beheaded Vogel with the sword.[174] More arrests followed as Nuremberg authorities worked to uproot this "unchristian error" in the countryside.[175]

Augsburg also cracked down on Anabaptists in 1527. For some time, Anabaptist preachers such as Ludwig Hätzer, Hans Denck, and Hans Hut had been making converts in the area, eventually founding a community of an estimated 800 souls.[176] Augsburg printers produced many tracts for Anabaptist authors, such that the city attracted brethren from neighboring areas looking to buy Bibles and Anabaptist writings.[177] By the summer of 1527, Augsburg had become a refuge for many Anabaptists fleeing the persecutions sweeping across the Empire. Beginning in August of that year, Augsburg authorities apprehended several local residents gathering in Anabaptist assemblies. The crackdown continued over the several months that followed, ultimately resulting in the arrests of such prominent Anabaptist leaders as Hans Hut and Eitelhans Langenmantel.[178]

In their interrogations of Hut, Augsburg officials uncovered his contacts with Müntzer and his support for the rebels in the Peasants' War. Echoing Müntzer, he had called on the peasants to take up the sword against the ungodly; since their defeat, he had preached a fiery vision of the End Times, when the faithful remnant would rise up to punish the wicked.[179] Many of the Augsburg brethren had rejected Hut's apocalyptic pronouncements, but his subversive message alarmed the local authorities.[180] In October

---

[174] Ibid., pp. 141–52.

[175] Schmid, *Täufertum und Obrigkeit*, pp. 26–134.

[176] Packull, *Mysticism and the Early South German-Austrian Anabaptist Movement*, pp. 92–99. On the Anabaptist movement in Augsburg, see Hans Guderian, *Die Täufer in Augsburg: Ihre Geschichte und ihr Erbe* (Pfaffenhofen: W. Ludwig Verlag, 1984); Christian Meyer, 'Zur Geschichte der Wiedertäufer in Oberschwaben,' *Zeitschrift des historischen Vereins für Schwaben und Neuberg* 1 (1874): pp. 207–53; Friedrich Roth, 'Zur Geschichte der Wiedertäufer in Oberschwaben, II' *Zeitschrift des Historischen Vereins für Schwaben und Neuburg*, 27 (1900); Roth, 'Zur Geschichte der Wiedertäufer in Oberschwaben, III' *Zeitschrift des Historischen Vereins für Schwaben und Neuburg* 28 (1901).

[177] See StAA, Strafamt, Urg. Georg Glaserle & Hans Farner, 11 Aug. 1533; Christof Schaff & Hans Miller, 20 March 1534; Hans Hartmann, 5–12 April 1535.

[178] Packull, *Mysticism and the Early South German-Austrian Anabaptist Movement*, pp. 118–119.

[179] On Hut, see Seebaß, *Müntzers Erbe*, p. 181–325.

[180] Ibid., pp. 258–80; 304–15.

1527, the city council issued a decree warning against the "forbidden, re-baptizing new sect" taking root in Augsburg.[181] The council recited a list of complaints against the new doctrine: it was "contrary to God, Christian order, good custom, honorable policy, and leads to quarrels, division, fighting, rebellion, and repudiation of the government ordained by God, as well as the destruction and sunderance of brotherly love." In principle, "it leads to no good."[182] The council ordered all Augsburgers to have their infants baptized and to reject re-baptism, as well as all sectarian sermons (*Winkelpredig*) and "evil, seductive doctrine." Residents were ordered to report to the *Bürgermeister* anyone who gave aid or shelter to Anabaptist preachers or who attended assemblies that might give rise to illegal sects or rebellion against the government.[183]

While many Anabaptists had suffered death for their beliefs in other jurisdictions, Augsburg's city council adopted a moderate policy. Most of the accused were released upon their recantation and oath of obedience to the council. Those who refused were expelled.[184] One man was executed for preaching Anabaptism, and Hans Hut died in Augsburg's jail while awaiting judgment.[185] While the arrests of 1527-28 broke up the local Anabaptist movement for a time,[186] the council's punishments establish that it was less interested in policing faith than in preserving its authority and public order.[187] The prisoners were given no instruction in how they should believe, for by 1527, there was no consensus within either the council or the city as to what Augsburg's orthodox faith should be. Prosecutions against Anabaptists continued sporadically for the next few decades, rising and falling with the activities of Anabaptist missionaries in the region.[188]

---

[181] SStBA, 2 S. 14, Kapsel I, 'Anschläge, 1524–1734, Nr. 1–201,' Nr. 10.

[182] Ibid.

[183] Ibid.

[184] See StAA, Ratsbuch Nr. 15, 1520–1529, fol. 143–153; Preu, 'Chronik,' pp. 37–9.

[185] Preu, 'Chronik,' pp. 39–40. Hut died of smoke inhalation after setting a fire in his jail cell in a botched escape attempt. His corpse was publicly burned on the gallows and his ashes were scattered in the Wertach river. Meyer, 'Zur Geschichte der Wiedertäufer in Oberschwaben,' p. 253.

[186] Packull, *Mysticism and the Early South German-Austrian Anabaptist Movement*, pp. 123–29.

[187] See Michele Zelinsky Hanson, *Religious Identity in an Early Reformation Community: Augsburg, 1517–1533* (Leiden: Brill, 2009) pp. 79–105.

[188] Another wave of arrests came in the early 1530s. The last major series of prosecutions occurred in the mid-1550s. See Hans Guderian, *Die Taufer in Augsburg: Ihre Geschichte und ihr Erbe* (Pfaffenhofen: W. Ludwig Verlag, 1984) pp. 75–106.

"Glorious Unity:" Enacting Reform in Augsburg

As the 1520s drew to a close, Augsburg was home to a wide spectrum of religious opinion. While the Anabaptists and other "sects" were officially outlawed, the city's churches offered services and sermons from widely divergent perspectives. The most popular preachers were the Zwinglian Michael Keller at the *Barfüsser* and Urban Rhegius at St Anna's. Frosch and Agricola preached the Lutheran view, while Mathias Kretz and Hans Nachtigall ministered to ever-dwindling Catholic congregations at the cathedral of Our Lady and the Fugger-controlled church of St Moritz. Augsburgers could hear services in German and take communion in both kinds in many of the city's churches, administered in some cases by married clergy.[189]

By the early 1530s, the clamor for reform in Augsburg had reached such a pitch that rumors of armed rebellion began to circulate. During the night of 17 June 1533, two bakers found an open letter to the council posted on the steps of the Perlach Tower. The letter warned the council that 1,926 men had pledged to overthrow the government if it did not immediately abolish the Mass, remove the images from the churches, expel the priests, and execute all adulterers and usurers.[190] Although no copy of the letter survives, it was "sharp and well-written, by a learned man," and caused an immediate sensation.[191] The council mustered 600 infantrymen to guard against the threatened revolt and offered a reward of 1,000 gulden for information as to the identities of the plotters. Although arrests were made, the source of the threats was never discovered.[192]

In January 1534, new council elections brought a reform party into the majority. A few months later, the council aligned itself openly with the evangelical cause, announcing a decree restricting the practice of Catholicism. The council closed those churches still preaching the Catholic faith, confiscating their liturgical goods until such time as a general council or national assembly resolved the religious status of the Empire. It outlawed any criticism of its mandate in public or in private, whether "by words or works," orally or in writing. The council's informants would

---

[189] Roth, *Reformationsgeschichte*, Bd. 1, pp. 289–99.

[190] Sender, 'Chronik,' p. 354; Preu, 'Chronik,' p. 54; Marcus Welser and Achilles Pirmin Gasser, *Chronica der weitberuempten Keyserlichen Freyen und deß H. Reichs Statt Augspurg in Schwaben / Von derselben altem Ursprung / Schöne / Gelegene / zierlichen Gebäuen und namhafften gedenckwürdigen Geschichten / in acht underschidliche Capitul* (Frankfurt am Main: Egenerben, 1595), Part III, p. 23.

[191] Sender, 'Chronik,' p. 354.

[192] Ibid, pp. 355–7.

report any dissent, it warned, and those who violated the prohibitions could face death for their crime.[193]

Augsburg's council sought to institutionalize the Reformation through increased governmental scrutiny in matters of public and private morality, family life, and religious observance and expression. It was not enough, the council declared, to simply remove the "idols" from the churches. Rather, it asserted, idolatry must be driven from the human heart and "a Christian, righteous change made in the community of God."[194] It therefore introduced a new "Discipline and Police Ordinance" (*Zucht und Policey Ordnung*), intended to enforce godliness in word and deed.[195]

In the Discipline Ordinance, the council prohibited all offensive books, songs, rhymes, and writings. Not only was it illegal to print such items, it was also forbidden to compose, adapt, write, sell, buy, sing, read, post, or otherwise "bring [them] to the light of day in any way."[196] Augsburgers were warned that a "hard punishment" would mercilessly follow every violation.

Augsburg's censorship apparatus was now harnessed to promote approved Protestant orthodoxy. Although the Catholic clergy were expelled, Catholic citizens were allowed to remain in Augsburg, provided they attended Protestant churches and outwardly conformed. The council banned Augsburgers from leaving the city to hear Mass or visit Catholic shrines in the countryside, ordering the city's gatekeepers to report those suspected of violating its orders.[197] The council also stripped midwives of their customary authority to baptize newborns, requiring that all children be brought instead to a clergyman for baptism under approved rites.[198]

The magistrates also sought to control the religious instruction of the citizenry. In order to align itself with the Lutheran powers of the Schmalkaldic League, the city council had agreed to accept the Augsburg Confession, and it pressured the city's preachers to teach a more Lutheran understanding of the Eucharist. To enforce uniformity in doctrine, the council required the preachers to agree to contracts regulating the content of their sermons. Under the contract, preachers undertook to preach the Gospel, relying only on Scripture for explanation. Although they were expected to decry sin, they agreed not to name individual sinners. More

---

[193] Ibid.
[194] StAA, Evangelisches Wesensarchiv Augsburg, Akten Nr. 147, Nr. 2, fol. Aiir.
[195] On the enforcement of Augsburg's Discipline Ordinance, see Lyndal Roper, *The Holy Household: Women and Morals in Reformation Augsburg* (Oxford: Clarendon Press, 1989).
[196] StAA, Evangelisches Wesensarchiv Augsburg, Akten Nr. 147, Nr. 2, fol. Aiiiᵛ.
[197] StAA, Ratsbuch Nr. 16, 1529–1542, fol. 122r–v.
[198] Ibid., fol. 122v.

significantly, preachers were bound to neither speak nor write on any innovations in doctrine without the prior consent of the council and the rest of the clergy. Under no circumstances was a preacher to criticize the council from the pulpit; rather, he might bring his concerns to one of the city's *Bürgermeister* in private. At all times, the preachers were to emphasize every subject's duty of obedience to the council as the city's lawful authority ordained by God. Parish elders were to oversee the preachers' compliance and report to the council on their performance throughout the year.[199] When preachers spoke out publicly against the council's policies or against each other, they could expect an official rebuke. Wolfgang Musculus, for example, earned a public reprimand in April 1540 for suggesting that the council was planning to appoint a Catholic preacher in one of the city's churches.[200]

As part of the effort to shape Protestant opinion, the council institutionalized the process for the review and approval of texts to be printed. In 1534, it had established a three-member committee of censors composed of Protestant clergymen and city officials.[201] These censors were charged with overseeing the printers and book shops, as well as the activities of foreign booksellers, to ensure that nothing was printed or sold in the city without their knowledge and permission.[202]

Although the city was officially Protestant, its censors did not single out Catholic writings for suppression, at least not initially. In 1538, the censors approved Johannes Dugo's *Libri Christianarum Institutionum Quattuor* for printing by the city's only remaining Catholic printer, Alexander Weißenhorn. The Catholic theologian reported in his dedicatory preface that he had submitted his manuscript for the censors' review, as Augsburg law required, and that they had promptly given their consent to the project.[203]

By 1541, however, the council was attempting to stop the import of Catholic books into the city. In June 1541, authorities arrested the Augsburg booksellers Hans Elchinger, Leonhart Purtenbach, and Hans Westermair for the unauthorized sale of a Latin text printed in the Catholic

---

[199] Philip Broadhead, '"One Heart and One Soul:" The Changing Nature of Public Worship in Augsburg, 1521–1548,' in *Continuity and Change in Christian Worship*, ed. R. N. Swanson (London: Boydell Press, 1999) pp. 122–3.

[200] StAA, Literalien, 'Schwenckfeldiana & Reformationsacten,' Decree dated 20 April 1540.

[201] Roth, *Reformationsgeschichte*, Bd. 2, p. 332; Volker Büchler, 'Die Zensur im frühneuzeitlichen Augsburg, 1515–1806,' *Zeitschrift des Historischen Vereins für Schwaben* 84 (1991): p. 77.

[202] Ludwig Greiff, *Beiträge zur Geschichte der deutschen Schulen Augsburg* (Augsburg: J.N. Hartmann'schen Buchdruckerei, 1858) p. 11; Büchler, 'Zensur,' p. 77.

[203] Künast, *Getruckt zu Augspurg*, p. 208.

printing center of Ingolstadt. Elchinger was imprisoned for four days, and the remaining books were confiscated.[204]

In August 1541, the council expressly banned non-Lutheran texts. It ordered the printers and booksellers to neither print nor sell anything, be it books, songs, writings, placards, or prints, in any language, contrary to "the pure teaching of the Holy Gospel and the Augsburg Confession." The council also banned any writings directed against the Schmalkaldic League or the other evangelical estates of the Empire. While attacks on the emperor were forbidden, political broadsides against other Catholic powers were not unlawful. Finally, the council reiterated its customary prohibition of texts which were "shameful, immoral, obscene, outrageous, or injurious."[205]

By 1541, the council was clearly seeking to suppress anti-Protestant writings, yet Dugo's case demonstrates that the censors themselves were not uniformly hostile to Catholic authors or texts. In fact, one of the censors serving at this time, Hans Jacob Fugger, was himself a Catholic. It appears that Augsburg's censorship system, as administered, was not focused exclusively on the religious credentials of authors, printers, and booksellers. On the issue of religion, as in all other matters, Augsburg's censorship system was focused far less on the text itself than on how it might be received in the community. It was the ideas contained within the text and their potential effect on the reader that censors were to evaluate—not the religious affiliations of the text's publishers.

It seems clear, however, that Augsburg's city council in the 1540s would have deemed any writing that the common man might recognize as explicitly "Catholic" to be contrary to "the pure doctrine of the Augsburg Confession" and therefore banned. Examining patterns of book production, Hans-Jörg Künast has concluded that the council's efforts to block the production of Catholic literature were largely successful. According to his findings, Catholic book production in Augsburg essentially disappeared after 1540.[206] As much as official hostility, though, the fall-off in Catholic text production in the 1540s may be equally reflective of the lack of any substantial demand for Catholic books in the local market. This fact may explain why Alexander Weißenhorn, Augsburg's only remaining Catholic printer, left the city for Bavaria in 1540. Whether attributable to official oversight, self-policing within the trade, or market forces, the effect on Augsburg through the end of its Reformation was the same: as

---

[204] StAA, Strafbuch Nr. 96, 1540–1543, fol. 33r–v.
[205] Ibid., fol. 67v–68r.
[206] Künast, *Getruckt zu Augspurg*, pp. 210–11; Graphik 16–17, p. 303.

Künast concludes, "censorship functioned almost seamlessly during the Schmalkaldic War."[207]

The Interim: A New Government and New Religious Order

Augsburg's adoption of the evangelical cause brought it into direct conflict with Emperor Charles V. With the outbreak of war in 1546, Augsburg sided with its allies in the Schmalkaldic League against the emperor. By September of that year, however, imperial troops encircled the city, and Augsburg soon capitulated.[208]

July 1547 brought the arrival of the emperor and bishop to the occupied city of Augsburg. At the emperor's command, electors, princes and dignitaries also gathered in Augsburg for a new Imperial Diet to consider the religious direction of the Empire. On 17 May 1548, Charles presented the Diet with his so-called "Interim," which he intended as a temporary solution to the Empire's religious troubles until the Council of Trent concluded its work. The Interim allowed concessions to both sides of the religious divide. While it permitted evangelical teaching on justification, clerical marriage, and the sacrament in both kinds, it also required reinstitution of the mass, oral confession, the wearing of clerical vestments, and the observance of Catholic feast days and fasts.[209]

Virtually all of the Protestant imperial cities in Swabia and Alsace had gone to war against Charles. Nuremberg, however, had remained loyal. Ever wary of imperial power, the city had refused to join the Schmalkaldic League, citing Luther's contention that subjects had no right to resist lawful secular authority.[210] Charles now held the others to account. "Woe to you, you miserable free cities," one ballad chided, "what a great miscalculation that you have ... set yourself against the pious emperor."[211] Charles held the urban trade guilds responsible for introducing reform and leading the free cities into rebellion. He suspected, also, that the same ruling parties that had made war against him could not be trusted to carry out the Interim. In Augsburg, Ulm, and in 26 other cities, Charles swept aside their civic constitutions and abolished their trade guilds. In their place, he established

---

[207] Ibid., p. 211.

[208] Zorn, *Augsburg*, p. 189.

[209] Ibid., p. 190.

[210] Moeller, 'Imperial Cities,' p. 107. By the 1530s, Luther conceded some defensive right of resistance. See David Mark Whitford, *Tyranny and Resistance: The Magdeburg Confession and the Lutheran Tradition* (St. Louis: Concordia Publishing House, 2001) pp. 37–57; 93–105.

[211] Thomas A. Brady, *Turning Swiss: Cities and Empire, 1450–1550* (Cambridge: Cambridge University Press, 1985) p. 220.

self-perpetuating patrician oligarchies.²¹² Most significantly for Augsburg, the new constitution effectively ensured that Catholic patricians would hold a slight majority of political offices, although Catholics comprised a mere 20 percent of the population at this time.²¹³

One day after the shakeup, Augsburg's new *Stadtpfleger* ("City Wardens") and Privy Council summoned the city's preachers before them and forbade them to speak out against either the new government or the new religious order.²¹⁴ Although many of the city's preachers left in protest, those who remained were ordered to resume the wearing of vestments. Mass was once again heard in the city's churches, and Catholic religious orders were re-established. Consistent with the Interim, the new government redirected the city's censorship policies toward the suppression of Protestantism and the re-introduction of Catholic observances. The council banned Protestant books and prosecuted individuals who spoke out against the Interim, insulted the Catholic clergy, or jeered at Catholic rites.²¹⁵ It punished Leonhart Bader, for example, for disparaging Catholicism in a public bathhouse. Priests did nothing but "go around with rogue's work (*Schelmwerk*)," he had supposedly said; the Mass was roguery, and all who attended it were rogues. Unfortunately for Bader, one of the other bathers happened to be a local bailiff. "I hear my lords the Cardinal and the Emperor also go in for this 'rogue's work,'" he warned, "so I advise you to keep silent because enough has already been said of these matters."²¹⁶ Bader was arrested, threatened with torture, and sentenced to eight days' imprisonment.²¹⁷ Catharina Frenkin fared worse: she was banished for insulting priests carrying the Host in procession. She was lucky, however, for the emperor's *alcalde* had demanded her death as an example to others who might dare such blasphemy.²¹⁸

---

²¹² Ibid., pp. 117–18, 221; Moeller, 'Imperial Cities,' pp. 108–9.

²¹³ Thomas Max Safley, *Charity and Economy in the Orphanages of Early Modern Augsburg* (Atlantic Highlands, New Jersey: Humanities Press, 1997) p. 37.

²¹⁴ Paul Hektor Mair, 'Zwei Chroniken des Augsburger Ratsdieners Paul Hektor Mair von 1548 bezw. 1547–1565 bezw. 1564,' in *Die Chroniken der Schwäbischen Städte: Augsburg*, Bd. 7, *Die Chroniken der deutschen Städte vom 14. bis ins 16. Jahrhundert*, Bd. 32, ed. Historische Kommission bei der Bayerischen Kommission der Wissenschaften. 1917. (Göttingen: Vandenhoek & Ruprecht, 1966), p. 41.

²¹⁵ SStBA, 2ʳ Aug. 10, 'Ordnungen, Decreten, Verrüffe und Anschläge, 1522–1677,' fol. 167; StAA, Strafamt. Urg. Leonhart Widenmann, 21–26 April 1549; Hans Löffler, 18 June 1549; Hieronymous Künig, 2 Jan. 1550; Leonhart Bader a/k/a Teuffel, 7 July 1550; Catharina Frenkin, 10 Sept. 1550.

²¹⁶ StAA, Strafamt, Urg. Leonhart Bader a/k/a Teuffel, 7 July 1550.

²¹⁷ StAA, Strafbuch Nr. 96.1, 1543–1553, fol. 10r.

²¹⁸ StAA, Strafamt, Urg. Catharina Frenkin, 10 Sept. 1550.

Chronicler Achilles Gasser recorded that the Interim was "nastily vilified" in "wonderful translations, interpretations, libels and copies in Latin and German."[219] Authorities traced one of these critiques in August 1549 to the Augsburg printer Narciss Ramminger and his apprentice, Marx Fischer. The men had printed a song about "King Antiocho" that the authorities considered critical of the Interim. The text was likely *A New Song About How King Antiocho Executed a Woman and Her Seven Sons on Account of God's Law* (*Ein Newes Lied/vom Könige Antiocho/ wie er ein Weyb mit siben Sönen so jammerlich ertödtet hat/von wegen deß Gsatz Gottes*).[220] Set to "Duke Ernst's tune," it told of the Syrian King Antiochus Ephiphanes, who persecuted the Jews and desecrated the Great Temple of Jerusalem during the time of the Maccabees. When a pious woman and her seven sons refused his command to break Jewish dietary laws, the tyrant ordered them each, in turn, slowly tortured and executed. This tale of Antiochus' attempt to force God's chosen to betray His laws was a transparent attack on Charles V's religious policies. Indeed, the 1550 *Magdeburg Confession*, published to justify that city's resistance to the Interim, explicitly linked resistance to the emperor and his Interim to the Maccabees' holy war against the tyrant Antiochus.[221]

Augsburg officials did not mistake the comparison, and they accused Ramminger of seeking to rouse the "common man" against the Interim. They also suspected that the city's Lutheran clergy were somehow involved. Ramminger denied all of this, insisting that his apprentice, Marx Fischer, had printed the song without his knowledge. The song was not new, he said, but a reprint of a song originally printed in 1538 by his former master, the late Hans Rogel. At that time, Ramminger said, Rogel had been given permission to print the song by the then *Bürgermeister*. He thought he would be permitted to reprint it because it had already been legally printed once before and was not offensive, at least in his opinion.[222] However, Ramminger overlooked the fact that Augsburg had been officially Lutheran when the song was first printed, and what the

---

[219] Welser & Gasser, *Chronica*, Part III, p. 69; for discussion of the many songs produced in protest of the Interim, see Oettinger, *Music as Propaganda*, 137–70; Nathan Rein, *The Chancery of God: Protestant Print, Polemic and Propaganda against the Empire, Magdeburg 1546–1551* (Aldershot: Ashgate, 2008); Thomas Kaufmann, *Das Ende der Reformation: Magdeburgs „Herrgotts Kanzlei" (1548–1551/2)* (Tübingen: Mohr Siebeck, 2003).

[220] *Ein Newes Lied/vom Könige Antiocho/wie er ein Weyb mit siben Sönen so jammerlich ertödtet hat/von wegen deß Gsatz Gottes. In Hertzog Ernsts Melodeye zusingen* ([n.p.: n.p., 1550?]) [BL, 11517 DE 8].

[221] Kaufmann, *Das Ende der Reformation*, pp. 195; 205–6; Oliver K. Olson, 'Theology of Revolution: Magdeburg 1550–1551' in *Sixteenth Century Journal* 3 (1972), pp. 69–70.

[222] StAA, Strafamt, Urg. Narciss Ramminger, (undated) Aug. 1549.

censors approved at the height of Augsburg's Reformation was unlikely to find favor under the Interim.

Ramminger's apprentice, Marx Fischer, stated that he had never heard that printers were required to obtain the censors' permission; in fact, his master had instructed him that he was free to print anything, as long as it was not "shameful" (*schandlich*). In his time with Ramminger, he said, he had done nothing but print "all kinds of bad songs;" so many, in fact, that he could not possibly name them all.[223] The council ordered his release, but Ramminger suffered one of the worst punishments that could befall a tradesman—he was forbidden to practice his trade.[224]

Ramminger had raised a common defense among printers: he had merely reprinted something that had previously been approved. Why should a further review be necessary? In Ramminger's case, the prior approval had been given by a government with an entirely different religious agenda, which was unlikely to be recognized by the new regime. Even in more stable times, however, printers expressed frustration with the requirement that every printing, even reprintings, be reviewed. From the council's perspective, however, its right of prior review asserted its ultimate authority over the trade. It also served an important regulatory purpose, for magistrates' censorship priorities continually shifted in response to circumstances within the community. In order to administer a system in which the targets of control frequently changed, authorities needed to police every edition, for what was legal yesterday might be forbidden today.

Opposition to the Interim continued to build, both in Augsburg and across the Empire. In the north, where Charles's military presence was less keenly felt, the Interim made little headway. Some northern princes introduced it only in modified form; here, Philip Melanchthon helped craft a more Lutheran settlement, the so-called Leipzig Interim. Other northern territories and cities rejected the Interim entirely. But the southern free cities that had fallen in the Schmalkaldic War had little choice but to comply, despite opposition from their clergy and citizenry. As in Augsburg, some Lutheran clergy, such as Strasbourg's Martin Bucer, chose exile over compliance. Others complied only partly. In August 1551, the imperial vice chancellor reported to the Augsburg city council that several of its clergy were not preaching in accordance with the Interim, and he demanded that the council expel them.[225] The council summoned the city's preachers

---

[223] StAA, Strafamt, Urg. Marx Fischer, 26 Aug. 1549.

[224] StAA, Strafbuch Nr. 96.1, 1543–1553, fol. 158r. Ramminger supported himself thereafter by selling fish and later served as the city's inspector of weights and measures (*Eichmeister*). Künast, *Getruckt zu Augspurg*, p. 212.

[225] StAA, Literalien, 'Schwenckfeldiana & Reformationsacten,' 25 Aug. 1551.

and laid before them a choice: accept either the Interim or exile. Most chose banishment, and were replaced with clergy more amenable to the government's policies.[226]

The expulsion of the clergy would loom large in the memories of the city's Lutherans for decades to come. At the time, and ever afterwards, the dissenting clergy were portrayed in songs and stories as martyrs to their faith, victims of an oppressive government under the sway of the Catholics. After the Interim, the city government would be almost continually haunted by rumors of another planned expulsion, as we shall see. The rumors generated suspicion of the city council among some disaffected elements of the Lutheran community, and eventually contributed to the "Calendar Conflict" protests of the 1580s.

In 1551, however, accommodating the emperor was the council's most pressing concern. Augsburg was again host to the Imperial Diet that year, and local officials were appalled to find "Lutheran books against the Interim" for sale in the city's book stalls. It was a public embarrassment and affront to both the council and the emperor, and magistrates quickly arrested local bookbinder Friedrich Thum for the crime. Thum testified that he had purchased the texts from two men, one of whom was from Magdeburg and had "all kinds of books" for sale.[227]

By 1551, the imperial city of Magdeburg had become a citadel of resistance to the emperor and his Interim. The books Thum purchased likely described that city's refusal to accept the Interim and the siege that the emperor's sometime ally, Moritz of Saxony, had consequently levied against it. Magdeburg's pastors and polemicists launched a massive propaganda campaign to justify the city's resistance, churning out hundreds of songs, pamphlets, and treatises that circulated widely throughout the Empire.[228] These prints asserted the magistrates' Christian duty of resistance to godless authority and legitimized the city's defiance as a defense of its traditional rights against the emperor's unjust abuse of his power.[229]

This assertion of a right of resistance in matters of conscience was unlikely to find favor with either the emperor or the Augsburg magistrates. Wishing to impress Charles with its severity, the council proposed banishing Friedrich Thum and banning him from the book trade. They were being lenient, they said, because many people had petitioned on his behalf and "this prohibition [against anti-Interim texts] is not so heavily

---

[226] Zorn, *Augsburg*, p. 193.

[227] StAA, Strafamt, Urg. Friedrich Thum, 23 Feb. 1551.

[228] Thomas Kaufmann has identified 360 such works published between 1548–1552. See Kaufmann, *Das Ende der Reformation*, p. 560.

[229] See Rein, *The Chancery of God*; Whitford, *Tyranny and Resistance*, pp. 77–91.

enforced in other places."[230] The emperor's advisor, the Bishop of Arras, asked the council to be merciful, for the emperor deemed Thum's books "not so dangerous."[231] With the emperor's consent, Thum was permitted to remain in the city and in his trade.[232]

Augsburg's printers followed Thum's sentencing with a petition seeking further reductions in the city's censorship controls. In a supplication to the council dated 19 March 1551, the city's printers complained that the council's censors denied them permission to print even apparently inoffensive texts that were in no way critical of the emperor or other authorities, much less contrary to the Holy Writ or the Interim. On the contrary, they argued, the censors were denying them permission to print even innocuous texts that served only to exhort their readers to "piety and an honorable way of life."[233] So intransigent were the censors that they might approve only one of every four or five exemplars the printers laid before them. The process was also far too slow, costing printers precious time and making it impossible for them to compete. Meanwhile, the printers claimed, they could only watch helplessly as the same texts were printed in Nuremberg, Dillingen, Ingolstadt, and in other cities, and then imported into Augsburg for sale to their customers. It was endangering their livelihoods, they said, and forced some to move their shops to other, less stringent cities, for they knew no other trade.[234]

The printers did not request a lifting of all the censorship requirements. They, too, agreed that certain dangerous and defamatory ideas should not be allowed to circulate. They asked, instead, that the council define certain "safe harbors" in which they would be allowed to print without threat of prosecution. The printers suggested that the council decree that they would be allowed to print anything that was neither "infamous," nor directed against the emperor or "our holy Christian faith."[235] They also conceded that there would continue to be a need for censors to police these standards. They simply asked that the review process be accelerated, so that compliance with the law would no longer bring economic loss to honest tradesmen.

The council was not altogether unsympathetic to the printers' complaints. As the council recorded in its judgment of Thum, Augsburg officials were aware that other cities were less exacting in their restrictions. The council was particularly concerned that Augsburg's artisans and

---

[230] StAA, Ratsbuch Nr. 25, 1551, Part I, fol. 26r.
[231] StAA, Strafbuch Nr. 96.1, 1543–1553, fol. 23r.
[232] Ibid.
[233] StAA, Censuramt, 'Die Buchdrucker betreffend, Tom I, 1550–1729.'
[234] Ibid.
[235] Ibid.

tradesmen not be crippled by restrictions their competitors in other cities did not face. The system that the printers envisioned, however, was no more practical than what the council had erected. If everything was to be allowed that was not "infamous" or opposed to the political status quo or "our holy Christian faith," who was to interpret those standards? The printers had already shown themselves to be poor judges when it came to self-policing, and the council likely had little confidence that they would be any more reliable in the future. Moreover, limiting the proscribed topics to the printers' narrow categories deprived the council of its discretion. While the lack of exact standards may have stymied the printers, it served the council's political interests perfectly. Without missing a day, the council rejected the printers' request, reiterating that they were to print nothing without the censors' prior approval.[236]

Above all, the council was not prepared to let the emperor be mocked. In April 1553, it arrested the bookseller Hans Elchinger for passing around a copy of a song lampooning Charles's defeat at Metz in the Princes' War. Elchinger testified that he received a manuscript copy of the song from a weaver he met in the Perlach Square. Always on the lookout for a marketable song, he left it with some men in a local tavern for their opinion. The men, some of whom could not read, told the authorities that they did not approve of the song; one said he was angry that Elchinger had even showed it to him.[237] When the weaver wanted his copy back, Elchinger went with him to a clerk named Reißmüller and asked him to transcribe another copy of the song. Upon reading the song, however, Reißmüller refused to have any involvement with it. "It is such a thing as might lead to trouble," he said; "I could not answer for it before my lords [in the council]."[238]

Elchinger claimed that he had never read the song and only first learned it was "defamatory" when Reißmüller refused to copy it. He then decided to get rid of it, but word of it had already reached the Augsburg magistrates. They found Elchinger's claim that he had not read the song to be simply incredible. He must have read the song and wanted to have it printed, the interrogators noted, otherwise he would not have asked Reißmüller to copy it.[239] Elchinger swore that he never had anything printed that he did not first show to the censors. The council ordered that he be tortured until he revealed the source of the song. Elchinger held to his story, however,

---

[236] StAA, Ratsbuch Nr. 25, 1551, Part I, fol. 31v.
[237] StAA, Strafamt, Urg. Hans Elchinger, 19–21 April 1553, Report of Witnesses.
[238] Ibid, Urg. 19 April 1553.
[239] Ibid.

and the council released him with a warning to stay out of the taverns for a year—a decidedly more lenient punishment than it customarily imposed.[240]

The testimony of the witnesses in Elchinger's case suggests the extent to which Augsburgers internalized and enforced the censors' standards. By 1553, almost all of the people who came in contact with Elchinger's song recognized it to be illegal and refused to have anything to do with it. Although the witnesses may have simply been telling the interrogators what they believed they wanted to hear, even Elchinger testified that Reißmüller was afraid to copy the song. If the witnesses are to be believed, they all seemed to have recognized that they could be criminally prosecuted in connection with the song. Moreover, some stated that they found it personally offensive. Not only were Augsburgers aware of the law's requirements, they claimed to accept its standards of propriety as their own.

Conclusions

The path that Augsburg and Nuremberg followed through the Reformation set the course for the administration of their censorship policies through the coming years. From the earliest years of the movement, civic censorship was motivated, above all, by a desire to keep order within the community and maintain good relations abroad. The magistrates' control of the religious debate was effectively limited by the need to meet these sometimes conflicting demands. While city officials were loath to challenge the emperor directly, they could not ignore the calls for reform coming from within their own communities. With no internal consensus on these issues, however, magistrates could keep order only by leaving open some room for debate on their city's religious future. What emerged in both Nuremberg and Augsburg was a system of censorship that accepted the local debate, but sought to suppress its most disorderly and politically dangerous elements.

Local printers and booksellers were eager to capitalize on the public appetite for news of the religious controversies sweeping the Empire, and the economic pressures of the trade ensured that some would overstep the local restrictions to meet the demand. This material was popular and profitable, and at least initially, printers lacked clear guidance on what was allowed. The censors' targets shifted continuously in response to external pressures and to forces at work within the community, and although this flexibility suited the magistrates' purposes, it bred confusion as to the scope of the law within the regional book trade. The uncertainty of the

---

[240] Ibid., 21 April 1553.

law encouraged individuals to police themselves and to enforce internal standards that mirrored the authorities' own definition of what was acceptable.

The magistrates' ability to police expression, however, was further compromised by the ease with which the unwanted ideas worked their way into the talk in the streets. The reformers' pamphlets and the preachers' sermons were dissected in the local taverns, halls, and guild houses. These ideas – often in quite different forms – found new life in the rumor and gossip that circulated through these communities. This "common talk" provided a means for even the most humble folk to comment on the local issues and it, in turn, shaped how they were prepared to understand them. This creative appropriation of the Word in the streets presented significant challenges for both reformers and magistrates, for neither could know how these ideas were being understood or effectively stop their spread.

The contests over censorship in the Reformation era reveal that the influence of both the magistrates and the reformers was far more limited in these communities than is often supposed. Like the cities' religious policies in general, censorship in Nuremberg and Augsburg evolved from a series of negotiations and compromises between the community and governing authorities. To build consensus and keep order, magistrates repeatedly adapted their censorship priorities to reflect communal expectations. In this, the control of expression became a means to contest and define the new civic order.

CHAPTER 3

Keeping the Peace: Censorship and Confessional Relations under the Peace of Augsburg

In 1555, the imperial estates gathered in Augsburg to craft a political solution to the religious divisions that had split the Empire for a generation. The Religious Peace of Augsburg, as the settlement came to be known, was presented as a temporary compromise until a more lasting peace could be negotiated. Discussions never resumed, however, and the Religious Peace of Augsburg would codify the rights of Catholics and Protestants within the Empire until the end of the Thirty Years' War.

Formally adopted on 25 September 1555, the Peace of Augsburg extended legal recognition within the Empire to the "old Catholic faith" and the "faith of the Augsburg Confession." In a principle jurists later summed up as *cujus regio, ejus religio*—"whose the rule, his the religion"— the treaty authorized the princes of the Empire to determine which of the two recognized faiths would be practiced within their territories. To secure the peace between the Empire's Catholic and Lutheran powers, each was compelled to recognize the other's religious rights:

> In order to bring peace to the Holy Empire of the German Nation ... let neither His Imperial Majesty nor the Electors, Princes, etc. do any violence or harm to any estate of the Empire on account of the faith of the Augsburg Confession ... but let them enjoy their religious beliefs, liturgy, and ceremonies as well as their estates and other rights and privileges in peace; and complete religious peace shall be obtained only by friendly, peaceful means of Christian understanding and agreement ...
>
> Likewise the Estates espousing the Augsburg Confession shall let all the Estates and the Princes who cling to the old religion ... live in absolute peace and in the enjoyment of all their estates, rights, and privileges ...[1]

---

[1] Karl Brandi, ed., *Der Augsburger Religionsfriede vom 25. September, 1555. Kritische Ausgabe des Textes mit den Entwürfen und der königlichen Deklaration* (Göttingen: Vandenhoeck & Ruprecht, 1927) pp. 36–8.

In its wording, the Peace of Augsburg invoked Christian ideals of concord and brotherly love—values that were presumably cherished across the confessional divide and could provide a foundation for a lasting peace. The treaty contained no express provisions on censorship, but its mandate that the parties leave each other in peace was widely construed as a general prohibition of polemical attacks by either side.[2] In both word and deed, Catholics and Lutherans were expected to keep the peace and respect each other's religious choices and legal rights. At both the imperial and local levels, authorities found in the Peace of Augsburg a powerful tool in policing interconfessional dialogue.

Imperial Censorship Under the Religious Peace

The regulation of expression under the Religious Peace was not unprecedented. Seventy years before, the 1485 settlement between the Catholic and Utraquist churches in Bohemia had banned religious invective between the parties;[3] similar proscriptions could be found in the Second Peace of Kappel of 1531, and later, in the Edict of Nantes.[4] In all of these cases, the censorship of religious invective drew on long-standing precedent outlawing works deemed libelous or potentially disruptive of the public peace.[5] By prohibiting religious libel, these treaties sought to incorporate the protected confessions into a single legal community, mutually bound to honor each other's rights as citizens and neighbors. As Debora Shugar has pointed out, the law of libel,

> Almost by definition, embodies and enforces an image of how people are tied together, or should be tied together, in a social setting. It articulates a society's rules of civility … defamation law defines obligations of respect, deference, and courtesy owed by members of a community to one another, and by so doing

---

[2] On the litigation of disputes over the Peace of Augsburg in the imperial courts, see Axel Gotthard, *Der Augsburger Religionsfrieden* (Münster: Aschendorff Verlag, 2004); Bernhard Ruthmann, *Die Religionsprozesse am Reichskammergericht (1555–1648)* (Köln: Böhlau Verlag, 1996).

[3] Zdeněk V. David, 'Confessional Accommodation in Early Modern Bohemia: Shifting Relations Between Catholics and Utraquists,' *Conciliation and Confession: The Struggle for Unity in the Age of Reform, 1415–1648*, eds Howard P. Louthan and Randall C. Zachman (Notre Dame, Indiana: University of Notre Dame Press, 2004) pp. 173–4.

[4] Ernst Walder, ed. *Religionsvergleiche des 16. Jahrhunderts, I, Quellen zur Neueren Geschichte*, Hft. 7 (Bern: Verlag Herbert Lang & CIE, 1960) pp. 5–13; Bernard Cottret, *1598: L'Edit de Nantes:pour en finir avec les guerres de religion* (Paris: Perrin, 1997).

[5] Günther Schmidt, *Libelli Famosi. Zur Bedeutung der Schmähschriften, Scheltbriefe, Schandgemälde und Pasquille in der deutschen Rechtsgeschichte* (Diss., Universität Köln, 1985) pp. 131–41, 253–4.

seeks to uphold both the identity of that community and the dignity of the individuals who constitute it.[6]

In the Holy Roman Empire, the long-standing prohibition of *Schmähschriften* (scandalous or libelous texts) quickly came to embrace religious polemic deemed contrary to the spirit of the Peace of Augsburg. However, the treaty's legal recognition of Lutheranism necessitated interpretative changes in existing legislation. The Peace of Augsburg ensured that imperial law could no longer simply prohibit Lutheran works; thus, prior legislation protecting Catholic doctrine now came to be understood as applying only to teachings common to both confessions.[7] The 1570 Diet of Speyer, accordingly, banned partisan polemical texts.[8] Further legislation adopted at the Frankfurt Diet of 1577 prohibited writings that violated doctrines common to both the Catholic faith and the Augsburg Confession, the "spirit" of the Peace of Augsburg, or that otherwise promoted unrest and breaches of the peace.[9]

The Peace of Augsburg, however, was a deeply flawed settlement: its terms were ambiguous and its protections limited. Indeed, the treaty was unclear by its very design. In their negotiations, the estates could find consensus on only the most general terms. Few expected all issues to be resolved, and had the parties fully discussed the treaty's particulars, settlement might never have been achieved.[10] For the Religious Peace struck a political bargain neither party could justify in theological terms: two religions legally recognized in one Empire.[11] In an age that saw religious uniformity as basic to the social and spiritual good of the community, the Peace was anomalous.[12] To the extent it had a religious basis, the treaty

---

[6] Debora Shuger, *Censorship and Cultural Sensibility: The Regulation of Language in Tudor-Stuart England* (Philadelphia: University of Pennsylvania Press, 2006) p. 140 (quoting Robert Post, *Constitutional Domains: Democracy, Community, Management* (Cambridge, MA: Harvard University Press, 1995)).

[7] Ulrich Eisenhardt, *Die kaiserliche Aufsicht über Buchdruck, Buchhandel und Presse in Heiligen Römischen Reich Deutscher Nation (1496–1806)* (Karlsruhe: Verlag C.F. Müller, 1970) pp. 55–6.

[8] Reichsabschied Speyer 1570, § 154, in *Neue vollständige Sammlung der Reichs-Abschiede, welche von den Zeiten Kayser Conrads des II. bis jetzo auf den Teutschen Reichs-Tagen abgefasset worden*, Bd. III (1747) (Osnabrück: Otto Zeller, 1967) p. 308.

[9] Reichspolizeiordung 1577, XXXV, § 3, ibid., p. 396.

[10] Gerhard Pfeiffer, 'Der Augsburger Religionsfrieden und die Reichsstädte,' in *Zeitschrift des historischen Vereins für Schwaben* 61 (1955): 215.

[11] Martin Heckel, 'Autonomia und Pacis Compositio: der Augsburger Religionsfriede in der Deutung der Gegenreformation,' *Zeitschrift der Savigny-Stiftung für Rechtsgeschichte, Kanonistische Abteilung XLV*, Bd. 77 (1959): pp. 140–90.

[12] Benjamin J. Kaplan, *Divided By Faith: Religious Conflict and the Practice of Toleration in Early Modern Europe* (Cambridge, MA: Harvard University Press, 2007)

drew on ideals presumably common to both faiths: peace, brotherhood, and Christian love. In origin and purpose, however, it was a political compromise: messy, deliberately vague, and open to debate.

Although it was clear that the Peace recognized only Catholicism and the Augsburg Confession, it was never made clear who was entitled to judge what did or did not constitute the practice of a protected faith. In the case of Lutheranism, for example, what exactly *was* the "faith of the Augsburg Confession" and who was entitled to interpret it authoritatively? The Peace of Augsburg never addressed these issues, nor did it provide any clear guidelines for their resolution.

The vagueness of the Religious Peace and the imperial censorship laws in general fostered much confusion. These ambiguities created considerable opportunities for circumvention of the law, as well as for arbitrary enforcement and political jockeying between the imperial estates. Substantial uncertainty existed, for example, as to the circumstances under which theological writings could be prohibited. Early modern Germany was awash in controversial theological literature, much of it couched in highly polemical terms. Was religious debate itself unlawful under the Peace of Augsburg? In these matters, the imperial courts typically held that debate over points of doctrine could legitimately occur, but that Lutherans and Catholics could not lawfully hold each other up to abuse and insult.[13]

Although the Peace of Augsburg was thought to prohibit confessional invective, authors on both sides of the religious divide questioned whether the imperial administration enforced the law impartially between Catholics and Lutherans. Lutheran clerics charged that censors were too often recruited from "vehemently Protestant-hating Papists" who struck out anything they judged too critical of the papacy.[14] This did not prevent some Catholic writers from also leveling charges of favoritism against imperial officials. The Bavarian-born jurist, Georg Eder, complained in 1573 that the imperial court in Vienna was so afraid of the perception of an anti-Lutheran bias that it gave Protestant polemicists license to attack the Catholic church in print. According to Eder, Lutheran writers used the Religious Peace of Augsburg to shield their attacks on Catholicism, while the emperor's own officials denied Catholic authors the right to respond in kind.[15]

---

pp. 60–72; Bob Scribner, 'Preconditions of Tolerance and Intolerance in Sixteenth-Century Germany,' *Tolerance and Intolerance in the European Reformation*, eds Ole Peter Grell and Bob Scribner (Cambridge: Cambridge University Press, 1996) p. 40.

[13] Eisenhardt, *Die kaiserliche Aufsicht über Buchdruck*, pp. 55–6.

[14] SStBA, 2° Cod. Aug. 53, "Chronica, darinen allerley wunderseltsame unnd underschidliche Sachen begriffen so alhier inn Augspurg vorgange," fol. 380r.

[15] Georg Eder, *Evangelische Inquisition Wahrer und falscher Religion. Wider Das gemain unchristliche Claggeschray / Das schier niemands mehr wissen künde / wie oder*

As if to prove his point, Eder's book, *Evangelical Inquisition of True and False Religion* (*Evangelische Inquisition Wahrer und Falscher Religion...*), was quickly condemned under the Peace of Augsburg.[16] The book offered a provocative point-by-point refutation of the Protestant "heresy" and an impassioned defense of Catholic belief. Eder insisted that his objective was not to demonize Protestantism, but to teach faithful Catholics how to discern truth from error. One month after its publication, however, Emperor Maximilian II ordered the book's confiscation and banned Eder from ever writing on religious subjects again.[17]

In his decree, Maximilian charged that the text had falsely claimed an imperial privilege, but this alone does not adequately explain the severity of Eder's condemnation. At the imperial court, officials saw the book as an attack on the emperor's irenic religious policies. Eder was an enthusiastic supporter of the Jesuits' Viennese mission and, like them, he looked askance at efforts to find compromise with Protestants.[18] He denounced the Catholic moderates at court as lukewarm Catholics and worse than heretics—an argument that was unlikely to endear him to Maximilian, a man known for his moderation and whose own religious loyalties were sometimes in doubt.[19] Moreover, Eder scorned the emperor's efforts to maintain a "false unity" between the Empire's Catholics and Protestants.[20] His *Evangelical Inquisition* attacked not only Maximilian, but also the notions of accommodation and coexistence on which the Peace of Augsburg rested. He mocked the emperor's constitutional role as the impartial guardian of the Religious Peace, suggesting that coexistence was not only impossible, but dangerous. The fact that Eder's book appeared to bear the imperial privilege only further undermined the emperor's position, suggesting as it did that Maximilian approved of Eder's views. To protect his public neutrality, Maximilian had little choice but to condemn Eder.

---

was er glauben solle: In forma aines Christlichen Rathschlags / Wie ein jeder Christen Mensch seines Glaubens halben gäntzlich vergwist und gesichert sein möge: Dermassen / daß er leichtlich nit künde betrogen noch verfürt werden. (Dillingen: Mayer, 1573(?)), pp. *iv(v)–**i(r). [SStBA, Th H 667].

[16] Paul von Stetten, *Geschichte der Heil. Röm. Reichs Freyen Stadt Augspurg, aus Bewährten Jahr-Büchern und Tüchtigen Urkunden gezogen, und an das Licht gegeben durch Paul von Stetten* (Frankfurt & Leipzig: Merz-und Mayerischen Buchhandlung, 1743) p. 606.

[17] BHStA, Kurbayern Äußeres Archiv Nr. 4240; Elaine Fulton, *Catholic Belief and Survival in Late Sixteenth-Century Vienna: The Case of Georg Eder (1523–87)* (Aldershot: Ashgate, 2007) p. 84.

[18] Howard Louthan, *The Quest for Compromise: Peacemakers in Counter-Reformation Vienna* (Cambridge: Cambridge University Press, 1997) pp. 127–33.

[19] Paula Sutter Fichtner, *Emperor Maximilian II* (New Haven: Yale University Press, 2001) pp. 135–55; Fulton, *Catholic Belief and Survival*, pp. 88–90. On irenicism at Maximilian's court, see Louthan, *The Quest for Compromise*, pp. 49–142.

[20] Fulton, *Catholic Belief and Survival*, p. 90.

The limits of imperial censorship law became even murkier as the Empire slid toward religious war in the seventeenth century. Historians have long noted the gradual crystallization of confessional identities in the late sixteenth century and the sharpening of religious discourse that accompanied it. The debates over the Peace of Augsburg reflected these tensions. Although many Lutheran commentators saw the Peace of Augsburg as guaranteeing them equal religious rights within the Empire, the relative legal status of the confessions—and the emperor's constitutional duties therein—increasingly came into question in this period. Some Catholic jurists and theologians argued that the Peace of Augsburg was never a law at all, but merely a contract between Emperor Charles V and the imperial estates—it was a temporary exception to the general law of the Empire recognizing Catholicism as the official faith of the realm.[21] As a contract, the Peace of Augsburg could have no application beyond the parties and the circumstances it expressly bound. In all other cases, these jurists invoked traditional imperial and canon law recognizing the primacy of the Catholic faith within the Empire.[22]

Censorship became one arena in which Catholics and Protestants fought their battles over the Peace of Augsburg. The legal uncertainties surrounding the treaty provided civil authorities with the opportunity to silence writers of the opposing confession if they deviated in any respect from the authorities' interpretation of the law. One notable example is the efforts of Emperor Ferdinand II to suppress the writings of the Tübingen theology professor Theodor Thumm. In 1627, the emperor ordered the Duke of Württemberg to arrest the Lutheran theologian and confiscate his books on the grounds that they were "*Famos-schriften*," or libels, which were long outlawed under the ordinances and constitution of the Empire. According to Ferdinand, Thumm's books belittled not only the emperor and the Catholic electors, princes, and estates of the Empire, but also insulted the entire Catholic faith. Moreover, Thumm had attacked Ferdinand's efforts to re-Catholicize portions of his Austrian patrimony.[23] Ferdinand demanded a full investigation, arguing that such books could

---

[21] See M. Frisch, 'Zur Rechtsnatur des Augsburger Religionsfriedens,' *Zeitschrift der Savigny-Stiftung für Rechtsgeschichte*, Kanonistische Abteilung, Bd. 79 (1993): pp. 448–58; Heckel, 'Autonomia und Pacis Compositio' pp. 140–249; Robert Bireley, 'The Origins of the 'Pacis Compositio' (1629): A Text of Paul Laymann,' *Archivum Historicum Sociatatis Jesu* 42 (1972): pp. 106–27.

[22] Robert Bireley, *Religion and Politics in the Age of the Counterreformation: Emperor Ferdinand II, William Lamormaini, S.J., and the Formation of Imperial Policy* (Chapel Hill: University of North Carolina Press, 1981).

[23] StAN, B-Laden SIL 196, Nr. 10, 'Buechtruckereysach. Der Röm. Kaÿ Mtt. Beveltschreiben Doctoris Theodori Thumÿ Prediacntens und Professoris zu Tübingen...,' Doc. Nr. 2.

serve only to create "more bitterness among the people and stir other disasters."[24] One month later, Ferdinand sent a similar order to the city councils of Nuremberg, Strasbourg, Ulm, and Augsburg.[25]

Clearly, the emperor wanted Thumm silenced, but what had he written to attract such attention in Vienna? Included in the emperor's mandate was a list of Thumm's offending works: most were dense Latin theological treatises, but some of their contents were incendiary. For years, Thumm had been locked in a vicious war of words with Jesuit theologians in Dillingen and Ingolstadt, in the course of which he had repeatedly attacked the papacy and counseled Ferdinand's Protestant subjects in Austria that they could by no means submit to their prince's efforts to enforce Catholicism in his lands. Thumm had also apparently questioned the pope's authority to bless marriages within prohibited degrees of kinship—an argument that cast doubt on Ferdinand's own legitimacy as a descendant of such unions.[26] But, more provocatively, Thumm had also argued that the pope was the Antichrist. In his defense, Thumm noted that he was merely reiterating a doctrine taught by the very founders of the Lutheran faith. In Nuremberg, Ulm, and Stuttgart, Lutheran politicians, jurists, and theologians sprang to Thumm's defense on this point: did the Peace of Augsburg guarantee Thumm—and other Lutherans—the right to call the pope the Antichrist?

The question turned on precisely what the Peace of Augsburg protected, but as noted, the document was itself far from clear. Ferdinand's advisors, and Thumm's Jesuit opponents, contended that his argument was prosecutable libel because the Peace of Augsburg protected only the exercise of the Augsburg Confession, and nowhere in that document could one find the teaching that the pope was the Antichrist. Thumm's defenders took a broader view of the Peace of Augsburg. For them, the treaty protected not merely the articles of faith outlined in the Augsburg Confession, but the Lutheran church's own understanding of its teachings as set forth in multiple sources. They noted that although the Augsburg Confession never identified the pope as the Antichrist, supporting documents and the writings of Lutheran reformers made that charge quite explicit.[27] The notion that the pope was the Antichrist was, to Thumm's supporters, a very *article* of the Lutheran faith, and under the Peace of Augsburg, they argued, it could not legitimately be suppressed.

---

[24] Ibid, fol. 1(v).

[25] Arnd Müller, 'Zensurpolitik der Reichsstadt Nürnberg,' *Mitteilungen des Vereins für Geschichte der Stadt Nürnberg*, 49 (1959): p. 103.

[26] Günther Franz, *Bücherzensur und Irenik: Die theologische Zensur im Herzogtum Württemberg in der Konkurrenz von Universität und Regierung* (Tübingen: J. C. B. Mohr, 1977), pp. 154–5.

[27] LKAN, MKA Nr. Gen. 18 I, Nr. 29, fol. 5(v).

It must be noted that Thumm's charges against the papacy were by no means new. The identification of the papacy with the Antichrist pre-dated the Protestant Reformation by many centuries; both Wyclif and Hus had made this charge, as did a great many lesser-known critics of the medieval and early modern papacy.[28] Luther's own conviction that the pope was the Antichrist is well documented, and the idea can be found in the *Schmalkald Articles*, Melanchthon's *Apology* in defense of the Augsburg Confession, and also in the Formula of Concord.[29] But did the Peace of Augsburg recognize these writings as definitive of the "faith of the Augsburg Confession"? The law simply was not clear.

At issue were matters of legal definition: the Peace of Augsburg recognized only two confessions but never specified what those faiths were thought to entail. When the treaty addressed the rights of the "old Catholic faith," there seemed to be little room for confusion. Centuries of tradition, interpreted authoritatively by popes and councils, defined the faith, however much its particulars might have been debated in the 1550s. But in the case of Lutheranism, the Peace of Augsburg did not so much protect a faith, but a faith defined by a document: the "faith of the Augsburg Confession." By the 1620s, however, it was not even clear which version of the Augsburg Confession was controlling for these purposes. Some jurisdictions within the Empire followed the so-called "Altered Augsburg Confession," or *Confessio Augustana Variata*; others accepted the Book of Concord. Some Catholic authors argued that the Peace of Augsburg protected only the Augsburg Confession in the form presented to Charles V in 1530.[30] Under this argument, the signatories to any other Lutheran statement of faith would have forfeited their rights. These definitional battles likewise embroiled the Reformed churches and any other non-Lutheran Protestant churches that sought to invoke the protections of the Peace of Augsburg.[31]

Even in its 1530 form, the Augsburg Confession left many questions unanswered. It was a basic statement of belief; it made no provision for church governance, liturgy, or other matters fundamental to religious life. It was never a comprehensive statement of Lutheran belief and practice. For that reason, Thumm's Lutheran supporters could not accept it as the

---

[28] Hans Preuß, *Die Vorstellungen vom Antichrist im späteren Mittelalter, bei Luther und in der konfessionellen Polemik* (Leipzig: J.C. Hinrichs, 1906).

[29] LKAN, MKA Nr. Gen. 18 I, Nr. 29, fol. 5(v)–6(v). On Lutheran views of the Antichrist, see Volker Leppin, *Antichrist und Jüngster Tag: Das Profil apokalyptischer Flugschriftenpublizistik im deutschen Luthertum 1548–1618* (Heidelberg: Gütersloher Verlagshaus, 1999).

[30] Heckel, 'Autonomia und Pacis Compositio', pp. 140–249; Bireley, 'The Origins of the "Pacis Compositio,"' pp. 106–27.

[31] Gotthard, *Der Augsburger Religionsfrieden*, pp. 218–20.

measure of their legal rights. They argued that the Peace of Augsburg embraced not merely the express language of the Augsburg Confession, but the Lutheran church's own understanding of its tradition and foundational documents. Under such an interpretation, Thumm's supporters believed they could credibly claim the law's protection. They emphasized that Thumm had merely reiterated a charge frequently made by Martin Luther himself—and presumably few people were in a better position to define the Lutheran faith than Martin Luther.

At the very heart of Thumm's case was the Lutheran church's legal autonomy within the Empire. In the late sixteenth and early seventeenth centuries, Lutheran clergy and officials repeatedly championed their church's right to define for itself what it believed. In the so-called "Calendar Conflict" (*Kalenderstreit*) of the 1580s, for example, they had legally challenged the emperor's authority to mandate the use of the new Gregorian calendar, arguing that, under the Peace of Augsburg, "the pope's new calendar" was an illegal intrusion on the Lutheran church's right to define its liturgical year.[32] The Imperial Cameral Court, at least initially, agreed.[33] In Thumm's case and in many others, Lutherans challenged the right of Catholic officials and theologians to define the Lutheran faith, for in defining the faith they effectively established the limits of its rights under the law.

Thumm's defenders also expressed concern that the very vagueness of the Peace of Augsburg presented the potential for abuse. Duke Johann Friedrich of Württemberg and his advisors worried that if imperial law did not protect Thumm's polemics, then perhaps all Lutheran preachers and theologians could one day be vulnerable to prosecution.[34] Indeed, jurists in Nuremberg warned the city council that if Thumm's writings were deemed illegal, it might eventually become impossible to buy Lutheran books in the Empire. The book sellers, they reasoned, would inevitably seek to limit their risk of prosecution by simply refusing to carry Lutheran works.[35] Moved by these arguments, Nuremberg joined with Ulm and the Duke of Württemberg to block Thumm's arrest and the delivery of his confiscated books to Vienna. In letters to the emperor and his agents, they complained that Thumm was being singled out unjustly. What Thumm had said was not unlike what many had said before him, they argued. Moreover, they said,

---

[32] On the Calendar Conflict, see Chapter 4.

[33] Ferdinand Kaltenbrunner, 'Der Augsburger Kalenderstreit,' *Mitteilungen der Institut für österreichische Geschichtsforschung* I (1880): pp. 504–8.

[34] Franz, *Bücherzensur und Irenik*, p. 155.

[35] StAN, B-Laden SIL 196, Nr. 10, 'Buechtruckereysach. Der Röm. Kaÿ Mtt. Beveltschreiben Doctoris Theodori Thumÿ Prediacntens und Professoris zu Tübingen...,' Prod. 7; Müller, 'Zensurpolitik der Reichsstadt Nürnberg,' p. 104.

the emperor applied the law unfairly against the Lutherans in general. If Thumm's books had violated the law in insulting Catholicism and inciting insurrection against the Catholic estates, then why, they asked, had the emperor not also proceeded against Catholic texts that stirred up sedition against the Lutheran powers?[36]

For Ferdinand and his advisors, what made Thumm particularly dangerous was not his recitation of age-old slanders against the papacy; it was his invocation of the Peace of Augsburg. Thumm had insulted the pope in print; as his defenders noted, he was hardly unique in this. But far more provocatively, Thumm had claimed that, under the Religious Peace, the emperor was legally powerless to silence him. His case, however, arose at a time when Ferdinand was increasingly disinclined to accept the Peace of Augsburg as a check on his authority. Thumm's Jesuit opponents urged Ferdinand to recognize that the Peace of Augsburg did not in any way alter the emperor's ancient role as defender of the papacy. Nothing in the Peace of Augsburg could protect Thumm, they argued, nor did it limit Ferdinand's power to defend the Catholic Church.[37]

By the late 1620s, Ferdinand was increasingly inclined to agree with such arguments. Due to the victories of imperial forces in the early stages of the Thirty Years' War, Ferdinand II was in 1627 at the height of his political power. He pressed this advantage in the Edict of Restitution of 1629, demanding that the Protestant estates restore Catholic ecclesiastical lands secularized after 1552.[38] Württemberg was among the states affected by the Edict, and the Duke decided to appease the emperor by sacrificing his controversial theologian, Theodor Thumm. As was so often the case in matters of censorship within the Empire, political calculations took priority. In due course, the Duke placed Thumm under arrest for six months and fined him 2,000 gulden.[39]

Thus ended Thumm's career as a Lutheran controversialist, but his case highlights the ways in which the Peace of Augsburg could serve as a weapon in the polemical war between the confessions. For both Catholics and

---

[36] StAN, B-Laden SIL 196, Nr. 10, 'Buechtruckereysach. Der Röm. Kaÿ Mtt. Beveltschreiben Doctoris Theodori Thumÿ Prediacntens und Professoris zu Tübingen...,' Prod. 3.

[37] See, e.g., *Zungenschlitzer. Das Ist: Außführliche, Gründliche Handlung Einer Wolbedencklichen Frag, Ob Auch Krafft Deß Religion Fridens Den Praedicanten Erlaubt Seye, Daß Sie Dem Papst Yu Rom Außrüffen Für Den Antichrist, Oder Aber Sie, Vermög Deß Kayserlichen Rechts, Von So Schädlichem, Und Den Gantzen Römischen Reich Schmählichen Lästerb, Sollen Abgehalten Werden. Auß Dem Lateinischen Buch De Compositione Pacis, C. 11 Edit. 2. Verteutscht. Cum Facultate Superiorum* (Dillingen: Lochner, 1629) pp. 1–21 [Freytag 5365]; Heckel, 'Autonomia und Pacis Compositio', pp. 142–4, 208–11.

[38] On the Thirty Years' War, see Chapter 5.

[39] Franz, *Bücherzensur und Irenik*, p. 155.

Lutherans, the treaty provided a means to silence opposition and advance political claims at the highest levels. But in the Empire's religiously mixed areas, the Peace of Augsburg could assume a very different role. Here, it could be a powerful tool for fostering confessional coexistence.

Censorship in the Biconfessional City

As promulgated in 1555, the Peace of Augsburg obligated those imperial cities with confessionally mixed populations to protect the rights of both confessions to live and worship within their communities. According to the treaty's so-called "City Article:"

> Because ... both religions, namely our old religion [i.e., Roman Catholicism] and the religion of the adherents to the Augsburg Confession, have been practiced for several years in many Free and Imperial Cities, the same should henceforth remain so observed in such cities, and the citizens and other residents of such Free and Imperial Cities, whether of the clerical or secular estate, should live peacefully and quietly with each other, and neither side shall attempt to abolish the other's religion, church practices, or ceremonies, or attempt to force them from them; rather, each side shall allow the other, according to this Peace, to remain quietly and peacefully in its religion, faith, church practices, ordinances, and ceremonies, as have been decreed and granted herein to both religions by the Imperial Estates.[40]

Those imperial cities that had always been officially Catholic, such as Cologne, were allowed under the City Article to remain so. Likewise, those Lutheran cities, such as Nuremberg, that had effectively resisted re-Catholicization under the Interim, also retained their religious status.[41] Augsburg and a handful of other imperial cities, however, had effectively become bi-confessional after the re-admission of Catholics after 1548. In these so-called "parity cities," magistrates were required to recognize both Catholicism and Lutheranism within their communities.

---

[40] Brandi, *Der Augsburger Religionsfriede*, pp. 49–50. For a contemporary printing of the text, see *Abschiedt der Römischen Königlichen Maiestat / und gemeiner Stendt / auff dem Reichsstag zu Augspurg / Anno Domini M.D.LV. auffgericht. Sampt/ der Keyserlichen Maiestat Cammergerichts Ordnung / wie die auff diesem Reichsstag / durch die Königliche Maiestat / und gemeine Stendt / widerumb ersehen / ernewert / und an vilen orten geendert* (Mainz: Behem, 1555) [SStBA, 2˚ Stw Abschied 1555].

[41] Paul Warmbrunn, *Zwei Konfessionen in einer Stadt: das Zusammenleben von Katholiken und Protestanten in den paritätischen Reichsstädten Augsburg, Biberach, Ravensburg und Dinklesbühl von 1548 bis 1648* (Weisbaden: F. Steiner, 1983) pp. 11–13. For discussion of the Interim and its implementation, see Chapter 2.

As in the Empire at large, the Peace of Augsburg called on the religiously mixed imperial cities to enforce Christian ideals of concord across confessional lines. The challenge these cities faced in keeping the peace is perhaps best illustrated in the city that gave the Peace of Augsburg its name. Of all the imperial cities subject to the Religious Peace, Augsburg was by far the largest and most prominent.[42] Its city council had officially adopted Protestant reforms in 1537 and erected an elaborate censorship apparatus to safeguard Protestant belief. The city's defeat at the end of the Schmalkaldic War and the subsequent imposition of the 1548 Interim, however, compelled the city to reintroduce Catholicism. A new urban constitution established by Charles V in that year also ensured that Catholics would hold a majority in the Augsburg city council, although they comprised only about 20 percent of the population. With the Religious Peace as the defining statement of the city's confessional status, the treaty's call for religious accommodation became the centerpiece of Augsburg's censorship policy in succeeding generations. It emerged as a powerful tool in the magistrates' efforts to police confessional conflict, as well as a touchstone of legitimacy for both the city council and its critics.

"Brotherly Love and Christian Peace:" Enforcing the Peace of Augsburg

Within days of the treaty's announcement, Augsburg's city council summoned the city's clergy before it and laid down the law that was to govern confessional relations under the new regime. The council decreed that, henceforth, both the adherents of the Catholic faith and the Augsburg Confession were to live together in peace and were in no way to hinder each other in the exercise of their religions. Rather, they were to leave each other to peacefully practice their respective faiths and ceremonies in accordance with the terms of the treaty. The council instructed both Lutheran and Catholic clergy to refrain from any insulting or incendiary preaching against each other, as such talk might stir up confessional hatred. Instead, the council ordered that they should, at all times, exhort their congregations to brotherly love and Christian peace. It decreed that:

> ... [The clergy of both faiths shall exhort] the common citizenry ... in dutiful obedience, to [that] Christian patience and humility, and also brotherly love,

---

[42] Of the imperial cities subject to the "City Article" of the Religious Peace, Paul Warmbrunn identifies only eight cities that can be properly considered "parity cities" in the sense that they protected the religious practices of both faiths, granted full civil rights to members of the minority faith, and allowed members of both faiths at least some participation in civic governance. These included: Ulm, Donauwörth, Kaufbeuren, Leutkirch, Augsburg, Biberach, Ravensburg, and Dinkelsbühl. See ibid., pp. 11–15.

which Christ so often and earnestly commanded, and which we are obligated, for the sake of our soul's salvation, to show to one another ... [43]

The Augsburg city council legitimized its censorship policies by invoking the Peace of Augsburg's call to Christian charity, but these measures also drew on deeply held notions of civility and community that had long had the force of law. Invoking the law of libel and defamation, the council sought to extend the limits of community, to affirm publicly that the obligations of civility and honor bridged the confessional divide.[44]

In Augsburg, the Religious Peace became a tool of indoctrination to educate the populace in an ethic of communal harmony and mutual respect. Catholics and Lutherans at all levels of society, the council urged, owed a duty to one another to co-exist peacefully and maintain the civic order. Magistrates reminded offenders that "both religions are practiced here and ... each resident [is] responsible to the other to uphold the peace, quiet, and rule of law."[45] However, the polemic between the confessions, and the disorder that sometimes accompanied it, severely tested this incorporative ideal. To combat the problem, the city council prosecuted individuals for words and writings that violated the Peace of Augsburg. Individuals dealing in anti-Catholic or anti-Lutheran polemical writings or overheard making religiously motivated insults or threats were subject to arrest. All such cases were referred to the city council for adjudication, as the expression of such views was considered likely to disrupt the fragile peace between the confessions and explode the city into violence.

The 1612 prosecution of Jacob Erhard illustrates how Augsburg magistrates used the Peace of Augsburg as both a didactic tool and a legal weapon to keep the peace. Erhard had been arrested for publicly calling a friend who had converted to Catholicism a "fallen Christian." He had compared him to Judas Iscariot and to Francesco Spiera, the notoriously conscience-stricken apostate made famous in pamphlets throughout the Protestant world.[46] In their interrogation, the council's deputies established first that Erhard understood that both Catholicism and Lutheranism were permitted religions in Augsburg and that it was forbidden to defame another person on account of his faith. Not content to simply appeal to Erhard's civic-mindedness, however, Augsburg officials underlined their message with the full power of the law. With the instruments of torture

---

[43] StAA, Literalien, 'Schwenckfeldiana & Reformations-Acten,' 4 Oct. 1555.

[44] Shuger, *Censorship and Cultural Sensibility*, p. 140; Schmidt, *Libelli Famosi*, pp. 131–41, 253–4.

[45] StAA, Strafamt, Urg. Hans Wagner, 11 Jan. 1581; Caspar Thoman, 11–13 Jan. 1581.

[46] On Spiera, see M.A Overell, 'The Exploitation of Francesco Spiera,' *Sixteenth Century Journal* 26(3) (1995): pp. 619–37.

arrayed before him, Erhard's interrogators sought to "re-educate" him in his duty to keep the Religious Peace. The interrogation reads almost as a kind of civic catechism; but while these questions teach a practical ideology of co-existence, it is one nonetheless deeply rooted in the religious ideal of Christian amity basic to the Peace of Augsburg. Erhard's interrogation records:

> ... He answers freely after an earnest warning:[47] ... Casper Hüber told him last Tuesday that he was going to Regensburg, and that if he or his two stepsons wanted something there, he would gladly take care of it. He [Erhard] served Hüber a drink, as a friend, because Hüber was very dear to him since he had served next to his own son in France. After they drank together ... he said to Hüber, "I hear you want to change from our religion." And Hüber said that was true because he believes the Augsburg Confession is not true, and then he, Erhard ... called him a fallen Christian and said he wanted to throw him down the stairs. He's sorry about all of it because they were good friends with each other...
>
> Q: Doesn't he know that it is forbidden here to insult or defame another person on account of religion or matters of faith?
>
> A: He knows that, and he confesses that he took the matter too far with his comments and that he has done wrong.
>
> Q: Is someone who becomes Catholic a fallen Christian?
>
> A: He says he spoke without thinking, and he was drunk and angry.
>
> Q: Is the Catholic religion so bad that no one can be of that faith without being a fallen Christian?
>
> A.: He is truly sorry about what he said; he has done wrong.
>
> Q: What wrongs does he know of about the Catholic religion and the Catholics living here, and how can he prove it?
>
> A: He doesn't know anything ill of them.
>
> Q: ... Were not his parents also Catholic? Were they wrong in their belief?

---

[47] That is, he testified without the use of torture but after a warning that torture would be applied if he proved uncooperative.

A: His parents were Catholic, and he asks once again for forgiveness for his unthinking comments.

Q: Are Catholics—those who were raised in that faith from childhood as well as those who freely convert—dishonorable people, such that no one can convert to the Catholic faith without disgracing themselves or becoming fallen Christians?

A: He holds the Catholics to be honorable people, and he has never [before] insulted them; he has only ever had good experiences with them.

Q: Does he know what a fallen Christian is? Would he call those who convert to Catholicism from another religion also fallen? On what grounds?

A: He is sorry enough that he used such heated words against Hüber.

Q: Why then did he speak so harshly to Hüber and call him a fallen Christian?

A: He has done wrong; he is sorry and it will be a lesson to him his entire life.

Q: Didn't he even compare him to Francesco Spiera and Judas Iscariot? Why?

A: He remembers the part about Francesco Spiera, but not the rest; perhaps it didn't happen, but he did wrong [in any case].

Q: Are the people who convert to Catholicism therefore comparable to this confused person [i.e., Spiera]?

A: He doesn't think that.

Q: He must be very opposed to Catholicism and have ill feelings toward Catholics in general to compare them to such people. Did he come to those conclusions himself, or did he learn them from others?

A: The Catholics have done him a lot of good, and they are dear to him. He asks for forgiveness.

Q: Did he also call Hüber a rogue?

A: He said this because he was angry because Hüber said his [Erhard's] religion wasn't true, but he went too far.

Q: What dishonorable things does he know about Hüber, and how can he prove it?

A: He knows nothing ill of Hüber; they were good friends ... he has been as dear to him as if he were his own son.

Q: Should he, as a citizen, be allowed to treat another citizen this way, when both owe obedience to my Lords [in the city council], and how does he propose to answer before the authorities for this?

A: [He] asks again, for God's sake, for mercy and forgiveness. He has done wrong.[48]

In its prosecution of Erhard, the council characteristically drew on the Religious Peace's invocation of commonly shared values of Christian brotherhood. Erhard's interrogators stressed these ideals relentlessly, challenging over and over Erhard's suggestion that Catholics were not Christians, and presumably, therefore, outside the bonds of Christian fellowship. The interrogators also underscored Erhard's civic obligation to treat his fellow citizen with honor. They reminded Erhard that the laws that protected Catholic citizens protected Lutheran citizens, too, and that both confessions shared the same duty to respect them.

In invoking shared rights and responsibilities under the Religious Peace, the city council wished to emphasize its impartiality between the confessions. Since 1548, a largely Catholic government had ruled mostly Lutheran Augsburg, and the city council had long been troubled by accusations of favoritism. Since the ratification of the Peace of Augsburg, such charges constituted a powerful attack on the government's very legitimacy and had, on occasion, shaken its authority.[49] To assert its legitimacy and ensure support across the religious spectrum, the Augsburg city council was ever careful to remind its citizens that it acted under *imperial* mandate in enforcing the Religious Peace. For Augsburg's magistrates, the treaty was a religiously neutral source of authority in an environment where the very perception of religious partisanship was potentially explosive.

Indeed, allegations of improper Catholic influence in the city's government were a frequent target of prosecution under the Religious Peace in the 1550s and 1560s. The council's critics blamed the Catholic clergy, in particular, for problems in Augsburg. Hans Weiss, for example,

---

[48] StAA, Strafamt, Urg. Jacob Erhard, 3 Feb. 1612.
[49] See Bernd Roeck, *Eine Stadt in Krieg und Frieden. Studien zur Geschichte der Reichsstadt Augsburg zwischen Kalenderstreit und Parität*, I (Göttingen: Vandenhoeck & Ruprecht, 1989) pp. 125-90; 201-70.

was arrested in 1556 after publicly denouncing the "monks and priests" as the source of all the city's problems. The only solution, he said, was to put them all to death.⁵⁰

Weiss's comments were extreme, but accusations of favoritism and political meddling by the clergy frequently bedeviled the city council in these years. Lutheran fears of the Catholic clergy seemed to center particularly on the newly established Jesuit mission in the city. In June 1559, the Jesuit missionary Peter Canisius arrived with a handful of associates to take up preaching duties in the city's cathedral.⁵¹ The Jesuits had been invited to Augsburg by the city's bishop, Otto Truchseß von Waldburg, with the hope that the fathers might establish a school for Catholic youth.⁵² Canisius and his colleagues were warmly received by the Catholic laity, who, according to the complaints of other Catholic clergy, flocked to the Jesuits "as if their masses were holier than the other priests'."⁵³

The popularity of the Jesuits also made them the focus of Protestant attack. One of the earliest and most public of these attacks came in 1561, when Caspar Hertzog was arrested for desecrating the Cathedral of Our Lady with vulgar anti-Canisius graffiti. Hertzog had allegedly scrawled "Peter Canisius can lick my ass!" on the door of the pulpit from which Canisius preached; he had also fouled the church's altars and fonts with horse manure.⁵⁴ Even after the offensive markings had been removed from the cathedral, Hertzog had reportedly scrawled similar graffiti against Canisius and the cathedral clergy throughout the city.⁵⁵ He did it, he said, because Canisius was "an enemy of Christ."⁵⁶ Hertzog claimed that he had been imprisoned in Munich for three months "on account of the Jesuits," and had nearly died as a result. Moreover, he said, Canisius was opposed

---

⁵⁰ StAA, Strafamt, Urg. Hans Weiss, 3–4 Dec. 1556; StAA, Strafbuch, 1554–1562, fol. 63r.

⁵¹ On Canisius in Augsburg, see J. Brodrick, *Saint Peter Canisius, S.J., 1521–1597* (London: Sheed and Ward, 1938) pp. 422–71; Julius Oswald and Peter Rummel, eds, *Petrus Canisius – Reformer der Kirche. Festschrift zum 400. Todestag des zweiten Apostels Deutschlands* (Augsburg: Sankt Ulrich Verlag, 1996) pp. 41–65.

⁵² Placidus Braun, *Geschichte des Kollegiums der Jesuiten in Augsburg* (Munich: Jakob Giel, 1822) pp. 1–11.

⁵³ Ibid., p. 7.

⁵⁴ StAA, Strafamt, Urg. Caspar Hertzog, 8 Aug. 1561.

⁵⁵ Paul Hektor Mair, 'Das Diarium Paul Hektor Mairs von 1560–1563,' in *Die Chroniken der Schwäbischen Städte: Augsburg*, bd. 8. *Die Chroniken der deutschen Städte vom 14. bis ins 16. Jahrhundert*, bd. 33, ed Historische Kommission bei der Bayerischen Kommission der Wissenschaften (1928) (Göttingen: Vandenhoek & Ruprecht, 1966) pp. 123–4.

⁵⁶ StAA, Strafamt, Urg. Caspar Hertzog, 8 Aug. 1561. Hertzog's comment recalls a favorite pun among German Protestants of the era substituting the German name "*Jesuiter*" with "*Jesuwider*," meaning literally, "against Jesus."

to Christ and all His followers, which Hertzog offered to prove by the Holy Writ, in writing if necessary. The City council was not convinced—it concluded that Hertzog was "soft in the head."[57]

Although there is scant evidence that the activities of the Jesuits were deliberately provocative, some in Augsburg's Protestant community saw their arrival as an attempt to undermine the confessional settlement established under the Religious Peace. Although Lutherans made up more than 80 percent of Augsburg's population at mid-century,[58] Catholics controlled the city's government. Indeed, Catholics held a majority in the Small Council every year from 1555 through 1569, and again from 1572 to 1632. Catholics also held a decisive majority in the politically important Privy Council, and were over-represented in most city offices at this time.[59] The Catholics' dominance in Augsburg's government was by design—in restructuring the city's constitution after his victory in the Schmalkaldic War, Emperor Charles V had favored the Catholic patriciate over the largely Protestant guild masters, believing that they could be better relied upon to ensure the city's loyalty to imperial interests. The system that he created effectively ensured a self-perpetuating Catholic majority in civic government.[60]

Many of Augsburg's wealthiest and most powerful families also adhered to the "old faith." The fact that many of these families were also public supporters of the Jesuit mission in Augsburg helped fuel Protestant rumors that the city's elites were conniving with the Jesuits against the Lutherans. Rumors circulated that the Catholic-controlled council was conspiring with the Jesuits in a secret plan to expel the Lutheran clergy and force the city's return to Catholicism,[61] or, at the very least, was giving the Jesuits free rein to tilt the confessional balance in the city back to the Catholic church.

---

[57] StAA, Strafbuch 1554–1562, fol. 44v; Mair, 'Diarium,' pp. 123–4.

[58] In a 1563 report, Canisius estimated Augsburg's population to be approximately 90 percent Protestant. By the 1580s, Catholics were thought to make up about 20 percent of the population. Carl A. Hoffmann, 'Konfessionell motivierte und gewandelte Konflikte in der zweiten Hälfte des 16. Jahrhunderts – Versuch eines mentalitätsgeschichtlichen Ansatzes am Beispiel der bikonfessionellen Reichsstadt Augsburg,' in *Konfessionalisierung und Region*, eds Peer Frieß and Rolf Kießling (Konstanz: Universitätsverlag Konstanz GmbH, 1999) p. 104.

[59] Lutherans held a one-person majority in the Small Council in 1570 and 1571, and held all seats during the Swedish occupation of 1632–1635. Warmbrunn, *Zwei Konfessionen*, pp. 106–11; 132–4.

[60] On this point, see Chapter 2.

[61] See, for example, StAA, Strafamt, Urg. Veit Goppoldt, 12–19 April 1564; Magdalena Geslerin, 17–19 April 1564; Gedeon Mair, 7–9 Nov. 1583; Christof Widenmann, 10–11 Nov. 1583; Christof Wörter, 22–29 Aug. 1584.

The explosive nature of these charges made such rumors the target of intense official scrutiny. In 1564, for example, magistrates investigated a rumor that the council was plotting to expel the Lutheran clergy, but that the two Lutheran *Bürgermeister* had been able to stop the plan. Lutheran pastors were said to be meeting in secret to plan a response, and there was talk of a coming riot in the city. Acting on informants' reports, the authorities arrested Veit Goppoldt, who admitted to recounting the story in a tavern. Goppoldt insisted, however, that no one had believed him because they all knew that the citizenry would riot over such a move, and, besides, "they'd heard such things before; the city was full of such stories."[62] The magistrates traced the rumor back to Magdalena Geslerin, who admitted under torture that she had spread such stories, ignoring her husband's warning to "keep such talk quiet and say nothing to anyone."[63] Geslerin claimed she had heard the story first from her neighbor's wife, and like Goppoldt, noted that similar rumors were circulating all over Augsburg.

If Goppolt and Geslerin are to be believed, rumors of a government-backed conspiracy against the Protestants were rife among Augsburg's Lutherans. These rumors exposed a deep sense of vulnerability within some segments of this community. Although the Peace of Augsburg mandated official neutrality, some feared that the Catholic-dominated council could not be trusted to respect Lutheran rights. Everyone understood that these charges were potentially explosive, and with good reason. Because Augsburg's post-1555 government drew its very legitimacy from the Peace of Augsburg, allegations of confessional favoritism undermined its political authority. The council was careful to publicly affirm its neutrality at every turn, but this did not prevent its detractors from suspecting its motives. Indeed, the conspiracy rumors assumed the council's need to appear publicly impartial—it was for this reason that it supposedly acted in secret, through agents like the Jesuits who stood outside the political process. These sorts of covert machinations were far more frightening, for they effectively side-stepped what political representation the Lutheran community had to protect its rights. In Goppoldt's story, for example, it was only the timely intervention of the Lutheran *Bürgermeister* that saved the clergy from expulsion. Lutheran officials had been able to thwart the plan this time, but who knew what other plots the council and its cronies were secretly hatching?

At the root of all of these rumors of favoritism and conspiracy were persistent anxieties about political representation and the Religious Peace. As we have seen, Catholics and Lutherans throughout the Empire often

---

[62] StAA, Strafamt, Urg. Veit Goppoldt, 12–19 April 1564.
[63] StAA, Strafamt, Urg. Magdalena Geslerin, 17–19 April 1564.

differed mightily in their interpretations of the treaty. In Augsburg, attempts to equalize the status of the confessions under the Religious Peace bred expectations that both sides would enjoy equal political representation as well—an expectation that ran head-long into the city's constitutional structure, and opened up significant debate as the century wore on.

Despite the council's efforts to suppress such talk, allegations of official bias continued to circulate, particularly as confessional lines hardened in the seventeenth century. As before, the city council prosecuted these cases under the Peace of Augsburg. In 1610, for example, the beer brewer Georg Graf was arrested for saying, among other "disgraceful words," that Lutherans had no chance against Catholics in the city's courts because the law favored Catholics. Graf, who was Lutheran, had been ordered by *Bürgermeister* Philip Jacob Rembold, a Catholic, to pay 435 gulden on a debt to Hans Fersen, also a Catholic. Neighbors testified that when Fersen's lawyer visited Graf to collect, he swore that the order was unjust, shouting angrily that "Fersen gets protection because he's Catholic, but the Lutherans have no backing against them!"[64] *Bürgermeister* Rembold had done him wrong, he said—"I shit on the council and the Catholics!," Graf shouted.[65]

Graf had plenty of experience with the law, having been arrested four times before for "disobedience," wife-beating, and keeping a "disorderly household" (*übel Haus*).[66] Graf was a cantankerous fellow with a loud mouth—many neighbors said they kept their windows shut because "they know well how rude he is when he's agitated."[67] As for the charges against him, Graf said he could not remember making such "blasphemous" statements because he had been drunk. Indeed, one of his neighbors testified that Graf was "all crazy and drunk" (*all toll und vol*).[68] However, according to other reports, Graf had shouted the next morning that "what he said yesterday, he says it still!"[69]

In Graf's interrogation, the council challenged Graf to show precisely how he had been unfairly treated. Had not the court ruled for Fersen consistent with the parties' own settlement? Had the court not heard his petitions as the occasion demanded? How then could he say that Catholics received more protection than others? Was it not true that the law treated both Catholics and Lutherans the same? How then could he use such "cruel insults" against the council and *Bürgermeister* Rembold, "the

---

[64] StAA, Strafamt, Urg. Georg Graf d. Ä., 22 March 1610.
[65] Ibid.
[66] Ibid.
[67] Report of Johannes Widenmann, dated 24 March 1610, filed ibid.
[68] Report of Mang Rudolf, dated 24 March 1610, filed ibid.
[69] Ibid.

authorities God had appointed over him?" What had the Catholics ever done to him, and what was he trying to incite with his "Godless and cruel blasphemy?"[70]

Graf swore he could not remember making these statements. Chastened after four nights in jail, he admitted in his second interrogation that, for the most part, he and Fersen had been treated fairly. He admitted he knew of no cases in which anyone had received preferential treatment on account of their religion. Moreover, he could think of no ill that any Catholic had ever caused him; indeed Catholics had been especially kind to him during his wanderings as a journeyman. He was truly sorry, he said, and begged for mercy.[71] The council ordered him expelled from the city, but allowed him to return four months later at the request of *Bürgermeister* Rembold.[72]

Later that year, Augsburg magistrates prosecuted a similar case, with far more destabilizing potential, against the weaver Maximilian Daniel. Daniel had been overheard spreading rumors of a Jesuit plot against Augsburg's Lutheran citizens. Allegedly, he had stood before the city hall one Saturday telling his listeners that there was a Jesuit going about saying,

> It would be good if [the council] drove all the Lutherans out of the city. But they shouldn't do it with force. Rather, since the government gives them no aid, some of them will have to leave, and some of them will convert. Thus, they will quit the city.[73]

Before the *Strafherren* ("Punishment Lords"), Daniel swore that he had not made up the story. He had heard it originally from his brother Stefan, who had died one and a half years before. Like Graf, Daniel claimed he had been unfairly treated in a dispute with a Catholic tradesman. Just like the Jesuits, Daniel said, this merchant was trying to drive him from the city.[74]

The explosive charge of governmental favoritism, linked with the popular suspicions of a Jesuit plot to undermine the Religious Peace, made Daniel's story a dangerous element in the streets of Augsburg. His interrogators were suspicious: "since this was a seditious, divisive thing to say, didn't he seek thereby to stir up rebellion and bitterness, at least among the weavers? What was his intent?" Daniel insisted he had spoken only in anger, and had no ill intent. He admitted having said, also, that

---

[70] Ibid.
[71] Ibid.
[72] StAA, Strafbuch Nr. 104, 1608–1615, fol. 87r–87v.
[73] StAA, Strafamt, Urg. Maximilian Daniel, 27 Aug. 1610.
[74] Ibid.

a "certain lord's" nose[75] was "too long," but again stated that he was merely angry. The magistrates demanded, "should an obedient citizen be allowed to speak so insultingly, contemptuously, and dishonorably against his government? Who does he think he is?"[76] Daniel said he had not understood what he was saying and begged, "very subserviently," for mercy.[77]

The council would have none of it. "Maxi Daniel," the council decreed, "had, without any given reason, poured out rebellious speech in front of the City Hall and evil speech against a prominent person. With these rebellious words, he began a punishable slander against the Lord Jesuits, and through this grave misdeed, could easily have roused something else."[78] In punishment for his crime, the council banished him from the city and the surrounding area.[79]

Protestant fears of political favoritism, combined with the high profile of the Jesuits' missionizing work, also fueled suspicions that the council actively supported the re-Catholicization of the city through conversion. By the early 1600s, Augsburg was still predominantly Lutheran, but the Catholic community had grown steadily through immigration from the countryside and high-profile conversions. With the relative representation of Lutherans and Catholics in Augsburg a sensitive issue, conversion was a concern on both sides. The city council was alert to these concerns, and invoked the Peace of Augsburg to regulate the clergy's missionizing. It interpreted the Peace of Augsburg's prohibitions against interference in the religious practices of another officially sanctioned confession to include efforts to proselytize members of the other faith. The council did not—and, practically speaking, could not—ban conversion, but it did discourage aggressive, high-profile missionizing likely to inflame confessional tensions. In the 1570s, for example, the council conditioned its approval of a planned Jesuit school and chapel on the Jesuits' promise to abide by the Religious Peace's mandate that each person be "allowed to remain peacefully in his own faith and religion."[80]

---

[75] According to a witness's report, the nose in question belonged to Matthäus Welser, a member of the prominent Welser family and *Reichspfenningmeister* to the emperor. Ibid. On the Welser family, see Günther Grünsteudel, Günther Hägele, and Rudolf Frankenberger, eds, *Augsburger Stadtlexikon 2* (Augsburg: Perlach Verlag, 1998) pp. 922–4.

[76] StAA, Strafamt, Urg. Maximilian Daniel, 27 Aug. 1610.

[77] Ibid.

[78] StAA, Strafbuch Nr. 104, 1608–1615, fol. 106v.

[79] Ibid.

[80] Wolfram Baer and Hans Joachim Hecker, eds, *Die Jesuiten und ihre Schule St. Salvator in Augsburg, 1582*. (Munich: Stadtarchiv Augsburg & Karl M. Lipp Verlag, 1982) pp. 20–21.

Returning anew to the 1612 confrontation between Jacob Erhard and his friend Caspar Hüber, these anxieties about conversion help explain the men's conflict and the council's response to it. What had so enraged Erhard was not so much Hüber's Catholicism—it was his apostasy. By Erhard's own account, Casper Hüber, the man he had called a "fallen Christian" and threatened to throw down the stairs, was "very dear to him;" he was "like a son" to him. They had lived peaceably together for many years; what had provoked him was his friend's decision to reject the Lutheran faith in favor of Catholicism. Erhard, however, was presumably himself a convert; as the interrogation revealed, his own parents had been Catholic. He had, at some point, rejected his family's faith to embrace Lutheranism. His outrage against Hüber perhaps reflected his own sense that conversion placed a person outside the conventional bonds of family, friendship, and community. In their questioning of Erhard, the Augsburg magistrates took aim at precisely this logic—they wanted to establish, above all, that the civic and Christian duties of accommodation transcended religious affiliation. Erhard had a duty to live peaceably with his neighbors, regardless of what religion they chose. In sentencing Erhard, the council was careful to note that Hüber himself had appealed for leniency on his behalf. Citing their long friendship, Hüber professed himself willing, out of Christian love, to forgive Erhard and "return good for bad."[81]

Erhard's case illustrates both the success of the Peace's call to religious accommodation and the very real obstacles it faced. The council implemented the Peace by invoking commonly shared values of brotherly love and Christian charity, and most Augsburgers in these years lived peaceably with their neighbors, whether Catholic or Protestant. Even those prosecuted under the Peace of Augsburg conceded (more or less freely) their duty to uphold its ideals, recognizing that it protected the rights of both confessions. Religious representation remained a problematic issue in the city, and like much of the rest of the Empire, Augsburg experienced its share of religious conflict in the confessional age. But these conflicts were the exception, not the norm, in Augsburg, and the confessions' mostly peaceful coexistence suggests that, to a large degree, Augsburgers internalized the values of the Religious Peace.

At all times, the Peace of Augsburg remained the touchstone of political legitimacy in public discourse in that city. In criticizing the council's confessional make-up or its religious policies, Augsburgers looked for support in the Peace of Augsburg. Debates about political representation and even fears of the Jesuit mission in Augsburg drew, in part, on the treaty's perceived guarantees of legal neutrality and religious self-determination. Although the disputes over the meaning of the Peace of Augsburg could

---

[81] StAA, Strafamt, Urg. Jacob Erhard, 3 Feb. 1612; Strafbuch Nr. 104, fol. 178r.

themselves serve confessional interests, these very debates nonetheless validated the ideal of communal harmony as a primary civic goal.

Fighting Words: Policing Confessional Conflict

Despite its successes, the council's efforts to keep the peace were in no small measure complicated by the proximity in which Catholics and Lutherans lived and the many opportunities for friction that such close contact created. Jacob Hötsch's 1601 prosecution highlighted the tensions that sometimes divided neighbors. Hötsch had been reported by a neighbor for singing "defamatory" songs about the pope and the Jesuits.[82] It all started, Hötsch told the *Strafherren*, when a Catholic neighbor boy punched a Lutheran girl in the face for singing a song about how Hell was full of priests and clerks (*Pfaffen und Schreibers*). Hötsch and his neighbors all lived in houses owned by the Jesuits, and the incident sparked a heated argument among the residents. One Catholic woman said that the neighborhood would only be peaceable if the Lutherans were evicted, whereupon Hötsch retorted, "we were citizens here before the Devil brought the Jesuits into the city!"[83]

The *Strafherren* challenged Hötsch to explain precisely how he thought the Jesuits had harmed the city. Hötsch replied that he knew nothing about the Jesuits themselves, but he objected to the way their students insulted and ridiculed the Lutherans and their pastors. It was divisive, he said, and he made a point of avoiding the students.[84] He admitted that he had sung a defamatory song describing the Jesuits as the hounds of Hell, stealing lambs for their papal master. He only sang it, he said, to retaliate against some Catholics who had ridiculed his singing of Psalms. He told the *Strafherren* that he knew very well that "defamatory" songs were banned in Augsburg, and that everyone was supposed to allow others to practice their own religion "without shame or humiliation."[85] He asked for forgiveness, insisting that he had only tried to defend himself against the "unjust talk" of his Catholic neighbors. He denied that he had written any of the offending songs, and insisted that he had no quarrel with the government.

Acting on information supplied by Hötsch, the authorities also arrested Ludwig Zimmermann, a 20-year-old student from Kaufering, near

---

[82] Unsigned report of Endris Hilbrant, dated 27 Aug. 1601, filed in StAA, Strafamt, Urg. Jacob Hötsch, 27–31 Aug. 1601.
[83] StAA, Strafamt, Urg. Jacob Hötsch, 27 Aug. 1601.
[84] Ibid., Answer Nr. 9.
[85] Ibid., Questions and Answers Nr. 10–11.

Landsberg. Zimmermann, a student of the Jesuits, was Hötsch's upstairs neighbor. Zimmermann admitted that he and his friends often sang chorales and "florid music" (that is, polyphonic music) in his rooms, and sometimes they laughed when Hötsch was singing his Psalms. Zimmermann stated that he had also belted out hymns in praise of the Virgin Mary to drown out Hötsch's singing.[86] The *Strafherren* asked him whether he did not yell at Hötsch out the window, "you're a bastard and a thief!" Zimmermann admitted that he had said this, and that Hötsch had yelled back that "I'm not insulted by the likes of you—you're just a janitor! If it weren't for the Jesuits, you'd have to beg!"[87]

Inquiries about Zimmermann revealed that he and several other students had allegedly hooted at the Lutheran pastor of St Georg and his wife as they made their way home one evening. Zimmermann was accused of threatening the pastor with physical injury, but he claimed that the pastor's wife had insulted them first.[88] The incident led to an exchange of insults with a group of weavers on the street, and later, a confrontation with a Protestant student from St Anna's school. The Catholic and Protestant students had evidently staked out separate turfs within the city, for the Catholic students demanded to know "what business do you have nosing about this place?"[89] Thinking that he had heard one of the Catholic students insult him, a Protestant student challenged them to fight him and his friends to the death. Zimmermann claimed that he simply challenged the Protestant student to bring his complaints before the authorities and leave them in peace.[90] He denied insulting any Protestants, other than those, like the weavers, who had insulted him, or like Hötsch, who had insulted the Jesuit fathers.

While most Catholics and Lutherans lived together peacefully in Augsburg, city magistrates worried that the city's youth were taking their religious differences to the extreme. In 1600, the council complained that the students of both the Lutheran school of St Anna's and the Jesuit school had been engaging in religious disputations. According to the council, they had been verbally abusive not only to each other but to the clergy of both faiths. Such conduct could easily lead to bitterness and unrest between the confessions, the council noted.[91] It ordered the schoolmasters

---

[86] StAA, Strafamt, Urg. Ludwig Zimmermann, 31 Aug. 1601, Answer Nr. 6. On singing as a form of confessional conflict in Augsburg, see Fisher, *Music and Religious Identity in Counter-Reformation Augsburg*, pp. 67–70

[87] StAA, Strafamt, Urg. Ludwig Zimmermann, 31 Aug. 1601, Answer Nr. 8.

[88] Ibid., Answer Nr. 5.

[89] Ibid.

[90] Ibid.

[91] StAA, Ratsbuch Nr.49, 1600–1602, fol. 49v.

of both faiths to rein in their students and teach them to avoid religious disputations, stop insulting the clergy, and show civility to all persons.[92]

The council's decree could not stop the problem, however. In February 1605, Augsburg authorities arrested Christof Lecherer, a 20-year-old student at the Jesuit school, for posting an insulting cartoon outside the lodgings of Simon Haderdey, the Lutheran pastor of Lützelburg.[93] Lecherer's drawing, with the glue residue still attached, is preserved with his *Urgicht* and shows the pastor being roasted in Hell by a gang of demons (see Fig. 3.1). Vulgar doggerel written at the top names the pastor and announces that the devils have dragged him to Hell, where he must remain forever to pay for his sins.

Didn't he know, the *Strafherren* asked him, that the council had announced "several times" in the Catholic schools that the students should not "disgrace or vex" the Lutheran citizenry, "especially the preachers?"[94] Lecherer admitted knowing this, and also that such pictures were prohibited in Augsburg, but that hadn't stopped him. In fact, Lecherer reported that he drew cartoons of Lutheran pastors in class and sold them to other students in exchange for food. His landlord, Thomas Meges, had encouraged him, asking him several times to draw a cartoon "against a preacher." It was Meges who had suggested that he add "a devil or something" to his drawing of Pastor Haderdey. According to Lecherer, Meges pointed out the house in which the pastor was staying, and he and another student posted the cartoon on the front door later that night. Both men, however, claimed to know nothing about Pastor Haderdey or to have anything against him personally. They apparently had singled him out only because they knew him to be a Protestant clergyman.[95]

Meges admitted that he had encouraged Lecherer to draw the cartoon, but insisted that he had never expected him to be so "fresh" as to actually tack it up in public. He also acknowledged that "both religions are equally recognized and protected in this city" and swore that he had never before defied the Peace of Augsburg.[96] He also knew that such "scandalous pictures and writings" were strictly forbidden. If only he hadn't headed home to bed, he would have torn down the placard himself, and then this "disaster" would not have befallen him.[97] He begged for mercy, pleading

---

[92] Ibid.
[93] Hans Wiedemann, *Augsburger Pfarrerbuch. Die evangelischen Geistlichen der Reichsstadt Augsburg, 1524–1806* (Nürnberg: Verein für bayerische Kirchengeschichte, 1962) p. 61; von Stetten, p. 782.
[94] StAA, Strafamt, Urg. Christof Lecherer, 3 Feb. 1605.
[95] Ibid; StAA, Strafamt, Urg. Thomas Meges, 11 Feb. 1605.
[96] StAA, Strafamt, Urg. Thomas Meges, 11 Feb. 1605.
[97] Ibid.

Figure 3.1 Christof Lecherer's drawing of Pastor Simon Haderdey (StAA, Strafamt, Urgichten, Christof Lecherer, 3–14 Feb. 1605).

that his pregnant wife would suffer a terrible shock if she were to see him imprisoned.[98] The council released him with a warning, finding that he had merely had knowledge of the placard and had helped in its making.[99] Lecherer, however, was expelled from the city.[100]

By 1603, the *Strafherren* feared that Catholics and Protestants were increasingly turning to violence to settle their disputes. Reporting to the council and *Stadtpfleger* on a May 1603 street fight between Catholic and Protestant men, they opined that the case was an especially bad one, as it involved people "molesting and irritating" one another on account of their religion. This problem, they noted, "had unfortunately now become very common and was completely out of control in almost all the inns and beer halls." Nothing good could come of it, the *Strafherren* concluded, if this "evil" were tolerated or allowed to worsen over time.[101]

The Augsburg criminal records document a marked upturn in prosecutions of confessional invective around the turn of the seventeenth century. Although the increase may simply reflect better record-keeping or closer policing, the *Strafherren*'s report indicates that at least some contemporary observers believed that confessional conflict was a worsening problem.[102] If the case records are to be believed, both the polemic and the potential for violence between Catholics and Protestants became more pronounced as the century progressed.

The testimony of witnesses to a 1610 disturbance in a local Lutheran church demonstrates the explosive potential of these cases. Hans Windbusch was accused of interrupting a sermon by slamming the door and shouting at the preacher, "if you're through lying, shut up!"[103] Windbusch continued to rail at the parishioners, and one of them, Melchior Cramer, slapped him in the face. As news of the disturbance spread through the *Jacober* quarter, a crowd of almost 400 people[104] gathered outside the church. Cramer testified that, as the crowd swelled outside, the mood inside the church grew increasingly anxious, as no one could predict how the mob would react.[105] Fortunately, the crowd dispersed without violence after Windbusch was arrested.[106]

---

[98] StAA, Strafamt, Urg. Christof Lecherer, 14 Feb. 1605.
[99] StAA, Strafbuch Nr. 103, 1596–1605, fol. 275v–276r.
[100] Ibid., fol. 275v.
[101] Report of *Strafherren*, filed in StAA, Strafamt, Urg. Hans Scheurer, 5 May 1603.
[102] Ibid.
[103] StAA, Strafamt, Urg. Hans Windbusch, 26 April 1610.
[104] The *Strafherren*'s estimate. Ibid.
[105] Report of Melchior Cramer, filed ibid.
[106] In view of Windbusch's drunkenness and allegedly "idiotic head", the council sentenced him to an additional eight days in the tower. StAA, Strafbuch Nr. 104, 1608–1615,

In the same year, Casper Koler also nearly started a riot with some anti-Lutheran comments. Koler, a soldier in the service of Marx Fugger, was accused of having ridden up and down the Bakers' Street shouting that the Lutherans were all "Mamelukes" who "belonged to the Devil body and soul," and that he did not want to leave the city until he had killed some.[107] According to the *Strafherren*, Koler drew a crowd of nearly 600 people, who created an "angry uproar and tumult" in the streets.[108] When the crowd began hurling stones at Koler, a member of the city guard, Hans Bair, came to his defense. Witnesses reported that Bair lashed out at the crowd with his halberd, striking several innocent bystanders in the process.[109] The witnesses complained that the Fuggers' servants received more protection from the law than did innocent citizens.[110]

Koler denied the charges, claiming that he had only been cursing at his lame horse. He admitted that he may have spoken "in anger" to a passer-by but denied insulting anyone else. For his part, Bair reported that he and his comrades were standing guard by the Red Gate (*Rotes Tor*) when Koler came riding up with 200 people on his trail. The crowd had taken Koler's weapon and was throwing stones at him, so the guard took him into custody to bring him before the *Bürgermeister*. Bair explained that the mob had the guard surrounded, and thinking themselves to be in danger, the guard captain ordered Bair to force the crowd back with his halberd. Although the council accepted that Bair acted in self-defense, it ordered him to remain in prison for another eight days.[111] Koler, however, was remanded into the custody of the *Strafherren* for punishment, along with the men accused of throwing stones.[112]

As Koler and Windbusch found out, religious insults could easily touch off mob violence in Augsburg in these years. If Augsburgers were becoming more belligerent and defensive, their language was also becoming more threatening. Koler had announced that he wanted to "kill some Lutherans;" Zimmermann's altercation with a Protestant student had ended with an offer to fight "to the death." Religious insult was not to be met with insult, but with violence, and the insults themselves were becoming more violent. Christof Peter, a soldier from Kronach, was arrested in June 1610 for threatening Christoph Nieschel, pastor of the

---

fol. 91v–92r.

[107] StAA, Strafamt, Urg. Casper Koler, 30 June 1610.

[108] Ibid.

[109] Report of Witnesses, dated 26 June 1610, filed ibid.

[110] Ibid.

[111] StAA, Strafbuch Nr. 104, 1608–1615, fol. 98v–99v.

[112] Ibid. Koler paid a fine of 1 gulden in lieu of imprisonment, together with a fine of 30 kreutzer for drunkenness. StAA, Strafamt, Zuchtbuch Nr. 199, 1600–1611 fol. 128.

Barfüsser church. Nieschel, dressed in his clerical robe, and his brother Daniel passed Peter and his comrades as they made their way to morning services at St Anna's. According to Pastor Nieschel, Peter pointed to him and told his fellow soldiers that if he had his rifle with him, he would shoot his cap off—and his head with it. "That's a fine cap for a fine thief," Peter allegedly told his comrades, "and if we took that thief out and hung him from a tree, we could share his clothes and cap between us!"[113]

"Bacon Boys & Alms Abusers"—Polemical Song and Religious Insult

It was apparent to everyone who had ears to hear that Augsburgers liked to sing. Indeed, there was so much singing on the street that delegates to the 1559 Imperial Diet in Augsburg had complained that they could still hear the din even in the quiet of their rooms.[114] Augsburgers also enjoyed writing songs, often on subjects the council did not wish discussed. As the new century dawned, Augsburg's streets and taverns were full of songs and stories about the city's newest religious order, the Capuchin Friars Minor. Neither the friars nor the council approved of this music-making, however, and the council wanted it stopped.

For years, Lutheran rumor-mongers had attributed the council's policies to the alleged covert machinations of the Jesuits. The Lutheran backlash against the Catholic religious orders only intensified after 1601, when the Fugger family helped the Capuchin order establish a mission in Augsburg.[115] The Capuchins' poverty and piety had won them much admiration among the city's Catholics and Protestants alike, but their public profile also provided a ready target for their detractors. Polemicists revived the long-standing Protestant caricature of the hypocritical, greedy friar, who begged alms from credulous believers to fund a life of excess. This image played on both the Protestant public's distrust of the Catholic clergy and its scorn for public begging. Thus, malcontents in Augsburg's Lutheran community found it a perfect vehicle through which to channel their resentment of the Catholic religious orders' presence in civic life.

The slanders against the Capuchins were merely one expression of the increasingly polemical and polarized relations between Catholics and Protestants in the early seventeenth century. Since the mid-sixteenth

---

[113] StAA, Strafamt, Urg. Christof Peter, 22 June 1610.

[114] Mair, 'Diarium,' p. 57 fn. 2.

[115] A small group of Capuchin friars first arrived in Augsburg in 1600 at the invitation of Marcus Fugger, but their presence was initially kept secret. In 1601, however, Fugger purchased property for a Capuchin church and cloister near the city's cathedral. The building was dedicated in 1602. See Grünsteudel et al, *Augsburger Stadtlexikon*, p. 546.

century, Catholic and Protestant authorities across the Empire had worked, with varying degrees of success, to define their churches' respective identities and shape the confessional consciousness of the common folk.[116] As confessional identities crystallized, religious divisions were thrown into sharper relief. In Augsburg, as in the rest of the Empire, the hardening of confessional boundaries tended to escalate the violence of the rhetoric between the communities. Through speech, symbols, prints, and songs, Catholics and Protestants in Augsburg each asserted the primacy of their own beliefs in the city's spiritual and public life. While the council tried to keep the peace, individual Catholics and Lutherans fought an increasingly hostile war of words and music.

The Capuchins, having stumbled into the fray in 1601, were soon the unwitting targets of a polemical assault. A nasty rumor about the Capuchins was circulating in Augsburg and kept reappearing in conversations, songs, and print. Where was it coming from, and how did it start? The council wanted to know.

An anonymous song, allegedly circulating in Augsburg since 1600, told how the Capuchins begged alms to finance their liaisons with prostitutes. Sung to the tune of the Lutheran hymn *Lord Keep Us Steadfast in Thy Word* (*Erhalt Uns Herr, Bei Deinem Wort*),[117] the *New Song about the Capuchins, Who Came to the City of Augsburg in the Year 1600* (*Neues Lied, von den Capußinern so Anno 1600: In die Statt Augspürg kommen*)[118] told how the Antichrist spawned the Capuchins to oppress the true church. The Capuchins were good Catholics, the song confirmed—they wear sheep's clothing, but have the hearts of wolves. They twist God's Word and call from the pulpit for the murder of Lutherans; they say Luther's teaching is damned and seduce the people. Begging from house to house, they use the alms they begged to seduce other men's wives and to pay their whores. The song denounced the Capuchins as "Bacon Boys" (*Spechbueben*)— in other words, slippery-tongued liars—and "Alms Abusers" (*Almueßen Schender*).[119] According to the song, the Capuchins' crimes were common

---

[116] On the confessionalization thesis and its limitations, see the Introduction.

[117] This hymn was itself banned in Augsburg and in many other areas as a violation of the Peace of Augsburg. See Robert Dollinger, 'Erhalt uns Herr, bei deinem Wort!' in *Zeitschrift für bayerische Kirchengeschichte*. 29 (1960): 33–42 and E. Hopp, 'Zur Geschichte des Liedes "Erhalt uns Herr bei deinem Wort,' *Beiträge zur bayerischen Kirchengeschichte* 7 (1901): 79–87.

[118] SStBA, 4° Aug. Cod. 196, *Capuziner nach Augspurg kommen anno. 1600. e. Neües Lied, von den Capußinern so Anno 1600: In die Statt Augspürg kommen. Im Thon. Erhalt uns her beÿ deinem Wort, unnd stürß des Bapsts, und Türckhens mord. Psalm: 84.*

[119] 'Speck,' in *An Historical Dictionary of German Figurative Usage*, ed. Keith Spalding, Fasc. 41–50 (Oxford: Blackwell Publishers, 1991), pp. 2288–9; 'Speckbube,' in

knowledge, but no one was allowed to discuss them. God, however, would preserve the faithful from their influence.

This portrait of the Capuchins as "Bacon Boys" enjoyed considerable popularity in certain quarters. In February, 1602, school teacher Johannes Eberhart was arrested after he repeated a story about the Capuchins in a local tavern. According to the accusation, Eberhart said that a Capuchin friar from the Catholic church of Holy Cross begged some pieces of bacon (*Speck*) from a merchant woman in Göggingen. He was next seen with a common prostitute in the Rosenau district, a notorious quarter of brothels and prostitutes.[120] The friar allegedly gave the prostitute the bacon he had begged in payment for her services. According to Eberhart, the prostitute unwittingly tried to sell the bacon back to the same merchant woman who had given it to the friar; the lady recognized it as from her own shop and realized what had transpired.

The twist at the end of the story lent it an air of veracity: the merchant woman could testify to the truth of the story because she saw the evidence. The addition of local names and places—the friar from Holy Cross, the merchant woman from Göggingen, and the whore from Rosenau—also gave the tale a touch of specificity to bolster its plausibility. However, the story also rehearsed time-worn stereotypes of lecherous, begging mendicants.[121] Thinking that the whole narrative was too neatly contrived, the council's deputies asked Eberhart, "isn't it far more likely that this is just an old fable, such as people have been spreading about monks for many years, before anyone had even heard of the Capuchins?"[122]

Eberhart said that he had first heard this story about six months before from an apprentice in the printer Hans Schultes's shop. The apprentice was a foreigner, whose name Eberhart claimed not to know.[123] Around the same time, Eberhart was drinking a beer with the illustrator (*Briefmaler*) Caspar Krebs in a tavern owned by the beer brewer Zollinger. There were other people there, and Eberhart regaled them with the story he had heard in Schultes's shop. Evidently one of the listeners informed on him, for Eberhart's tale came to the attention of the *Bürgermeister*.[124]

With Eberhart, the council suspected they might have the author of the anonymous song circulating about the "Bacon Boys." Eberhart admitted

---

Deutsches Wörterbuch von Jacob Grimm und Wilhelm Grimm (32 vols. Leipzig: S. Hirzel 1854–1960) vol. 16, p. 2039.

[120] On prostitution in Augsburg, see Lyndal Roper, *The Holy Household: Women and Morals in Reformation Augsburg* (Oxford: Clarendon Press, 1989) pp. 56–89.

[121] Ibid, pp. 104–7.

[122] StAA, Strafamt, Urg. Johannes Eberhart, 25 Feb. 1602, Question Nr. 10.

[123] Ibid.

[124] See Report of *Bürgermeister*, filed ibid.

he had heard of the song, but had never seen it. The *Strafherren* pressed: "didn't he write the song himself?" they asked, "for it certainly wouldn't be too hard for him, since he goes about saying the same thing."[125] He swore that he had never written a song in his life, but the council did not believe him. They wanted the name of the mysterious printer's apprentice and the author of the song. Threatened with torture three days later, Eberhart stood by his story, denying any further knowledge of the song or the apprentice who told him the story.[126] Unable to proceed further, the council released him with a warning, accounting his imprisonment as a punishment.[127]

The council had evidently hoped that Eberhart's testimony would lead them to the source of the scandalous song making the rounds in Augsburg, and the evidence suggests that they may have had good reason to suspect him. Eberhart's presence in Hans Schultes's print shop and his beer drinking with Caspar Krebs indicates that he had contacts in the book world, and may have had reason to know who was dealing in the prohibited song. He may also have been the author and used his contacts with Schultes and Krebs to get it printed. On the other hand, both Eberhart and the printer's apprentice may have simply repeated and expanded upon a story that was already "in the air" in Augsburg, as so many others later did. Unfortunately, the source of the song remains unclear, although the testimony of later witnesses suggests that many in Augsburg traced its story to Zollinger's tavern.[128]

After 1602, the story of the Capuchin "Bacon Boys" began showing up in many different guises. Tobias Wunderer was arrested in 1603 on charges that he had told a young Catholic apprentice in a tavern that the Capuchins "have bacon" and that they kept whores with it.[129] Wunderer denied it, noting that he had only observed that everyone in the city said the Capuchins lied like "crooks and thieves."[130]

The story appeared again in 1604, this time in the medium of song. The council arrested Jacob Bentele in February 1604 for repeating "here and there" that the Capuchins "have bacon" and that they and their faith

---

[125] Ibid, Question Nr. 14.
[126] Ibid., 28 Feb. 1602.
[127] StAA, Strafbuch Nr. 103, 1596–1605, fol. 167r.
[128] Bernd Roeck concluded that Krebs took the story Eberhart told him in the tavern and published it as a song, but there is no evidence that Krebs ever printed it. Roeck, *Eine Stadt in Krieg und Frieden*, p. 370.
[129] StAA, Strafamt, Urg. Tobias Wunderer, 17 Jan. 1603.
[130] Ibid. Wunderer was sentenced to eight days' imprisonment in a tower for his comments. StAA, Strafbuch Nr. 103, 1596–1605, fol. 200v.

were devoted to the Devil.[131] Under questioning by the *Strafherren*, Bentele confirmed that there was also a song circulating in Augsburg on this very theme. He identified the author as a local master named "Zochelin," but stated that he had not learned the song personally from Zochelin; he had only heard it sung by strangers. He also admitted telling people that the author of this song had been arrested for it, but that the council had been forced to release him after the song's accusations against the Capuchins had been proven to be true. He admitted that he did not know whether the story was true and swore that he would not repeat such rumors again. The council ordered him expelled from the city.[132]

Several months later, the authorities confiscated copies of the song in connection with the arrest of the weaver Michael Sangel. Sangel had been hauled before the *Bürgermeister* in December 1604 for calling Hans Schuester, a convert to Catholicism, a "thieving Capuchin" and a "fallen Christian" during a quarrel.[133] During the course of his interrogation, Sangel admitted that he had sung a "shameful song about the Capuchins," and claimed that he had gotten the song from young Hans Knöpflin. Sangel stated that he had given his only copy away to another weaver, Sixt Eherer. Eherer gave the song, in Sangel's handwriting, to the *Bürgermeister* and testified that Sangel had left the copy in his house against his wishes.[134] Knöpflin denied giving Sangel the song, but admitted that he heard Sangel sing it about four years before (that is, around 1600). He had been too young at that time to fully understand it, he told the *Bürgermeister*, but now he found it offensive.[135]

The song Eherer turned over, entitled *A New Song About the New Creatures of the Antichrist in Rome* (*Ein Newes Lied von den Newen Creathuren des Antechristens zu Rohm*)[136] was a slightly re-worked version of the earlier *New Song about the Capuchins, who came to the City of Augsburg in the Year 1600*.[137] Although sung to a different tune (the Lutheran Christmas song *Praise Be To You, Jesus Christ* (*Gelobet Seist Du, Jesu Christ*)),[138] the song recited many of the same accusations made against the Capuchins in the earlier song, including that the Capuchins were

---

[131] StAA, Strafamt, Urg. Jacob Bentele, 11 Feb. 1604.
[132] StAA, Strafbuch Nr. 103, 1596–1605, fol. 237v.
[133] StAA, Strafamt, Urg. Michael Sangel, 29 Dec. 1604 to 7–12 Jan. 1605.
[134] Statement of Sixt Eherer and Hans Knöpflin, dated 31 December 1604, filed ibid.
[135] Ibid.
[136] *Ein Newes Lied von den Newen Creathuren des Antechristens zu Rohm*, filed ibid.
[137] SStBA, 4° Aug. Cod. 196, *Capuziner nach Augspurg kommen anno. 1600. e. Neües Lied, von den Capußinern so Anno 1600: In die Statt Augspürg kommen*. See discussion, above.
[138] *Deutsches Evangelisches Kirchen-Gesangbuch* (1854) (Köln: Themen, 1995) p. 7.

"Bacon Boys" amassing great wealth from their begging and collecting both money and sexual favors from their female benefactors. The song also charged that the Capuchins were building a "nest" in Augsburg, thanks to the Fuggers' endowment of a cloister for them, and planned to expel other citizens to make room for them.

Two days later, *Bürgermeister* Welser sent a report to the *Stadtpfleger*, along with the song and Sangel's *Urgicht*. Welser noted that the sixth verse—criticizing the Fuggers—was particularly offensive.[139] Since the authorities were coming across so many of such "calumnies and lampoons," the *Bürgermeister* felt that a full investigation was warranted.[140]

The *Stadtpfleger* evidently agreed, for Sangel was questioned on two more occasions, including one interrogation under the threat of the *strappado*. The *Strafherren* confronted Sangel with the song turned over by Eherer: since the song was in his handwriting, they noted, he must be the author. Sangel denied it, swearing that he had merely copied it from the text Knöpflin had given him. He gave his copy to Eherer, at Eherer's request, and Knöpflin's copy to Ludwig Mair; he had otherwise distributed the song to no one else. The *Strafherren* then confronted him with Knöpflin, but both men held to their contradictory stories. Five days later, the *Strafherren* interrogated Sangel again. This time, the council instructed that Sangel be questioned while bound in the *strappado*, "but not lifted." Sangel stuck to his story even under the threat of torture, swearing that he had never given Knöpflin "so much as a single letter of the alphabet."[141] Five days later, Knöpflin got a taste of the *Strafherren*'s questioning.[142] Knöpflin, however, also stuck to his story, insisting that Sangel had given him the song. Faced with conflicting testimony and no confessions, the council had no alternative but to release them both.[143] By that time, Sangel had been jailed for almost a month.

The testimonies of Bentele and Sangel, although not revealing the source of the song, provide clues as to how it circulated through Augsburg. Bentele had learned the song, he said, "from strangers." They may indeed have been strangers to him, or he may have wished to keep their names from the *Strafherren*. Whoever they were, they told Bentele that the author was a master in Augsburg and was named "Zochelin." They also told him that the author had been arrested for it but released. This account of the origin of the song recalls the case of Johannes Eberhart, who had been

---

[139] Unsigned report dated 2 Jan. 1605, filed in StAA, Strafamt, Urg. Michael Sangel, 29 Dec. 1604 to 7–12 Jan. 1605.
[140] Ibid.
[141] Ibid., 12 Jan. 1605.
[142] StAA, Strafamt, Urg. Hans Knöpflin, 17 Jan. 1605.
[143] StAA, Strafbuch Nr.103, 1596–1605, fol. 271v–272r.

arrested for repeating its story but released with merely a warning. Eberhart had told the story in the tavern of Zollinger, a master beer-brewer.[144] It is possible that, by the time the story worked its way to Bentele, the master Zollinger had become the master "Zochelin," and "Zochelin's" story had been conflated with Eberhart's. Like Eberhart, "Zochelin" had been arrested on suspicion of writing the song, and like Eberhart, the council had released him. By the time Bentele heard the story, the author's release had been substantially reworked. Instead of the warning and sentence of "time served" the council gave to Eberhart, "Zochelin" was fully vindicated, having convinced even the council that the song told the truth. Despite the triumphal ending, the "Zochelin" story preserves enough of Eberhart's story to suggest a connection. It is very likely that word of Eberhart's case had spread in the community and that he was assumed to have been the author. He was, after all, convicted for it.

It would be tempting to speculate that, somewhere in the rumors, there may have been some element of truth, for Eberhart's neighbors might be expected to know whether he was the author or not. It is equally likely, however, that the rumor simply grew out of the council's prosecution of Eberhart and reflects nothing more about his authorship than the council's own judgment against him. Still, the cases establish how stories circulated and developed within Augsburg. By the time Sangel was arrested, the song had been reworked and circulated in numerous manuscript versions from hand to hand. No one could say for sure where the song originated or even where he got his copies. The story of the song's origin had become almost as much of a polemical myth (heroic songwriter vindicated for speaking the truth about evil Capuchins) as the song itself. In the Augsburg streets, myth built upon myth, such that the authorities had only a slim chance of tracing the truth to its source.

Conclusions

While modern historians have sometimes hailed the Peace of Augsburg as a milestone in the history of religious toleration,[145] early modern Germans understood it to be a narrowly crafted and fragile compromise. It endorsed

---

[144] StAA, Strafamt, Urg. Valentin Sollinger, 7 Jan. 1598.

[145] For recent analyses of the treaty's historical and contemporary significance, see Wolfgang Wüst, Georg Kreuzer, and Nicola Shümann, eds, *Der Augsburger Religionsfriede 1555. Ein Epochenerignis und seine regionale Verankerung* (Augsburg: Wißner, 2005); Heinz Schilling and Heribert Smolinsky, *Der Augsburger Religionsfrieden 1555* (Münster: Aschendorff, 2007).

neither liberty of conscience nor the equal dignity of all faiths.[146] Nor was the Peace of Augsburg particularly innovative. In many ways, the treaty looked backwards, recalling age-old values of Christian brotherhood. It also found its legal force in long-held understandings of the law of libel. By joining the ideal of Christian amity with the legal proscription of defamation, the Peace of Augsburg emerged as a potent weapon in the confessional battles of the early modern age.

The debates over the use of the Peace of Augsburg to regulate confessional discourse and mold opinion nonetheless help to explain how the ideal of religious self-determination and confessional peace came to be elevated as a constitutional mandate to later generations. Whether authorities used the Peace of Augsburg to fight their confessional battles or bridge the religious divide, all sides justified their actions in the treaty's call for "Christian amity" between the two faiths. The Peace of Augsburg's fundamental principle—that Catholics and Lutherans should each be allowed the peaceful practice of their faiths without interference or intimidation—quickly evolved into an imperial prohibition on polemical insult and invective between the confessions.

As the scope of the treaty's protections were far from clear, it gave both Catholic and Lutheran authorities the legal mandate to silence their confessional critics in the name of keeping the Peace. These conflicts over the meaning of the Peace of Augsburg put the treaty's call to religious accommodation at the very center of debate within the Empire. As these conflicts found resolution in the courts and in the political settlements ending the Thirty Years' War, they helped not only to clarify the scope of the Peace of Augsburg's protections but also to affirm its principles of religious self-determination and co-existence within the Empire's constitution.

In the biconfessional cities, the Peace of Augsburg was both a legal weapon to suppress religious invective and a didactic tool to foster confessional coexistence. By policing the making of converts and the conduct of religious discourse under the Peace of Augsburg, the Augsburg authorities sought to both preserve the peace between the confessions and undergird the religious settlement that defined the bounds of both groups and protected their rights.

The authority of the Peace of Augsburg, first invoked by the council in the 1560s, became an ever more important instrument in the council's efforts to keep the peace in the confessional age. When religious tensions erupted in Augsburg, however, the Peace of Augsburg would also become an important symbol and propaganda weapon for opponents of the council's policies.

---

[146] On the history of religious toleration in the early modern era, see Kaplan, *Divided By Faith*.

Despite the council's efforts to preserve the Religious Peace, its carefully crafted religious policies were increasingly contested. The confessional boundaries that had been drawn in the sixteenth century hardened in the early years of the seventeenth century, and with them, the war of words between Catholics and Protestants in Augsburg grew increasingly more intense. As the violence of the rhetoric between both communities escalated, so too did the level of the council's surveillance.

CHAPTER 4

"A Fire Started:" Sedition, Censorship, and the Calendar Conflict

By 1582, it seemed that time itself had gone awry. Over the centuries, errors in the Julian calendar's dating of the vernal equinox had skewed the calculation of the date of Easter, and, as a result, the entire religious year. To address the problem, Pope Gregory XIII commissioned a panel of astronomers to undertake a thorough calendar reform. Adopted by papal decree in February 1582, this new "Gregorian" calendar required that ten days be dropped from the old calendar to bring the year into proper measure. In those lands adopting the new calendar, 4 October 1582 was to be followed immediately by 15 October 1582.[1]

The Gregorian calendar was hailed by astronomers and readily adopted in most Catholic lands. To many Protestants, however, the calendar was suspect. Not only did the pope presume to dictate when the Christian world was to celebrate Easter, he meant to do so by fundamentally reordering the measure of time itself. With papal power deeply contested across Europe, the new calendar was a sweeping assertion of Gregory's authority.[2] Protestant critics worried that it marked a dangerous first step in the pope's eventual reassertion of spiritual authority over their churches. If the pope was permitted to dictate *when* Protestants would worship, might he soon be telling them *how* to worship?

These fears galvanized Protestant opposition to the introduction of the new calendar within the Empire and led the imperial city of Augsburg into one of the most turbulent periods in its history.[3] In the confessionally mixed city, the new calendar became a lightning rod for

---

[1] August Ziggelaar, 'The Papal Bull of 1582 Promulgating a Reform of the Calendar,' in G. V. Coyne, Michael A Hoskin, and O. Pedersen, eds, *Gregorian Reform of the Calendar: Proceedings of the Vatican Conference to Commemorate its 400th Anniversary, 1582–1982* (Vatican City: Pontificia Academia Scientiarum Specola Vaticana, 1983) pp. 201–39.

[2] Ibid., pp. 226–32; Robert Poole, *Time's Alteration: Calendar Reform in Early Modern England* (London: UCL Press, 1998) pp. 38.

[3] Opposition to the Gregorian calendar delayed its adoption in many of the Protestant and eastern churches for some time. See Michael Hoskin, 'The Reception of the Calendar by Other Churches,' in G. V. Coyne, Michael A Hoskin, and O. Pedersen, eds, *Gregorian*

religious confrontation. At stake for the calendar's Protestant critics was the independence of Augsburg's Lutheran churches from Catholic control, a division that they saw as basic to the political settlement of the Peace of Augsburg. This so-called "Calendar Conflict" (*Kalenderstreit*) unleashed mob violence and widespread protest, ultimately culminating in the city council's expulsion of Augsburg's Lutheran clergy and the appointment of replacements more amenable to its control. The ensuing debate over the council's right to appoint and discipline Lutheran clerics helped redefine the scope of governmental authority in spiritual affairs. The Calendar Conflict also exposed serious rifts regarding the council's implementation of the Peace of Augsburg. Given that the Peace of Augsburg undergirded the council's bi-confessional policies, any doubts about the council's commitment to that settlement fundamentally called its legitimacy into question. The disorder accompanying the new calendar helped crystallize confessional identity in the city, widening the divide between Catholic and Protestant and severely testing the council's incorporative policies. In the public controversy surrounding the calendar, Augsburgers revealed how deeply they had internalized the Peace of Augsburg's values, but also how differently they had come to interpret that document's guarantees.

Augsburg's Calendar Conflict also highlights the ways in which rumor, song, and print combined to feed dissent and frustrate official control. While the storm of protest sharpened governmental watchfulness over the expression of dissent, the magistrates' investigations laid bare the social networks through which seditious rumor and gossip traveled, as well as the inter-regional channels through which illegal prints moved in and out of the city. For historians, this tumultuous episode gives us a unique glimpse into how public opinion evolved and responded to official control. For Augsburg, the lessons of the Calendar Conflict guided the city's censorship policies for decades to come.

"The Pope's Lying New Calendar:" Rumor and Rebellion over Calendar Reform

In its public pronouncements, the city council presented its adoption of the new calendar as a matter of simple economic necessity. The Gregorian calendar had already been introduced in neighboring Bavaria, and Augsburg's commercial interests dictated that the city operate on the same timetable. Moreover, the council noted, the Lutherans' own *Book of Concord* affirmed that the celebration of feast days was *adiaphora*, an

---

Reform of the Calendar pp. 255–65, and Owen Gingerich, 'The Civil Reform of the Gregorian Calendar,' ibid., pp. 265–79.

inessential matter of religious custom on which Protestants could remain indifferent. Given the compelling economic need and the religiously neutral nature of the changes, a majority in the council saw no ground for confessional division on the issue. The leaders of Augsburg's Lutheran community, however, argued that acceptance of the new calendar would require them, in essence, to acknowledge the Pope's authority to define the celebration of the ritual year within the Lutheran churches. To these critics, the calendar violated the terms of the Religious Peace of Augsburg, which they interpreted as granting the Lutheran churches exclusive authority to define their own rituals and practices without interference or hindrance from the Catholic Church. As a violation of the Religious Peace, it represented a breach of the consensus on which the very community was thought to have been founded.

In protest of the council's decision, four Lutheran members of the Great Council made public their opposition. The three church wardens (*Kirchenpfleger*) appointed to oversee the city's Lutheran clergy also presented a *Supplicatio* to the council setting forth their objections, which the clergy affirmed in a joint protest read from their pulpits during Sunday services.[4] In March 1583, the Imperial Cameral Court, acting on a petition from the Augsburg church wardens, set aside the city council's January decision to adopt the calendar, holding it a violation of the Religious Peace of Augsburg. The Cameral Court enjoined the council from implementing any changes until the calendar was either approved by an assembly of the Imperial estates or clearly accepted by the Lutheran side.[5]

In October 1583, however, Emperor Rudolf II ordered implementation of the new calendar throughout the Empire. By now, debate on the calendar had moved out of the churches and courts and into the city's streets. Murmuring against the new calendar reached such a pitch in Augsburg that the council found it necessary to issue a public warning. Noting that seditious talk was now being heard even from the city's pulpits, the council cautioned its subjects against sowing unrest.[6]

Fearing that the controversy could topple the city government, the emperor appointed a commission in late October 1583 to investigate.[7] Others shared the emperor's assessment of the danger. A placard found

---

[4] Ferdinand Kaltenbrunner, 'Der Augsburger Kalenderstreit,' in *Mitteilungen der Institut für österreichische Geschichtsforschung* I (1880): pp. 504–5.

[5] Ibid., pp. 507–8. On this litigation, see Ehrenpreis, *Kaiserliche Gerichtsbarkeit*, pp. 196–203.

[6] SStBA, 2′ Aug. 10, "Ordnungen, Decreten, Verrüffe und Anschläge, 1522–1677," fol. 238–62.

[7] Kaltenbrunner, 'Der Augsburger Kalenderstreit,' p. 514. The Imperial Commissioners were Duke Wilhelm of Bavaria, Count Philipp Ludwig of the Palatinate, and the Imperial *Reichspfennig-Meister*, Johann Achilles Ilsung.

at the city hall warned ominously of a revolution if the calendar were adopted. According to the writer, Augsburg's civic order hinged on the council's repudiation of "the pope's lying new calendar":

> We in the community have long seen, my Lords, what sort of peace the Pope's lying new calendar makes in the city of Augsburg, and [we will see to it that] it will not make a priests' city of Augsburg. If the calendar is not done away with, then we in the community will become strong enough to take action. This should give my Lords cause to consider, so that you may preserve yourselves from harm, and so that we may live together in peace still longer. [Otherwise] you will see a fire started against those who have helped in this, both secular and clerical, especially the Devil's dogs, the Jesuits. We will break down again what they and their supporters have built up. God will support it, and [establish] a Christian government.[8]

The threatening placard raised a number of charges that would bedevil the city council throughout the Calendar Conflict. The calendar's association with the papacy made it suspect in Lutheran eyes;[9] in the broadsheets and rumors that circulated in the Augsburg streets, it was simply "the pope's calendar," and, as such, it was inherently unsound, ungodly, and perhaps even diabolical. The council's adoption of "the pope's calendar" confirmed, for some of its detractors, the government's connivance in a Jesuit-backed conspiracy to reassert papal control over the city. For those Protestants who resented the political hegemony of the Catholics in the city council, such rumors reinforced their doubts of the council's evenhandedness between the confessions. To some, a rebellion seemed to offer the only hope of restoring legitimate government.

Throughout the Calendar Conflict, such rumors swirled through the Augsburg Lutheran community, fueled by fiery preachers and polemical prints. While the city council took steps to squelch the talk spreading throughout the city, these efforts were stymied by the ease with which the stories spread. Despite the authorities' efforts, subversive stories and seditious texts were widely circulated. Together, they fed speculation in the taverns and workshops where people gadded and gossiped.

---

[8] Bernd Roeck, *Eine Stadt in Krieg und Frieden: Studien zur Geschichte der Reichsstadt Augsburg zwischen Kalenderstreit und Parität* (Göttingen: Vanderhoeck & Ruprecht, 1989) p. 128.

[9] Even commentators who claimed to support the new calendar predicted a Protestant backlash against its papal associations; see, for example, *Kurzer Bericht/von gemeinem Kalender, Woher er kommen/wie er mit der zeit verrückt/ob und wie er widerumb zuersetzen sey. Auß anlaß der Päpstlichen newlich außgegangen Kalenders Reformation* (Neustadt: Harnisch, 1583), p. Biir [StBU, Schad 4322].

While rumors were a basic feature of urban life, the political and religious environment of the Calendar Conflict created a particularly fertile breeding ground for rumors of the most dangerous sort. As social psychologists have noted, rumors thrive in times of crisis, when events are of vital interest but news is typically lacking or unreliable.[10] While many saw Augsburg's basic political and religious order at issue in the adoption of the new calendar, the confusion surrounding its introduction invited speculation as to its real purpose. Although the council tried to explain its rationale in public pronouncements and shows of authority, its deliberations were far removed from the public eye, and its policy unfolded in fits and starts. Throughout the 1580s, the introduction of the new calendar proceeded haltingly, subject to continued interference by imperial officials, neighboring princes, and violent protesters. The new calendar was thus introduced into a political climate of confusion and mistrust. In these bewildering times, some people manufactured explanations in stories of political intrigue and religious favoritism. In such an environment, rumors of conspiracy and rebellion fed the public's thirst for news and reassurance.

One favored theme of these rumors, as reflected in the placard at the city hall, was the time-worn Lutheran complaint faulting the Society of Jesus for all the confessional divisions in Augsburg.[11] All had been peaceful before the Jesuit fathers arrived, these critics contended, but they and their supporters on the city council had been bent on returning the city to the Catholic fold. Indeed, Protestant polemics stemming from the Calendar Conflict complained bitterly of the council's alleged violations of Lutheran rights under the Religious Peace and blamed the Jesuits explicitly for the current trouble.[12] In one anonymous dialog from the period, a Protestant weaver complained to a Jesuit that, although Catholics and Protestants had once lived together quietly under the Peace of Augsburg, the Jesuits had sown only discord in the city. This was all the Pope's doing, the weaver exclaimed, for the pope had sent the Jesuits into Augsburg to undo the Religious Peace and to build him a new kingdom.[13] The new calendar was a key element of the pope's plan, these tracts contended: with it, the Jesuits

---

[10] Gordon W. Allport and Leo Postman, *The Psychology of Rumor* (New York: Henry Holt & Co., 1947), p. 2.

[11] On the Jesuit mission in Augsburg and the polemic concerning them, see Chapter 3.

[12] See, for example, Georg Müller, *Augspurgische Handel, So sich daselbsten wegen der Religion/und Sonderlich jüngst vor zwey Jahren im werenden Calender Streit mit Georgen Müller D. Pfarrer und Superintendenten daselbst zugetragen... Sampt Nottwendiger rettung der Unschuld und ehren/wider allerhand beschwerliche Anklag und ungegründte Bezüchtigung/damit die Papisten eine zeitlang ihn D. Müllern fürnemlich beleget haben*. (Wittenberg: Matthes Welack, 1586) [SStBA, 4° Aug 735/2, "Kalenderstreit II," Nr. 25].

[13] StAA, Chronik Nr. 19, 'Chronik der Stadt Augsburg in Sachen der Reformation, 1583–1589,' *Ein gespräch, das ein weber Guet mit einem Jesuwider thuet*, fol. 333(v)–338(r).

would sow discord and confusion, weakening the papacy's opponents and mustering its loyal followers.[14]

How widespread was the "rumor public" sharing in these stories?[15] Those arrested for voicing opposition to the new calendar were almost uniformly Lutheran, but were otherwise a diverse lot. While the majority of individuals arrested were tradesmen and artisans, opposition to the calendar reached across the social spectrum. Indeed, almost all of the city's Lutheran clergy were publicly opposed to the new calendar, as were several prominent members of the patriciate, including some members of the Great Council itself.[16] While it is impossible to measure what proportion of the city's Protestant population shared these views, an imperial investigation into the unrest revealed fairly widespread complaints about the council's policies within the Protestant community, although these grievances were by no means uniform. Far from being marginalized, the calendar's critics found a sympathetic ear in the Protestant princes and estates of the Empire. Indeed, even the Imperial Cameral Court had ruled the calendar violated the Peace of Augsburg.[17] It seems plausible, therefore, that these rumors found a receptive audience among wide segments of the city's Protestant community, and should not be dismissed as simply the agitation of a few isolated troublemakers. Precisely because these stories were accepted and repeated so widely, they proved particularly hard to control.

The city council took steps to squelch the incendiary talk spreading throughout the city, but the rumors seemed to grow with each re-telling, taking on a life of their own in the city streets. By early November 1583, for example, Gideon Mair was telling his neighbors that the Duke of Bavaria, the Bishop of Augsburg, both *Stadtpfleger*, and the "priests' lackeys" in the council had conspired to massacre the Lutherans in their churches as a prelude to forcibly converting the city to Catholicism. His source for this information? Some Bavarian farmers he had met at the local baker's shop. Under torture, he confessed that a shoemaker named Widenmann had also told him that the Duke, the bishop, and the council had agreed to expel the Lutheran clergy and force all citizens to accept Catholicism. He spread

---

[14] *Newe Zeytung/Warhafftige und eigentliche Beschreibung/von den view geistlosen Meüdmachern/unnd auffrürischen Jesuwidern und Pfaffen/So den Newen Calendar erdacht und zugericht haben/die gantze Welt damit in unrüh zubringen*. (n.p.: n.p., 1584) [BL, T. 731.(8)]; Eric Nelson, 'The Jesuit Legend: Superstition and Myth-Making,' in *Religion and Superstition in Reformation Europe*, eds Helen Parish and William G. Naphy (Manchester: Manchester University Press, 2002) pp. 94–115.

[15] Allport and Postman, *The Psychology of Rumor*, pp. 180–84.

[16] See, for example, Christof Hörmann's account of the widespread opposition to the calendar among the city's patriciate at StAA, Strafamt, Urg. Christof Hörmann, 11 Jan. 1588, discussed infra.

[17] Kaltenbrunner, 'Der Augsburger Kalenderstreit,' pp. 507–8.

the story through the neighborhood, and soon every house on the street was armed against the expected attack.[18] A local smith named Peter Eisele reportedly even went from shop to shop, organizing resistance, and said that if they were strong enough, they could overtake the city guard and attack the *Stadtpfleger* and the council members.[19]

Mair's testimony led the authorities to the shoemaker Christof Widenmann, who admitted, under threat of torture, having told Mair that the city council planned to forcibly impose Catholicism in Augsburg. He had also boasted that, when the trouble started, he wanted to help kill all the monks, priests, and Jesuits. Widenmann had told Mair "roughly" that if fighting broke out, he himself wanted to help throw the council members out of the city hall windows. He denied any intent to incite a riot, however, and expressed his hope that the council would not take his comments seriously.[20]

Unfortunately for Widenmann, the council always took threats of violence extremely seriously, and talk of insurrection even more so. The council suspected him to be the author of a seditious placard left at the city hall, the jail, and St Anna's church a few days before. Widenmann denied any knowledge of it, but after three hoists in the *strappado*, he admitted that he had seen the pasquinade posted on St Anna's, but had not read it. Threatened with further torture, Widenmann admitted posting it himself, and even admitted writing it when the executioner added weights to the rope. He could not, however, describe the contents of the placard and ultimately admitted he had confessed to writing and posting it only to escape further torment. His interrogators sent him back to his cell, noting "the longer he is tortured, the more inconstant in his speech he becomes."[21]

Acting on the rumors of rebellion, the council in late 1583 ordered the city's *Stadtvogt*, Augustin Weissier, to enlist a troop of soldiers for the city's defense.[22] Rumors of an impending attack against the Lutheran churches continued to circulate, however, despite the council's aggressive prosecution of individuals repeating such talk. By January 1584, the story had been embellished even more—the servant Hans Schwemmer claimed, for example, to have heard the details of the planned attack from city officials privy to the plot. According to Schwemmer, council member Octavius Fugger had told Dr Lucas Stenglin that the council "would teach the Protestants well to accept the new calendar" by attacking them in their

---

[18] StAA, Strafamt, Urg. Gideon Mair, 9 Nov. 1583.
[19] Ibid.
[20] StAA, Strafamt, Urg. Christof Widenmann, 10 Nov. 1583.
[21] Ibid., Urg. 11 Nov. 1583.
[22] Roeck, *Eine Stadt in Krieg und Frieden*, p. 129.

churches.²³ Schwemmer admitted to the *Strafherren* that he had made up much of the story, but explained that the tense situation in the city had made him anxious.²⁴ By falsely attributing the story to the prominent patricians Stenglin and Fugger, however, Schwemmer had lent the rumor an air of authority that dramatically bolstered its credibility, for named witnesses in a position to know the facts could presumably confirm the truth of the story. This kernel of apparently hard evidence could be a persuasive factor in public acceptance of rumor,²⁵ a reality that the *Strafherren* recognized as "no small matter, but something that might develop into a greater evil."²⁶

Where had these stories originated? The rumors of a Catholic conspiracy perhaps fed on Protestant memories of the notorious St Bartholomew's Day massacre of 1572, which, as was well known, Pope Gregory XIII had celebrated with a public *Te Deum* and the issuance of commemorative medals.²⁷ Those who remembered Gregory's public exultation over the murder of Protestants in France might doubt his good intentions now.²⁸ Was the calendar merely a prelude to another attack against unwitting Protestants? Should Augsburg's Protestants plan to strike first for their own defense?²⁹

Fearing trouble, the Austrian Archduke Ferdinand II directed the recruitment of another 1,000 soldiers in March 1584. The presence of expensive foreign troops stirred up further resentment among the financially strapped citizens of Augsburg,³⁰ but further troubles were in store. Within two months, the Imperial Cameral Court reversed itself, concluding that the new calendar did not infringe on the Peace of Augsburg. While many of the Protestant members of the council accepted the court's decision, some of the Protestant citizenry did not. On 3 June 1584, the Lutheran clergy announced from their pulpits that they would celebrate the coming Ascension Day

---

²³ StAA, Strafamt, Urg. Hans Schwemmer, 20 Jan. 1584.

²⁴ Ibid.

²⁵ Tamotsu Shibutani, *Improvised News: A Sociological Study of Rumor* (Indianapolis: Bobbs-Merrill,1966), pp. 76–86; R. W. Scribner, *For the Sake of Simple Folk: Popular Propaganda for the German Reformation* (Cambridge: Cambridge University Press, 1981) p. xxiii.

²⁶ Undated report of *Strafherren*, filed in StAA, Strafamt, Urg. Hans Schwemmer, 20 Jan. 1584. Schwemmer was expelled from the city. StAA, Strafbuch Nr. 101, fol. 107r.

²⁷ Tlusty, *The Martial Ethic in Early Modern Germany*, pp. 249–51.

²⁸ On public perceptions of the massacre, see Robert M. Kingdon, *Myths About the St. Bartholomew's Day Massacres 1572–1576* (Cambridge, MA: Harvard University Press, 1988) pp. 41–2; 107–24; Peter Burschel, 'Das Heilige und die Gewalt. Zur frühneuzeitlichen Deutung von Massakern,' in *Archiv für Kulturgeschichte* 86(2) (2004) pp. 341–68.

²⁹ For an analysis of the role of rumors of an planned assault on Protestants in fueling the Calendar Conflict, see Tlusty, *The Martial Ethic in Early Modern Germany*, pp. 251–64.

³⁰ Roeck, *Eine Stadt in Krieg und Frieden*, pp. 129–30.

according to the old calendar. Recognizing the power of the pulpit, the council's informants had been monitoring the contents of sermons preached at the city's Lutheran churches. The city attorney, Dr Georg Tradel, dutifully collected the preachers' more subversive remarks and passed them on to the *Stadtpfleger*, Anton Christoph Rehlinger.[31] The council responded with an order banning observance of the announced holiday.[32]

The following day, the council ordered the expulsion of Dr Georg Müller, the Lutheran superintendent of St Anna's and the council's most vehement critic.[33] In its order, the council noted that Müller had publicly condemned the council members as "tyrants" and "hypocrites" and had fomented unrest and disobedience against the government. The council condemned Müller with his own writings, noting that he had published a text in Cologne in which he had argued that the citizenry had the right to both create and overthrow its own government.[34]

For this seditious talk, the council ordered the *Stadtvogt* to eject Müller from Augsburg on the afternoon of 4 June 1584. Müller's arrest had evidently been expected, however, and a large crowd gathered in protest outside his home. As the *Stadtvogt* escorted Müller away, the mob blocked the carriage and freed him (See Fig. 4.1). Müller's supporters smuggled him to safety, while news of the riot spread throughout the city.[35] A crowd assembled in the poor *Jacober* neighborhood and attempted to push their way into the upper city, where the council had ordered the closing of the city's interior gates. Finding an opening, the crowd rushed into the heart of the city. Assembling before the Jesuit school, the protestors made their way toward the city hall, where the council had assembled its troops. Warning shots were fired, answered by musket fire from some of the rioters. The *Stadtvogt* was wounded in the arm. With the help of the Lutheran clergy, the crowd eventually dispersed, although the city remained tense for several days.[36]

---

[31] See, for example, the series of notes reporting on the contents of sermons preached at St Anna's during this period collected at StAA, Religionsakten, 1574–1793.

[32] Roeck, *Eine Stadt in Krieg und Frieden*, p. 130.

[33] Müller sometimes published under the name Georg Mylius.

[34] StAA, Ratsbüch Nr. 44, 1584–1586, fol. 38r; Georg Mylius, *Christlicher Sendtbreiff an einen ersamen wolweisen Raht, der uhralten loblichen frei Reichsstadt Cölln, welcher hiemit trewhertzig vermanet und hochflehenlich gebeten wirdt, der Unterthanen daselbs, so der Augspurgischen Confession ... zugethan, mit Verfolgung zu verschonen ...* (Heidelberg: Johann Spies, 1582).

[35] Müller fled first to Ulm and ultimately took up posts on the theological faculties at Wittenberg and Jena. He continued to publish for the remainder of his life, including treatises directed against the Augsburg city council. On Müller, see Kenneth G. Appold, *Orthodoxie als Konsensbildung. Das theologische Disputationswesen an der Universität Wittenberg zwischen 1570–1710* (Tübingen: Mohr Siebeck, 2004) pp. 193–204.

[36] Roeck, *Eine Stadt in Krieg und Frieden*, pp. 130–31; Tlusty, *The Martial Ethic in Early Modern Germany*, pp. 258–62.

Figure 4.1 Broadsheet depicting the rescue of Georg Müller and ensuing riot in Augsburg, April 1584 (SStBA, Graphik 22/12, *Wahrhaffte fürstellung der begebenheit so sich A 1584 d. 25 Mai mit Herrn D. Georg Müller gewesenen Pfarrer beÿ St. Anna, auch Superintendens und Rector des Evangelische Collegii zugetragen...* [np: np, nd]).

In response to the riot, representatives from Ulm and Duke Ludwig of Württemberg arrived in Augsburg to help negotiate a settlement of the Calendar Conflict. Pursuant to a compromise reached on 14 June 1584, the council extended a general pardon to all except the leaders of the riot, and the Lutheran clergy agreed to accept the new calendar. The Lutheran church wardens were released from house arrest but relieved of their offices.[37]

Although the feared revolution had never materialized and significant bloodshed had been averted, the so-called "Müller riot" profoundly affected Augsburg for decades to come. Müller's expulsion and the ensuing riot became a rallying point for Augsburg's disgruntled Lutherans, who celebrated it in song and verse as righteous resistance to a tyrannical city council seeking to trample Protestant rights. In these texts, Müller became a Protestant hero; his wife, who had suffered a miscarriage and died after the riot, was celebrated as a martyr. As a symbol of resistance to the council's oppression, Müller galvanized popular dissent on a scale far greater than his work as a mere preacher and occasional author had ever allowed.

The council tried repeatedly to suppress all mention of Müller and the anti-government, anti-Catholic cause he came to symbolize. The council tried also to monitor public dissent more closely. Murmuring against the council had preceded the riot, and it clearly saw this seditious talk as the seed of the revolt. For years to come, memories of the Müller riot sharpened the city council's response to dissent and led to a regulatory environment of increasing suspicion and control.

In the weeks following the riot, the council tried to silence Müller's supporters. Many citizens, however, made no secret of their support for Müller. Martin Heigele, a carpenter from Pfersee, was accused of having told his neighbors that the magistrates had acted like "rogues and oppressors" in their treatment of Müller. Under torture, Heigele admitted having said that the council members responsible for Müller's expulsion should be thrown out the windows of the city hall.[38] Although Heigele claimed he was "not at all right in the head," the council ordered him whipped out of the city and banished for life.[39] Georg Fischer was also banished after he was heard to say that "he would stand by the pastors and

---

[37] SStBA, 2° Aug. 10, 'Ordnungen, Decreten, Verrüffe und Anschläge, 1522–1677,' fol. 263–70; Max Radlkofer, 'Die volkstümliche und besonders dichterische Litteratur zum Augsburger Kalenderstreit,' *Beitrage zur bayerischen Kirchengeschichte*. 7 (1901): pp. 8–9; Warmbrunn, *Zwei Konfessionen*, p. 367.

[38] StAA, 'Ad Kalenderstreit Criminalia, 583–1589,' Urg. Martin Heigele, 6 July 1584.

[39] StAA, Strafbuch Nr. 101, 1581–1587, fol. 126v–127v.

give his life for Dr Müller," and that he wanted to kill those responsible for Müller's expulsion.[40]

Support for Müller's cause got a boost from a new conflict between the council and the Lutheran clergy over the appointment of new church wardens. Breaking with a longstanding tradition allowing Lutheran clergy to select their own officials, the Privy Council appointed its own candidates to the two vacant posts. To its critics, the council's assertion of its unilateral authority to appoint Lutheran church officials undermined the independence and privileges of the Lutheran church in violation of the Religious Peace of Augsburg. At stake in this so-called "Vocation Conflict" (*Vokationstreit*) were the same issues looming in the Calendar Conflict: the independence of the Lutheran churches from the interference of a supposedly Catholic-leaning council. One Augsburger accused of speaking out against the council testified that he heard the preachers cry "daily" that the council intended to give them preachers who were not of their religion, and that the entire city was buzzing with reports that the council meant to "wrest from them their religion and their freedom."[41]

Despite the protests, the council's appointees took over as new wardens for the Lutheran churches. Those clergy unwilling to accept the council's authority were ordered to resign their posts and leave the city.[42] All but two of the pastors resigned, and the council replaced them with its own appointees. It ordered the new church wardens to ensure that the new pastors did not preach against the council or otherwise promote unrest or disobedience among the Protestant citizenry.[43] The church wardens were to attend every preachers' assembly to ensure that nothing was discussed that might be deemed "political, disruptive, or otherwise against the government."[44] The council also reminded the new church wardens that both Lutherans and Catholics were permitted in Augsburg; they were to see to it that the new clergy did not preach against the Catholics or otherwise violate the spirit of the Religious Peace of Augsburg.[45]

Despite its efforts, the council faced continuing opposition, and it appealed to Emperor Rudolf II to appoint another imperial commission to help resolve the controversy. The emperor appointed Duke Wilhelm of Bavaria and Count Wilhelm of Öttingen in July 1584 to look into

---

[40] StAA, Strafamt, Urg. Georg Fischer, 9 July 1584; StAA, Strafbuch Nr. 101, 1581–1587, fol. 126r–v.

[41] StAA, 'Ad Kalenderstreit Criminalia,' Urg. Leonhard Österreicher, 1 Nov. 1585.

[42] SStBA, 2° Cod. H. 18, 'Augspurgischer Calendar Streitt von Anno 83 Bis 90,' fol. 479.

[43] Ibid., fol. 480, ¶ ii.

[44] Ibid., fol. 480, ¶ xi.

[45] Ibid., fol. 480, ¶ i.

Augsburg's troubles. As part of their investigation, the commissioners interviewed representatives from the Privy Council, the patriciate, the merchants, and "the community" in early August 1584. Using a standard set of questions with each respondent, the commissioners focused on four essential points:

1. Did they know that some members of the community had sought to overthrow the government?
2. Had the council ever attempted to hinder members of the Lutheran community in the practice of their religion?
3. Did any of them have reason to believe that the council had treated them unjustly?
4. Did they wish to be obedient to this government, and promote unity within the community?[46]

To encourage the deponents to speak freely, the interviews were conducted in secret, and many voiced strong opinions on the issues. The interviews reveal not only the range of opinions within the group, but highlight some of the fundamentally divergent perspectives that divided Protestants from Catholics and the rulers from the ruled on these points. In the eyes of some Catholics, the root of the problems lay simply in Georg Müller's rabble-rousing. He and the other Lutheran clergy had stirred up "the common man" with their intemperate preaching, convincing the common folk that the government sought to force them from their religion.[47] In their view, the Lutheran community was rife with disobedient troublemakers who needed to be taught a lesson.[48] Like many of the Catholic patricians interviewed, Hans and Jacob Fugger saw the Protestants' complaints as a political gambit: a move to force greater control over the city's government into Lutheran hands. "Dr Müller wants to have one foot in the city hall and one foot in the pulpit," Hans Fugger quipped.[49]

The responses of Protestant leaders suggest that political representation was, indeed, a major concern. For Lutheran patricians Anton Felix Welser and Hans Herwart, the problem lay in the Catholics' long domination of

---

[46] StAA, Kalenderstreitacten Nr. 28, 'Relatio. Der Ro: Kay: Mt: verordneter Comissarien der alhie anno 1584 nach dem auflauf verrichter Inquisition und Commission,' fols. 129r–174v. Members of the council and the patriciate were also asked an additional set of questions, essentially fleshing out their answers on the basic points.

[47] Ibid., fol. 131r–132r.

[48] See, for example, StAA, Strafamt, Urg. Onophrius Ursenthaler, 25 April 1586; Martin Krüger, 16 May 1586.

[49] StAA, Kalenderstreitacten Nr. 28, 'Relatio. Der Ro: Kay: Mt: verordneter Comissarien,' fol. 131v–132r: Answer 16.

the council. Emperor Charles V had decreed that power in Augsburg should be shared between Catholics and Protestants "half and half," they said, but they believed the Catholics had manipulated council elections to ensure their control of the government.[50] In fact, Charles V's 1548 constitution had purposely engineered Catholic predominance on the council, but the prevalence of this particular complaint among the Protestant respondents suggests that many in the Lutheran community had a quite different understanding of their legal rights. Relying on the Peace of Augsburg, they were arguing for a strict power-sharing between the confessions that was not in fact established in Augsburg for another 64 years, when the Peace of Westphalia ended the Thirty Years' War. In anticipating a system of true confessional parity in government, the Lutherans were advancing a claim to political participation rooted in the Peace of Augsburg, but well beyond its express guarantees.[51]

Not all of the problems centered on politics, however. Many respondents mentioned the poverty and economic disparity in the city as a factor contributing to the unrest.[52] Others cited the presence of foreign troops.[53] For many, the council had simply been too heavy-handed in its treatment of Müller and the church wardens. Respondents cited the rumors swirling in the city about the Jesuits and the council's supposed plans to forcibly impose Catholicism—in such a climate, they suggested, the expulsion of Müller and the other clergy naturally aroused concern.[54]

Many of the interviewees laid blame on the council's efforts to oversee Lutherans' religious expression. According to some, the council's prohibition of *Lord, Keep Us Steadfast in Thy Word* (*Erhalt Uns Herr Bei Deinem Wort*) and other popular Lutheran hymns contributed to the riot.[55] According to the Protestant patrician Hans Honold, the council simply watched the Lutherans too closely:

> A great mistrust has existed among the citizenry for a while now, and especially since the recent riot ... If someone of the Augsburg Confession drinks a beer

---

[50] Ibid., fol. 138v, 142v.

[51] On the evolution of constitutional parity in Augsburg, see Eberhad Naujoks, 'Vorstufen der Parität in der Verfassungsgeschichte der schwäbischen Reichsstädte (1555–1648). Das Beispiel Augsburgs,' in *Burgerschaft und Kirche*, ed. Jürgen Sydow (Sigmaringen: Jan Thorbecke Verlag, 1980) pp. 39–63.

[52] StAA, Kalenderstreitacten, Nr. 28, fol. 131r, 168r.

[53] Ibid, fol. 142v, 150r–v.

[54] Ibid, fol. 142v, 155r, 159r.

[55] Ibid, fol. 137r, 149v. On the banning of this hymn, see Dollinger, 'Erhalt uns Herr, bei deinem Wort!' in *Zeitschrift für bayerische Kirchengeschichte*. 29 (1960): pp. 33–42; Hopp, 'Zur Geschichte des Liedes "Erhalt uns Herr bei deinem Wort",' in *Beiträge zur bayerischen Kirchengeschichte* 7 (1901): pp. 79–87.

with a good, honest man a mere half a mile out of the city, one of them will be reported to the authorities the next day and be punished for it, while the Catholics, on the other hand, would go unpunished.[56]

The interviews highlighted a deep divide between the council and some segments of the Protestant community. In part, this mistrust arose from the very policies the council had worked so hard to advance since 1555. In stressing the mutual rights and obligations of Catholics and Lutherans under the Peace of Augsburg, the council had sought to promote a spirit of accommodation between the confessions, one in which respect for the Religious Peace was a duty shared by every citizen. The aftermath of the riot revealed that many Protestants also looked to the Peace of Augsburg with the expectation that the confessions would share power, as well. However, the council's rhetoric of civic cooperation did not match the reality of civic governance. Augsburg's 1548 constitution contemplated precisely the opposite of power-sharing, and the council had no mind to change it. Resentful of their comparative disenfranchisement, some members of Augsburg's Protestant community expressed their distrust in wild rumors of Jesuit conspiracies and forced conversion. The council's efforts to suppress such talk only confirmed these suspicions, while widening the divisions between the confessions.

Many Augsburgers feared that the tension between the council and the Protestant citizenry could be resolved only through another violent confrontation. Rumors thrive on fear, and in the unstable aftermath of the Müller riot, some residents expressed their anxiety in speculation and hearsay. The markets were buzzing with rumors of another expulsion of the clergy and another uprising. The fact that both events had already once occurred confirmed the plausibility of these stories in the public mind, making them all the more difficult for the authorities to discount. Warning against those with "poisonous, evil, impudent tongues," the council banned all divisive talk about the riot and the new calendar and ordered all residents to report those who violated its decree.[57]

Rudolph Bosshart's neighbors reported him in August 1584 for talking of another riot. As he was standing in the street in front of his house, Bosshart was allegedly overheard to say that there was no hope for peace in Augsburg and that he could hardly wait until the revolt began. He reportedly vented a litany of complaints against the council and the Roman Catholic clergy, but knew his comments would be betrayed to the council. "I'm not allowed to speak out," Bosshart reportedly said, "because there's

---

[56] StAA Kalenderstreitakten, Nr. 28, fol. 155r.
[57] SStBA, 2° Aug. 10, 'Ordnungen, Decreten, Verrüffe und Anschläge, 1522–1677,' fol. 263–70.

a spy in our midst, but I won't keep silent!"[58] He boasted that even if he were arrested, he would soon be released, for "a community is stronger than a council."[59] Bosshart was indeed reported and arrested, and under questioning, admitted saying that the council had treated Dr Müller "like a thief and a knave," that the council's army wanted only to plunder the citizenry, and that the citizenry would fight to defend themselves. He denied, however, any intent to foment insurrection. He was simply venting his frustrations over the current situation, he said. Under threat of torture, he explained his unease:

> It's true that he has often complained about the unrest here. He is very worried that this will not be settled and everything will fall apart because it has been going on for too long and the tradesmen have no solution, as they didn't solve anything with the last riot; so, he did say that if it will never change, something has to happen soon, but he never said that he wanted it to happen. He would be sad if anything happened, and he meant what he said only as a warning.[60]

For disaffected citizens such as Bosshart, repeating the rumors of a revolt provided a means to critique their government without overtly challenging the council. Given the profound moral imperative of loyalism and public order in civic life, open advocacy of rebellion would have deeply offended communal norms.[61] Hearsay, however, offered a safe means to speculate about unrest without seeming to condone it. As social psychologists have noted, rumors provide an outlet for ideas and emotions that often cannot be faced directly. The rumors' explanatory fictions also help to protect and justify disagreeable ideas.[62] The council's opponents could therefore couch their dissent in the form of hearsay—while safely disclaiming responsibility for their statements.

---

[58] Statement of witnesses, dated 21 Aug. 1584, filed in StAA, Strafamt, Urg. Rudolph Bosshart, 22–31 Aug. 1584. The "spy," Bosshart later explained, was the Catholic priest who lived next door and eavesdropped on all his conversations. Indeed, Bosshart's criminal file contains a sworn statement from three priests, dated one day before his first interrogation, testifying as to the seditious remarks they had overheard Bosshart make against the council, as well as various threats and insults he made against the Roman Catholic clergy.

[59] This slogan had also been a rallying cry during the 1524 protests demanding religious reform. See Chapter 2.

[60] StAA, Strafamt, Urg. Rudolph Bosshart, 31 Aug. 1584.

[61] See Ethan Shagan, *Popular Politics and the English Reformation* (Cambridge: Cambridge University Press, 2003), p. 51.

[62] Allport and Postman, *The Psychology of Rumor*, p. 38.

Opposition to the calendar and the council also thrived on a lively trade in prohibited pamphlets, ballads, and broadsheets, along with a clandestine exchange of illegal manuscripts. These texts moved within an inter-regional network that proved exceedingly difficult for Augsburg authorities to control. The ideas they contained also moved freely between the printed page and the oral culture of the city's streets.

" ... This Müller-ish Zeal and Devotion:" The Spread of Polemic and Protest

While the council worked to stop the rumors flying about the city, it also took steps to suppress the many songs and woodcuts lauding Georg Müller. Müller's expulsion had made him a hero and a martyr in the eyes of his supporters, and the songs and images they made to honor him invariably cast the council and its deputies as godless persecutors. Songs about Müller and woodcuts of him remained popular in Augsburg long after the riot, and the council vigorously prosecuted anyone caught circulating them.

Müller and most of the other exiled clergy found refuge in Ulm, an easy journey from Augsburg.[63] From there, they continued to publish tracts critical of the Augsburg city council and the new clergy. The "old" clergy urged their supporters in Augsburg to boycott the services of the "new" clergy and otherwise resist the council's authority over church affairs. The Augsburg exiles found a welcome reception in Lutheran Ulm, where some of the local pastors even wrote and published ballads on Müller's behalf.[64] Indeed, Ulm proved a valuable source of material for Augsburg booksellers looking for texts commenting on the unrest in Augsburg. While such material was too dangerous to produce at home, it could be easily printed in Ulm or other neighboring cities and imported for sale in Augsburg. Although Ulm had its own censorship apparatus overseeing its book trade,[65] local officials seldom intervened to stop the stream of pro-Müller propaganda flowing through the city. To the extent local censors ruled on this material at all, they tended to favor Müller's cause. In 1584, for example, the Ulm city council investigated a local bookseller for peddling a tract directed *against* Müller.[66] In 1586, local censors allowed Ulm's

---

[63] Müller married his second wife in Ulm in 1583. StAU, G1 1590/2, 'Chronik von Jerg Kraumer,' fol. 41r.

[64] On Ulm's religious policies in these years, see F. Fritz, *Ulmische Kirchengeschichte vom Interim bis zum dreißigjährigen Krieg (1548–1612)* (Stuttgart: Chr. Scheufele, 1934).

[65] Elmar Schmitt and Bernhard Appenzeller, 'Die Ulmer Bücher und Zeitungszensur,' in *Balthasar Kühn. Buchdruckerei und Verlag Kühn, Ulm 1637–1736* (Weißenhorn: Anton H. Konrad Verlag, 1992) pp. 62–85.

[66] StAU, Ratsprotokoll 1584, fol. 903r.

printers to re-print Müller's *Augspurgische Handel* (*Augsburg Affairs*), an apologia for his opposition to the new calendar that the Augsburg city council was extremely keen to suppress.[67] Although the Ulmer church wardens ultimately reprimanded their censors for authorizing the re-prints, Augsburg authorities could hardly have been pleased.[68] In fact, the stream of criticism from Ulm vexed the Augsburg city council to such an extent that it ultimately protested to an assembly of the imperial cities that Ulm was harboring and giving aid to its disobedient subjects.[69]

Because Ulm had become the haven for the exiled pastors, Augsburg's council closely scrutinized its subjects' contacts with that city, suspecting that they might be acting as couriers between the expelled clergy and their local sympathizers. One individual who brought back dangerous ideas from Ulm was Jonas Losch, arrested in September 1584 for writing "scandalous" songs and rhymes about Müller and the riot. Losch, a weaver, testified that he supplemented his income by composing songs and singing at weddings. He claimed to have written up to thirty songs on various subjects, some of which had been confiscated from him by the *Bürgermeister* Christof Ilsung. Fearing arrest, Losch had fled to Ulm after the riot, where he remained for several weeks. After his return, he was arrested for singing a defamatory song about the Jesuits in the city streets. He was also accused of writing a song about Müller's expulsion and the ensuing riot that was sharply critical of the authorities. He testified that, approximately a week before his arrest, a boy named Michael Karg from Memmingen loaned him a printed song about the riot, which Losch copied out in his own hand, revising several verses in the process.[70] The song had originally been printed in Ulm, where people openly sang a song about the riot supposedly written by a local preacher named "Herr Peter." In his own version of the song, Losch claimed to have substantially revised the last verse and to have added a 25th verse about the death of Müller's wife. He also set his version to a tune, *Praise God, Ye Pious Christians* (*Lobt Gott, Ihr Frommen Christen*).[71]

Although Losch claimed he had not considered his song to be seditious, he had taken the precaution of tearing up his only copy of it while in his

---

[67] SStBA, 4° Aug 735/2, 'Kalenderstreit II,' Nr. 25, Müller, *Augspurgische Handel*.

[68] StAU, [6875], 'Religionsprotokoll of the Kirchenbaupflegerampt, 1570–1587,' fol. 359v; 361v.

[69] Radlkofer, 'zum Augsburger Kalenderstreit,' p. 12.

[70] This sort of borrowing from printed songs was apparently a common practice for Losch, as he testified that other songs he had written were based on printed rhymes he had seen. See StAA, 'Ad Kalenderstreit Criminalia,' Urg. Jonas Losch, 3 Sept. 1584, Answer Nr. 13.

[71] For further discussion of this song, see Fisher, *Music and Religious Identity in Counter-Reformation Augsburg*, pp. 37–49.

jail cell, "so that it would not be found on him."[72] Under torture, however, he admitted having given a copy of his song to a painter named Lutz; he had also let his friend Leonhart Deisenhofer read it.[73] Losch identified the copy confiscated from Lutz as his composition, but identified another song about the riot as the work of one Abraham Schedle, which was printed in Ulm and circulated in Augsburg.[74]

The authorities also questioned Losch about anonymous libels against the authorities posted on the weavers' guild hall and elsewhere about town. They forced him to supply a writing sample, but could not establish a definitive link to the illegal placards. The council ordered his release upon his oath, under penalty of death or maiming, not to write, sing, or distribute any songs in the future. Losch swore also not to participate in any assemblies against the government and to promptly report any information he might have regarding others who did.[75]

Losch's testimony led the authorities to Leonhard Deisenhofer, who had read Losch's song, and according to Losch, had spoken out against the council. Deisenhofer was no friend of the council's, having taken part in the riot and called for the Catholics in the city government to be thrown out of the city hall.[76] He also owned copies of several of Losch's songs, along with an anonymous, printed song about Georg Müller and the riot which he had bought from the bookseller Aaron Stier.

Although he could barely write, magistrates questioned Deisenhofer about a handwritten libel posted on the door of St Anna's church. Addressed to the "Rebellious Doctor Thief," Georg Müller, the placard heaped abuse on Müller and the other "heretical" pastors of the "Augsburg Confusion." The pasquinade hinted darkly at violent retribution against Müller for fomenting rebellion against the emperor and the council, God's appointed secular authorities.[77] Since its first appearance in October 1583, handwritten copies of the libel had circulated among Müller's supporters as proof of a Catholic conspiracy to silence Müller. Deisenhofer swore that he had not written the libel, but identified the handwriting on the copy shown to him as belonging to his brother, Hans.[78] Hans, however, claimed

---

[72] StAA, 'Ad Kalenderstreit Criminalia,' Urg. Jonas Losch, 5 Sept. 1584, Answer Nr. 7.

[73] Ibid.

[74] Ibid., Urg. 10 Sept. 1584; Confession and Supplication of Jonas Losch, dated 6 Sept. 1584.

[75] StAA, Strafbuch Nr. 101, 1581–1587, fol. 136v.

[76] StAA, 'Ad Kalenderstreit Criminalia,' Urg. Leonhart Deisenhofer, Sept. 10, 1584.

[77] Copies of the text may be found in Deisenhofer's file. Additional copies are extant in SStBA, 2 Cod. Aug. 311, 'Catholische Lästerpredigten und Pasquille,' Nr. 2 and in StAA, Historische Verein von Schwaben und Neuberg, Nr. H. 140, 'Pasquille, 16. Jrhdt.'

[78] StAA, 'Ad Kalenderstreit Criminalia,' Urg. Leonhart Deisenhofer, 10 Sept. 1584, Answer Nr. 7.

to have simply copied the text from a copy shown him by Ulrich Müller, the watchman on the Perlach Tower.[79]

The following day, authorities questioned Ulrich Müller. Müller, who denied having written or revised anything, claimed not to know how Deisenhofer came into possession of the libel. Under threat of torture, however, he admitted that he had gotten a copy of the placard from a former student at St Anna's, and that Deisenhofer had asked him for a copy some six months previously. Müller denied distributing any other copies, and claimed that he had heard that the author of the libel was a man identified only as "Hans Georg." Subsequent questioning of the student failed to turn up any evidence leading to "Hans Georg" or the source of Müller's copy.[80]

The investigation of Losch and the Deisenhofers revealed some of the difficulties the Augsburg authorities faced in trying to control the dissemination of songs and libels. As Losch's testimony indicated, songs circulated rapidly and widely—within weeks of the riot in Augsburg, songs about it were rolling off the presses and being sung in the streets of Ulm. Losch also confirmed how easily existing songs could be adapted to new purposes with the simple substitution of new words and meanings for the existing text. Borrowing the words and melodies of popular songs made it simple for anyone to comment on the local unrest,[81] and the ease with which such songs were appropriated made it all the more difficult for authorities to identify the authors and stamp out the adaptations. As Deisenhofer and Müller demonstrated, such material was readily copied out and passed from hand to hand. Demand for copies spread by word of mouth, and manuscripts could be copied so frequently and distributed so far afield that no one could say for sure where they had originated. The circulation of such manuscripts within the city was virtually impossible to regulate, for such texts changed hands beyond the purview of the censors and without the intervention of the printers and booksellers charged with securing the censors' review.

These texts also enjoyed a long life. Two years after Losch's arrest, the song that had served as the basis of his illegal composition surfaced again. In November 1586, the council arrested Regina Hurter for peddling door-to-door a song "about Dr Müller and other pastors."[82] Like most such peddlers, Hurter was a poor woman, and pregnant with her sixth child. She and her husband received alms from the public coffers, and her husband

---

[79] StAA, 'Ad Kalenderstreit Criminalia,' Urg. Hans Deisenhofer, 13 Sept. 1584.

[80] StAA, Urg. Ulrich Müller, 14–17 Sept. 1584.

[81] On *contrafacta* songs in the Reformation, see Rebecca Wagner Oettinger, *Music as Propaganda in the German Reformation* (Aldershot: Ashgate, 2001), pp. 89–136.

[82] StAA, 'Ad Kalenderstreit Criminalia,' Urg. Regina Hurterin, 11 Nov. 1586.

had bought the songs in Ulm in hopes that they might earn a bit of money selling them. Hurter herself knew little of the song's origin, other than that it was supposed to have been printed in Ulm and distributed by a "Herr Peter" there. "Herr Peter," of course, was the pastor in Ulm whom Jonas Losch had identified in 1584 as the author of a subversive song about the Müller riot.[83] Hurter's testimony establishes that "Herr Peter" and his distributors were exporting printed copies of the song into Augsburg for years after the riot.

Who was Herr Peter? What little anyone seemed to know about him was that he was a pastor in Ulm. The records of the Ulm church wardens suggest that he was probably Peter Schumann, also known as Peter Hypodemander, who served as pastor of the city's hospital church from 1576 until his death in 1589.[84] In addition to his pastoral duties, Schumann also found time to write, publishing a number of religious poems and songs in Latin and German in the 1580s. His verses, typically dedicated to pastors or other local worthies, championed the triumph of the Lutheran faith amid adversity. In his 1583 poem *Halcyon*, for example, Schumann likened the Lutheran church to a storm-tossed seabird. True faith being a rarity, the fabulous bird Halcyon was a rare creature, but although it was buffeted by sea winds and threatened by strange beasts, divine grace kept its nest safe from all earthly threats.[85] Appended to a 1585 reprint of the poem were several songs, to the tune of popular hymns, praising a local pastor who had been exiled in the 1540s for his opposition to the Interim.[86] Several other German songs and Latin poems celebrated pious Lutherans for their constancy in times of trial.[87]

---

[83] See the discussion of the Losch case, above.

[84] StAU, H. Kammerer, *Consignatio Chronologica Ministorum Ecclesiarum Ulmensium Tempore Reformationis Lutheri Ad nostra usq Tempora ...* fol. 40.

[85] SStBA 4° LD 398, Peter Schumann, *Halcyon. Ein Schöne Christliche betrachtung/ deß herrlichen und grossen wunderwercks Gottes/im Wintervogel Halcyon, und von seiner wunderbaren Natur unnd eygenschafft/mit der hayligen Schrifft auß gelegt/Gaystlich erklert/ und auff die Christliche Kirch gezogen. Hierbey das Evangelion/vom ungestümen Meer/ Math 8. Sampt der Gaystlichen Deytung D.M. Luthers gleiches inhalts/alles in Reymen unnd gebundne Red gefast. Zu end etliche Schöne throst Sprich/Von der Christlichen Kirchen.* (Ulm: Ulhart, 1583).

[86] SStBA, Th Pr 4721, [Peter Schumann], *Halcyon. Ein Schöne Christliche betrachtung des herrlichen unnd grossen wunderwercks Gottes/im Winter Vogel Halcyon/mit der heyligen schrifft außgelegt/geistlich erkleret/unnd auff die Christliche Kirch gezogen. Hierbey das Evangelion/vom Ungestimmen Meer. Matth. am 8. sampt der gesitlichen deutund D. M. Luth. Item/Trost spiegel der Christen/in irem Creutz. Ein Christliche betrachtung/der gleichnus Christi. Joan. 16. vom geberenden Weib/darin der Christen Creutz/Leid und Frewd/ sehr tröstlich abgebildet und erklert wirt. Alles in Reimen und gebundene Rede verfast. Anno M.D. LXXXV.* ([n.p.: n.p.,] 1585).

[87] See, for example, StBB, Hymn. 195, Peter Schumann, *Die Unschuld Davids/darvon er sang dem Herrn/von wegen der Wort des Moren/des Jeminiten. Ist der Sibend Psalm Davids/von newen außgesezt inn Bund unnd Melodei.* (Ulm: Ulhart, 1581).

Schumann's pious verses appeared under his name and the imprint of his printers,[88] but none of the songs relating to Georg Müller or the Calendar Conflict bear his name. Schumann, however, was not above writing illegal verses, and had already been punished once before by the Ulm authorities for such activities. In 1570, while he was still a pastor in the neighboring town of Kuchen, he was disciplined by the Ulm church wardens for helping another pastor write a defamatory song mocking his parishioners.[89] The songs that bore his name thereafter were unobjectionable, but decidedly Lutheran. The anonymous songs in praise of Müller resemble Schumann's known songs sufficiently in form and content to suggest that one or more may have come from his pen. With their simple rhyme schemes and borrowing of popular tunes, Schumann's songs followed essentially the same format as the anonymous songs written in support of Müller. Moreover, Müller's story was precisely the sort of theme dear to Peter Schumann. His known songs were of two main types: songs celebrating Lutheran pastors who had suffered persecution for their faith, and songs of consolation exhorting Lutherans to stay true to their church. The songs in praise of Müller combined both themes, celebrating a principled man of God who had suffered exile for the Lutheran cause, and exhorting Augsburg's Lutherans not to let the city council force them from their faith.

Although Schumann was likely the author behind at least one of the Müller songs, there is no evidence that the Augsburg authorities ever tried to identify him—or any other Ulm pastor—as "Herr Peter." Indeed, it appears that Augsburg's magistrates never followed up on the evidence supplied by Losch and Hurter regarding this source, even though they proved keen to track down the authors of such songs in other cases. Perhaps they doubted Ulm's willingness to proceed against its own clergy, or perhaps the case simply fell through the cracks. With an unpaid, under-staffed magistracy, many leads were destined to be ignored. In other cases, however, Augsburg officials proved quick to enlist the aid of neighboring governments to apprehend suspects dealing in pro-Müller propaganda. In 1587, for example, the city council wrote to Bamberg, Würzburg, Dinkelsbühl, Bavaria, and Trier for help in suppressing Müller's *Augspurgische Handel*.[90] Their efforts netted Georg Schloher, who was arrested in Bavaria on suspicion of distributing Müller's book there. Although Schloher admitted he had done some gardening for Müller

---

[88] Most of Schumann's known works bear the imprint of the Ulm printer Johann Anthony Ulhart.

[89] StAU, A[6875]; Religionsprotokoll Kirchenbaupflegerampt, 1570–1587, fol. 49r; 60v–61r; 72r.

[90] StAA, Literalien 1585–1587.

after his move to Wittenberg, there was no evidence that he had brought anything back with him other than a stack of personal letters.[91]

The widespread copying and sharing of songs could result in their circulation far beyond the author's intended audience, as Abraham Schedle learned in 1585. Schedle was a weaver with a penchant for songwriting, and Jonas Losch had identified him in his 1584 interrogation as the author of a song about the riot that had been printed in Ulm.[92] Schedle admitted writing the song, but swore he had not distributed it, other than to let a friend write out a copy for his wife. Soon more copies were circulating, and Schedle fled to Ulm fearing his imminent arrest. Hoping for a merciful settlement, he turned himself in to the Augsburg authorities in April 1585.

Schedle testified that his song about the Müller riot described, in 47 verses, "the whole Dr Müller business."[93] Schedle's description suggests that he may have been referring to *A New Lament about the Sorrowful State of the Honorable, Highly-learned Georg Müller* (*Ein Newes und Klägliches Lied / von dem Betrübten Zustand / deß Ehrwürdigen / hochgelehrten herrn Georgii Miller*), which appeared in print in 1584. Set to the tune of the Lutheran hymn, *If the Lord God Forsakes Us* (*Wo Gott Der Herr Nicht Bei Uns Hält*),[94] the song tells the story of Müller's expulsion, the death of his pregnant wife, and the ensuing riot. According to the song, God had rescued Augsburg from the false teaching of the pope, but the Devil had sent the Jesuits to Augsburg to do his work under the guise of the new calendar. Müller had been a bulwark against the Devil's advances, for which he was expelled. The song ended with a description of the persecution of Christians by the Roman emperors, and encouraged Augsburgers to patiently suffer for their faith, reminding them that the tyrants who persecuted the righteous would be justly punished by God.[95] With its association of the calendar with the Devil and the Jesuits, the song rehearsed charges common to Augsburg's rumor mill, helping to spread these stories still further.

If this was the song Schedle had written, he had reason to expect he would be arrested for it. Not only did the song champion the cause of

---

[91] Ibid.

[92] See StAA, 'Ad Kalenderstreit Criminalia,' Urg. Jonas Losch, 10 Sept. 1584.

[93] Ibid., 10 Sept. 1584, Answer Nr. 6. On Schedle and his songs, see Fisher, *Music and Religious Identity in Counter-Reformation Augsburg*, pp. 27–37.

[94] *Das Babstsche Gesangbuch von 1545*, 1545 (Kassel: Bärenreiter, 1988) XL–XLI.

[95] SStBA, 4° Aug 735/1, 'Kalenderstreit I,' Nr. 3, *Ein Newes und klägliches Lied/von dem Betrübten Zustand/deß Ehrwürdigen/hochgelehrten herrn Georgii Miller/Doctor der h. Schrift/unnd gewesnen Pfarrhern/der Euangelischen Kirchen zu S. Anna inn Augspurg. Namblich/wie Ihn Gott Wunderbarlicher weiß/auß seiner feinden hännden/erlediget hat. Neben einer Tröstlichen Vermanung/zu der Gedult/inn der Verfolgung. In der Melodia. Wo Gott der Herr nicht bey uns helt / etc.* ([n.p.: n.p.], 1584).

Georg Müller; it implied that the council was under the sway of the Jesuits and, worse still, the Devil. The *New Lament* thus reiterated the favorite Protestant charge that the new calendar was merely a device to reintroduce papal control over their churches, with the Catholic-dominated council merely an obedient arm of the papacy. The account of the Roman persecution of Christians cast the council in the role of a godless tyrant, which deserved divine punishment.

Schedle also admitted writing another song against the council's adoption of the new calendar, *The Peasants' Lament about the Pope Gregory XIII's New Calendar* (*Die Baurenklag uber des Bapst Gregorii XIII. Newen Calendar*), which had also appeared in print in 1584.[96] *The Peasants' Lament* complained that, under the new calendar, the farmers no longer knew when to plant. Religious holidays and traditional church practices had been thrown into disarray. Christmas wasn't on Christmas Day anymore, and nobody knew when the Imperial Diet should be. The new calendar even purported to change the time when Christ is to return in Judgment. All this, the song asserted, was the pope's doing, to determine who was loyal to him.[97]

Both songs were sharply critical of the new calendar and the council, and both proved popular enough that they were published in multiple editions.[98] The council noted that, on the basis of "unfounded complaints,"

---

[96] SStBA, 4° Aug. 735/1, 'Kalenderstreit I,' Nr. 2 & Nr. 3; SStBA, 4° Aug. 956, 'Georg Müller Btf.,' [Abraham Schedle], *Baurenklag uber des Bapst Gregorii XIII. Newen Calendar / Namlich/was für grosse unordnung (beides in Geistlichen / wie auch im Weltlichen Regiment / inn Kirchenyebungen / und inn anndern Politischen Sachen / Händlen unnd Gewerb) Darauß entprungen / gewachßen und herkommen sey. Kürzlich und einfaltig in gebundene reden gestellet und verfasset. Ein New Lied / vom newen Calendar / auch was sich zu Augspurg / den 4. Tag Brachmonats / inn disem 84. Jar hat zugetragen. Im Ton / Es wonet Lieb bey Liebe, etc. 1584* ([n.p.: n.p.], 1584).

[97] See, SStBA, 4 Aug. 956, 'Georg Müller Btf.,' *Die New vermehrte / und gebesserte Bawrenklag / uber den Newen zugerichten Gregorianischen Bäpstische Kalender. In wölcher kurzlich angedeutet wirdt / das nicht allein under dem Bawensvolk / sondern auch in den Kirchen übungen und Polittischen sachen / für unordnungen / auß disem newen Kalender entsprungen und erwachsen seyen. Neben einem sonderlichen begern an den Bapst / da er anderst wölle / das amn sich nach seinem Kalender halten solle.* ([n.p.: n.p.], 1584).

[98] The Peasants' Lament also generated a Catholic response, which argued that the new calendar was not a cause for complaint among the peasantry, but a useful and much-needed reform. See, StAA, Reichsstadt Chroniken, Nr. 19, "Chronik der Stadt Augsburg in Sachen der Reformation, 1583–1589," fol. 200r–209v, *Newe Zeittung: Und Warhafftiger bericht Sampt entschuldigung der Jüngst in Truckh außgegangen Bawren klag, des Newen Calender halben, So wider unns Römische Catholische Bawren, durch ein unriehige auffrierische Person, ist Fälschlich angeben worden, als ob wir Bauren so hefftig wider den Newen Callender Klagten, unnd Bäpstliche H: darinen zue schmächen bedacht weren, welliches khein ehrlicher Baur nie In synn genomen hat, oder Nemen wirdt, allen Fromen Römischen Cathollische Christen zue verantwortung, und hiemit uns zuentschuldigen an tag Geben.*

Schedle had "somewhat harshly attacked and injured" the government in his song. Schedle, however, had cooperated with the authorities by turning himself in and voluntarily confessing his guilt. As a result, the council released him upon his oath, under penalty of death or maiming, not to compose, sing, copy, or distribute any scandalous songs or rhymes, or to participate in any anti-government activities. If he were to learn of any such writings or activities, he was obligated to report them immediately to the *Stadtpfleger*.[99]

Despite the council's efforts, songs about Müller and the riot remained popular in Augsburg long afterwards. Four years after the riot, Anna Borst and Sabina Preiss were expelled from the city in 1588 for simply singing a song about Georg Müller in the city hospital. Preiss, a young patient there, had refused to pray the *Ave Maria* as required of other patients.[100] The housemother, Anna Borst, recognized Preiss as a fellow Lutheran, and offered to loan her a copy of a printed song about Dr Müller that her son had given her. Borst, who apparently could not read, wanted Preiss to memorize the song so that she could sing it for her. Preiss testified, however, that she had been unable to learn the song because "there were very hard words in it."[101] On St Martin's Night, Preiss overheard Borst's son talking with a guest about the new calendar, and Borst asked Preiss to sing "the song about Dr Müller." According to Borst, the other patients clamored for them to sing the song, with one elderly lady saying she wanted to hear them sing of Dr Müller "one last time before she died."[102]

Borst admitted knowing that Müller's "teaching" had been banned in Augsburg, but both women claimed not to know that they were forbidden to sing of him.[103] The song that Preiss and Borst sang was included in

---

[99] StAA, Strafbuch Nr. 101, 1581–1587, fol. 155v. Schedle's subsequent history is unclear. Although Schedle identified himself as a weaver, he supported himself in Ulm as a writer and clearly some of his compositions found their way into print. The Urgichten register in the Augsburg Stadtarchiv lists him as "Abraham Schädlin" (although this spelling does not, in fact, appear in any of his records), linking him with one Abraham Schädlin, who served as a Catholic schoolmaster in Augsburg after converting to Catholicism in 1586. This Schädlin was a *Meistersinger* and songwriter who also wrote several Catholic polemical tracts. Unfortunately, not enough is known about Schädlin's early life to confirm the identification. See, Max Radlkofer, *Die schriftstellerische Tätigkeit der Augsburger Volksschullehrer im Jahrhundert der Reformation* (Augsburg: Verlag der Schwäbischen Schulausstellung, 1903) pp. 21–32; Grünsteudel et al, *Augsburger Stadtlexikon*, p. 776.

[100] Patients in the hospital of Heilig Kreuz who received alms from Catholic donors were required to pray the *Ave Maria* as directed by the donors, over the objections of some patients and the hospital director. StAA, Katholisches Wesens Archiv, Nr. J19⁴, fol. 12v–13v.

[101] StAA, 'Ad Kalenderstreit Criminalia,' Urg. Sabina Preiss, 13 Jan. 1588.

[102] StAA, Strafamt, Urg. Anna Borst, 13 Jan. 1588.

[103] In expelling Preiss and Borst for their crime, the council noted that Borst, as the housemother, "should have known better." StAA, Strafbuch Nr. 102, 1588–1596, fol. 2v.

Preiss's criminal file and sported the descriptive title of *Augsburg Calendar News—A Short Historical Tale of the Calendar Conflict and the Ensuing Riot in Augsburg, including the Firing, Expulsion, and Rescue of the Honorable and Highly-Learned Georg Müller, Doctor of the Holy Writ* (*Augspurgische Calendar Zeitung. Kurze Historische erzölung deß Calendar Streits / und darauß entstandenen Entpörung zu Augspurg…*). As the title promised, the song, to be sung to "Duke Ernest's Tune," summed up in 19 verses the entire history of the Calendar Conflict in Augsburg: its origins, the wrangling in the imperial courts, the expulsion of Müller, the riot, and the imperial commission that eventually brokered the peace. Interspersed with the history were sharp jabs at the city council for forcing the new calendar upon the people against their will.[104]

Just as reading aloud proved instrumental in conveying printed information to the unlettered,[105] performance helped teach songs to a non-reading audience. Sabrina Preiss's song, therefore, had the potential to spread Müller's story exponentially, making her performance all the more dangerous in the magistrates' eyes. The city council's efforts to suppress these texts were stymied by the popular demand for them and the many booksellers eager to exploit it. The June 1586 arrests of a circle of booksellers revealed the extent of the underground market for books about Müller. The prisoners had all been caught peddling woodcuts of Georg Müller and songs about the expulsion of the Lutheran clergy. Under separate interrogation, they admitted that they had been previously warned by the *Bürgermeister* not to sell certain "inflammatory pictures and writings serving only to incite unrest," and that the sale of "pictures and rhymes about Dr Müller" was particularly prohibited.[106] They explained, however, that although they had observed the ban for some time, their customers kept asking for materials about Georg Müller. They noticed that many others openly sold such items, and they wondered why they

---

Sabina Preiss's father, Leonhart Preiss, was also expelled for threatening the hospital housefather for reporting his daughter to the authorities. StAA, 'Ad Kalenderstreit Criminalia,' Urg. Leonhart Preiss, 13 Jan. 1588; StAA, Strafbuch Nr. 102, 1588–1596, fol. 2v.

[104] Anon., *Augspurgische Calender Zeitung. Kurze Historische erzölung deß Calendar Streits / und darauß entstandenen Entpörung zu Augspurg 25. Maij / 1584. Darinnen auch gedacht wirdt / der Enturlaubung / hinführung / und Errettung deß Ehrwürdigen unnd hochgelerten Herrn Georgÿ Miller / der Heiligen Schrifft Doctorn. Zusingen inn Herzog Ernsts Ton.* ([n.p.: n.p., n.d.]), filed in StAA, 'Ad Kalenderstreit Criminalia,' Urg. Sabina Preiss, 13 Jan. 1588. On this song, see Fisher, *Music and Religious Identity in Counter-Reformation Augsburg*, pp. 49–54.

[105] See Bob Scribner, 'Is a History of Popular Culture Possible?,' *History of European Ideas* 10(2) (1989): pp. 175–91; Adam Fox, *Oral and Literate Culture in England, 1500–1700* (Oxford: Oxford University Press, 2000), pp. 1–50.

[106] StAA, 'Ad Kalenderstreit Criminalia,' Urg. Anthony Schneider, Margaret Helblingen, and Barbara Zollingerin, 11 June 1586.

should not also profit from the demand. Margaret Helblingin, the widow of the pamphleteer Martin Schrot,[107] testified that she had even seen the sexton at St Anna's selling woodcuts of Müller from the church shortly after the *Bürgermeister*'s announcement.[108] Anton Krug, too, testified that since he had seen the sexton at St Anna's openly selling Müller's picture, he had assumed that he could also sell such woodcuts without penalty.[109] They acted not out of any hostility to the council, they insisted, but only to earn a few pennies.[110]

The booksellers stated that they had gotten the smaller woodcuts of Müller from the Augsburg woodcut artist (*Formschneider*) and printer Hans Schultes. Anton Krug testified that the Augsburg pamphleteer Samuel Dilbaum[111] had had the larger woodcut printed in Ulm and imported back to Augsburg by way of neighboring Pfersee.[112] Others thought the larger image of Müller had come from Nuremberg, allegedly sold by one of Schultes's former apprentices.[113] Helblingin and Zollinger were even less sure of the origin of the song, thinking that it had been printed in Ulm or Tübingen.[114] Anthony Schneider testified that he had purchased the song about the expulsion of the clergy from the late bookseller Michael Hermann, who often engaged the printer Josias Wöhrle to print for him. Schneider revealed how sought-after this material could be. Fearing that the magistrates would search his goods for more forbidden imports, Schneider told his interrogators that prohibited texts were just too lucrative to pry out of the Frankfurt distributors' hands:

> if they were to search his shipments from Frankfurt, perhaps they might find something [but] the Frankfurt traders don't normally let him have such

---

[107] Martin Schrot had been the author of the *Destruction of the Papacy*, the text for which David Dannecker was prosecuted in 1559. See discussion of this case in Chapter 1; see also Friedrich Roth, 'Zur Lebensgeschichte des Augsburger Formschneiders David Danecker u. seines Freundes, des Dicters Martin Schrot; ihr anonym herausgegebenes "Schmachbuch" *Von Erschrocklichen Zustörung unnd Niderlag deß gantzen Bapstumbs*,' in *Archiv für Reformationsgeschichte* 9 (1912): pp. 189–230.

[108] StAA, 'Ad Kalenderstreit Criminalia,' Urg. Margaret Helblingen, 11 June 1586.

[109] StAA, 'Ad Kalenderstreit Criminalia,' Urg. Anton Krug, 13 June 1586.

[110] StAA, 'Ad Kalenderstreit Criminalia,' Urg. Anthony Schneider and Margaret Helblingen, 11 June 1586.

[111] Dilbaum had once been a teacher at the Protestant school of St Anna's, and went on to a career as a pamphleteer and publisher. Grünsteudel et al, *Augsburger Stadtlexicon*, pp. 353–4.

[112] StAA, 'Ad Kalenderstreit Criminalia,' Urg. Anton Krug, 13 June 1586.

[113] StAA, 'Ad Kalenderstreit Criminalia,' Urg. Anthony Schneider and Barbara Zollinger, 11 June 1586.

[114] StAA, 'Ad Kalenderstreit Criminalia,' Urg. Anthony Schneider, 18 June 1586; Urg. Margaret Helblingen and Barbara Zollinger, 11 June 1586.

things, because when there's something "secret" available, they keep it for themselves.¹¹⁵

Acting on the information provided by the booksellers, the authorities arrested Hans Schultes and the printer Josias Wöhrle. Schultes admitted that he had printed approximately 1,500 woodcut portraits of Müller two years before. He acknowledged knowing that nothing was to be printed or sold in Augsburg without the approval of the censors, but testified that he had not expected any trouble, as woodcuts of Müller were "so very common" in Augsburg.¹¹⁶ He had not acted out of any contempt for the council or intent to stir up unrest, he said, but simply to make a bit of money.¹¹⁷

Schultes identified the maker of the larger woodcut of Müller as the apprentice Lucas Mair, who had made the copies in Nuremberg and brought them to Augsburg. Schultes denied any knowledge of the song about the expulsion of the clergy confiscated from the booksellers. To prove his good faith, Schultes reported that he knew of two prohibited pieces circulating in Augsburg: one piece about the riot, sold by the merchant Hans Amman, and another with a standing figure of Georg Müller, sold by Sigmund Müller.¹¹⁸ For his part, Josias Wöhrle also denied any knowledge of the song about the expulsion of the clergy. Although he admitted he had printed items for the bookseller Hermann, he insisted these projects were limited to "in general, bad stories and secular songs."¹¹⁹ Wöhrle also testified that he had heard that a new song about the calendar being sold about town had been written by Abraham Schedle, and printed in Ulm.¹²⁰

Since the songs Schedle confessed to writing had appeared in Augsburg two years before, this "new" song about the calendar must have been either a reprint of Schedle's 1584 songs or a new composition.¹²¹ Whatever the truth was, the Augsburg authorities were evidently unable to trace the offending songs back to their source, as the records contain no further investigations into the matter. Wöhrle was cleared of suspicion and released, while Schultes was ordered to surrender the offending wood

---

115 StAA, 'Ad Kalenderstreit Criminalia,' Urg. Anthony Schneider, 18 June 1586.
116 StAA, 'Ad Kalenderstreit Criminalia,' Urg. Hans Schultes d. Ä, 18 June 1586.
117 Ibid., Urg. 13 June 1586.
118 Ibid., Urg. 18 June 1586. There is no record of any subsequent action taken against Amman or Müller.
119 StAA, 'Ad Kalenderstreit Criminalia,' Urg. Josias Wöhrle, 25 July 1586.
120 Ibid.
121 An "expanded and improved" *Peasant's Lament* appeared in 1584, and was reprinted by the Augsburg printer Michael Manger in 1585. See *Die new vermehrte und gebesserte Bawrenklag, uber den Newen zugerichten Gregorianischen Baepstischen Calendar*. (Augsburg: Manger, 1585).

blocks and made to swear, under penalty of banishment, not to make, print, or sell any further pictures, writings, or songs "serving to promote unrest."[122]

The prosecution of Schultes and the booksellers made clear that tracts about Müller and the Calendar Conflict were being imported into Augsburg from all over. Their testimony also confirmed the high demand in Augsburg for this material. If the booksellers are to be believed, practically everyone was openly flouting the law—even church functionaries were selling illegal prints about Georg Müller. Although the booksellers and printers may have overstated the case to excuse their own guilt, the evidence does suggest that such materials were readily available in Augsburg, notwithstanding the ban. In this instance, the dynamics of the book market essentially required sellers to flout the law. With customers demanding news about Müller and competitors ready to supply it, booksellers and printers could not afford to remain on the sidelines. Indeed, Schneider's account of the Frankfurt competition in the underground book market attests to the money that could be made from illegal prints. Open disregard for the law both accelerated the scramble to cash in and lowered the risk that the authorities would target any one seller. In such an atmosphere, the risks of the forbidden book market seemed lessened, and the financial rewards increased.

If Augsburgers had any difficulty purchasing books about Müller from local booksellers, they could arrange with private couriers to smuggle them in. In October, 1586, Augsburg officials intercepted Wolf Eisenkramer, a messenger from Dresden, with a shipment of Georg Müller's 1586 epistle to the Augsburg Lutheran community, *An Open Letter of Consolation* (*Send und Trostbrief*).[123] In his *Open Letter*, Müller attacked the new clergy appointed by the council as "hirelings" ("*Mietlinge*") who did not preach in accordance with the Augsburg Confession. Müller advised his Augsburg readers to avoid the services of the new clergy and to gather instead in each other's homes to read "pure books" and sing psalms.[124]

---

[122] StAA, Strafbuch Nr. 101, 1581–1587, fol. 191v–192r; 192r.

[123] SStBA, 4° Aug 735/1, 'Kalenderstreit I,' Nr. 10, Georg Müller, *Send und Trostbrief / Georg: Müllers Doct. Und Professorn zu Wittenberg / an seine liebe Landsleut unnd Pfarrkinder / die Euangelische Burgerschafft in Augspurg uber irem betrübten Zustande / da inen ire liebe Seelsorger / und Prediger abgeschafft / und alle zumal auff einen Tag zur Stadt ausgetrieten worden*. (Wittenberg: Welack, 1586).

[124] Müller, *Send und Trostbrief*, p. Biir. For the answer of the "new" clergy, see SStBA, 4° Aug 735/2, 'Kalenderstreit II,' Nr. 27, *Gegründte Christliche Antwort der jetzigen Euangelischen Predicanten in der Statt Augspurg. Auff Doctor Georgen Müllers newlich in Truck außgegangen vermainten Send und Trostbrieff. Sampt einem außführlichen Bericht / auß weilund des Ehrwirdigen herrn D. Martin Luthers / und anderer furnemen Euangelischer / der wahren Lehrer Schrifften / was man vom Berüff der Kirchendiener derselben Confession unnd der Lutherischen Lehr gemeß halten solle. An die Euangelische Burgerschaft zu Augspurg*

Müller's treatise was of course prohibited in Augsburg, as it encouraged Augsburgers to boycott the new clergy in contravention of the council's orders. Eisenkramer testified that he had purchased a dozen copies of this text in Kempten, and had distributed several copies among the Augsburg customers for whom he carried letters.[125] Eisenkramer stated that his Augsburg clients frequently asked him if he carried prints about Müller, and he thought that he might find plenty of buyers there for Müller's latest work. Eisenkramer was evidently not the first to have that thought: he testified that he had not expected any trouble for distributing the *Open Letter*, since "people here have had this same *Letter* for a long time already."[126] The council threw him out of the city, with the order that he "spend his pennies elsewhere."[127]

The link between the exiled clergy and the Augsburg booktrade was further exposed with the arrest of the bookseller Anton Krug in February 1589. Krug had been arrested before, in 1586, for selling prohibited songs and woodcuts of Georg Müller. Released with a warning at that time,[128] three years later he was back before the *Strafherren* for selling an unauthorized German translation of a Latin treatise on the clerical office by the Lutheran theologian Aegidius Hunnius. The text was probably the *True and Thorough Report of the Proper and Orderly Selection and Vocation of the Protestant Preacher* (*Warhaffter und Gründtlicher Bericht von Rechter, Ordenlicher Wahl unnd Beruff der Evangelischen Prediger*), which appeared in print in 1589.[129] Contrary to both Augsburg and imperial censorship decrees, the *True and Thorough Report* did not set forth the name of the author or its place of printing. More significantly, the *Report*'s commentary on the proper appointment of the Lutheran clergy was an implicit critique of the city council's role in the "Vocation Conflict." Krug admitted that he knew it was forbidden to sell such books in Augsburg, but had assumed that he would not be prosecuted for it, since

---

Sendbrieffs weyß / derselben zum besten / zu auffdeckung der warheit / unnd widerlegung des ungrunds / getrewhertziger mainung gestellt und Publicirt / damit sich nyemandt in Sünd füren / oder darinn zu seinem ewigen verderben auffhalten lasse (Augsburg: Schönig, 1586).

125   StAA, 'Ad Kalenderstreit Criminalia,' Urg. Wolf Eisenkramer, 13 Oct. 1586.
126   Ibid.
127   StAA, Strafbuch Nr. 101, 1581–1587, fol. 204v–205r.
128   Ibid., fol. 191r–191v.
129   HAB, A:751.25 Theol. (3), [Aegidius Hunnius], *Warhaffter und Gründtlicher Bericht von rechter, ordenlicher Wahl unnd Beruff der Evangelischen Prediger. Darzu fürnemlich angezeigt wirdt / durch welche Personen / vermög Gottes Worts und Exempel der Ersten Kirchen / selbinger soll verrichtet werden. Erstlich: Durch den Ehrwürdigen/ hochgelehrten Herren Egidium Hunn / der H. Schrifft Doctorn und Professorn/bey der Hohenschul Marpurg in Hessen / in Latein gestelt / und in Truck verfertiget. Jetz aber: Den Evangelischen Kirchen / bey welchen solcher Beruff diser zeit streitig / zu nothwendigem Bericht / trewlich ins Teutsch gebracht* ([n.p.: n.p.], 1589).

the booksellers Georg Willer and Johann Georg Burtenbach had openly sold the Latin version without incident in Augsburg a year before.[130] Evidently, interest in the book had been great, for Krug stated that several people had asked him for it even before he had begun to offer it for sale. Of the 100 copies he received from Bernhard Zobin in Strasbourg, he had sold 25 in Memmingen, 15 in Kempten, and all the rest in Augsburg, including two to the patrician Hans Herwart.[131]

Krug claimed initially not to know who the translator was, but in his second interrogation the following day, he testified that he had gone to Ulm "to buy honey" and had been approached on the street by Matthaeus Herbst, one of the Lutheran clergymen expelled from Augsburg. Herbst told him that he had translated Hunnius's treatise about the clerical office and asked him to get it printed for him. Herbst had already published a book in Tübingen, which had sold well in Augsburg.[132] Herbst told Krug that he had tried unsuccessfully to get his translation printed in Lauingen, and suggested that they have it printed in Strasbourg and shipped to Augsburg. Krug admitted that after Herbst sent him the manuscript, he sent everything to Zobin in Strasbourg through a courier.[133]

The *Strafherren* asked Krug whether it had not been "his intent to cause more unrest here through these books and strengthen the disobedient [clergy]?"[134] Denying any intent to cause trouble, he insisted that his dealings with "the disobedient" had been limited to his book deal with Herbst. He had never even been in their houses, he swore, and had not been back to Ulm in two years. Krug affirmed his willingness to cooperate and, after he swore that he would never again sell or print anything without the censors' approval, the council ordered his release.[135]

In its efforts to intercept the pastors' couriers, practically anyone with contacts to Ulm became a suspect. Joseph Karg and Hans Widenmann were both arrested in May 1587 for allowing the wives of two of the expelled pastors to stay with them during a secret visit to Augsburg. The *Strafherren* interrogated both men as to whether the women brought

---

[130] StAA, Strafamt, Urg. Anton Krug, 27 Feb. 1589.

[131] Ibid.

[132] Ibid. Krug identified this book as the *Spiegel des gotlosen und fromen* (*Mirror of the Godless and Pious*). He was probably refering to Herbst's 1589 *Geistlich Gemaeldt In welchem allerley Eygenschafften der Gottlosen und Frommen in gedancken, geberden, worten und wercken fuergemalet sein* (Tübingen: Alexander Hock, 1589) [HAB, A:751.25 Theol. (3)].

[133] StAA, Strafant, Urg. Anton Krug, 28 Feb. 1589.

[134] Ibid., Urg. 3 March 1589.

[135] StAA, Strafbuch Nr. 102, 1588–1596, fol. 34r.

books and writings with them from Ulm for distribution in Augsburg. Both men denied receiving any books or manuscripts from the women.[136]

Despite the surveillance, the exiled clergy in Ulm were still somehow communicating with their supporters in Augsburg. The January 1588 arrest of Christof Hörmann provided the council with a glimpse into the workings of the exiles' support network. Hörmann, from a wealthy patrician family,[137] had been arrested for publicly snubbing two prominent council members at a funeral by refusing to shake their hands. The magistrates suspected he meant to demonstrate his solidarity with Georg Müller and the expelled clergy and questioned him regarding his possible contacts with the exiles. They asked about the tracts flowing into Augsburg from Ulm, the names of the smugglers carrying them, and how many he himself had written. Hörmann insisted he had no contact with the exiled clergymen and knew nothing of any writings they distributed. He did report, however, that in the Perlach neighborhood he had heard that several Augsburg scriveners' offices (*Schreibstuben*) were supposedly collecting money for the exiles' support. He identified some of them as associated with the prominent mercantile firms of the Protestant Krafter, Weiss, Hainhofer, and Cristell families.[138] Hörmann stated that he had heard that a group of the clergy's supporters had met six months previously, but he claimed to know nothing else about their activities. He stated that he had never given them any money, and he did not know how they transported materials to and from Ulm.

Hörmann knew a lot about the group's supporters, however, and testified, after some thought, that he had also heard that the clergy's supporters were not limited to the Perlach area, but also included the wives of the patricians Mattheus Rehlinger and Hieronymus Imhof, as well as Mattheus Stenglin and Endris Merzen.[139] If Hörmann is to be believed, support for the exiled clergy reached into the highest levels of Augsburg society. With local notables offering material and moral support to their cause, the city council's efforts to stem the expelled clergy's influence in Augsburg faced formidable, but quiet, opposition.

---

[136] StAA, 'Ad Kalenderstreit Criminalia,' Urg. Joseph Karg and Hans Widenmann, 21 May 1587.

[137] On the Hörmann family, see Grünsteudel et al, *Augsburger Stadtlexikon*, pp. 506–7.

[138] StAA, Strafamt, Urg. Christof Hörmann, 11 Jan. 1588. On these families, see Grünsteudel et al, *Augsburger Stadtlexikon*, pp. 336; 470–71; 577; 919–20.

[139] StAA, Strafamt, Urg. Christof Hörmann, 11 Jan. 1588.

"Impudent Tongues:" Print, Gossip and Social Control

In addition to reading their books and sending them money, many Augsburgers supported the exiled clergy by boycotting the services of the new pastors. In the council's view, parishioners could not demonstrate their loyalty to their old pastors without showing disloyalty to the council that had replaced them. Therefore, the council investigated non-attendance at church as a symbolic act of protest against its authority.[140] Suspecting that the bookseller Anton Krug supported the boycott of the new clergy, for example, the council had made inquiries about his church attendance, questioning him as to why he and his family avoided services. He insisted that he had worshiped often at the Franciscan *Barfüsser* church, Holy Cross, St Anna's, and St Ulrich's, as his fellow parishioners would attest. Melchior Hafner, who had resigned his 20-year post as sexton at the *Barfüsser* after the clergy were expelled, was also suspected of supporting the boycott. Under torture, he insisted that he had simply decided the change in pastors was a convenient juncture to retire, but the council saw his resignation as a public protest against the clergy's expulsion.[141] Having been seen carrying letters "hither and yon," Hafner was also suspected of acting as a courier for the exiles in Ulm.[142]

The boycott was enforced within Augsburg's Lutheran community by public denunciation and gossip against those who broke rank. The January 1587 arrest of Hans Geiger and Balthasar Kling demonstrates how illegal texts and social pressure combined to fuel the boycott. Geiger and Kling, both shoemakers, were arrested for shouting abuse at parishioners accepting communion from the new clergy at the Holy Cross church on Christmas Day.[143] One witness, Gregory Schick, reported that Kling had called the new clergy "renegade traitors and knaves" and said that the Protestant princes should invade Augsburg to rectify the situation. According to Schick, "whatever is against the authorities, is [Kling's] greatest joy."[144] Geiger was also supposed to have called the new clergy "hirelings" and to have insulted the parishioners as they took communion. Both men denied the charges under torture, but Geiger reported that a student he knew only as "Johannes" had come recently into his shop and read to him and his journeymen from a letter denouncing the new clergy as "hirelings." Geiger also reported that he had heard, "in general," that

---

[140] See, for example, the case of the bookseller Anton Krug, discussed above.
[141] StAA, 'Ad Kalenderstreit Criminalia,' Urg. Melchior Hafner, 4 Aug. 1586.
[142] StAA, Strafbuch Nr. 101, 1581–1587, fol. 197v.
[143] StAA, 'Ad Kalenderstreit Criminalia,' Urg. Balthasar Kling, 12 Jan. 1587.
[144] Statement of witnesses, dated 13 Jan. 1587, filed ibid.

the old clergy would soon be restored, and that the new ones would be expelled.[145]

Geiger and Kling were both released with a warning,[146] but a third shoemaker, Jacob Herbst, was arrested four months later in connection with the same incident. Herbst was the brother of the preacher Mattheus Herbst, who had taken refuge in Ulm after his expulsion from Augsburg. Jacob Herbst testified that he had fled to his brother's house in Ulm when he heard of the arrests of Geiger and Kling, but had voluntarily returned to face the charges against him. He admitted that he had attended communion at Holy Cross on Christmas Day, but denied reports that he had called the new clergy "hirelings" or the parishioners "Mamelukes" and "fallen Christians."[147] The *Strafherren* told Herbst that they could prove that he had, "in several places," publicly read from a letter which argued that Augsburgers could not in good conscience attend the services of the new clergy, and that he should report the source of this letter, "better voluntarily, than under torture."[148] Herbst admitted that his brother Mattheus had given him a copy of a letter in Ulm that set forth eight reasons why Augsburgers should not attend the services of the new clergy, and that he, Jacob, had allowed others to read it. After he had returned to Augsburg, however, he had not shown it to anyone because he had heard that "they would proceed harshly against him."[149]

The denunciation of the new clergy as "hirelings" recalled a similar charge that Georg Müller had made against them in his 1586 *Open Letter* to Augsburg. While it is impossible to know whether Geiger and Kling had read Müller's book, it is clear from the 1586 testimony of the courier Wolf Eisenkramer that it was circulating in Augsburg. The persistence of this specific charge against the new clergy may thus betray Müller's influence. Geiger's and Herbst's testimony also establishes the importance of the expelled clergy's writings in encouraging the boycott; it is clear from their accounts that some people in Augsburg were reading pastor Mattheus Herbst's letters, or were having them read to them. The intersection of the oral culture of the shoemakers and the lettered world of the pastors illustrates the importance of public reading and discussion in mediating the written word and the reciprocal exchange between them.

As Geiger and Kling's conduct demonstrates, public condemnation was a powerful force behind the boycott. Fearing their neighbors' scorn and gossip, some Lutherans took care to stay away from church. Hans Loher,

---

[145] StAA, 'Ad Kalenderstreit Criminalia,' Urg. Hans Geiger, 12 Jan. 1587.
[146] StAA, Strafbuch Nr. 101, 1581–1587, fol. 214r–214v.
[147] StAA, 'Ad Kalenderstreit Criminalia,' Urg. Jacob Herbst, 11 May 1587.
[148] Ibid.
[149] Ibid.

a fustian weaver accused of speaking against the new clergy, reported that "when someone goes to church nowadays, people are liable to shout that he's a 'Mameluke' for it."[150] His friend Mang Hüber agreed that the only people who attended the new clergy's services were men in the council's employ.[151] Both men stated that they avoided the services because they feared the condemnation of their neighbors, and they noted that "others with more understanding" did the same. Hüber added that the general consensus in the community was that, if everyone boycotted the services, the council would have no alternative but to reinstate the old clergy.[152]

The public pressure behind the boycott testifies to the power of gossip in enforcing communal norms. Within close-knit social networks, fear of scandal can be particularly powerful, ensuring conformity with agreed values and strengthening group solidarity.[153] In urban environments, gossip also calls down the surveillance and regulatory power of the authorities.[154] Within Augsburg's Lutheran community, fear of denunciation enforced the boycott of the new clergy, but also attracted the attention of the magistrates.

Jacob Martin, for example, was so unwilling to show support for the new clergy that he boycotted his sister-in-law's funeral. Martin had scrupulously avoided the services of the new clergy, preferring to read the Gospel at home rather than attend church.[155] When his wife's sister died, her pastor, Elias Ehinger, accused Martin of trying to prevent the family from having a funeral sermon delivered in accordance with the dead woman's wishes. Knowing that the new pastors would have to officiate at the funeral, Martin evidently preferred not to have the funeral at all rather than be seen to publicly endorse them before all the family's friends and neighbors. Under interrogation, Martin admitted that he had boycotted the funeral to protest the participation of the new clergy. He insisted that he stayed home as a matter of conscience and to avoid giving offense to any of his like-minded friends and neighbors, whom he feared might interpret his presence as an abandonment of their cause.[156] Others evidently felt the same, for many of the invited guests stayed away.[157]

---

[150] Ibid.

[151] StAA, 'Ad Kalenderstreit Criminalia,' Urg. Hans Loher and Mang Hüber, 25 May 1587.

[152] Ibid.

[153] Jörg R. Bergmann, *Discreet Indiscretions: The Social Organization of Gossip*, trans. John Bednarz, Jr. (New York: Aldine de Gruyter, 1993) pp. 140–44.

[154] Sally Engle Merry, 'Rethinking Gossip and Scandal,' in *Toward a General Theory of Social Control*, Vol. 1, ed. Donald Black (New York: Academic Press, 1984), pp. 271–96.

[155] StAA, Strafamt, Urg., Jacob Martin, 30 Jan. 1588.

[156] Ibid., Urg. 1 Feb. 1588.

[157] Ibid.

Martin freely admitted that he prayed for the peaceful return of the old clergy, but denied any disobedience to the council or intent to encourage resistance to its policies. He stated that he had thought he could remain true to his oath of obedience to the government if he simply stayed at home and kept silent.[158] The council, however, demanded to know how he thought he could be loyal when he refused to attend the services of the clergy it had appointed. The *Strafherren* asked, "since he reads the Gospel so diligently, why did he not follow the instructions of St Paul to keep to the good and attend church to see for himself if their doctrine was sound or not?" Did he not know that these pastors had preached the Gospel in other imperial cities and followed the Augsburg Confession? The new pastors may be good men, Martin replied, "but [I] stay home because others stay home."[159]

Hüber's and Martin's cases testify to the importance of communal pressure in shaping opinion and behavior. Both men testified that they participated in the boycott of the new clergy in part because they feared the condemnation of their neighbors if they refused. Indeed, Martin was so aware of his neighbors' scrutiny that he placed his solidarity with them above his family commitments. This identification with communal interests presented a challenge to the council's efforts to forge a consensus between Catholics and Protestants, for the judgment of the religious community could sometimes prove more persuasive than the calls to civic unity.

By the early 1590s, the conflict over the clergy was finally winding toward a resolution. In 1591, several Protestant members of the council facilitated a compromise, which the emperor approved. Under the agreement, the council had the right to appoint three church wardens to oversee the Lutheran churches with the help of three assistants appointed by representatives of the Protestant citizenry. In the future, the church wardens and Lutheran clergy were to make recommendations to the council on prospective appointees, but the council was to confirm them.[160] The church wardens were to examine all appointees to ensure that they preached only the Augsburg Confession in the form adopted in 1530—no "Calvinist, Zwinglian, Flaccian, Schwenckfeldian, Anabaptist, or other secretarian doctrine" was to be tolerated. Moreover, the church wardens were to ensure that the Lutheran clergy did not speak out against the *Stadtpfleger* or the council "under the guise of commenting on church affairs."[161]

---

[158] Ibid, Urg. 30 Jan. 1588.

[159] Ibid., Urg. 1 Feb. 1588.

[160] Radlkofer, 'Augsburger Kalenderstreit,' p. 12.

[161] SStBA, 2° Aug. 10, 'Ordnungen, Decreten, Verrüffe und Anschläge, 1522–1677,' fol. 271–8, 274.

To finally put an end to the longstanding murmuring about the new clergy's Lutheran credentials, the council decreed that the church wardens and "impartial and experienced, peace-loving, learned theologians of the Augsburg Confession" were to examine the pastors on their doctrinal orthodoxy and moral fitness. Any Lutheran clergymen found to be preaching unsound doctrine or engaging in inappropriate behavior were to be immediately dismissed.[162] All this, the council stated, was done with the blessing of the emperor and under the authority of the Religious Peace of Augsburg.

Conclusions

The controversy surrounding Augsburg's adoption of the new calendar cast the city's divisions in sharp relief. Fueled by seditious rumor, polemical prints, and fiery preaching, the storm of protest exposed the fears and frustrations of broad segments of the urban population. To some Lutherans, the controversies of the 1580s confirmed their suspicions that the council was aligned with Catholic interests to dismantle the city's religious settlement and usurp control of the Lutheran churches. At the extreme, these fears manifested themselves in rumors of a council-backed plot to re-Catholicize the city, prompting calls for an insurrection. For their part, some Catholic citizens came to regard their Lutheran neighbors as disobedient troublemakers unwilling to compromise for the common good. By underscoring these divisions, the Calendar Conflict and the Vocation Conflict helped to crystallize confessional identities in Augsburg. In the coming years, this hardening of confessional boundaries would help deepen the religious divide within the city and sharpen the polemical rhetoric between both communities.

While the city council worked to suppress these ideas, its efforts were frustrated by the ease with which subversive songs, prints, and stories circulated through the city. In this, oral and print culture formed a single circuit: the talk in the streets fed on the steady stream of polemic flowing from the city's presses and book stalls, and fed back into the ballads and broadsheets hawked about town. As dissent flowed between the spoken and the written word, it proved exceedingly difficult for authorities to identify its source and control its spread. Throughout the Calendar Conflict, songs, prints, and rumors combined to consolidate opposition to the council's policies and frustrate its control.

The conflicts of the 1580s and 1590s also underscored the rift between the council and broad segments of the community over the limits of civic

---

[162] Ibid., fol. 277–8.

participation. The council had presented the maintenance of the Religious Peace of Augsburg as a shared communal responsibility. In the aftermath of the Calendar Conflict, it became clear that important elements of the Protestant community also looked to the Religious Peace to legitimize their claim to equal political representation. The clash between the council's incorporative ideal and the city's political reality would not be resolved until the 1648 Peace of Westphalia guaranteed full legal parity to the confessions.

These years of conflict cast a long shadow over Augsburg's course through the new century. As confessional divisions deepened in Augsburg and throughout the Empire in the prelude to the Thirty Years' War, memories of the tumultuous 1580s contributed to an atmosphere of increased suspicion and surveillance. In the new century, the lingering mistrust found expression in a more strident tone of debate in Augsburg as the Empire slid toward religious war.

CHAPTER 5

"The Times, They are so Troubled:" Censorship in Wartime, 1618–1648

The city of Augsburg came to a standstill on the afternoon of 8 August 1629. Awaiting a "special command" from Emperor Ferdinand II, the city council had ordered a general curfew until early the following morning. With the streets empty, councilors assembled to hear the emperor's edict: as they had feared, it outlawed the Lutheran faith in Augsburg. When Augsburgers emerged from their homes the following day, they found troops stationed before their city hall. There they learned that all "un-Catholic" teaching was now banned in Augsburg, the Lutheran churches had been padlocked, and their clergy had been dismissed. Next to the city hall, residents found a gallows, newly erected in the night, complete with nooses ready to receive those who questioned the new order.[1]

For the city council, the emperor's edict marked the total collapse of the bi-confessional settlement it had long attempted to maintain in Augsburg. The council's representatives had urged the emperor not to take this step, but given the harsh sanctions now threatening the city, they knew Augsburg could not resist. As magistrates implemented the imperial command, a Lutheran diarist recorded an extraordinary phenomenon in the heavens. For three nights in a row, people said, angels could be heard singing in the skies over Augsburg. The angels sang the popular Lutheran hymns, *A Mighty Fortress Is Our God* (*Ein Feste Berg ist Unser Gott*) and *Lord Keep Us Steadfast in Thy Word* (*Erhalt Uns Herr, Bei Deinem Wort*), both of which had been prohibited as an exercise of the now illegal Lutheran faith. The singing was duly reported to Augsburg's top official, the *Stadtpfleger*, who arrived with a band of armed men to arrest the singers. "Seize them!" he shouted to his men, but when the troops advanced, the angels disappeared.[2]

This story of the angelic sing-in against the emperor's edict no doubt offered some comfort to Lutherans laboring under what they saw as an unjust abuse of imperial authority. The angels raised the only voice of

---

[1] StAA, Chronik 32, fol. 4r; Chronik 28, fol. 1v; SStBA, 4° Cod. S 8, 'Chronik der Stadt Augsburg bis 1634,' fol. 62r.

[2] SStBA, 4° Cod. S 8, 'Chronik der Stadt Augsburg bis 1634,' fol. 66v.

protest in Augsburg that could not be silenced. Heaven itself, it seemed, promised justice for the Lutheran cause. But, whether he knew it or not, the diarist's story was not new. In fact, the story of Augsburg's angelic visitors had been circulating in print a good ten years before the emperor's edict. Print had evolved into rumor, and in the process, become a far sharper attack on the government's legitimacy.

The story of the singing angels appeared in Augsburg at the height of the emperor's victories in the Thirty Years' War. Throughout the war, political power and religious policy in Augsburg fluctuated with the military fortunes of the combatants. As power changed hands between Catholic and Protestant factions, the targets of censorship also shifted. For Augsburg, this period marked the near total collapse of the bi-confessional settlement previous governments had tried to achieve. For decades, the city council's regulatory policies had focused on preserving communal order and consensus. Obligated under the Religious Peace of Augsburg to recognize both Lutheranism and Catholicism, the city council had appealed to commonly held notions of neighborliness and civic cooperation to bridge divisions between the confessions and keep the peace. As the bonds of community ruptured in wartime, confessional hostilities came to the fore. Catholic and Lutheran factions in their turn harnessed the city's censorship laws to advance their agendas, policing both public expression and private belief.

As the second decade of the seventeenth century was winding to a close, events far from Augsburg presaged the coming of a major war. With the Spanish-Dutch treaty due to expire in 1621, many expected a renewed war on the Lower Rhine.[3] Tensions were also building in Bohemia. In 1617, Holy Roman Emperor Matthias had persuaded the Bohemian Estates to crown Ferdinand of Styria as their king-designate. Ferdinand was known for his zealous propagation of Catholicism within his territories, and his regents in Prague enacted a series of measures to curtail Protestantism in the kingdom.[4] When Matthias died the following year, the Bohemians refused to accept Ferdinand as their king, ultimately tossing his regents out of the window of Prague Castle and offering the crown to the Elector Palatine, Frederick V.[5] With Bohemia still in open revolt, Ferdinand was unanimously elected as the new Holy Roman Emperor in August 1619, and the stage was set for war within the Empire.[6]

---

[3] Geoffrey Parker, ed., *The Thirty Years' War*, 2nd ed., (London: Routledge, 1997), p. 38.

[4] Ibid., p. 39; Peter H. Wilson, *The Thirty Years War: Europe's Tragedy* (Cambridge, MA: Harvard University Press, 2009), pp. 70–3; 269–72.

[5] Wilson, *The Thirty Years War*, pp. 269–89.

[6] Parker, *The Thirty Years' War*, pp. 57–60; Wilson, *The Thirty Years War*, pp. 281–4.

Although far removed from the conflict in Bohemia, Augsburgers feared that war might soon visit their land. In response to the Bohemian uprising, the city council mobilized troops for the city's defense.[7] The city was abuzz with news of the revolt. In August 1619, the weaver Hans Haßler was arrested for publicly predicting that soon the Augsburgers would "do as the Bohemians had done" and throw the council and its soldiers out the window.[8]

"Lies as Truth"—Controlling News, Defining Truth

In November 1618, the city council of Augsburg ordered its deputies to root out the source of news-sheets and songs reporting on the revolt in Bohemia.[9] The whole city—indeed, the whole Empire—was rife with rumors about the uprising. In Augsburg, the gossip was generally not kind to Ferdinand: people said he was a laughing stock as a military leader, the son of a whore, and a puppet of the Jesuits.[10] Even members of the city guard were arrested for repeating the rumors. They'd rather hang themselves, they said, than have Ferdinand as their emperor.[11]

Much of this gossip fed on information reported in news-sheets and songs about the conflict. The problem, as the Augsburg city council saw it, was that these reports were often simple fabrications; the common folk, however, were presumably not savvy enough to know that. "The poor," the council declared flatly, "believe lies to be the truth."[12] They simply accepted what they read (or, more likely, heard) and as a result, the council concluded, they had been "moved to anger, hate, envy, unrest, and quarreling."[13]

Augsburg was by no means alone in confronting the problem of wartime rumors in these years. The confusing political and religious environment of the Thirty Years' War, combined with the lack of regular and credible news about it, bred speculation and rumors throughout the

---

[7] Bernd Roeck, *Eine Stadt in Krieg und Frieden: Studien zur Geschichte der Reichsstadt Augsburg zwischen Kalenderstreit und Parität* (Göttingen: Vanderhoeck & Ruprecht, 1989), pp. 524–5.

[8] StAA, Strafamt, Urg. Hans Haßler, 26 Aug. 1619. Haßler claimed his accuser had lied, but the council banished him on the oath of a sworn witness. StAA, Strafbuch Nr. 105, 1615–1632, fol. 226.

[9] SStBA, 2° Aug. 324, 'Statutes,' Bd. 4, Nr. 8.

[10] StAA, Strafamt, Urg. Hieronymus Erhard, 16 Aug. 1619; Anna Stierlerin, 21 Aug. 1619; Sigmund Müestig, et al., 4 Sept. 1619; StAA, Strafbuch Nr. 105, 1615–1632, fol. 226.

[11] StAA, Strafamt, Urg. Sigmund Müestig, et al., 4 Sept. 1619.

[12] SStBA, 2°Aug. 324, 'Statutes,' Bd. 4, Nr. 8.

[13] Ibid.

German cities and in the news accounts of the popular press. Magistrates feared the effects of these stories among "the common folk," for it was widely assumed that they lacked the means to distinguish truth from falsehood. False reports were especially dangerous in wartime, as they might spread panic, and as the Augsburg decree suggests, they might also undermine good government. In these dangerous times, when traditional loyalties were so publicly contested, magistrates feared that their own legitimacy might come under attack. To define what the common man perceived as legitimate, therefore, urban officials sought to define what he perceived to be *true*. These efforts went far beyond simply controlling news of the war to regulating how truth was presented before the public in general.

Urban magistrates across the Empire shared a common concern to regulate the public's access to and evaluation of the printed word. In particular, they sought to influence the "common man's" perception of the credibility of information. This contest over truth was necessitated, in part, by the lack of any clear consensus as to how accuracy was to be achieved or evaluated in the press. This problem was by no means isolated to the print trade in this era—similar debates on questions of truth and reliability were ongoing in natural philosophy, history, law, and in many other fields.[14] But the search for truth in print was complicated by several factors.[15] In the early modern news trade, ostensibly true facts were quite promiscuously and deliberately mixed up with apparently false information. Fiction was very often presented as fact, and fact was often purposely distorted. In this environment, it was exceedingly difficult to know what to trust.

As is well known, the popular literature of the age was awash in cheap broadsheets and songs reporting spectacular wonders. These *Zeitungen* were usually brief, easy to read, and could be had for the price of a few pennies. Awesome miracles and lurid accounts of crimes, monstrous births, and ominous portents were the typical fare, usually ending with an edifying moral lesson or admonition to the reader. Much of this literature put a heavy emphasis on the strange and fantastical, but all of it purported to be *true*, to have *really happened...* somewhere. Indeed, the

---

[14] See Stephen J. A. Ward, *The Invention of Journalism Ethics: The Path to Objectivity and Beyond* (Montreal: McGill-Queen's University Press, 2004) pp. 60–64; Steven Shapin, *A Social History of Truth: Civility and Science in Seventeenth-Century England* (Chicago: The University of Chicago Press, 1994); Brendan Dooley, 'Veritas Filia Temporis: Experience and Belief in Early Modern Culture,' *Journal of the History of Ideas*, 60(3) (1999): pp. 487–504.

[15] On the unique problems of "credibility" in print, see Adrian Johns, *The Nature of the Book: Print and Knowledge in the Making* (Chicago: University of Chicago Press, 1998).

very strangeness of these events was what made them important, for it was in the momentary breach of the natural order that the hidden truth was revealed.[16] The more incredible these accounts seemed, therefore, the more they should be heeded.

Mixed within all this sensational fare, news vendors also peddled accounts of noteworthy political and military events. Although these news-sheets took a much more sober and straightforward factual tone, they were not necessarily what they purported to be. Early modern governments and military leaders fully understood the value of disinformation and routinely paid publishers to plant stories favorable to their interests.[17] Astute readers had to understand that reported facts might very well be fiction.

Even without deliberate manipulation, standards of accuracy in early modern news reports were not high, in part because the facts themselves were somewhat elusive. At the start of the Thirty Years' War, the German periodical newspaper was only in its infancy. In cities such as Strasbourg, Wolfenbüttel, Frankfurt, and Hamburg, weekly news-sheets related news sent in from correspondents along the postal routes linking Europe's major cities.[18] Coverage was spotty, however, and readership was fairly restricted at this stage. The average person was more likely to get their news from one of the many ephemeral news ballads or pamphlets that occasionally appeared. These reports were sporadic and unpredictable, appearing largely when an enterprising printer came across a bit of information that seemed marketable.[19] Without a dedicated staff to ferret out news, facts were, quite simply, scarce, and some publishers took the opportunity to fill in the gaps with rumor and speculation. Above all, news vendors focused on what would *sell*, not necessarily what was *true*. Assuming, therefore, that "the common man" even knew how to read news-sheets, the information he could hope to get from

---

[16] See Robin Bruce Barnes, *Prophecy and Gnosis: Apocalypticism in the Wake of the Lutheran Reformation* (Stanford: Stanford University Press, 1988).

[17] Else Bogel and Elger Blühm, eds, *Die deutschen Zeitungen des 17. Jahrhunderts*, Bd. 1 (Bremen: Schünemann Universitätsverlag, 1971) pp. IX–X; Göran Rystad, *Kriegsnachrichten und Propaganda während des Dreissigjährigen Krieges: Die Schlacht bei Nördlingen in den gelichzeitigen gedruckten Kriegsberichten* (Lund: C W K Gleerup, 1960).

[18] Wolfgang Behringer, 'Veränderung der Raum-Zeit-Relation. Zur Bedeutung des Zeitungs- und Nachrichtenwesens während der Zeit des Dreißigjährigen Krieges,' in *Zwischen Alltag und Katastrophe. Der Dreißigjährige Krieg aus der Nähe*, eds Benigna von Krusenstjern and Hans Medick (Göttingen: Vandenhoeck & Ruprecht, 1999), pp. 40–55. On the imperial postal system and its role in the early modern "communication revolution," see Wolfgang Behringer, *Im Zeichen des Merkur. Reichspost und Kommunikationsrevolution in der Frühen Neuzeit* (Göttingen: Vandenhoeck & Ruprecht, 2003).

[19] C. John Sommerville, *The News Revolution: Cultural Dynamics of Daily Information* (Oxford: Oxford University Press, 1996), pp. 20–21.

them might be factually spotty, frequently sensationalized, or sometimes simply fabricated.

In this context, the public confusion that the Augsburg officials lamented is hardly surprising. Publishers recognized this uncertainty, and sought to assure the public of their accuracy. This was, in part, simply good marketing, for since accurate news was perceived to be in short supply, those who had it stood out from the rest. But information that appeared more accurate could also seem more persuasive, and this attracted the censor's eye, for early modern authorities were ever wary of what their subjects were being persuaded to believe. A look at the target of the Augsburg's city council's ire helps to explain how these reports claimed credibility and why magistrates found it so necessary to discount them before the public.

Augsburg's 1618 decree seems to have been prompted by the confiscation of an illustrated news ballad on the siege of Pilsen called *A True New News Report from Bohemia on the Siege, Taking, and Conquest of the Catholic City of Pilsen* (*Warhafftige Newe Zeitung auß Böhmen/Von Belagerung/einnemung und eroberung der Catholischen Stad Pilsen*).[20] City officials characterized it as "mostly fabricated," but a review of the lyrics reveals why the song, whether true or not, would have seemed inflammatory in bi-confessional Augsburg. It asserted that the revolt in Bohemia was due entirely to the pope's attempts to suppress "Luther's pious teaching" through the machinations of the Jesuits, whom it likened to the spawn of vipers.[21] In blaming the Jesuits, the song was rehearsing already time-worn rumors that the Jesuits were secretly conspiring to foment religious war and forcibly re-Catholicize the Empire.[22] The song, nevertheless, claimed to be telling the whole truth; even more than that, it purported to supply that rarest of commodities: accurate news about the war. Indeed, the ballad took pains to distinguish

---

[20] HAAB, 4°XXV:133, *Warhafftige Newe Zeitung auß Böhmen/Von Belagerung/ einnemung und eroberung der Catholischen Stad Pilsen/ Wie dieselbe durch der Böhmischen Stände ihrem Obersten Feld Herren/dem Wolgebornen und Edlen Herrn/Grafen zu Mansfeld/ den 2. Octoberis mit einem gewaltigen und mächtigen Sturman gelauffen/und darüber uber drey hunder Mann verloren/und an in die drey hunderert tödlich beschödigt worden/Item wie die ganzte Bürgerschaffe auff die Knie gefallen und umb Gnade gebeten/welche ihnen auch vom Grafen widerfaren/etc. Wie ihr ferner in diesem Gesang sollet berichtet worden? Zu singen im Thon: Kompt her zu mir spricht GOttes SON/etc ...* Erstlich Gedruckt in der Alten Stadt Prag/bey Samuel Adam/im Jahr/1618.

[21] Ibid.

[22] See, for example, BL, T. 731.(8), *Newe Zeytung/Warhafftige und eigentliche Beschreibung/von den view geistlosen Meüdmachern/unnd auffrürischen Jesuwidern und Pfaffen/So den Newen Calendar erdacht und zugericht haben/diegantze Welt damit in unrüh zubringen.* (n.p.: n.p., 1584); Nelson, 'The Jesuit Legend: Superstition and Myth-Making,' pp. 94–115.

itself from the sensationalist miracle stories that passed for news in these troubled times. "Wherever we turn," the song noted, "one hears of all kinds of wondrous things, but one hears nothing of the war cries."[23] This song, however, was different. The title said it all: it was true, it was new, and it was *news*.

In laying claim to the public's trust, this *True, New News Report from Bohemia* was entering a highly fraught area. For what did it mean in this age for news to be "true"? How did the reading public know that the information printed in these accounts was, in fact, an objectively accurate depiction of the events recounted? This was—and remains—a highly contested point. Today, readers rely on the professionalism of trained journalists, whom they trust are dedicated to principles of objectivity and accuracy. But, modern notions of objectivity and journalistic ethics were still only evolving in the seventeenth-century print trade, and very often the desire for profits outweighed the commitment to accuracy.[24] In a news trade focused on the sensational and the wondrous, readers could judge the accuracy of news reports only by certain internal clues—and by what the community held about them.

Readers had to judge the credibility of news, in part, by an account's own representations about itself. Did it *say* it was true? Such a standard would have offered only limited help, for one thing almost every news account of this period claimed to be was "true."[25] Indeed, the words "true" or "truthful" had pride of place in many titles, appearing in accounts of everything from the most mundane events to the most fantastical fables.[26]

Increasingly in the seventeenth century, news accounts claimed to be "impartial." Of course, by the start of the Thirty Years' War, the literary marketplace had long since been flooded with polemical prints, particularly on religious themes, which were anything but impartial; this was the legacy of the pamphlet wars of the Reformation and the increasingly strident confessional debates of the late sixteenth century. Seventeenth-century readers would have been accustomed—and may well have expected—to receive their news through an explicitly partisan, confessional

---

[23] HAAB 4°XXV:133. *Warhafftige Newe Zeitung auß Böhmen*
[24] See Joad Raymond, *The Invention of the Newspaper* (Oxford: Oxford University Press, 1996) pp. 233–8; Anthony Smith, 'The Long Road to Objectivity and Back Again: The Kinds of Truth We Get in Journalism,' in *Newspaper History: From the Seventeenth Century to the Present Day*, eds George Boyce, James Curren, and Pauline Wingate (London: Constable, 1978) pp. 153–71.
[25] Ward, *The Invention of Journalism Ethics*, pp. 91, 100–07.
[26] See, for example, the titles compiled in *Flugschriften-Sammlung Gustav Freytag*, ed. Paul Hohenemser (Hildesheim: Georg Olms Verlagsbuchhandlung, 1966).

filter.²⁷ But the fact that news reports increasingly claimed an impartial stance testifies to the growing value placed on "objectivity" and verifiable accuracy in the evaluation of information.²⁸ We can see this reflected in another account of the siege of Pilsen, the *True Report of the Siege and Conquest of the City of Pilsen*.²⁹ This account trumpeted its credibility on multiple points, announcing in its title that it was—as usual—"a true report," but that it was, additionally, the work of an "impartial person," who had actually been there, and who had personally written down everything, first in the original language, and only then carefully translated it into German. Nothing could be closer to the source or more faithful to the facts. To underscore its accuracy, the report warned against the unfounded rumors that passed for news in other accounts:

> I have no doubt, dear Reader, that many and various things are said of this siege in many places, in which, in many cases, the rumor is worse than the facts themselves ... But since lovers of truth want something certain, I have brought this summary report to print, not with the thought that I have described everything (for who would or could be in every place?), but rather that I can truly relate what I have seen myself or learned through reliable information.³⁰

The preface stressed its impartiality with a final, poetical flourish: "Friend and foe may read me/Love and Truth rule me."³¹ But despite the *True Report*'s claims to be fair and balanced, it included many of the partisan details given in the more explicitly polemical 1618 song banned in Augsburg: readers would still learn here that a Jesuit conspiracy caused the unrest in Bohemia, for example.³² But the *True Report* was also careful to explode some of the more sensational rumors circulating about atrocities supposedly committed during the siege and its aftermath: so you've

---

²⁷ Ward, *The Invention of Journalism Ethics*, pp. 99–100; Luc Racaut, *Hatred in Print: Catholic Propaganda and Protestant Identity During the French Wars of Religion* (Aldershot: Ashgate, 2002).

²⁸ Ward, *The Invention of Journalism Ethics*, pp. 106–15; Raymond, *The Invention of the Newspaper*, pp. 126–83; Peter Dear, 'From Truth to Disinterestedness in the Seventeenth Century,' *Social Studies of Science*, 22(4) (Nov. 1992): pp. 619–31.

²⁹ BSB, Res. 4° Eur. 349, 22, *Warhaffter Bericht/Von der Belägerung und mit gestrümter hand eroberung der Stadt Pilsen inn behem/Von einer unpartheyischen Person/so selbsten darbey gewesen/soviel ihm müglich/erstlich in Behmischer Sprach zusammen geschrieben: Jetzt aber auß dem Behmischen Original getreulich verteuscht/etc. Mit befgefügtem Kupfferstuck/inn welchem der Abriß gemelter Stadt und Belägerung zu sehen/etc. Erstlich Gedruckt zu Prag/etc.* [n.p.: n.p., n.d.]

³⁰ Ibid, fol. Aiir.
³¹ Ibid.
³² Ibid., fol. Aiiv.

heard that the women and children of Pilsen were all burned alive in the church where they sought shelter? Even the Pilseners would tell you that's not true. And the nuns would tell you that they weren't raped, either, contrary to common report. And to make the report's factuality even more compelling, readers could refer to an attached map showing all the events that really *did* take place.

Although the *True Report* reiterated some of the same themes that had characterized the more polemical reporting on the siege of Pilsen, it couched them in language that appealed to standards of truth emerging in scientific and philosophical circles of the day.[33] Such standards were increasingly being applied to the press, and the *True Report*'s presentation reveals several basic assumptions about how accurate news was to be judged: accurate reporting was based either on first-hand knowledge or reliable information from credible eye-witnesses. Where certain knowledge could not be had, speculation must be avoided. Above all, the facts were not to be pre-judged and were to be evaluated without bias. Finally, information was to be presented in clear and accurate language and had to be backed up with demonstrable data.[34]

Readers alert to these signs of accuracy might be able to pick out credible reporting from the misinformation so common to news accounts of the day. But even if truth *could* be identified, authorities worried that most people were not savvy enough to recognize it and, in any case, might be too comfortable with fiction to accept hard fact. As one Venetian author put it, "those too accustomed to lies will never believe or heed the truth."[35] Print, whether true or not, carried authority in the eyes of the public. Once enshrined in print, even the basest falsehood could become a widespread, tenaciously held "truth" that local officials found extremely hard to counteract.[36] And here was the rub: governments keen to retain public confidence feared that their legitimacy might be eroded by inflammatory misinformation which they might be powerless to combat. This fear, above all, explains the Augsburg city council's 1618 prohibition of news-sheets on the war. These accounts were "poisonous" in the council's view not only because they misled the simple but, more importantly, because they made them ungovernable. In the council's words, the poor had been "moved to anger, hate, envy, unrest and quarreling" by these news-sheets—in short, they grumbled, they questioned, and they undermined the council's

---

[33] Dear, 'From Truth to Disinterestedness,' pp. 621–28; Dooley, '*Veritas Filia Temporis*,' pp. 495–503.
[34] Ward, *The Invention of Journalism Ethics*, p. 102.
[35] Dooley, 'Veritas Filia Temporis,' p. 495.
[36] Ibid.

rule.[37] By outlawing such materials, the council hoped to control both the news residents received and the way they understood the council's own authority. Such prohibitions would, ideally, ensure that the public encountered only those versions of "truth" that endorsed the traditional authority of council and emperor.

These prohibitions extended not only to news of the war, but to any material authorities deemed likely to confuse the public perception of credible truth. Thus, even seemingly inconsequential texts on subjects entirely unrelated to the war came under scrutiny. One target was the stories of miracles, signs, and wonders so popular in the pulp press. Although the stories might seem patently fantastical and untrue to the learned reader, officials did not expect "the common man" to know better. If left unchecked, these spurious stories and rumors could potentially encourage readers to believe anything, or to question everything—even their government. In order to keep the public's confidence, therefore, authorities attempted to police the truth, even in the smallest matters.

In February 1625, for example, Augsburg officials arrested the peddler Hans Meyer, called "Gallmeyer" after his father, for peddling "false, made-up" songs and news-sheets throughout the city.[38] Gallmeyer made his living mostly by selling "heart or chest candy" (*Herz oder Brusstzukher*)—that is, medicinal lozenges—but sang and sold songs when he had to. He was forced to wander the byways of Southern Germany, for Augsburg's officials had denied him permission to sell his cough drops in the city. Gallmeyer may have been a quack, but his questionable news-sheets confronted authorities with the same basic issue as his questionable medicines: how could the buyer know that either were what they purported to be? That is, could they be trusted? Gallmeyer's printed offerings ran heavily toward the fantastic and the moralistic. Among them were a song about a captain's wife in Feldkirch who had given birth to three evil demons,[39] and a song about a fabulous

---

[37] SStBA, 2°Aug. 324, 'Statutes,' Bd. 4, Nr. 8.
[38] StAA, Strafamt, Urg. Hans Meyer a/k/a Gallmeyer, 1 Feb. 1625.
[39] *Eine warhafftige erschrockliche newe Zeitung. Die erste / am tag Simonis und Jude / hat in d' Statt Veldkirch eines hauptmans Weib seines Namens Berengard Schmid / dises Weib hat in ihrer Geburt drey bose Geister gebracht / welche gestalt / wie ein mensch / aber lange Schwaif / wie die Schlangen / die lebe noch auff den heutige Tag / und Pfarrhern haben sich beschworen wollen / warumb sie da seyen / hat einer auß inen anfangen zu sagen mit Worten warumb sie da seyen biß irer Mutter sechs wochen furuber kommen / was nun weiter geschehen worden / werdet ihr inn disem Gesang ferner vernemmen. Im Thon. Hüff Gott das mir gelinge etc. Ein Schönes newes Anklopff lied Zur warnung allen Trewzigen Christen / in diser letsten betrübten zeit / sehr trostlich Zusingen. Im Thon. Von grund des Herzen mein / hab ich. Gedruckt zu Hohen Ems / durch Bartholomeum Schnell / Im Jahr Christi 1623* ([n.p.: n.p., n.d.]), filed in ibid.

apparition near Neustadt in which people not only saw Christian and Turkish soldiers in the sky, but actually heard them insult each other.[40] Another song told of a lake in Switzerland in which the water had changed to blood. As part of his sales pitch, Gallmeyer displayed a glass of red water and told his customers that it was actually blood from the very pond.[41] He swore to the Augsburg magistrates that this was a true story and had actually occurred about three miles from Schaffhausen. He and his partner, Thomas Kern, had bought the "changed water" at the St Vitus's Day market in Mehingen, and the people there affirmed that it was all true. Recognizing the story's commercial potential, Kern wrote a song about it and had it printed in Ulm.[42] Whether the song was actually true or not was beside the point for Gallmeyer: he made a good living selling these songs, and in any case, they made their readers better people. The strange stories they told warned of divine wrath, and all the songs ended with a tidy moral lesson. When the Augsburg magistrates asked him why he sold "such clearly and intentionally fabricated stories,"[43] Gallmeyer replied that "Kern always said that, 'even if it's not true, it's sure a good admonition!'"[44]

The city council, however, had another word for it—they called it "fraud." Of particular concern to the city officials was that Gallmeyer duped the public into believing that his "false, lying news sheets" were absolutely true.[45] Not only was Gallmeyer enriching himself through fraud, he was spreading confusion among a gullible public. They banished him from the city,[46] but it was not long before his name again came before the Augsburg magistrates. In late November 1626, they received a letter from the city council of Regensburg complaining that a printed broadsheet was circulating in Ulm under the false imprint of a Regensburg printer. Hearing that the seller was headed toward Lake Constance, the Regensburgers had written to nearby cities asking them for help. Noting

---

[40] *Ein warhaffte / doch erschrockliche newe Zeitung. Wie Sie den 20. Septebris / zur Newstatt an der hart / auch an viel andern orden mehr / zu nacht umb 10. Uhr / biß auff 2. Uhr / gegen tag am hohen Himmel / zwen Christliche feld Obristen / und ein Türckischer Obrister gesehen wordt / gleichsam / als wann Sie mit ein ander gar hotigs Sprachorten / und zwey Kriegsherr / mit einandder gar schröcklich gescharmieziert / auch ein Stim / fünffmal / inn lifften ist gehort worden / welche also geschrien / O Ihr gottlosen thut bueß. Zu Singen / Im thon. Ewiger Vatter im Himmelreich. Wie volgt Darbey der Tittel und Uberschrifft deß Türckischen Keyser. Wie auch die verzeichnuß der Gewaltigen Statt Constantinopel mit al ihrer gelegenheit. Gedruckt in Erfurt / bey Tobias Frisch. 1623* ([Augsburg: David Franck, n.d.]), filed ibid.
[41] StAA, Strafamt, Urg. Hans Meyer a/k/a Gallmeyer, 6 Feb. 1625, Question 11.
[42] Ibid.
[43] Ibid., Question 6.
[44] Ibid., Answer 6.
[45] Ibid., Question 8.
[46] StAA, Strafbuch Nr. 105, 1615–1632, fol. 470.

that "all kinds of inconvenience" could easily stem from such false news sheets, the Regensburg magistrates asked the Augsburg city council to investigate the local booksellers at Regensburg's expense.[47] The trail led back to Hans Gallmeyer, still dealing in fantastical stories printed under false imprints, and still swearing that they reported "certain, recent news events."[48]

Although a colorful character, Gallmeyer was by no means unique. The region's highways and byways were home to many such peddlers, who made a living satisfying the public's appetite for sensational, diversionary stories, usually with an edifying moral lesson to be learned from them. Gallmeyer and his printers all testified that they regarded these prints—and their fabrications—as essentially harmless, maybe even helpful to the extent they encouraged readers to mend their ways. Modern scholars, too, have emphasized the essentially conservative tone of this literature, seeing them as affirmations of the existing moral, social, and political order.[49] The reaction of the Regensburg and Augsburg authorities, however, indicates that early modern officials saw these stories in a far more sinister light. The problem, in the magistrates' view, was not so much the stories that these prints told, but that they offended official standards of truth and accuracy. These stories, even if patently untrue to the learned eye, were likely to be accepted as true among the simple. Fantastical stories fostered credulity among the common folk, making them willing to believe all manner of things, good or bad. Subversive rumor, in particular, might gain ground. The danger was thought to be particularly critical in wartime, when the threat to public order was highest, but facts were scarce and only dimly understood. Authorities responded by trying to define what should be taken as true. The goal here was not to train the public in critical judgment—early modern authorities were by no means inviting their subjects to critically evaluate their government. Rather, censorship of the news aimed to make the public more tractable—to foster their receptivity to officially sanctioned "truths" at a time when truth itself was contested. By regulating the news, officials sought not simply to control the information that was received, but to shape the public's evaluation of it.

---

[47] Letter dated 20/30 Nov. 1626, from Regensburg to Augsburg, filed in StAA, Strafamt, Urg. Hans Meyer a/k/a Gallmeyer, 1–6 Feb. 1625.

[48] Ibid.

[49] See Robert Mandrou, *De la culture populaire aux 17e et 18e siecles: La Bibliotheque bleue de Troyes* (Paris: Stock, 1975); Jerome Friedman, *The Battle of the Frogs and Fairford's Flies: Miracles and the Pulp Press in the English Revolution* (New York: St. Martin's Press, 1993).

The dangers that the magistrates feared in the public's embrace of the fantastic were realized in the strange and long-spun story of the three heavenly visitors to Augsburg with which we began this chapter. In 1619, as war raged in Bohemia, a printer in Lauingen printed a "beautiful new song of lamentation" (*Klaglied*) about three angels seen in Augsburg around New Year's Day. Sung to the tune of "How Lovely Shines the Morning Star," the song recited that God had sent the angels to Augsburg to warn the city against the false doctrine spread there by the Jesuits. The angels sang a woeful song over the city, but disappeared before anyone could approach them.[50]

The song also revealed that the Jesuits were able to suppress the news of the angels' warning through their control of the Augsburg city council. Indeed, the song alleged that the Jesuits so thoroughly controlled the council that it did nothing without their approval. But this would not protect the Augsburgers from God's wrath, the song warned. Instead, they should harken to God's word and reject the Jesuits, lest the troubles besetting the Empire be visited on their own city.

With its attacks on the Jesuits, the 1619 "song of lamentation" rehearsed the time-worn charge that the Jesuits held Augsburg's city council in thrall. Almost since the Jesuits first established their Augsburg mission in 1559, they had been dogged by rumors that they were attempting to upset the city's confessional settlement through improper political influence.[51] The song fed on these rumors, and in the context of the Bohemian war, it invited comparisons between the Jesuits' alleged dominance of the city council and their supposed influence over the new emperor—a theme also recited in the 1618 ballad of the siege of Pilsen. The song thus introduced the frightening prospect that God would soon visit his wrath on Augsburg, just as he had on the Empire. Augsburg could only be saved from war if its government were cleansed of the Jesuits' pernicious influence.

In attacking both the Jesuits and the city council, the 1619 song would have been doubly illegal in Augsburg. It was a violation of the council's ban on confessional polemic, which the council had sought to suppress under the Peace of Augsburg of 1555. In challenging the

---

[50] BL, Tab. 597.d.2(13), *Ein Schönes neues Klaglied/von der lezten Zeit/was sich auch für Wunder zeichen alle Tag begeben/Wie sich auch zu Augspurg drey Engel haben sehen lassen Wie ihr solches in diesem Lied werdet vernemen/den andern Tag Jenner/Anno 1619. Im Thon: Wie Schone leicht uns der Morgenstern, etc. Die ander Zeitung. Von dem newen Cometstern/so in dem 1618. Jahr/den 1. Decembr. erschienen/welcher zu Augspurg und in vielen Landen ist gesehen worden/Gesangweiß gestellt/Im Thon: Kompt her zu mir spricht GOttes Sohn/etc.* (Lauingen: Jacob Senft, 1619).

[51] See, for example, StAA, Strafamt, Urg. Veit Goppoldt, 12 April 1564; Magdalena Geslerin, 17 April 1564; Gedeon Mair, 7 Nov. 1583; Christof Widenman, 10 Nov. 1583; Christof Wörter, 22 Aug. 1584.

council's impartiality between the confessions, it was also a powerful attack on the council's political legitimacy. Thus, the song would have had to circulate surreptitiously in Augsburg. This perhaps explains why it appeared under a Lauingen imprint; the song may have been printed in the nearby town—outside the purview of the Augsburg censors—and then smuggled into Augsburg. Alternatively, it may have been secretly printed in Augsburg under a false imprint to mislead the local authorities. In either case, the song about the three angels was known in Augsburg, as evidenced by the fact that it was still grist for the city's rumor mill a full ten years later. By this time, the story had picked up several new additions responsive to the new problems facing the city's Protestant community.

When the singing angels next appeared in the Augsburg sources it was 1629. In March of that year, Ferdinand II issued the Edict of Restitution, which mandated the return of all property confiscated from the Catholic church throughout the Empire since 1552. The emperor claimed that the Edict merely restored the status quo as it existed in 1555, at the time of the signing of the Religious Peace of Augsburg. However, the Edict reflected some of the more extreme Catholic interpretations of that ambiguous document and, in fact, it went far beyond the Peace of Augsburg in declaring that ecclesiastical princes had the same right to enforce religious conformity on their subjects as did secular princes.[52]

Although the Edict was law throughout the Empire, Augsburg was chosen as a test site for the implementation of a far more sweeping policy of re-Catholicization. In May 1628, the bishop of Augsburg, Heinrich von Knöringen, had lodged a formal complaint with the imperial court, arguing that the city council discriminated against Augsburg's Catholics.[53] In view of the Catholics' longtime majority in the city council, Bernd Roeck has characterized the bishop's charges as "completely absurd."[54] Nonetheless, the bishop's complaint prompted Ferdinand to issue a "special command" in August 1629 ordering that all "un-Catholic" teachings should be set aside in Augsburg.

In the weeks that followed, the council issued a series of decrees closing the Lutheran churches, mandating the observance of Catholic feast days,[55] banning teaching of the Lutheran catechism,[56] and prohibiting the sale of "un-Catholic" books and images.[57] To ensure

---

[52] Wilson, *The Thirty Years War*, pp. 446–54.
[53] Roeck, *Eine Stadt in Krieg und Frieden*, pp. 658–9.
[54] Ibid., p. 659.
[55] StAA, Schätze 16, fol. 346v.
[56] SStBA, 2° Cod. 208, 'Bernhard Rehlinger, Stadtpfleger, Reformations Protocoll, 1629–1631,' fol. 5v.
[57] Ibid., fol. 6r; StAA, Chronik 28, fol. 2r.

compliance with its decrees, the council ordered the *Stadtvogt*, Hans Voit von Berg, to instruct his informants to be on the lookout for anything, "be it words, writings, or works," that could be construed as critical of the pope, the bishop, other Catholic clergy, the emperor or city council, or which might blaspheme against God and the saints.[58] The *Stadtvogt* was to keep a list of those who vowed to attend Catholic services, and those who failed to attend faithfully were to be punished with fines.[59] Moreover, the *Stadtvogt* and his men were to patrol the city listening at the windows for the sounds of Lutheran singing and preaching coming from the houses. If they came upon anyone singing psalms or reading aloud from Lutheran books, they were to warn them that such activities were now prohibited. They were also to warn the offenders' neighbors to report them if it happened again. Repeat offenders would be arrested, and depending upon their wealth, could be subject to fines ranging from 4 to 25 gulden, with two-time offenders receiving doubled fines.[60]

The council also made the *Stadtvogt* and his men responsible, along with the city guard, for seeing to it that street singers—"aside from the usual Catholic choirboys"—either stayed off the street or were locked up in the beggars' house.[61] They and the market inspectors were to ensure that no Lutheran or Calvinist books or images were sold in the city's markets and shops.[62] If Protestants jeered at fellow Protestants for attending Catholic services "by calling them 'fallen Mamelukes' and the like," they were to be reported.[63]

It was these measures that prompted a Lutheran diarist to record the story of the angelic sing-in with which we began this chapter. The diarist's account was likely adapted from the 1619 Lauingen ballad of the three angels seen over Augsburg at the start of the war. Indeed, the stories share several common elements: three singing angels, their sorry lament over Catholic influence in Augsburg, and their mysterious disappearance. As recorded by the diarist, however, the story making the rounds in 1629 added several entirely new elements that spoke directly to the city's new reality. By now, the angels had taken on a more explicitly Lutheran stance. No longer did the angels sing a song of lamentation—they now triumphantly sang out Luther's own hymns in the Augsburg skies.

---

[58] SStBA, 2° Cod. Aug. 123, 'Singularia Augustana,' Nr. 25.
[59] Ibid., ¶¶ 3, 10.
[60] Ibid., ¶¶ 4, 10.
[61] Ibid., ¶ 6. For an analysis of Protestant songs protesting these measures, see Fisher, *Music and Religious Identity in Counter-Reformation Augsburg*, pp. 54–70; 279–87.
[62] Ibid., ¶ 7.
[63] Ibid., ¶ 12.

There could be no clearer assertion of the Lutheran faith or defiance of the emperor's edict. Moreover, the angels were now given a specific adversary—the city *Stadtpfleger*. In this account, the *Stadtpfleger*'s assault on the angels confirmed the city council's complicity in an injustice so unchristian that it did not hesitate even to raise arms against the Heavenly Host. Here, the angels themselves bore witness to the justness of the Lutheran cause, proclaiming in the heavens that, no matter what the emperor and the city council might decree, Augsburg was and would remain a Lutheran city.

The transformation of the angels' story within Augsburg's rumor mill highlighted the adaptive power of hearsay. Stories that had dropped out of circulation were resurrected to speak to new events; in the re-telling, people dropped the seemingly unimportant elements of the story, accented more meaningful details, and added all new elements relevant to the current circumstances.[64] While rumors were always a basic feature of urban life, the fraught political and religious environment of the Thirty Years' War created a particularly fertile breeding ground for subversive hearsay. Rumors thrive in times of crisis, when events are of vital interest but news is typically lacking or unreliable.[65] With the very survival of Augsburg's Lutheran churches at stake in the Restitution Edict, fear and confusion prevailed among the city's Protestants. In these troubled times, rumors—even improbable ones—fed the public's thirst for news and reassurance. As much as the city council worked to discount stories like that of the singing angels, they found acceptance among a public conditioned to look for divine aid in times of crisis. The angels' appearance provided a powerful and reassuring explanation of confusing events. And the stories these rumors told promised divine protection of the Lutheran cause.

These adaptations to the 1619 print provided Augsburg's Lutheran community with not only a consolatory story of divine aid, but also an image of safe resistance to authority. Given the close surveillance accompanying the announcement of the edict, fears of reprisal checked most protests. But protest is clearly evident in the story, and the angels feared no one—the appeal of this story lay not just in the angels' message, but in the fact that they were untouchable in their protest. The printed story, as filtered through rumor, had become an almost unassailable critique of the council's policy.

---

[64] Gordon W. Allport and Leo Postman, *The Psychology of Rumor* (New York: Henry Holt & Co., 1947), pp. 134–6.

[65] Ibid., pp. 1–2; Sally Engle Merry, 'Rethinking Gossip and Scandal,' in *Toward a General Theory of Social Control*, Vol. 1, ed. Donald Black (New York: Academic Press, 1984) p. 275.

The story of the singing angels highlights the complex interaction of print and oral culture in the communication networks of the early modern city. The story's evolution from print into rumor demonstrates how ideas were appropriated and creatively adapted, giving rise to messages sometimes quite unlike their original sources. Although city magistrates worked to block access to ideas they deemed disruptive, their efforts were often frustrated by the ease with which these messages were absorbed and transformed in the oral culture of the streets. To combat this problem, officials sought to define the public's very perception of truth. But as the angels' protest made clear, defining truth often lay beyond the magistrates' reach.

"The Psalter is in Fetters"—Song as Protest

Now expelled from their churches, some Augsburg Lutherans consoled themselves with stories of Lutheran angels triumphantly singing in the Augsburg skies. In November 1629—not long after the supposed angelic "sing-in"—Lutherans gathered in the Protestant graveyard of St Stephan's for a sing-in of their own. According to several chroniclers, people began to gather over the graves on Friday and Sunday afternoons to sing psalms and listen to a young boy read from the Bible.[66] Many accounts identified the boy as Daniel Pantier, the seven-year-old son of a local goldsmith. Since many in the group could not read, they gave the boy money to read to them and lead them in song.[67] With the crowd growing into the hundreds, the gravedigger, Bernhard Baum, reported the gathering to the *Bürgermeister*. He identified some people in the crowd, but stated that many of the participants must have come over from the wealthy Upper City, for he could not recognize them.[68] When the council sent a small contingent of guardsmen to disperse them, the crowd resisted, forcing the guards to draw their weapons in self-defense. Someone in the crowd spirited Daniel Pantier away while the rest of the group carried on with their singing, telling the guardsmen that they would allow no one to stop them.[69] Threatened with the loss of his position, the gravedigger saw to it that the gates of the cemetery remained locked thereafter.[70]

---

[66] StAA, Chronik 32, fol. 6; SStBA, 4° Cod. S 8, 'Chronik bis 1634,' fol. 69v; 2° Aug. 10, 'Ordnungen, Decreten, Verrüffe und Anschläge, 1522–1677,' fol. 475.
[67] StAA, Chronik 32, fol. 6v.
[68] StAA, Strafamt, Urg. Mathaus Weiss & Balthasar Hein, 27 Nov. 1629, Report of Bernhard Baum, dated 26 Nov. 1629.
[69] Ibid; StAA, Chronik 32, fol. 6v; SStBA, 4° Cod. S 8, fol. 69v.
[70] StAA, Chronik 32, fol. 6v.

Several chroniclers recorded this incident, and for them, the "sing-in" in St Stephan's graveyard was clear evidence of the tyranny of the new regime. Peaceful citizens worshiping God under the open sky, with a little child to lead them: only a godless and oppressive regime could criminalize that. Like the miraculous story of the singing angels, little Daniel Pantier's precocious mastery of the Scriptures was taken as a sign of divine favor and a moral rebuke to Augsburg's governors. God's innocents, it seemed, knew better than the magistrates what was right, and anyone who would persecute them was guilty of the greatest injustice. As one diarist commented on the event,

> Never before in Augsburg has praying been forbidden or the government required that you vow to deliver your children into blasphemy ... No sin has ever been so great in Augsburg as now, when they have banned so many good prayers of the children and so many beautiful songs in the churches and the schools. This is sin enough, and it would be no be wonder if God sent some special punishment to those responsible, like in the songs about Sodom.[71]

The testimony of those arrested at the assembly suggests that, for some at least, the gathering was not necessarily the outpouring of Lutheran piety and protest the chroniclers made it out to be. Although little Daniel Pantier had escaped,[72] the guards did arrest two men at the assembly. Matthaus Weiss and Balthasar Hein, both cloth workers, were on their way to a tavern when a friend, Hans Wickhaus, invited them to go with him to St Stephan's graveyard, where he had heard that people had gathered to sing and pray. This was not their first visit to the cemetery. In fact, Weiss testified that he and several of his comrades had twice been paid to sing at Lutheran funerals in St Stephan's after the emperor's edict was announced. The families of the deceased paid Wickhaus, formerly a cantor at St Ulrich's, to recruit singers at the funerals, and the men shared the money between them. As trained *Meistersinger*, Weiss and Hain had participated along with seven other comrades, all of them paid.[73] Anticipating wages, the men returned to the churchyard "to help with the singing" and found a large crowd assembled there.[74] Fearing trouble, Hain slipped away as soon as he saw the guards arrive.[75] Both Hain and Weiss stated that they had not

---

[71] SStBA, 4° Cod. S 8, fol. 70r.
[72] One chronicler reported that Pantier and his father were arrested the following day, and that the boy received a "high penalty." Ibid. However, there is no official record of these arrests.
[73] StAA, Strafamt, Urg. Mathaus Weiss and Balthasar Hein, 27 Nov. 1629.
[74] Ibid., testimony of Mathaus Weiss.
[75] Ibid., testimony of Balthasar Hain.

heard any preaching and had not seen the little boy who supposedly read to the crowd. They claimed the gathering had left no impression on them. "Sure, I heard singing there," Hain commented, but "of course, I didn't understand anything."[76]

The city council issued a decree warning against future assemblies. The St Stephan's gathering could easily have led to "riot, tumult, and bloodshed," the council concluded, and it reminded the citizenry that such assemblies were prohibited under the emperor's edict.[77] The council also banned singing at funerals. It warned everyone to show obedience in the future, noting that the council preferred to be mild rather than strict "this time."[78]

In the following year, Thomas Schueler was arrested for holding illegal prayer meetings in his home, punctuated by hymn singing so loud that the entire neighborhood not only heard them, but sang along.[79] It was a loud assertion of Lutheran rights to worship in Augsburg. While Schueler insisted that he had not intentionally disobeyed imperial law, the neighbors' response was clearly intended to show their solidarity with their Lutheran neighbor. Much as the story of the "angels" had done, the neighborhood sought to assert Lutheran rights to worship in Augsburg by filling its streets with song.

Eavesdropping neighbors were not always so supportive, as the weaver Hans Schmalzer soon discovered. He had participated in the St Stephan's assembly, but had not been arrested. Rather, two of his neighbors, Hans Christof Diez and Ulrich Pfundt, reported him to the *Bürgermeister* after they overheard him complaining about the emperor's edict to his apprentices.[80] According to their statements, they had heard him tell his apprentices that the authorities had searched many Protestant homes and confiscated their "un-Catholic" books. He, however, swore to fight to the death if anyone ever came for his books. The neighbors also accused him of predicting that the Protestants would ultimately triumph and would soon take even the Jesuits' church from them.[81]

Before the *Strafherren*, Schmalzer stated that the whole matter started when his Catholic apprentice Jacob had remarked that the authorities would soon confiscate the Protestants' books. Schmalzer angrily exclaimed that he had only three books, but he would lay down his

---

[76] Ibid.
[77] SStBA, 2° Aug. 10, 'Ordnungen, Decreten, Verrüffe und Anschläge, 1522–1677,' fol. 475.
[78] Ibid.
[79] StAA, Strafamt, Urg. Thomas Schueler, 8 Oct. 1630.
[80] StAA, Strafamt, Urg. Hans Schmalzer, 29 Nov. 1629, report of *Bürgermeister* to Jeronimus Imhof.
[81] Ibid., report of Hans Christof Diez and Hans Ulrich Hofsteter, dated 28 Nov 1629.

life for them. He admitted that he and Jacob had said many "vexing" things to each other that day, but he could not recall any talk against the government.[82]

Jacob's recollection of the conversation was somewhat different. He stated that Schmalzer had started complaining to him and his co-worker Hans about the Catholic preaching in the formerly Lutheran churches of St Anna's and the *Barfüsser*. Schmalzer supposedly said that if the Protestants were "as vengeful and bloodthirsty" as the Catholics, they would have ripped the priests right out of the pulpits, but the Protestants were too obedient to the authorities to attempt such a thing. He then told Jacob that "[the priests] might be preaching in our churches now, but soon we'll be preaching in your churches, maybe St Moritz' or even the Jesuits' church!"[83] Jacob said Schmalzer also boasted that if anyone tried to confiscate his books, "he had an executioner's sword and a killer's rapier" and would defend his books with them.[84]

Schmalzer told the *Strafherren* that, looking back on their conversations, he could see how it all sounded like "pure foolishness," but his apprentice Hans was very simple-minded and one could not talk seriously with him.[85] He did admit that he had speculated about a possible revolt, telling them ominously, "who knows what tonight might bring?" He swore that he had not meant to imply that an uprising was imminent, and indeed "every day of his life he has feared, loved, and honored the authorities and has prayed to God for them every day."[86] He also denied saying that there was "curious talk" circulating in the community, although he had heard people saying that Protestant preachers would be installed in the Catholic churches by Easter.[87]

The council was not convinced, and ordered that the executioner stand by in his second interrogation "to help bring the truth out of him."[88] The *Strafherren* noted that he must be very opposed to the government if he was willing to die to keep his books, especially since he could not even read them. How did he suppose to defy the authorities without help? Schmalzer swore he had no accomplices nor any knowledge of any conspiracy. He confessed that "his heart was not with his mouth" when he had spoken out.[89]

---

[82] Ibid., testimony of Hans Schmalzer.
[83] Ibid., report of Jacob Holls.
[84] Ibid.
[85] Ibid., testimony of Hans Schmalzer.
[86] Ibid.
[87] Ibid.
[88] StAA, Strafamt Urg. Hans Schmalzer, 4 Dec. 1629.
[89] Ibid.

The *Strafherren* asked whether he still refused to turn over the books the authorities wanted from him—and just what kind of books were they, anyway? "God forbid that I should ever defy the authorities!" Schmalzer replied. He would do whatever they asked of him, he said, for he feared that "he will be handled like the others."[90] As for his books, they were a Bible, a *Hauspostill*, and a prayer book printed by "Herr Albrecht." Although he could not read them himself, his wife read to him.[91] He begged forgiveness, noting that his wife was pregnant and that he had spoken only out of "vexation," not with the intent to disobey. As a "merciful" punishment, the council ordered his expulsion.[92]

The testimony in the Schmalzer case suggests that confiscations of "un-Catholic" books from private homes were underway by November 1629, or were at least under consideration. For Schmalzer, this threat to take away his books—even though he could not read them—was tantamount to taking away his religion. Like the prohibition on public assembly and singing, the prohibition of reading was, to men like Schmalzer, an illegitimate coercion of conscience. However, the control of reading was just part of a broader effort to control access to "un-Catholic" texts. The city council had also ordered the *Stadtvogt* and the market inspectors to ensure that no Protestant books were sold in the city's shops and markets.[93] In March 1630, *Stadtpfleger* Rehlinger ordered that no religious books were to be printed in Augsburg without the permission of Catholic church censors.[94]

One anonymous Catholic commentator noted that, although the booksellers were no longer dealing in Protestant texts, forbidden books were nonetheless being smuggled into the city by "particular persons."[95] Pictures of the Protestant clergy were also apparently for sale in Augsburg, for the same commentator recommended that the *Stadtpfleger* ban the images to prevent "further seduction" of the citizenry.[96] The arrest of Christof Glatz in March 1630 proved that "un-Catholic" texts were indeed circulating—and multiplying—through a clandestine network in Augsburg. Glatz, a fisherman, had been arrested for singing a song in a tavern about the prohibition of the Augsburg Confession and confiscation of the Lutheran churches. Glatz admitted

---

[90] Ibid.
[91] Ibid.
[92] StAA, Strafbuch Nr. 105, 1615–1632, fol. 671. He was pardoned and readmitted to the city the following month to support his pregnant wife and two children. Ibid.
[93] SStBA, 2° Cod. Aug. 123, 'Singularia Augustana,' Nr. 25, ¶ 7.
[94] SStBA, 2° Cod. 208, 'Bernhard Rehlinger, Stadtpfleger, Reformations Protocoll, 1629–1631,' fol. 8v.
[95] SStBA, 2° Cod. Aug. 123, 'Singularia Augustana,' Nr. 14, ¶ 29.
[96] Ibid., ¶ 8.

that he had discussed the song with two other men in the tavern, Michael Dirr and Christof Obermeyer. Obermeyer claimed that he had already heard that song many times, especially in the flower market, whereupon Glatz bet him a taler that he hadn't.[97] Obermeyer later showed him a printed song which he claimed was identical to Glatz's song. Glatz denied it and demanded his taler; Obermeyer refused—he threatened instead to report Glatz for singing a forbidden song unless he paid *him*.[98]

Glatz claimed that he had gotten a handwritten song from a local butcher. This was the same song that Obermeyer had in print, but Glatz had reworked it "according to his pleasure."[99] Many people had copies of Obermeyer's song, he boasted, but no one had a copy of *his*. He gave the song to no one, he said, nor did he let anyone read it. That was why he set his version down on paper: so that,

> if he was ever questioned by the authorities or the *Bürgermeister* about this song, he would have something ready to show them so that he could defend his case, for he knows that they could read something illegal into it.[100]

This was not the first account that Glatz had given of the origin of his song, however. After his arrest, he had told the *Bürgermeister* that he had gotten the song from a student at St Anna's school. When confronted by the jailor, however, he claimed he made it all up himself. The *Bürgermeister* recommended that he be interrogated about other prohibited texts circulating in the city "because he has a bad reputation and frequents the taverns."[101] In Glatz's second interrogation, Glatz admitted that he had falsely accused the student "to get himself out of trouble."[102]

Turning to the text they'd confiscated from Glatz, the *Strafherren* noted that Latin words were written in the margins (see Fig. 5.1). Surely he must have had help with this; who and where was his accomplice? Glatz swore that he was the sole author, but he had asked a local student named "Johann" to write some Latin words on it so that "he would be better able to defend his crime before the authorities."[103] Evidently, Glatz had hoped that the Latin writing would either convince the authorities that he could not possibly have been the author or, more implausibly, persuade them

---

[97] StAA, Strafamt, Urg. Christof Glatz, 7 March 1630.
[98] Ibid., Answer Nr. 10.
[99] Ibid., Strafamt, Urg. 11 March 1630, Answer Nr. 1.
[100] Ibid., Strafamt, Urg. 7 March 1630, Answer Nr. 12.
[101] Ibid., report of *Bürgermeister* Rehlinger.
[102] Ibid., Strafamt, Urg. 11 March 1630, Answer Nr. 1.
[103] Ibid., Answer 2.

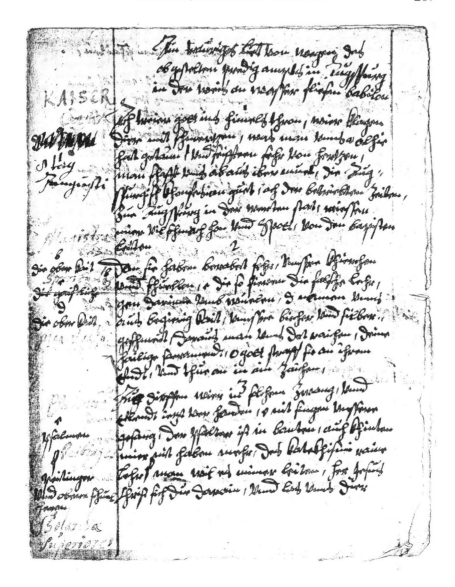

Figure 5.1 Christof Glatz's song, *A Sad Song About the Abolished Ministry in Augsburg*, showing his marginal notes and the Latin words written by "Johann." (StAA, Strafamt Urgichten, Christof Glatz, 7–11 March 1630).

that it was a serious work of scholarship. Whatever his intent, it did not work. The *Strafherren* accused him of trying to "stir up resistance among the common man" and incite a revolt.[104] Glatz swore that he had never intended to let the song out of his own hands. He had only written it, he said, as "a song of lamentation, to comfort himself," and had never had the slightest intent to foment rebellion.[105]

Glatz's song, with "Johann's" Latin notations, is included in his criminal file and reveals the lengths to which Glatz went to conceal his true meaning. Titled *A Sad Song About the Abolished Ministry in Augsburg* (*Ein trauiges liedt von wegen des abgestelten predig ampts in Augspurg in der weis an Wasser fliesen Babilon*), it was to be sung to the tune of the hymn *By the Rivers of Babylon* (*Am Wasserflüssen Babylon*).[106] Also included in Glatz's file are two anonymous printed prayer books containing the song Glatz evidently used as his model, *A Consolatory Song of Lamentation to Sing in These Times* (*Ein tröstlich Trawer-Lied / zu dieser Zeit zu singen*) also set to the tune of *By the Rivers of Babylon*.[107] Both songs mourned the loss of Protestant rights and complained of the mockery and oppression they allegedly suffered from the Catholics. By relying on the hymn *By the Rivers of Babylon*, both songs reinforced their claims by drawing on the hymn's evocation of the words of the 137th Psalm, in which the enslaved Hebrews mourned their lost homeland and lamented their persecution at the hands of their Babylonian captors.

In associating the Protestants of the Empire with God's chosen people, the songs called for divine retribution against their Catholic oppressors. Both songs echoed the Hebrews' patient suffering under the mockery and gloating of their persecutors. Glatz's song, however, brought the persecution home to Augsburg and was more sharply critical of the local authorities. Fearing prosecution, Glatz avoiding naming the targets of his criticism directly, identifying them only with italic letters in the text. Unfortunately for Glatz, his zeal to record his song as "evidence" exposed him, for the authorities had confiscated his copy with the notes explaining the meaning of the letters. Notations in the margins of the song identified the subjects keyed to the letters. Read with the text, the marginal notes leave no doubt about Glatz's meaning:

---

[104] Ibid., Question Nr. 8.
[105] Ibid., Answer Nr. 8.
[106] Christof Glatz, *Ein trauiges liedt von wegen des abgestelten predig ampts in Augspurg in der weis an Wasser fliesen Babilon*, filed in StAA, Strafamt, Urg. Christof Glatz, 7–11 March 1630.
[107] *Ein tröstlich Trawer-Lied / zu dieser Zeit zu singen. Im Thon: An Wasserflüssen Babylon / c.*, in *Für die Betrangte Christen*. ([n.p.: n.p., n.d.]), filed ibid.

I – August 8th[108]	1. Oh true God on heaven's throne, Painfully we lament to you Over what has been done to us here on *I*, And sigh from our very hearts. In their arrogance, They forbid to us the good Augsburg Confession. Oh, the sorrowful times in the worthy city of Augsburg! We must suffer much disgrace, mockery and insult from the Catholics.
b – the Government *e – the [Catholic] Clergy* *d – the Government*	2. For *b* has stolen our churches and schools, *e*, who teach false doctrine, go in to take them over. *d* has taken our books and silver plate From which we administered your holy sacrament. Oh God, punish them for their sin And make of them a sign.
e – Psalms[109]	3. Under this duress and misery, We are not allowed to sing *e* among our songs. The psalter is in fetters Nor are we allowed our property anymore.
f – [Conrad] Peutinger & the Upper School Masters[110]	*f* denies us the catechism of the pure doctrine. Lord Jesus Christ, let us be your people when we depart this life.
	4. They speak of order in such times, while they are on top, And cause us much heartbreak: "You may never again sing 'Erhalt Uns Herr, bei deinem Wort, und steir des Papsts und Türken Mord,'[111] It can be easily forbidden to you. You must come to our churches

---

[108] The emperor's "special command" suppressing Lutheranism in Augsburg was announced on 8 August 1629. StAA, Chronik 32, fol. 3v.

[109] The singing of psalms was forbidden, as it was deemed to be an exercise of the Lutheran faith. See, SStBA, 2° Aug. 10, 'Ordnungen, Decreten, Verrüffe und Anschläge, 1522–1677,' fol. 475; SStBA, 2° Cod. Aug. 123, 'Singularia Augustana,' Nr. 25; SStBA, 2° Cod. 208, 'Bernhard Rehlinger, Stadtpfleger, Reformations Protocoll, 1629–1631,' fol. 5–6.

[110] Peutinger and the Upper School Masters oversaw efforts to ban the teaching of the Lutheran catechism in Augsburg schools. StAA, Chronik 32, fol. 13r.

[111] On the banning of this hymn, see Dollinger, 'Erhalt uns Herr, bei deinem Wort!,' in *Zeitschrift für bayerische Kirchengeschichte*. 29 (1960): 33–42; Hopp, 'Zur Geschichte des Liedes "Erhalt uns Herr bei deinem Wort", *Beiträge zur bayerischen Kirchengeschichte* 7 (1901): 79–87.

	and not hinder us in what has already or may yet happen."
	5. Before I convert and fall away from my faith
	I would prefer many more times
	to flee from my Fatherland.
	Therefore, Oh God, stand by me
a – the Jesuits	So that *a* do not convert me.
	Helper and Protector,
	Oh God my Lord,
	Restore to us the pure doctrine
b – Psalms	So that we may honor you again with *b*
	…
	7. They want to force us into their faith and idolatry.
	If their faith were the Word of God,
	They would not need to compel people
r – the Jesuits	However *r* cannot prove their evil poison
	Out of the Scriptures,
	Therefore they have to use the hangman's noose and sword
	So that the Pope will be honored higher than God on earth.[112]

The council decided that Glatz deserved to be whipped out of the city for his crime, but in view of the petitions it had received on his behalf, they granted him the "special mercy" of exposure in the pillory, followed by banishment.[113] Several diarists recorded Glatz's disgrace, but concluded he had been unjustly punished. Commenting on Glatz's fate, one Lutheran diarist objected that he had "told the truth" in his song,[114] while another chronicler judged that the song was "entirely spiritual and proved by God's Word."[115]

On the day of Glatz's punishment, the city council also posted a decree publicizing a mandate from the emperor and the Bishop of Augsburg ordering that the Lutheran citizenry attend Catholic church services.[116] While the Protestant council members sought to block enforcement of the decree, ordinary Augsburgers showed their contempt in more subtle ways. During the night, someone ripped up a copy of the decree posted on the

---

[112] Ibid.
[113] StAA, Strafbuch Nr. 105, 1615–1632, fol. 682. Glatz was pardoned and allowed to return to Augsburg four months later. Ibid.
[114] StAA, Chronik Nr. 32, fol. 7v.
[115] SStBA, 4° Cod. S 8, 'Chronik der Stadt Augsburg bis 1634,' fol. 73v.
[116] StAA, Chronik Nr. 28, fol. 3r.

Weavers' Hall,[117] and a few days later authorities apprehended Melchior Cramer running off with another copy posted on the Franciscans' Gate. Cramer was a shoemaker and perhaps something of a hothead where his religion was concerned. Twenty years earlier, Cramer had silenced Hans Windbusch's heckling of the preacher in the Franciscan church with a punch in the mouth, sparking an altercation that nearly resulted in a serious riot outside the church.[118] This time, Cramer testified, he was standing under the Franciscans' Gate when the combination of drink and "the scourges of Satan" moved him to steal the decree.[119] Unfortunately for Cramer, the impulse came upon him in broad daylight, and he was quickly apprehended by the gate-keepers and brought before the *Bürgermeister*. With the decree recovered, the soldiers searched Cramer, finding a handwritten copy of a forbidden song hidden in his pants pocket.[120]

The song Cramer was carrying bore no title nor indication of the melody to which it was to be sung. The structure of the song, however, suggests that it was a contrafact of a popular hymn. In 13 verses, Cramer's version calls on God the Father, God the Son, and God the Holy Spirit to sustain the author in the true faith while his enemies seek to force him into false doctrine.[121] In this, Cramer's song recalled the theme of Glatz's song: the oppressed people of God patiently enduring the persecution of the faithless until God sends them their deliverance. Cramer claimed he got the song about a week before from his daughter Barbara, but had not sung it or allowed other people to copy it. In fact, Cramer said, he really could not even read it very well.

Cramer's friends and family petitioned the city council on his behalf, arguing that he was almost 70 and "at times so confused in the head that he doesn't know what he's doing, especially when he's drunk a little beer."[122] Although it stated that Cramer deserved death for his crime, the council determined to be merciful, ordering that Cramer be whipped on the pillory and banished.[123] As Cramer stood in the pillory, official heralds read aloud the decree he had tried to steal. Although the crowd was warned once more to attend Catholic services, one

---

[117] Michael Bökh was expelled for falsely accusing a member of the Protestant patrician Thenn family of having torn the decree. StAA, Strafbuch Nr. 105, 1615–1632, fol. 684; Chronik Nr. 28, fol. 3v; Chronik Nr. 32, fol. 8v.
[118] For discussion of Hans Windbusch's case, see Chapter 3, above.
[119] StAA, Strafamt, Urg. Melchior Cramer, 20 March 1630.
[120] Ibid.
[121] See untitled song filed ibid.
[122] See petition dated 21 March 1630, filed ibid.
[123] StAA, Strafbuch Nr. 105, 1615–1632, fol. 683.

diarist noted, "nobody goes to them, rather they avoid churches and sermons."[124]

The arrests of Glatz and Cramer demonstrated that, despite the council's efforts to ban "un-Catholic" songs and pamphlets, texts protesting the emperor's edict were secretly circulating through the Augsburg Lutheran community in manuscript form. Indeed, so many songs seem to have been available that Glatz took pride in being the owner of a song none of his neighbors had yet heard. Even the barely literate Melchior Cramer was collecting such songs, although he could not read them. Glatz's elaborate efforts to conceal his meaning and manufacture an alibi establish, however, that Augsburgers well understood the illegality of these texts and had developed strategies to keep them hidden from the authorities.

The Politics of Smuggling

In the summer of 1630, Augsburg officials identified one of the channels through which Lutheran texts were entering the city. On 2 July 1630, the *Bürgermeister* interviewed the printer Johann Gottlieb Morhart, who confessed to reprinting a tract by the former superintendent of the Lutheran churches in Augsburg, Johann Conrad Göbel. Titled *Instruction and Consolation to the Highly-Grieved Lutheran Citizenry of Augsburg* (*Unterricht und Trostschrift ... an die hochbetrubte Evangelicsch Burgerschafft zu Augspurg*), the original was supposed to have been printed in Stuttgart in 1630.[125] Morhart stated that he had reprinted the text for the respected Protestant physician Johann Rimmele. According to Morhart, Rimmele had persuaded him to undertake the work with promises to indemnify him against any losses. Morhart was worried about the danger, but needed work to support his sick wife. To keep the printing a secret and speed up the work, Rimmele himself helped Morhart set the text, coming to his shop under the pretense of treating his wife.[126]

---

[124] StAA, Chronik 32, fol. 7v.

[125] See, SStBA, S 563, M. Johann Conrad Göbel, *Underricht und Trostschrift / Neben trewhertziger Vermahnung / in gegenwärtigem kläglichen Zustand / zu wahrer Gedult / und Christlicher Beständigkeit bey der erkanten und bekanten Lehr deß heiligen Evangelii. An die hochbetrübte Evangelische Burgerschafft in Augspurg / welche auß Gottes verhängnuß ihrer getrwen lieben Seelenhirren / jetziger Zeit in mangel gesetzt ist. Geschriben Durch M. Johannem Conradum Goebelium, gewesnen Pfarrer bey S. Anna / und Seniorem daselbsten. Getruckt in Stuttgart / im Jahr Christi 1630. Durch Johann Weyrich Rößlin* (Stuttgart: Rößlin, 1630).

[126] See report of Bürgermeister Hans Felix Ilsung dated 2 July 1630, filed in StAA, Strafamt, Urg. Johann Rimmele, 8–13 July 1630.

Rimmele at first denied Morhart's accusations. He noted that his son, also named Johann, had taken up the book trade and had recently received a letter from Tübingen asking him to ship 1,000 copies of Göbel's *Instruction* to Frankfurt. As far as Rimmele knew, the book was already openly sold in Augsburg; in fact, his son was to send the books to Frankfurt because "so many had already been sent to Augsburg from Stuttgart that they didn't need any more here."[127] He claimed he had not known it was illegal to reprint or sell something that had already been printed, and he assured the *Strafherren* that his son had only been trying to earn a living.

When confronted with Morhart's testimony, Rimmele ultimately admitted that he helped set some of the pages "to help his son."[128] However, he denied any involvement with two other texts seized by the authorities, *When Will You Become Catholic? (Wann Wiltu Einmal Catholisch Werden?)* and *So You Still Won't Accommodate? (Wilt du dich noch nicht accomodieren?)*.[129] His son had received some of these tracts from Nuremberg and Ulm, Rimmele said, and sold them to the bookbinder Gabriel Mehlführer.[130]

After further investigation, the authorities re-examined Rimmele. This time, he admitted his involvement and promised his cooperation. He reported that the two anonymous tracts, *When Will You Become Catholic?* and *So You Still Won't Accommodate?* were written by Peter Meiderlin, the former preceptor at St Anna's. He had seen Meiderlin's drafts himself, and had helped Morhart set the texts and correct the proofs.[131]

Although the search for Meiderlin proved fruitless, authorities arrested bookbinder Gabriel Mehlführer. He admitted that he had bought 200 copies of *When Will You Become Catholic?* and 50 copies of *So You Still Won't Accommodate?* from the younger Rimmele. He bound the tracts and sold them, making only a "bad profit."[132] The *Strafherren* demanded to know how Mehlführer could be so "fresh" as to sell such

---

[127] Ibid.
[128] StAA, Strafamt, Urg. Johann Rimmele, 8 July 1630.
[129] SStBA, Th Pr 4091, *Ferrners Gespräch Uber die Gewissens Frag / Wilt du dich noch nicht accomodieren? Das ist: Anhange weiterer Fragen: und Beantwortungen / Dem Gesprech Wann wiltu einmal Catholisch werden? Zu zusetzen / Männiglichen dieser Zeit zu betrachten nützlich unnd nothwendig* ([np: np,] 1630). For the Catholic response, see SStBA, Aug 2571, Andreas Wagner, *Wann wilt du Catholisch werden? Das ist Gesprach zwischen einem Catholischen unnd Lutherisch Evangelischen: So newlich von einem unbenambten Lutherischen Zeloten durch den Truck außgesprengt worden: jetzund aber durch fleißigs examen gezogen / und auff Catholischer Seiten mit einem starcken Zusag vermehrt / und wider den Gegentheil kurzlich doch gründlich beantwortet.* (Augsburg: Aperger, 1631).
[130] StAA, Strafamt, Urg. Johann Rimmele, 8 July 1630.
[131] Ibid.
[132] StAA, Strafamt, Urg. Gabriel Mehlführer, 8 July 1630, Answer 7.

texts in violation of the express ban on "un-Catholic" books. These two tracts were especially bad, they noted, because they allegedly compared the Catholic churches to murderers' dens (*Mördergrueben*), accused the *Stadtpfleger* and the Privy Council of perjury, rallied the "un-Catholic" citizenry against the published imperial decrees, and spread vicious lies "hither and yon" about Catholics and the Catholic religion.[133] Mehlführer countered that he had read none of these points in the texts, but had only found "good compassion and consolation" in them. Finding nothing objectionable in the texts, he had not feared to sell them, especially since he had received them from "a prominent lord."[134] That lord was the wealthy merchant Jeremias Österreicher, a member of one of Augsburg's most prominent Protestant families.[135] According to Mehlführer, Österreicher had given him 600 copies of Göbel's *Instruction* to sell in Augsburg and, given his patron's high position, Mehlführer assumed the books were legal to sell.[136]

On the same day, the magistrates summoned Österreicher to appear before the *Bürgermeister* to answer Mehlführer's charges. Österreicher admitted that he had given Mehlführer some 600–700 copies of Göbel's *Instruction*, which his friend Antony Stenglin had received from Stuttgart. According to Österreicher, he and other Lutheran patricians had decided to distribute the book among "the common man," hoping that they would heed Göbel's instruction that they show respect to the authorities.[137]

Österreicher's testimony proved troublesome to the Privy Council. He and Stenglin belonged to two of the city's wealthiest and most politically prominent Protestant families. They had also both been members of the council, and their involvement in the distribution of illegal "un-Catholic" books was deeply embarrassing to the government. How could the council demand the compliance of the "common man" if the very leaders of the community flouted the law? Moreover, a secret alliance of Protestant patricians for illegal ends raised the fears of conspiracy and, possibly, insurrection.

In a departure from usual practice, Österreicher and Stenglin were each examined in "*Secreti Senatus Secretiorius*," that is, during a closed meeting of the Privy Council. The Privy Council's questions focused on who had orchestrated the plan to distribute Göbel's book. Was the clergy involved? Which council members participated? How often did they

---

[133] Ibid., Question 5.
[134] Ibid., Answers 4 and 5.
[135] On the Österreicher family, see Grünsteudel et al, *Augsburger Stadtlexikon*, p. 694.
[136] StAA, Strafamt, Urg. Gabriel Mehlführer, 8 July 1630, Answer 4.
[137] Report of *Bürgermeister* Hans Felix Ilsung, dated 8 July 1630, filed in StAA, Strafamt, Urg., Jeremias Österreicher, 18 July 1630.

meet? Who was their leader? Had they asked Göbel to write this tract to encourage boycotts of Catholic services? Österreicher and Stenglin both testified that they had not engaged Göbel to write the *Instruction*; rather Göbel had sent the books to Stenglin through his trade correspondent Johann Hörmann. Stenglin admitted he had corresponded with Göbel about other matters but had neither asked for nor expected to receive the books.[138] Both Österreicher and Stenglin described the plan to distribute the books as an informal affair. According to Österreicher, Stenglin had simply approached him and a group of other men speaking together on a street near the Perlach Tower. Stenglin passed along greetings from Pastor Göbel and told them that he had about 200 copies of his *Instruction* for distribution among the Protestant leadership. The group, which included several other prominent men, suggested that he send the books to Österreicher's friend Gabriel Mehlführer.

According to Österreicher, Mehlführer had been his bookbinder for years, and the two men had become friends. He asked Mehlführer to sell the books for them because, he said, he "didn't know anything about books."[139] He claimed that he had not anticipated any trouble with the authorities because Göbel's book exhorted the Augsburg Lutheran community to show obedience to their government while waiting for God's deliverance. "He did not think there was anything evil in it," he said, "because it said that the citizenry should show respect and obedience to the authorities and refrain from all rebellion."[140] He stated that even Mehlführer seemed unconcerned about the danger. Although Mehlführer *had* pointed out that the text was illegal, he was evidently satisfied that the texts would pass scrutiny because they properly bore the author's name on the title page. Far from having to talk Mehlführer into the plan, Österreicher insisted that he knowingly accepted the risks.[141]

For his part, Stenglin claimed not to have known that "un-Catholic" books had been banned in Augsburg or that the censors' approval was a prerequisite to the sale of books. In any case, he noted, he had not known what the books were about because they were all packed up in their shipping crates.[142] Österreicher admitted, however, that the men often talked of the suffering of the Lutheran community and decided to distribute the texts to encourage patience among the "common man."[143] Although Österreicher

---

[138] StAA, Strafamt, Urg. Anthony Stenglin, 16 July 1630.
[139] StAA, Strafamt, Urg. Jeremias Österreicher, 18 July 1630, Answer 6.
[140] Ibid.
[141] Ibid., Answer 8.
[142] StAA, Strafamt, Urg. Antony Stenglin, 16 July 1630, Answer 4.
[143] Report of *Bürgermeister* Hans Felix Ilsung dated 8 July 1630, filed in StAA, Strafamt, Urg. Jeremias Österreicher, 18 July 1630.

denied any organized meetings among them, he affirmed that "there was no time when some of the [Protestant leaders] got together when they did not talk about their distress in religious matters."[144] They met only when "something important happened," he said, and were often joined by several members of the council and the city attorney.

To keep its proceedings against Stenglin and Österreicher a secret, the Privy Council did not record its judgment against them in the city's Punishment Books (*Strafbücher*), as it did in most criminal matters. It also could not impose the usual penalties of imprisonment or expulsion, as such punishments might provoke speculation. Rather, as "a merciful punishment" it assessed a hefty fine of 300 gulden against Österreicher and 100 gulden against Stenglin, which they were ordered to pay into the city's alms coffers.[145] The matter did not remain a secret from everyone, however, for at least one contemporary diarist recorded the lords' punishment.[146]

Despite the council's efforts, illegal Protestant texts were relatively easy to distribute through private channels. Although the council had dispatched the city guards and inspectors to search the markets for merchants selling illegal Protestant texts, such texts could enter the city through private couriers and easily change hands in homes and taverns outside public view, particularly if given the protection of prominent lords and officials. Indeed, despite wide gaps in wealth and station, it seems Augsburg's printers and booksellers had close connections to the city's social and political elite. The bookmen could rely on these contacts to shield their work, and their patrons could call on them to help spread messages that they themselves could not be publicly seen to endorse. The arrangement suited the interests of both parties, even if it violated the laws of the government these councilmen served. Combined with the sharing of manuscript songs and texts in the city's streets and taverns, these channels ensured that prohibited Protestant writings would continue to find an audience in Augsburg despite the efforts of the emperor, the city council, or its deputies.

"The Swedish Time:" Censorship Serves the State

By April 1632, the Swedish army was camped in Lechhausen, across the river from Augsburg. Augsburg's imperial defenders had already burnt the Lechhausen bridge, but found themselves grossly outnumbered. With Swedish guns trained on the city, Augsburg representatives attempted to

---

[144] StAA, Strafamt, Urg. Jeremias Österreicher, 18 July 1630, Answer 4.
[145] StAA, Geheime Ratsbuch Nr. 9, 1628–1639, fol. 92.
[146] StAA, Chronik 28, fol. 4.

organize a settlement. On 20 April, the Swedish king Gustavus Adolphus led his army into Augsburg, where the city's Protestants greeted them as liberators sent from God.[147] The Catholics in the city council, however, had no cause to celebrate. Gustavus Adolphus announced his intention to oust all of them, along with their deputies.

The king repeatedly stressed his desire to restore Augsburg's Lutherans to their full rights, but he assured the Catholic citizenry that they would find him their merciful lord so long as they remained loyal. Catholics would be free to worship in Augsburg, but their processions and ceremonies would be restricted.[148] Despite his conciliatory promises, however, the king appointed an exclusively Protestant city council, elevating several prominent Protestant families to the patriciate in the process.[149]

When Gustavus Adolphus left Augsburg in late April, he left the city with a Swedish garrison and an obligation to pay a monthly subsidy of 30,000 taler into the royal coffers.[150] With the advent of the so-called "Swedish Time" (die Schwedenzeit) in Augsburg, the city's censorship policies shifted focus once more. Emperor Ferdinand II's edict against "unCatholic" teaching was set aside, and magistrates shifted from enforcing religious conformity to policing internal security and political loyalty to the occupying forces. To this end, the new Swedish-backed city council, or "Swedish Council" (Schwedenrat) as it was sometimes known, used its regulatory powers to suppress anti-Swedish talk within the community.

Beginning soon after the departure of Gustavus Adolphus, the new, all-Lutheran city council also took steps to restrict the activities of Augsburg's Catholic residents. Rumors circulated that Augsburg's Catholics were sending secret messages to imperial and Bavarian forces regarding the recapture of the city.[151] Government proclamations denounced those holding "suspicious" assemblies, making threatening comments against the city and the members of the Protestant faith, distributing "made up" news accounts, and sending aid to the enemy armies. The magistrates ordered that anyone, "especially the members of the Papist religion, both clerical and lay," who engaged in such "machinations" would be removed from their offices and confined to their houses or monasteries. Moreover, they were forbidden to send any letters or provisions out of the city

---

[147] Ibid., pp. 684–6.
[148] Horst Jesse, *Die Geschichte der Evangelischen Kirche in Augsburg* (Pfaffenhofen: W. Ludwig Verlag, 1983) p. 222.
[149] Roeck, *Eine Stadt in Krieg und Frieden*, pp. 688–95.
[150] C. V. Wedgwood, *The Thirty Years War* (Garden City, New York: Anchor Books, 1961), p. 307.
[151] StAA, Chronik 32, fol. 31v.

without official permission. Masterless servants, "including *the Jesuits' students*" (emphasis original) were no longer welcome in Augsburg and were ordered to leave within two days.[152]

One of the "made up news accounts" that troubled the authorities was published by the city's only remaining Catholic printer, Andreas Aperger. In the spring of 1632, before Augsburg had fallen to the Swedes, Aperger had printed a news-sheet containing extracts from war reports written by imperial partisans. Among the reports was a brief description of how the imperial commander defending the nearby Protestant city of Nördlingen had disarmed the Lutheran citizenry there after discovering them to be in communication with the Swedes.[153] Aperger's print had been duly approved by the Catholic censors Hans Felix Ilsung and Hans Wolf Zeehen, appointed by the then all-Catholic council. Unfortunately for Aperger, the change in government also ushered in a change of censors, who had very different ideas of how the law should be applied.

In early July 1632, both Aperger and the author of the piece, Michael Ulrich Oleus, came under investigation for publication of the tract. The city council's records suggest that the prosecution may have originated with an official complaint from the now Swedish-controlled city of Nördlingen. Although the transcript of Aperger's interrogation does not survive, Oleus's case suggests that the source of the council's ire was a passage describing the Protestant citizens of Nördlingen as "the well-known eternally rebellious Nördlingers."[154] The new city council held the tract to be a defamatory libel, long forbidden under imperial law.[155]

In his defense, Oleus insisted that he and Aperger had fully obeyed the law as it existed at the time they published the news-sheet. Oleus believed that the account had come directly from the imperial commander at Nördlingen and had no reason to doubt its veracity. While at mass one day in the cathedral of Our Lady, Oleus had shown the letter to Aperger, who was looking for something to print on some empty sheets he had left over from another job. As required under the city's censorship laws, Aperger first showed the text to the censors. The censors reviewed the materials twice, finally giving him permission to print them.[156]

---

[152] StAA, Schätze Nr. 16, 'Anschläge,' fol. 378v; StAA, Chronik 32, fol. 30v.

[153] SStBA, 4° Gs. Flugschriften 1437, *Extract, Auß glaubwürdigen Schreiben / von Ihr Excellent Herrn General Tilly / u. an Ihr Fürstl: Gnad: Herzog Rudolph Maximilian von Sachsen Lawenburg de dato 12. Martii 1632 auß Bamberg / sampt noch andern gewisen Berichten / so von underschidlichen Orthen außgeschrieben worden / Wie hernach zusehen.* (Augsburg: Aperger, 1632), p. Aiiv.

[154] Ibid.; StAA, Strafamt, Urg. Michael Ulrich Oleus, 9 July 1632.

[155] StAA, Strafbuch Nr. 105, 1615–1632, fol. 752.

[156] StAA, Strafamt, Urg. Michael Ulrich Oleus, 9 July 1632.

Oleus insisted that he and Aperger had acted out of no improper motives and would not have published the reports if they had known they were punishable. The news seemed reliable, Oleus protested, and what was more, they had the express permission of the *Bürgermeister* and the censors.[157] In the new council's eyes, however, this was not enough to excuse Aperger and Oleus. It concluded that the text was patently defamatory and therefore illegal under any reading of the law. To support its position, the council looked not to Augsburg's own laws, but to the imperial recesses. Imperial law dating back to the early sixteenth century had banned defamatory libels; the fact that the Catholic censors of the prior regime had nevertheless approved the anti-Nördlingen tract only proved *their* illegal bias, the council reasoned. In prosecuting a pro-imperial text under the Empire's own laws, the new government presented its actions as an attempt to restore even-handed justice. According to the council, it had not changed the law after the fact against its political enemies—it had simply removed the official bias that had allowed illegal activity to go unpunished in the past.

The council accordingly instituted proceedings against the former censors, Hans Felix Ilsung and Hans Wolf Zeehen von Deibach, charging them with dereliction of their duties. In addition to serving as censors, both men had also been *Bürgermeister* under the prior Catholic-controlled regime. They were also rumored to have been among the former government officials in secret correspondence with imperial and Bavarian forces.[158] Perhaps because of their social prominence and the sensitive charges against them, the case was handled outside the usual criminal process. The men were interviewed in private, and the council's judgment against them was not recorded in the city's official punishment rolls. In its own minutes, however, the council recorded that the men had failed in their duties as censors by allowing a defamatory text to be printed in violation of longstanding imperial law. What was more, the council found, they not only failed to confiscate the tracts, but approved them for immediate sale, "thereby to publicize their own intentions and concerns."[159] In other words, the council alleged, they had illegally subverted imperial law to further their own political and religious agenda. As punishment, the council ordered each man to pay 50 imperial taler into the city's alms coffers.[160] Oleus and Aperger were both expelled.[161]

---

[157] See supplications of Michael Ulrich Oleus, filed ibid.
[158] StAA, Chronik 32, fol. 31v.
[159] StAA, Ratsbuch Nr. 63, 1631–1633, fol. 186.
[160] Ibid.
[161] Ibid.; StAA, Strafbuch Nr. 105, 1615–1632, fol. 752; StAA, Chronik 32, fol. 32r.

The prosecution of Oleus and Aperger demonstrated, once again, that printers and authors could not rely on the censors' approval to protect them from changes in government policy. Although they had complied with all legal requirements, the clearances they received provided them no security after the fall of the old regime. This was a long-standing problem, as booksellers and printers had been similarly prosecuted after the change in government at the end of the Schmalkaldic War.[162] These reversals of policy were merely the most dramatic examples of the system's unpredictability. Even in peacetime, printers complained that officials changed standards after the fact, prosecuting them for texts that had once been permitted. This problem was basic to a system that was vague by design. The laws did not change, but their official interpretation fluctuated in response to changing times. Those interpretative changes were typically not announced, but once adopted, they completely negated the decisions made under prior policy.

In November 1637, Gustavus Adolphus fell in the battle of Lützen, ending a string of Protestant victories.[163] The fall of Nördlingen to imperial forces in September 1634 had destroyed the Swedish army in the region, leaving the imperial and Bavarian armies in command of the field. Rejecting calls to negotiate a surrender, the Augsburg city council resolved to hang on. Meanwhile, the citizens starved. One chronicler noted that his "poor dog is not even safe in the streets, for whoever wants to will shoot him down and eat him."[164] Rumors of cannibalism circulated; one soldier's wife was said to have cooked and eaten the remains of her own child.[165] Finally, with deaths mounting and no more provisions to be found, the city council treated with the imperial commander in Leonberg for the surrender of Augsburg.

The so-called "Leonberger Accord" returned Augsburg to its legal status in 1629. Although the emperor's 1629 edict was once again operative and Augsburg's churches were to be returned to Catholic control, imperial negotiators allowed Augsburg's Lutheran community the right to construct a new church and employ a pastor at their own cost. A new military commander, Ottheinrich Fugger, took control of the city's defenses.[166] Soon thereafter, the emperor dissolved the "Swedish council" and ordered the installation of a new, exclusively Catholic council. Catholic clergy assumed control of all of Augsburg's churches, with the exception of the *Barfüsser*, where some Lutheran baptisms were still performed. Until the new church allowed under the Leonberger Accord could be built,

---

[162] See Chapter 2, above.
[163] Parker, *The Thirty Years' War*, pp. 117–8.
[164] StAA, Chronik 32, fol. 59r.
[165] StAA, Chronik 28, fol. 17v.
[166] Roeck, *Eine Stadt in Krieg und Frieden*, pp. 763–7.

Augsburg's Lutherans worshiped under the open sky in the courtyard of St Anna's.[167]

Although Catholics ruled in Augsburg until the end of the war, the council's policies were more inclusive, appointing representatives from the Lutheran community and setting aside the re-Catholicizing zeal that characterized the regime from 1629 to 1632.[168] For the community and the council, the years that followed were a time of rebuilding and reconsolidation. Public expression in Augsburg, and official oversight of it, adopted a milder, more pragmatic tone.

The ravages of the war had taken a heavy toll on Augsburg. The city's experience under both the 1629 edict and the "Swedish Time" had demonstrated the ultimate failure of both confessions' efforts to impose their political will upon the city. By the 1630s, Augsburgers had come to understand their city as effectively bi-confessional. Catholics and Lutherans may not have genuinely embraced the truths of each other's faiths, but both groups had come to understand the practical necessity of accommodating both confessions' traditional claims on the city. Both Catholics and Lutherans had learned their rights under the Peace of Augsburg, and neither group would accept the restriction of their privileges or the legitimacy of one confession's exclusive rule.

Parity Confirmed: The Peace of Westphalia

With Augsburg in imperial hands, officials conducted an official census of the city in the autumn of 1635. The results were grim: with a total population of merely 16,442 souls, Augsburg had lost 65 percent of its pre-war population. Of the survivors, 73 percent identified themselves as Lutheran; only 4,405 Catholics remained in the city.[169] With refugees flooding in from the ravaged countryside, Augsburg's officials struggled to find enough food to feed the hungry. While famine stalked the city, 1646 brought the return of war to Augsburg. In October of that year, a French and Swedish army stormed the city's northern gates. To secure the aid of all members of the community in the defense, the city council promised the Protestant citizenry representation in the council and recovery of their churches. The Bavarian elector likewise pledged the full restoration of the Lutheran community's political and religious rights.[170] The defenders

---

[167] Ibid., pp. 771–5.
[168] On political developments during this era, see ibid., pp. 869–80.
[169] Ibid., pp. 775–89.
[170] Wolfgang Zorn, *Augsburg: Geschichte einer deutschen Stadt* (Augsburg: Hieronymus Mühlberger Verlag, 1972), p. 219.

repelled the attacking army, and a truce in March 1647 secured a few months' peace for Augsburg.

In the meantime, representatives of the warring powers had been negotiating in the Westphalian cities of Münster and Osnabrück for an end to the war. The Augsburg city council sent a Catholic representative to the assembly, while Augsburg's Lutheran community appointed its own delegates to represent its interests. Despite initial opposition from the representatives of the city and the bishop, they finally reached an agreement in March 1648 guaranteeing equal rights to Augsburg's Protestants and Catholics in religion and political participation. The parties' agreement was memorialized in Article V of the Osnabrück treaty. The treaties of Osnabrück and Münster, known collectively as the Peace of Westphalia, were signed simultaneously on 24 October 1648, bringing the long years of war finally to an end.[171] After decades of fighting, the Empire finally had peace, and Augsburg's two confessions finally had the legal parity over which they had so long contested.

Riders bearing the news first reached Augsburg around midnight on Sunday, 1 November. The initial rejoicing was tempered with anxiety over whether the peace would last, and whether its terms would be fully executed.[172] News-sheets broadcasting the terms of the Peace enjoyed a brisk sale.[173] In these accounts, readers would have learned that the Peace of Westphalia ratified the Religious Peace of Augsburg, recognizing it as "valid, and to be held sacred and inviolate."[174] The Peace mandated a return to the religious status of the "normal year" of 1624. In Augsburg and other confessionally mixed cities, religious practices and church property reverted to their status as of 1 January 1624, well before the Edict of Restitution.[175] In political matters, the Peace required that all offices in Augsburg be filled by equal numbers of Lutheran and Catholic officials, or in the case of civic offices having unequal numbers of members, that the majority position be rotated annually between the confessions. Thus, Augsburg was to have one Catholic and one Lutheran *Stadtpfleger* at all times. Correspondingly equal appointments were to be made to the council and all other city offices, from the *Bürgermeister*

---

[171] Ibid., p. 220.

[172] Claire Gantet, 'Die ambivalente Wahrnehmung des Friedens: Erwartung, Frucht und Spannungen in Augsburg um 1648,' in *Zwischen Alltag und Katastrophe. Der Dreißigjährige Kriege aus der Nähe*, eds Benigna von Krusenstjern and Hans Medick (Göttingen: Vandenhoeck & Ruprecht, 1999), pp. 359–73.

[173] Ibid., p. 361.

[174] Instrumentum Pacis Osnabrugense, Art. V, § 1, in *Kaiser und Reich: Verfassungsgeschichte des Heiligen Römischen Reiches Deutscher Nation vom Beginn des 12. Jahrhunderts bis zum Jahre 1806 in Dokumenten*, Teil II, ed. Arno Buschmann, 2nd ed. (Baden-Baden: Nomos Verlagsgesellschaft, 1994), p. 34.

[175] Ibid., Art. V, §§ 2–3.

and the city's judicial officers all the way down to the most menial functionaries. Catholics and Lutherans were to have exclusive authority over their respective schools and churches, and neither confession was permitted a voting majority with respect to religious matters. Both sides were forbidden to use civic authority to oppress members of the other confession.[176]

The Peace also reordered Augsburg's censorship system, mandating the appointment of equal numbers of Catholic and Protestant censors. To ensure the independence of both churches, all Catholic religious texts were to be reviewed solely by Catholic censors, while all Protestant texts were to be reviewed solely by Protestants. Secular writings, however, were to be reviewed by all four censors. The censors were instructed to ensure that nothing was printed that was contrary to the imperial Police Ordinances, the Religious Peace of Augsburg, the political treaties of the Empire, or the Peace of Westphalia. Moreover, they were to suppress any works critical of the emperor, the electors, or the other estates of the Empire, as well as anything shameful, defamatory, or disruptive of the public peace.[177]

The city council followed the changes to the censorship system with a new decree governing public expression. The text of the council's 20 May 1649 decree made clear that the arrival of confessional parity under the Peace had not brought peace between the confessions. The council stated,

> It has been publicly decreed at various times in many City Police and Punishment ordinances that everyone should refrain from all defamations, insults, and threats, especially in religious or governmental matters, and should allow each other to live in peace and quiet. However, reliable reports have come forward, to the council's extreme displeasure, that for a while now, especially since the changes in the All-Holy Religious and Political Order, all kinds of evil and entirely irresponsible speech, gossip, defamations, and insults are put about by members of both religious groups, not just in the beerhalls and taverns, but rather in the public lanes and imperial streets. Not only are neighbors and fellow citizens sorely injured by this, but the Worthy Government is critically attacked; above all God Himself is not spared ... Such [conduct] is deeply contrary to good policy, the welfare of the citizenry, and communal harmony, and is to be even less tolerated in this Praiseworthy Imperial City, because it offends God, above all, and both religions, as well as the Worthy Government, and in general serves only to create mistrust, embitterment, breakdown, and disaster, destroys the peaceful life of the citizenry, and gives cause to all kinds of dangers. According to the command of the Great Council, each and

---

[176] Ibid., Art. V, §§ 4; 6–9.
[177] SStBA, 2° Aug. 10, 'Ordnungen, Decreten, Verrüffe und Anschläge, 1522–1677,' fol. 508, 519–20.

every citizen and resident of both religions is to refrain from all defamations and insults and all that goes with them ... They shall show to everyone all appropriate decorum, peaceful and neighborly trust, and above all shall avoid all blasphemous and irresponsible speech against God, the exercise of both religions, the Praiseworthy Government and the newly-established civic order.[178]

As it had before the war, the new government sought to use its regulatory powers to promote acceptance of the new political and religious order, looking this time to the Peace of Westphalia to instruct Augsburgers in their mutual rights and obligations to keep the peace. Although this regulatory strategy had a long history in the city, events in Augsburg since the end of the Calendar Conflict had crystallized confessional identities and deepened the rifts within the community. The confirmation of legal parity between the confessions was expected to provide Augsburg authorities with a more effective means of policing and negotiating some of these conflicts. However, as Etienne François has pointed out in his study of post-1648 Augsburg, to the extent that parity defined each group's political rights in confessional terms, it also reinforced religious division within the community, creating an "invisible boundary" that separated Catholic from Protestant Augsburg.[179] In this, the new order in Augsburg fostered the organization of communal life around exclusive, confessional identifications.

Conclusions

The coming of the Peace of Westphalia officially enshrined the principle of legal parity between the confessions in Augsburg. This was an issue that had divided Augsburgers for over a generation, since the Calendar Conflict had exposed the deep differences between Catholics and Protestants on participation in civic governance. Since 1629, however, it had become evident that the civic ideal of communal cooperation the council had sought to foster under the Peace of Augsburg had collapsed for want of a more reliable legal foundation. The war had also demonstrated that the efforts of both groups to police conformity would ultimately be unsuccessful. Although Catholic and Lutheran governments both used the city's censorship apparatus to control dissent, these ideas continued to find expression in speech and song. Even strict controls on book production and ownership could not halt the circulation of forbidden messages

---

[178] SStBA, 2' Aug. 324, Bd. 4, 'Statutes,' Nr. 21.
[179] See Etienne François, *Die unsichtbare Grenze: Protestanten und Katholiken in Augsburg 1648–1806* (Sigmaringen: Jan Thorbecke Verlag, 1991).

through private channels and personal networks. In part, the failure of these governments to control expression suggests the success of prior governmental efforts to shape opinion. Although the Peace of Augsburg had proved unworkable in practice, both Catholics and Lutherans in Augsburg had internalized the standards that it was supposed to enforce. Both groups expected that their rights to live and worship in Augsburg would be legally recognized, and that their neighbors would be bound to accommodate them. Neither side was prepared thereafter to accept the legitimacy of either group's exclusive rule.

Confessional parity, with its guarantee of equal participation for both religious groups, was expected to provide a new basis on which to rebuild the community. In the months and years following the war, Augsburg's new government directed its controls to ensure that the principles of the Peace were communicated and reinforced throughout society. However, in a community where civic participation was organized around religious affiliation, parity also ensured that confessional identity would come to be seen as the defining element of individual and communal life. Rather than bridging the divide between the confessions, it helped to accentuate it.

Conclusion

Viewed from a historical perspective, the study of censorship implicitly raises the question as to what role it may have played in directing or impeding the transmission of ideas and in shaping public opinion. For the historian, this is a delicate matter, for how are we to determine what ideas *might have been* expressed and what *might have* occurred had censorship not been in place? At its heart, however, this inquiry may be somewhat misguided, for it presupposes that the most authentic expression of a culture is to be found in critical inquiry freed from external constraints. The urban experience in the confessional era suggests that these constraints were in some sense intrinsic to the culture itself; it was, in short, a society that was at once both censored and censoring. Throughout the period, these cities were forced to adapt their censorship policies to political and social forces at work within their communities. In such an environment, the consequences of "official" or "external" constraints on expression cannot be fully separated from the controlling impulses penetrating the society itself. In the early modern German city, censorship was as much a product of public opinion as a force acting upon it.

These currents of opinion, and official responses to them, shifted substantially over the course of the sixteenth and seventeenth centuries. As political power shifted and religious policy evolved, the targets of official control changed with the shifting religious and political climate. Despite these changes, censorship remained an expression of a broader, long-standing civic effort to create and preserve an orderly and integrated society. Ideally, all members of society were to be integrated into a single community, united in belief and opinion for the common good. The magistrates' fundamental authority to regulate expression and suppress dissent was therefore generally accepted as integral to the spiritual and social good of the community.

In its practical effects, censorship in the early modern German city was often adapted to accommodate communal expectations and demands. We have seen that the first impulses toward reform in the 1520s were accompanied by increased public questioning of previously accepted religious norms. Official attempts to control the spread of Reformation ideas in the cities, however, reveal that the authorities were often less interested in preserving religious orthodoxy than in suppressing controversy and communal division. In this effort, official policies were geared toward balancing the growing demand for reform with prevailing standards of civil discourse and magisterial authority.

The official adoption of Protestant reforms was typically accompanied by more aggressive efforts on the part of the governing authorities to shape religious opinion among the citizenry. As imperial cities, these communities had to struggle to balance their perceived duty to teach and uphold the Word of God with their duty of loyalty to their Catholic emperor and overlord. The cities' censorship policies, therefore, had to be sufficiently flexible to allow them to meet the communal demand for religious uniformity at home without directly challenging the interests of the emperor or their Catholic neighbors abroad.

Although magistrates sought to control what information was permitted to circulate, the techniques used to skirt the law's requirements demonstrate that official control was by no means absolute. As centers for the exchange of ideas and information, these cities' regulatory capacities were often overwhelmed by the stream of texts and information flowing into and out of the community. The economic risks inherent within the book trade, and the inefficiencies within the censorship bureaucracy, also ensured that some would seek the financial rewards to be found in the clandestine book market. Illegal texts and ideas also circulated outside the book trade in manuscripts, songs, and speech. Those skirting the margins of the law understood that city officials lacked the resources to adequately police expression and therefore exploited the system's weaknesses.

We cannot assume, however, that censorship was ineffectual because it did not suppress everything; nor can we assume that it was unrelentingly oppressive because it may have prevented access to certain ideas and information. Rather, we have seen that authors and speakers to some degree internalized and helped to enforce the very standards the authorities tried to legislate. Given the significant obstacles to policing a large and diverse community, official control was, by necessity, dependent upon citizen reporting and voluntary compliance. Residents participated in this system as informants, but we have also seen that many residents undertook to police their own conduct and opinions, as well as those of their neighbors. Although individuals often did not fully understand the scope of the law, they had a general sense of the broad areas that were off-limits to public discussion and were quick to warn their neighbors against the dangers of dissent.

The cooperation of the citizenry was secured, in part, by a general acceptance of the magistrates' asserted right to regulate expression to protect communal values and the public peace. To encourage compliance, the magistrates also relied upon the vagueness inherent within the system's shifting standards. We have seen in the regulation of the urban print trade that its apparently arbitrary standards were to some degree intended to create uncertainty as to the scope of the law. As a result, printers and booksellers would be encouraged to exercise a degree of protective self-censorship in questionable cases. Economic interest also fostered self-regulation within the trade. While the economic pressures of the book trade may have enticed some printers and booksellers into the clandestine book market, financial self-interest also encouraged conservatism among printers looking to protect their livelihood from official backlash. Although it is evident that many book dealers and printers nevertheless chose to flout the law, it is also clear that many feared prosecution. Consequently, they either refused to deal in illegal prints or altered the texts to limit their risk. In assessing the consequences of censorship, we must recognize not only the many opportunities for evasion the system created, but also the defensive self-regulation that the system fostered within the community.

The devices that early modern Germans used to circulate their messages also provide some insight into the spectrum of opinion swirling beyond the officials' mandate and the means by which these ideas were transmitted. The urban trial transcripts, together with the songs, speeches, and texts preserved within the case records, document a complex interaction of oral and print cultures in the transmission of ideas. It is perhaps impossible to assess whether the texts and stories discussed here created and shaped public opinion or merely reflected the popular mood. The evidence does indicate, however, the circularity between high and low cultures, in which communication proceeded through a network of channels, each referring to and influencing the others. These messages contributed to the mix of ideas discussed within the community and were frequently adapted into new forms, for new purposes. The authorities appear to have understood this interaction, and sought to control the transmission of ideas and information at every level. To the extent that prohibited texts and ideas were able to circumvent official controls, however, the community's absorption and appropriation of these messages allowed them to penetrate the city to a degree perhaps neither the original authors nor the city magistrates could have expected.

At the heart of these cities' censorship policies, throughout all the shifts in confessional politics, was an overriding concern to foster and preserve communal consensus. The communal focus underlying these censorship controls thus undermines traditional models of social disciplining and confessionalization to the extent that they presuppose a unilateral extension of state and church authority over the urban population. We have seen, instead, that negotiation and cooperation between the censors and the censored was basic to the system of control. Indeed, the system's apparent inconsistencies in enforcement often stemmed directly from official efforts to adapt to the expectations and demands of large segments of the community. In highlighting this mediation, this study contributes to an emerging new paradigm of the urban Reformation and the consolidation of confessional identities. Whereas past models of the "magisterial Reformation" and confessionalization would attribute formative influence in these processes to the efforts of church leaders and government officials, we have seen just how fragmentary and limited the influence of reformers and magistrates often was in these communities. While we must appreciate the limits of official control, we must not thereby underestimate the significance of either church or state in influencing the course of change in the early modern city. Clearly, urban magistrates played a critical role in articulating, shaping, and enforcing communal standards of discourse. The sources also establish that church leaders and reformers, through their pamphlets, preaching, and institutions, exerted an indisputable influence over the course of religious change in the cities. However, the contests over censorship in these communities also show that the ideas and prescriptions of church and civic leaders did not directly translate into action. Rather, they were mediated, and in some cases modified, through a process of accommodation and negotiation at multiple levels within the community. Within this framework, the cities' censorship controls served as both a forum for negotiating competing demands and a vehicle for creating and enforcing new concepts of civic order. The magistrates' efforts to police this order within an often fractious, confessionally divided population thus suggests a more nuanced, and perhaps more realistic, paradigm for the process of change in the early modern city.

Bibliography

Archivalia

Bayerisches Hauptstaatsarchiv (BHStA)

'Kasten schwarz'
    Nr. 12676 – Visitation der Buchläden (1558–1607)
'Kurbayern Äüßeres Archiv'
    Nr. 77–82; 4240–4242; 4268; 4273
'Staatverwaltung'
    Nr. 2288; 2299, 2778; 2797; 3019; 3188; 3221

Frankfurt am Main, Institut für Stadtgeschichte (FaM ISG)

'Buchdruck und Zensur'
    Nr. 11; 14; 20; 31; 40; 55; 91; 98; 105; 113
'Bürgermeisterbücher'
    1521–23; 1621–22; 1627; 1630
'Ratsprotokolle'
    1621–22; 1627; 1630–31

Landeskirchliches Archiv Nürnberg (LKAN)

'Landalmosenamt Nürnberg' Nr. 466
'Markgräfliches Konsistorium Ansbach'
    Nr. Gen. ad 1; Gen. 18 I

Staats- und Stadtbibliothek Augsburg (SStBA)

2° Aug. 10, 'Ordnungen, Decreten, Verrüffe und Anschläge, 1522–1677'
2° Aug. 324, Bd. 2, 'Statutes'
2° Aug. 324, Bd. 4, 'Statutes'
2° Aug. 324, Bd. 7, 'Decreta Civitatis Augustana'
4° Aug. 735/1, 'Kalenderstreit I'
4° Aug. 735/2, 'Kalenderstreit II'
4° Aug. 956, 'Georg Müller btf.'
4° Aug. 1021, 'Statuta Civitatis Augustanae Tomus VIII'

2° Aug. Cod. 437, 'Acta Augustana d. i. Amtshandlung und Amtliche Correspondenz der Stadt Augsburg, 1566–1745'
4° Aug. Cod. 196, 'Neües Lied, von den Capußinern so Anno 1600: in die Statt Augspürg kommen'
2° Cod. 208, 'Bernhard Rehlinger, Stadtpfleger, Reformations Protocoll, 1629–1631'
2° Cod. Aug. 53, 'Chronica, darinen allerley wunderseltsame unnd underschidliche Sachen begriffen so alhier inn Augspurg vorgange'
2° Cod. Aug. 123, 'Singularia Augustana'
2° Cod. Aug. 311, 'Catholische Lästerpredigten und Pasquille'
4° Cod. Aug. 147, 'Jesuiter Lied'
2° Cod. H. 18, 'Augspurgischer Calender Streitt von Anno 83 bis 90'
2° Cod. S. 65, 'Anon: Cath: Diar: Aug. ab anno 1633'
4° Cod. S. 8, 'Chronik der Stadt Augsburg bis 1634'
2° S. 14, Kapsel I, 'Anschläge, 1524–1734, Nr. 1–201'
2° Stw Abschied 1555, 'Reichsabschied 1555'

Staatsarchiv Nürnberg (StAN)

'B-Laden SIL 196,' Nr. 6; Nr. 7; Nr. 10; Nr. 12
'B-Laden SIL 296,' Nr. 12
'Ratsbücher,' Nr. 12–13

Stadtarchiv Augsburg (StAA)

'Reichsstadt'
    Ad Kalenderstreit Criminalia, 1583–1589
    Anschläge und Dekrete, 1490–1649, Nr. 1–86, Teil I
    Baumeisteramt: Nr. 152 (1559); Nr. 181 (1590)
    Burgermeisteramt:
        'Instruction die Herren Burgermeister betreffend'
        'Amts-Protokolle des Bürgermeister Hans Bächler, 1576–1588'
        'Amts Protokolle des Bürgermeister Michael Mair, 1584–1589'
        'Hieremiae Österreichers Ambts Prothocoll 1632'
        'Protocollum 1625–1630…Herrn Burgermaister Sebastian Christoph Rehlinger'
    Censuramt:
        'Die Buchdrucker betreffend,' Tom I, 1550–1729
        Nr. XVI (1474–1756)
        Nr. XVIII (1551–1798)
        'Evangelia betreffend,' 1649–1753

'Pasquillen und Öffentlich Angehaftete oder Ausgebreitete Zettel und Scripten,' 1552–1795
Chroniken:
> Nr. 18, 'Wahrhafftige klägliche erzelung von dem trawrigen zustandt der Evangelischen kirchen zu Augspurg nach dem sie von den vorigen kirchen dienern verlassen worden von Iohannes Rößler, der zeit pfarher beÿ S. Anna, und senior der Evangelishen Ministerÿ daselbst.'
> Nr. 19, 'Chronik der Stadt Augsburg in Sachen der Reformation, 1583–1589'
> Nr. 28, 'Gründtliche Beschreibung dessen was sich von A°: 1629 biß A° 1648 In Gaist: und Welttlichen händlen Zwischen beeden Religionen zue Ausgpurg begeben und zuegetragen durch Eine wahrhaffte und der sachen selbst erfahrne Persohn aufgezaichnet'
> Nr. 32, 'Augspurgische Cronica, 1629–1660 von Ludwig Hainzelmann d. Ä, deutscher Schulhalter zu Augsburg'

Criminalakten Beilagen, 16. u. 17. Jhdt.
Geheime Ratsbücher:
> Nr. 2 (1527–1529); Nr. 3 (1530–1537); Nr. 5 (1539–1540);~ Nr. 6 (1540–1542); Nr. 9 (1628–1639)

Handwerkakten: Briefmaler, Illuministen & Formschneider, 1529–1645
Kalenderstreitacten: Nr. 28, 'Relatio. Der Ro: Kay: Mt: verordneter Comissarien der alhie anno 1584 nach dem auflauf verrichter Inquisition und Commission.'
Literalien Sammlung:
> 1522; 1524; 1528; 1555; 1585–87
> 'Schwenckfeldiana & Reformations-Acten'

Ordnungen und Statuten: Karton 9, 'Marktordnungen'
Ratsbücher:
> Nrs. 14–16 (1501–1542); Nrs. 18–19 (1544–1545); Nrs. 21–28 (1547–1554); Nrs. 30–32 (1557–1562); Nrs. 35–36 (1566–1570); Nr. 38 (1572–1573); Nr. 41 (1578–1579); Nr. 44 (1584–1586); Nr. 49 (1600–1602); Nrs. 61–63 (1627–1633); Nr. 65 (1635–1637); Nr. 67 (1638–1640); Nr. 71 (1648–1650)

Ratserlasse, 1507–1599
Religionsakten, 1574–1793
Schätze:
> Nr. 16, 'Anschläge'

Nr. 31, 'Sammlung reichsstädtischer Verordnungen und geschichtlicher Notizen der Stadt Augsburg, 1575–1600.'
Nr. ad 36/3, 'Zucht unnd Execution Ordnung, 1553'
Nr. ad 36/7, 'Zucht und Policey Ordnung, 1580'
Nr. ad 36/9, 'Zucht und Policey Ordnung, 1621'

Spreng'sche Notarialsarchiv 1574: Nr. 76 1/4
Steuerbücher: 1562; 1583; 1604; 1625
Strafamt:

Strafbücher: Nr. 94 (1509–1526); Nr. 95 (1533–1539); Nr. 96 (1540–1543); Nr. 96.1 (1543–1553) Nr. 97 (1553–1554); Nr. 98 (1554–1562); Nr. 99 (1563–1571); Nr. 100 (1571–1580); Nr. 101 (1581–1587); Nr. 102 (1588–1596); Nr. 103 (1596–1605); Nr. 104 (1608–1615); Nr. 105 (1615–1632); Nr. 106 (1633–1653).

Urgichten: 1521–1526; 1533–35; 1539; 1541–1544; 1547–1549; 1550–1553; 1556; 1559; 1561; 1563–1564; 1568–1569; 1571–1573; 1578–1581; 1583–1584; 1586–1592; 1594–1595; 1598; 1601–1606; 1608; 1610–1615; 1617; 1619; 1624–1625; 1628–1632; 1636; 1638–1640; 1645–1646; 1648–1650.

Zuchtbücher: Nr. 170 (1537–1539); Nr. 171 (1539–1540); Nr. 172 (1540–1542); Nr. 173 (1542–1543); Nr. 174; (1544–1545); Nr. 178 (1548–1549); Nr. 183 (1554–1557); Nr. 186 (1564–1567); Nr. 188 (1571–1575); Nr. 190 (1577–1580); Nr. 192 (1582–1584); Nr. 193 (1584–1588); Nr. 199 (1600–1611).

Wiedertäufer und Religionsacten

'Evangelisches Wesensarchiv Augsburg'
Nr. 1561, 'Öffentliche Anschläge und Verrufe, 1490–1599,' Tom. 1 & 2
Nr. 147, 'Öffentliche Anschläge und Verrüfe der Ehemaligen Reichs-Stadt Augsburg, Theil I & II.'
Nr. 503
Nr. 1046

'Historische Verein für Schwaben'
Nr. N6, 'Greiff Sammelband'
Nr. N13, 'Sammelband'
Nr. H. 140, 'Pasquille, 16. Jrhdt'
Nr. H. 239, 'Neue Zeitungen von 1521 bis 1570'

'Katholisches Wesensarchiv Augsburg'
    Nr. A38[5]; Nr. J19[4]; Nr. Lii[i]

Stadtarchiv Ulm (StAU)

A 1203 – 'Acta und Correspondenz die von Kayser begehrte Einführung des Gregorianischen Calenders betreffend 1583–1584'
A 3530 – 'Ratsprotokolle' 1548–1549; 1558; 1584
A 6875 – 'Religionsprotokoll of the Kirchenbaupflegerampt, 1570–1587'
G1 1590/2 – 'Chronik von Jerg Kraumer'
Kammerer, H., *Consignatio Chronologica Ministorum Ecclesiarum Ulmensium Tempore Reformationis Lutheri Ad nostra usq Tempora...*
U 5483 – 'Pfarrkirchenbaupflegamt'

Printed Works to 1650

Abschiedt der Römischen Königlichen Maiestat / und gemeiner Stendt / auff dem Reichsstag zu Augspurg / Anno Domini M.D.LV. auffgericht. Sampt/ der Keyserlichen Maiestat Cammergerichts Ordnung / wie die auff diesem Reichsstag / durch die Königliche Maiestat / und gemeine Stendt / widerumb ersehen / ernewert / und an vilen orten geendert. Mainz: Franz Behem, 1555. [SStBA, 2° Stw Abschied 1555]
Augspurgische Calender Zeittung. Kurze Historische erzölung deß Calender Streits / und darauß entstandenen Entpörung zu Augspurg 25. Maij / 1584. Darinnen auch gedacht wirdt / der Enturlaubung / hinführung / und Errettung deß Ehrwürdigen unnd hochgelerten Herrn Georgÿ Miller / der Heiligen Schrifft Doctorn. Zusingen inn Herzog Ernsts Ton. Omnis Mutation Periculosa [n.p.: n.p., n.d.]. [StAA, 'Ad Kalenderstreit Criminalia,' Urg. Sabina Preiss, 13 Jan. 1588].
Die New vermehrte / und gebesserte Bawrenklag / uber den Newen zugerichten Gregorianischen Bäpstische Kalender. In wölcher kurzlich angedeutet wirdt / das nicht allein under dem Bawensvolk / sondern auch in den Kirchen übungen und Polittischen sachen / für unordnungen / auß disem newen Kalender entsprungen und erwachsen seyen. Neben einem sonderlichen begern an den Bapst / da er anderst wölle / das amn sich nach seinem Kalender halten solle. [n.p.: n.p.], 1584. [SStBA, 4° Aug. 956, 'Georg Müller Btf.'].
Eder, Georg. *Evangelische Inquisition Wahrer und falscher Religion. Wider Das gemain unchristliche Claggeschray / Das schier niemands mehr wissen künde / wie oder was er glauben solle: In forma aines Christlichen Rathschlags / Wie ein jeder Christen Mensch seines Glaubens halben gäntzlich vergwist und gesichert sein möge: Dermassen*

/ daß er leichtlich nit künde betrogen noch verfürt werden. Dillingen: Sebald Mayer, 1573. [SStBA, Th H 667].

Ein Newes Lied/vom Könige Antiocho/wie er ein Weyb mit siben Sönen so jammerlich ertödtet hat/von wegen deß Gsatz Gottes. In Hertzog Ernsts Melodeye zusingen. H.R. [n.p., n.p., n.d.– 1550?] [BL, 11517 DE 8].

Ein Newes und klägliches Lied / von dem Betrübten Zustand / deß Ehrwürdigen / hochgelehrten herrn Georgii Miller / Doctor der h. Schrift / unnd gewesnen Pfarrhern / der Euangelischen Kirchen zu S. Anna inn Augspurg. Namblich / wie Ihn Gott Wunderbarlicher weiß / auß seiner feinden hännden / erlediget hat. Neben einer Tröstlichen Vermanung / zu der Gedult / inn der Verfolgung. In der Melodia. Wo Gott der Herr nicht bey uns helt / etc. [n.p.: n.p.], 1584. [SStBA, 4° Aug 735/1, 'Kalenderstreit I,' Nr. 3].

Ein Schönes neues Klaglied/von der lezten Zeit/was sich auch für Wunder zeichen alle Tag begeben/Wie sich auch zu Augspurg drey Engel haben sehen lassen Wie ihr solches in diesem Lied werdet vernemen/den andern Tag Jenner/Anno 1619. Im Thon: Wie Schone leicht uns der Morgenstern, etc. Die ander Zeitung. Von dem newen Cometstern/so in dem 1618. Jahr/den 1. Decembr. erschienen/welcher zu Augspurg und in vielen Landen ist gesehen worden/Gesangweiß gestelt/Im Thon: Kompt her zu mir spricht GOttes Sohn/etc. Lauingen: Jacob Senft, 1619. [BL, Tab. 597.d.2(13)].

Ein tröstlich Trawer-Lied / zu dieser Zeit zu singen. Im Thon: An Wasserflüssen Babylon / c. Für die Betrangte Christen. [n.p.: n.p., n.d.]. [StAA, Strafamt, Urg. Christof Glatz, 7–11 March 1630].

Ein warhaffte / doch erschrockliche newe Zeitung. Wie Sie den 20. Septebris / zur Newstatt an der hart / auch an viel andern orden mehr / zu nacht umb 10. Uhr / biß auff 2. Uhr / gegen tag am hohen Himmel / zwen Christliche feld Obristen / und ein Türckischer Obrister gesehen wordt / gleichsam / als wann Sie mit ein ander gar hotigs Sprachorten / und zwey Kriegsherr / mit einandder gar schröcklich gescharmieziert / auch ein Stim / fünffmal / inn lifften ist gehort worden / welche also geschrien / O Ihr gottlosen thut bueß. Zu Singen / Im thon. Ewiger Vatter im Himmelreich. Wie volgt Darbey der Tittel und Uberschrifft deß Türckischen Keyser. Wie auch die verzeichnuß der Gewaltigen Statt Constantinopel mit al ihrer gelegenheit. Gedruckt in Erfurt / bey Tobias Frisch. 1623. [Augsburg: David Franck, n.d.]. [StAA, Strafamt, Urg. Hans Meyer a/k/a Gallmeyer, 1–6 Feb. 1625].

Eine warhafftige erschrockliche newe Zeitung. Die erste / am tag Simonis und Jude / hat in d' Statt Veldkirch eines hauptmans Weib seines Namens Berengard Schmid / dises Weib hat in ihrer Geburt drey bose Geister gebracht / welche gestalt / wie ein mensch / aber lange Schwaif

/ wie die Schlangen / die lebe noch auff den heutige Tag / und Pfarrhern haben sich beschworen wollen / warumb sie da seyen / hat einer auß inen anfangen zu sagen mit Worten warumb sie da seyen biß irer Mutter sechs wochen furuber kommen / was nun weiter geschehen worden / werdet ihr inn disem Gesang ferner vernemmen. Im Thon. Hüff Gott das mir gelinge etc. Ein Schönes newes Anklopff lied Zur warnung allen Trewzigen Christen / in diser letsten betrübten zeit / sehr trostlich Zusingen. Im Thon. Von grund des Herzen mein / hab ich. Gedruckt zu Hohen Ems / durch Bartholomeum Schnell / Im Jahr Christi 1623. [n.p.: n.p., n.d.]. [StAA, Strafamt, Urg. Hans Meyer a/ k/a Gallmeyer, 1–6 Feb. 1625].

Ein warhafftige / und doch erschröckliche newe Zeitung. Von vier gottlose / verfluchten gelt Küpperer / welche sich zu Bayrischen Wathofen / ein halb Jar sich auff gleichem gewin oder verlust verbunden / Als sie aber den 20 Jannuarÿ angestelt mit einander ab zu rechnen / wie schrocklich der Teuffel mit inen umbgangen / werdet ihr in disem Lied vernemmen. Im Thon. Hilff Gott das mir gelinge etc. Gedruckt zu Regenspurg / bey Johann Miller. ANNO 1624. [n.p.: n.p., n.d.]. [StAA, Strafamt, Urg. Hans Meyer a/k/a Gallmeyer, 1–6 Feb. 1625].

Ein Warhafftige und erschrockliche newe Zeitung / welche begeben unnd zugetragen in dem flecken Steüne / zwo Meyl von Halbrunn in dem Wirtenberger Land / wie allda ein Reicher Mann / an Sanct Andreas seine Kinder bevoll den Segen zu thon. Was aber fur herzleyd darauß entstanden / wirst ein Frommer Christ fleissig in diesen Lied vernemmen. Im Thon: Hiff GOtt das mit gelinge / etc. Das Ander: Ein schön new Geistlich Weihenacht Lied. Im Thon: Mein Fröhlich Herz das treibt mich an: etc. Gedruckt zu Stuttgart / bey Johann Weyrich Rößlin / Im Jahr Christi / 1624. [n.p.: n.p., n.d.]. [StAA, Strafamt, Urg. Hans Meyer a/k/a Gallmeyer, 1–6 Feb. 1625].

Extract, Auß glaubwürdigen Schreiben / von Ihr Excellent Herrn General Tilly / u. an Ihr Fürstl: Gnad: Herzog Rudolph Maximilian von Sachsen Lawenburg de dato 12. Martii 1632 auß Bamberg / sampt noch andern gewisen Berichten / so von underschidlichen Orthen außgeschriben worden / Wie hernach zusehen. Augsburg: Andreas Aperger, 1632. [SStBA, 4° Gs. Flugschriften 1437].

Ferrners Gespräch Uber die Gewissens Frag / Wilt du dich noch nicht accomodieren? Das ist: Anhange weiterer Fragen: und Beantwortungen / Dem Gesprech Wann wiltu einmal Catholisch werden? Zu zusetzen / Männiglichen dieser Zeit zu betrachten nützlich unnd nothwendig. [np: np,] 1630. [SStBA, Th Pr 4091].

Göbel, M. Johann Conrad. *Underricht und Trostschrift / Neben trewhertziger Vermahnung / in gegenwärtigem kläglichen Zustand / zu wahrer Gedult / und Christlicher Beständigkeit bey der erkanten und bekanten Lehr deß heiligen Evangelii. An die hochbetrübte Evangelische Burgerschafft in Augspurg / welche auß Gottes verhängnuß ihrer getrwen lieben Seelenhirren / jetziger Zeit in mangel gesetzt ist.* Stuttgart: Johann Weyrich Rößlin, 1630. [SStBA, S 563].

Gegründte Christliche Antwort der jetzigen Euangelischen Predicanten in der Statt Augspurg. Auff Doctor Georgen Müllers newlich in Truck außgegangen vermainten Send und Trostbrieff. Sampt einem außfürlichen Bericht / auß weilund des Ehrwirdigen herrn D. Martin Luthers / und anderer furnemen Euangelischer / der wahren Lehrer Schrifften / was man vom Berüff der Kirchendiener derselben Confession unnd der Lutherischen Lehr gemeß halten solle. An die Euangelische Burgerschaft zu Augspurg Sendbrieffs weyß / derselben zum besten / zu auffdeckung der warheit / unnd widerlegung des ungrunds / getrewhertziger mainung gestellt und Publicirt / damit sich nyemandt in Sünd füren / oder darinn zu seinem ewigen verderben auffhalten lasse. Augsburg: Valentin Schönig, 1586. [SStBA, 4° Aug 735/2, 'Kalenderstreit II,' Nr. 27].

Herbst, Matthaeus. *Ein Geistlich Gemäldt. In Welchem allerley Eygenschafften/der Gottlosen und Frommen/in gedancken/geberden/worten und wercken/fürgemalet sein. Item wie es zeitlichen glücks halben/auff Erden/under ihnen ungleich zu geht: aber doch endlich/die Gottlosen hie und dort gestrafft/die frommen aber getröstet/und ewig erfrewt werden. Gestelt und auffgericht/auß dem Psalter deß Königlichen Propheten Davids/allen frommen zum trost/Den bösen aber zu nohtwendiger Christlicher warnung.* Tübingen: Alexander Hock, 1589. [HAB, A:751.25 Theol. (3)]

[Holtzmann, Ulrich]. *Ain New Lied Wie die Predicanten der Statt Augspurg geurlaubt und abgeschafft seind, den 26. Augusti... 1551 geschehen.* [Augsburg: Hans Zimmermann, 1551]. [SStBA, Aug. 1035].

[Hunnius, Aegidius]. *Warhaffter und Gründtlicher Bericht von rechter, ordenlicher Wahl unnd Beruff der Evangelischen Prediger. Darzu fürnemlich angezeigt wirdt / durch welche Personen / vermög Gottes Worts und Exempel der Ersten Kirchen / selbinger soll verrichtet werden. Erstlich: Durch den Ehrwürdigen / hochgelehrten Herren Egidium Hunn / der H. Schrifft Doctorn und Professorn / bey der Hohenschul Marpurg in Hessen / in Latein gestelt / und in Truck verfertiget. Jetz aber: Den Evangelischen Kirchen / bey welchen solcher Beruff diser zeit streitig / zu nothwendigem Bericht / trewlich ins Teutsch gebracht.* [n.p.: n.p.], 1589. [HAB, A:751.25 Theol. (3)]

[Kern, Thomas]. *Ein warhafftige und kurtzweilige newe Zeittung der gantz newe verbindtnuß / Etlicher fürnemme Länder unnd Reichstatten / wider den Türcken in Ungern / gar starckhen widerstand zu thun. Was aber für hilff oder rath von jeder Statt oder Land soll geschehen,*

Hat ein fürnemer Mann mit der Feder geschriben / unnd under die Preß in Truck kommen lassen. Wie folget ... Gedruckt under der Preß / mit Schwarzen Buchstaben / Im Jahr / 1625. Bratwürst. [Augsburg: Mathaus Langenwalter, 1625]. [StAA, Strafamt, Urg. David Franck and Matthaus Langenwalter, 12 Feb. 1625].

Kurzer Bericht/von gemeinem Kalender, Woher er kommen/wie er mit der zeit verrückt/ob und wie er widerumb zuersetzen sey. Auß anlaß der Päpstlichen newlich außgegangen Kalenders Reformation/Gestelt in Fürstlicher/pfaltgräuischer Schul zu Newstadt an der Hardt. Neustadt: M. Harnisch, 1583. [StBU, Schad 4322]

Luther, Martin. *Ain underricht der beychkünder über die verbotten bücher D.M. Luther. Wuittemberg. Im Jar. M.D.XXI.* [Augsburg: Melchior Ramminger], 1521. [HAB, A:151.26 Theol. (9)]

Luther, Martin. *Wider den falsch genanten gaystlichen Stand des Bapsts und derBischofe. D. Martin. Luther Ecclesiasten zu Wittenberg. M.D. XXII.* [Augsburg: Silvan Othmar], 1522. [BSB, Res 4° Th. U. 103 XXX, 3]

Luther, Martin. *Widder den falsch genantten geistlichen Stand des Bapst und der Bischoffen. D. Martinus Luth. Ecclesiasten zu Wittemburg.* [Wittenberg: Lotter, 1522]. [BSB, Res 4° Th. U. 104 VII, 41]

Marschalck, Haug. *Das Hailig ewyg wort gots/was dz in im kraft/strecke/ tugendt/frid/fred erleüchtung/unnd leben/in aym rechten Christen zu erwecken vermag, etc. Zu gestelt dem edlen Gestrengen Riter und Kaiserlichen hauptman Hern Jörgen vonn Fronsperg zu Mündelhain, etc. Im Jahr M.D. XXiii.* Augsburg: Melchior Ramminger, 1523. [BL, 3906.e.70].

Marschalck, Haug. *Ein Spiegel der Plinden/wan Christus der her hat geredt/Ich wird mein glory von den/hochweisen verberge/und/wird es den kleine/verkünden und offbaren./Dann ee mein glory und eer solt undergon/es musten die steyn und holtz/reden lernen. Uff solichs ist uffgericht anzuschauwe dises Spiegel der Blinden.* 1523.

Müller, Georg. *Augspurgische Handel, So sich daselbsten wegen der Religion / und Sonderlich jüngst vor zwey Jahren im werenden Calender Streit mit Georgen Müller D. Pfarrer und Superintendenten daselbst zugetragen... Sampt Nottwendiger rettung der Unschuld und ehren / wider allerhand beschwerliche Anklag und ungegründte Bezüchtigung / damit die Papisten eine zeitlang ihn D. Müllern fürnemlich beleget haben. Beschrieben Durch Doct. Georgen Müllet / Professoren und Cancellarium bey der löblichen Universitet / auch prapositum in der Stifftkirchen zu Wittemberg.* Wittenberg: Matthes Welack, 1586. [SStBA, 4° Aug 735/2, 'Kalenderstreit II,' Nr. 25].

Müller, Georg. *Send und Trostbrief / Georg: Müllers Doct. Und Professorn zu Wittenberg / an seine liebe Landsleut unnd Pfarrkinder / die*

Euangelische Burgerschafft in Augspurg uber irem betrübten Zustande / da inen ire liebe Seelsorger / und Preidiger abgeschafft / und alle zumal auff einen Tag zur Stadt ausgetrieten worden. Wittenberg: Matthes Welack, 1586. [SStBA, 4° Aug 735/1, 'Kalenderstreit I,' Nr. 10].

Musculus, Wolfgang. *Wie weyt ein Christ Schuldig sey / gewalt zu leyden. W. Meüßlin. Gedruckt zu Augspurg / durch Hans Zimmerman. M.D. Lii.* Augsburg: Hans Zimmermann, 1552 [SStBA, Aug. 1563].

Mylius, Georg. *Christlicher Sendtbreiff an einen ersamen wolweisen Raht, der uhralten loblichen frei Reichsstadt Cölln, welcher hiemit trewhertzig vermanet und hochflehenlich gebeten wirdt, der Unterthanen daselbs, so der Augspurgischen Confession ... zugethan, mit Verfolgung zu verschonen...* Heidelberg: Johann Spies, 1582.

Newe Zeytung/Warhafftige und eigentliche Beschreibung/von den view geistlosen Meüdmachern/unnd auffrürischen Jesuwidern und Pfaffen/ So den Newen Calendar erdacht und zugericht haben/die gantze Welt damit in unrüh zubringen. n.p.: n.p., 1584 [BL, T. 731.(8)]

Nicolai, Philip. *Kurtzer Bericht von der caluinisten Gott vnd jrer Religion ... sampt angehengter kurtzer Form, wie ein christlicher einfältiger Haussvatter sein Kindt vnnd Haussgesind für demselbigen vnseligen Caluinismo trewlich warnen vnd davon abhalten soll.* Frankfurt am Main: Johann Spiess, 1597.

Richsner, Utz. *Ain Schöne Underweysung/wie und wir in Christo alle gebrüder und schwester seyen/dabey angezaigt nicht allain die weltlichen/wie sy es nennen/sonder auch die gaistlichen zustraffen/wa sy anders in den leybe dessen haubt Christus ist wöllen sein auff die geschrift gottes gegründt und darauß gezogen/zu nutz allen die das götlich wort leiben seindt: Utz Rychßner Weber. M:D:XXiiii. Jar.* [BL 3906.c.98/14].

[Schedle, Abraham]. *Baurenklag uber des Bapst Gregorii XIII. Newen Calendar / Namlich / was für grosse unordnung (beides in Geistlichen / wie auch im Weltlichen Regiment / inn Kirchenyebungen / und inn anndern Politischen Sachen / Händlen unnd Gewerb) Darauß entprungen / gewachßen und herkommen sey. Kürzlich und einfaltig in gebundene reden gestellet und verfasset. Ein New Lied / vom newen Calendar / auch was sich zu Augspurg / den 4. Tag Brachmonats / inn disem 84. Jar hat zugetragen. Im Ton / Es wonet Lieb bey Liebe, etc. 1584.* [n.p.: n.p.], 1584. [SStBA, 4° Aug. 735/1, 'Kalenderstreit I,' Nr. 2 & Nr. 3].

[Schrot, Martin]. *Von der Erschrocklichen Zurstörung unnd Niderlag deß gantzen Bapstumbs / geproheceyet und geweissagt / durch die propheten / Christum / und seine Apostoln / und auß Johannis Apocalypsi Figürlich und sichtlich gesehen. Durch ain hochgelehrten / dise gegen würtige ding / vor sehr vil Jaren beschriben / und der wellt trewlich / auffs kürtzest hiermit fürgehallten / zü Nutz unnd güt / der Seelen / zum Ewigen Leben. Mathei am 7. Weicht ab ir ubeltheter all behendt Dan ich hab euch noch nie kain mal erkent.* [Augsburg: David Danecker, 1558]. [SStBA, Rar 78].

Schumann, Peter. *Die Unschuld Davids/darvon er sang dem Herrn/von wegen der Wort des Moren/des Jeminiten. Ist der Sibend Psalm Davids/ von newen außgesezt inn Bund unnd Melodei.* Ulm: Johann Antoni Ulhart, 1581. [StBB, Hymn. 195]

Schumann, Peter. *Halcyon. Ein Schöne Christliche betrachtung/deß herrlichen und grossen wunderwercks Gottes/im Wintervogel Halcyon, und von seiner wunderbaren Natur unnd eygenschafft/mit der hayligen Schrifft auß gelegt/Gaystlich erklert/und auff die Christliche Kirch gezogen. Hierbey das Evangelion/vom ungestümen Meer/Math 8. Sampt der Gaystlichen Deytung D.M. Luthers gleiches inhalts/alles in Reymen unnd gebundne Red gefast. Zu end etliche Schöne throst Sprich/Von der Christlichen Kirchen.* Ulm: Ulhart, 1583. [SStBA 4° LD 398]

[Schumann, Peter]. *Halcyon. Ein Schöne Christliche betrachtung des herrlichen unnd grossen wunderwercks Gottes/im Winter Vogel Halcyon/mit der heyligen schrifft außgelegt/geistlich erkleret/unnd auff die Christliche Kirch gezogen. Hierbey das Evangelion/vom Ungestimmen Meer. Matth. am 8. sampt der gesitlichen deutund D. M. Luth. Item/Trost spiegel der Christen/in irem Creuzt. Ein Christliche betrachtung/der gleichnus Christi. Joan. 16. vom geberenden Weib/ darin der Christen Creutz/Leid und Frewd/sehr tröstlich abgebildet und erklert wirt. Alles in Reimen und gebundene Rede verfast.* [n.p.: n.p., 1585] [SStBA, Th Pr 4721]

[Schwenckfeld, Caspar], *Ein Christlich Bedencken: Von dem Gemeynen Geschrey / so man jetzt außgibt: Das man nyemandts soll leyden unnd gedulden / der nit in allem / ohne all widerred / Bäpstisch / oder Lutherisch ist. Den Oberkeyten unnd Predicanten zur warnung geschriben / damit sie nit unschuldig Blüt auf sich laden / und meynen / sie thüen Gott ein dienst daran. Matthaei xiij. Cap. Lassets beyde mit einander wachssen / biß zu der Erndt. Matthaei vij. Cap. Alles nun was ir wollend / das euch die Leüth thün sollend / das thüt inen auch / das ist das Gesetz und die Propheten. Lucae vj. Cap. Liebet ewere feind / Richtet nicht / so werdet ir auch nit gerichtet: Verdammet nicht / so werdet ir nicht verdampt.* [Augsburg]: [Hans Gegler],[n.d.] [SStBA, 4ThH 242].

Suarez, Francisco. *Metaphysicarum disputationum: in quibus et universa naturalis theologia ordinate traditur, et questiones omnes ad duodecim Aristotelis libros pertinentes, accuratè disputantur.* Venice: Baretium, 1599.

Thumm, Theodor. *Christlicher wolgegründter Bericht/Auff die Frag: ob ein Evangelischer Christ/auff begehren und nötigen weltlicher Obrigkeit/mit gutem Gewissen/zur Papstischer Religion sich begeben könde? Darinnen auß GOttes Wort/und bewehrten Scribenten/clärlich erwiesen/daß die Papisten/nahend in allen Glaubens-Articuln/hoch schadlich irren/alle drey haupstand der Christenheit wider Gottes Ordnung/unverantwortlich verwirren/beneben mit ihrer Lehr wider alle Gebot Gottes/ein Lasterhafft strafflich Leben einführen. Zur Warnung und Trost allen Evangelischen under dem Pabsthum/sonderlich aber in under-und ober Oesterreich/Böhmen/Merren/in der undern-und obern Pfalz/Marggraffschafft Baden und andern Orten betrangen Christen/ gestelt Durch Theodorum Thumm, der H. Schrifft D. und Professorn zu Tübingen. Zum andernmal uffgetegt/und mit einer Vorred an Christlichen Leser vermehrt.* Tübingen: Philbert Brunn, 1625. [HAB, A:1287.1 Theol.(2)]

Vogel, Wolfgang. *Ain trostlicher Sendbrieff und christliche Ermanung zum Evangelio an ain Erbarn Radt und gantze Gemain zu Bopfingen, und an alle die, so vom Evangelio und Wort Gotes abgefallen seind.* [Augsburg]: [M. Ramminger], 1526. [StAN, SIL 59, Nr. 21].

Wagner, Andreas. *Wann wilt du Catholisch werden? Das ist Gesprach zwischen einem Catholischen unnd Lutherisch Evangelischen: So newlich von einem unbenambten Lutherischen Zeloten durch den Truck außgesprengt worden: jetzund aber durch fleißigs examen gezogen / und auff Catholischer Seiten mit einem starcken Zusag vermehrt / und wider den Gegentheil kurzlich doch gründlich beantwortet.* Augsburg: Andreas Aperger, 1631. [SStBA, Aug 2571].

Wahrhaffte fürstellung der begebenheit so sich A 1584 d. 25 Mai mit Herrn D. Georg Müller gewesenen Pfarrer beÿ St. Anna, auch Superintendens und Rector des Evangelische Collegii zugetragen ... [np: np, nd]. [SStBA, Graphik 22/12].

Warhaffter Bericht/Von der Belägerung und mit gestrümter hand eroberung der Stadt Pilsen inn behem/Von einer unpartheyischen Person/so selbsten darbey gewesen/soviel ihm müglich/erstlich in Behmischer Sprach zusammen geschrieben: Jetzt aber auß dem Behmischen Original getreulich verteuscht/etc. Mit befgefügtem Kupfferstuck/ inn welchem der Abriß gemelter Stadt und Belägerung zu sehen/etc. Erstlich Gedruckt zu Prag/etc. [n.p.: n.p., n.d.] [BSB, Res. 4° Eur. 349, 22]

Warhafftige/Erbärmliche New Zeitung. Von der Schönen Statt Bülsen/ wie die selbige von den Böhmen ist eingenommen worden/und wie sie auch ein Schlacht mit dem Keyser gethan/unnd ime viertausent Mann erschlagen/und in der flucht getriben/die Keyserische abr drey Predicanten mit ihnen hin weg gefüihrt/und erbärmlich mit jnen umbgangen sind. Solches alles werdet ihr in disem Gsang außführlich vernemmen/geschehen den 3.Octobris/dises 1618. Jahrs. Im Thon Hilff Gott das mir gelinge/etc. Gedruckt zu Nürnberg/bey Ludwig Lochner/ Anno 1618. [HAB, Xfiche 32:1]

Warhafftige Newe Zeitung auß Böhmen/Von Belagerung/einnemung und eroberung der Catholischen Stad Pilsen/ Wie dieselbe durch der Böhmischen Stände ihrem Obersten Feld Herren/dem Wolgebornen und Edlen Herrn/Grafen zu Mansfeld/den 2. Octoberis mit einem gewaltigen und mächtigen Sturman gelauffen/und darüber uber drey hunder Mann verloren/und an in die drey hunderet tödlich beschödigt worden/Item wie die ganzte Bürgerschaffe auff die Knie gefallen und umb Gnade gebeten/welche ihnen auch vom Grafen widerfaren/etc. Wie ihr ferner in diesem Gesang sollet berichtet worden?Zu singen im Thon: Kompt her zu mir spricht GOttes SON/etc... Erstlich Gedruckt in der Alten Stadt Prag/bey Samuel Adam/im Jahr/1618. [n.p.: n.p.], 1618. [HAAB 4°XXV:133].

Welser, Marcus & Achilles Pirmin Gasser. *Chronica der weitberuempten Keyserlichen Freyen und deß H. Reichs Statt Augspurg in Schwaben / Von derselben altem Ursprung / Schöne / Gelegene / zierlichen Gebäuen und namhafften gedenckwürdigen Geschichten / in acht underschidliche Capitul (dero Innhalt vor anfang dieser Chronicken / sampt Abbildung und Deutung gedachter Statt alter Monumenten zufinden) abgetheilt: Auß Deß Edlen und Ehrenvesten Marx Welsers deß Jüngern / Patricii und Burgermeisters daselbsten acht Büchern (so er in lateinischer Spraach beschrieben / und vor einem Jhar in offnen Truck ausgehen lassen) gezogen / und derselben Burgerschafft / sampt dero benachbarten zu sondern Ehren und gefallen in unser teutschen Spraach in Truck verfertigt / Durch Engelbertum Werlichium, der Historien liebhabern, Frankfurt.* Frankfurt am Main: C. Egenerben, 1595.

Zungenschlitzer. Das Ist: Außführliche, Gründliche Handlung Einer Wolbedencklichen Frag, Ob Auch Krafft Deß Religion Fridens Den Praedicanten Erlaubt Seye, Daß Sie Dem Papst Yu Rom Außrüffen Für Den Antichrist, Oder Aber Sie, Vermög Deß Kayserlichen Rechts, Von So Schädlichem, Und Den Gantzen Römischen Reich Schmählichen Lästerb, Sollen Abgehalten Werden. Auß Dem Lateinischen Buch De Compositione Pacis, C. 11 Edit. 2. Verteutscht. Cum Facultate Superiorum. Dillingen: Erhard Lochner, 1629. [Freytag 5365]

Zwo Warhaffte Newe Zeitung / Die erst: Ein Warhafftige / doch erschröckliche Newe Zeitung / welche sich begeben und zugetragen / den 2. Jenner in disem 1625. Jahr / von einem grausamen und erschrocklich Wetter und Sturmwind / welche sich begeben und zugetragen / im undern Bayerlandt / inn der Blangtensteinerischen Herrschafft / als namblich zu Gerhausen / unnd inn dem Dorff Mihlsteten / auch an andern ortten mehr / vil Hauser und Stadel eingerissen / auch das Wetter etlich mal eingeschlagen / Menschen und Vich verlezet und verderbet / was weitters werdet ihr in disem Gesang vernemen. Im Thon: Der grimmig Todt mit seinem Pfeil / etc ... Dinder / Ein sehr erschrocklich doch warhaffte Newe Zeittung / welche sich begeben und zutragen hat / inn einem Flecken Feldtbach / zwo meil von Chur / wie allda der 6. Mann außgemustert / unnd endlich einen armen Mann getroffen mit sechs kleinen Kinden / die er vor herzleid gestorben / und wie seinem Weib in der Not ein Engel erschinen / was sich weitter begeben / werdet ihr in disem Gesang vernemen / etc. Geschehen den 28. Demb. Anno 1624. Im Thon: Warumn betrubst mich mein Herz / etc. Getruckt zu Straubingen / durch Simon Han / Anno 1625. [n.p.: n.p., n.d.]. [StAA, Strafamt, Urg. Hans Meyer a/k/a Gallmeyer, 1–6 Feb. 1625].

Edited Primary Sources

Alexander, Dorothy and Walter L. Strauss, eds. *The German Single-Leaf Woodcut. 1600–1700: A Pictorial Catalogue*. New York: Abaris Books, 1977.

Böckel, Otto. *Handbuch des Deutschen Volksliedes*. Hildesheim: Georg Olms Verlagsbuchhandlung, 1967.

Brandi, Karl, ed. *Der Augsburger Religionsfriede vom 25. September, 1555. Kritische Ausgabe des Textes mit den Entwürfen und der königlichen Deklaration*. Göttingen: Vandenhoeck & Ruprecht, 1927.

Constitutio Criminalis Carolina, in *Die Peinliche Gerichtsordnung Kaiser Karl V. von 1532*, ed. Gustav Radbruch. Stuttgart: Philipp Reclam, 1996.

Das Babstsche Gesangbuch von 1545. 1545. Kassel: Bärenreiter, 1988.

Deutsches Evangelisches Kirchen-Gesangbuch. 1854. Köln: Themen, 1995.

Geisberg, Max. *The German Single-Leaf Woodcut: 1500–1550*. Rev. and ed. Walter L. Strauss. New York: Hacker Art Books, 1974.

Hampe, Theodor, ed. *Nürnberger Ratsverlässe über Kunst und Künstler*. Vienna: Karl Graeser, 1904.

Hohenemser, Paul, ed. *Flugschriften-Sammlung Gustav Freytag*. Hildesheim: Georg Olms Verlagsbuchhandlung, 1966.

Instrumentum Pacis Osnabrugense, in *Kaiser und Reich: Verfassungsgeschichte des Heiligen Römischen Reiches Deutscher Nation vom Beginn des 12. Jahrhunderts bis zum Jahre 1806 in Dokumenten, Teil II*, ed. Arno Buschmann. 2nd ed. Baden-Baden: Nomos Verlagsgesellschaft, 1994.

Kant, Immanuel. 'An Answer to the Question: "What is Enlightenment?",' in *Kant: Political Writings*, ed. Hans Reiss. 2nd ed. Cambridge: Cambridge University Press, 1991.

Liliencron von, Rochus. *Die historischen Volkslieder der Deutschen vom 13. bis 16. Jahrhundert*. 1867. Hildesheim: Georg Olms Verlagsbuchhandlung, 1966.

Luther, Martin. 'Of the Holy Ghost.' CCXLI. *Table Talk*. Trans. William Hazlitt. London: G. Bell, 1902.

Luther, Martin. 'The Second Sermon, March 10, 1522, Monday after Invocavit,' in *Luther's Works*, vol. 51, ed. and trans. John W. Doberstein. Muhlenberg Press, Philadelphia, 1959.

Luther, Martin. 'Secular Authority: To What Extent It Should Be Obeyed,' 1523, in *Martin Luther: Selections From His Writings*, ed. John Dillenberger. New York: Doubleday, 1962.

Luther, Martin. 'Sermon for Pentecost Wednesday; John 6:44–5,' in *The Sermons of Martin Luther*, vol. III, ed. John Nichols Lenker. Grand Rapids, MI: Baker Book House, 1992.

Luther, Martin. 'Wider den falsch genannten geistlichen Stand des Papsts und der Bischöfe,' in *D. Martin Luthers Werke*, Bd. 10. Weimar: Hermann Böhlaus Nachfolger, 1966.

Mair, Paul Hektor. 'Das Diarium Paul Hektor Mairs von 1560–1563,' in *Die Chroniken der Schwäbischen Städte: Augsburg*, Bd. 8. *Die Chroniken der deutschen Städte vom 14. bis ins 16. Jahrhundert*, Bd. 33, ed. Historische Kommission bei der Bayerischen Kommission der Wissenschaften. 1928. Göttingen: Vandenhoek & Ruprecht, 1966.

Mair, Paul Hektor. 'Zwei Chroniken des Augsburger Ratsdieners Paul Hektor Mair von 1548 bezw. 1547–1565 bezw. 1564,' in *Die Chroniken der Schwäbischen Städte: Augsburg*, Bd. 7. *Die Chroniken der deutschen Städte vom 14. bis ins 16. Jahrhundert*, Bd. 32, ed. Historische Kommission bei der Bayerischen Kommission der Wissenschaften. 1917. Göttingen: Vandenhoek & Ruprecht, 1966.

Müntzer, Thomas. *Thomas Müntzers Schriften und Briefe. Kritische Gesamtausgabe*, ed. Günter Franz and Paul Kirn. Göttingen: Vandenhoeck & Ruprecht, 1968.

Neue vollständige Sammlung der Reichs-Abschiede, welche von den Zeiten Kayser Conrads des II. bis jetzo auf den Teutschen Reichs-Tagen abgefasset worden. 1747. Osnabrück: Otto Zeller, 1967.

Pfeiffer, Gerhard, ed. *Quellen zur Nürnberger Reformationsgeschichte von der Duldung liturgischer Änderungen bis zur Ausübung des Kirchenregiments durch den Rat (Juni 1524–Juni 1525)*. Nürnberg: Selbstverlag des Vereins für bayerische Kirchengeschichte, 1968.

Preu der Ä., Georg. 'Die Chronik des Augsburger Malers Georg Preu des Älteren, 1512–1537,' in *Die Chroniken der Schwäbischen Städte: Augsburg*, Bd. 6. *Die Chroniken der deutschen Städte vom 14. bis ins 16. Jahrhundert*, Bd. 29, ed. Historische Kommission bei der Bayerischen Kommission der Wissenschaften. 1906. Göttingen: Vandenhoek & Ruprecht, 1966.

Rem, Wilhem. 'Cronica newer geschichten von Wilhelm Rem, 1512–1527,' in *Die Chroniken der Schwäbischen Städte: Augsburg*, Bd. 5. *Die Chroniken der deutschen Städte vom 14. bis ins 16. Jahrhundert*, Bd. 25, ed. Historische Kommission bei der Bayerischen Kommission der Wissenschaften. 1896. Göttingen: Vandenhoek & Ruprecht, 1966.

Sender, Clemens. 'Die Chronik von Clemens Sender von ältesten Zeiten der Stadt bis zum Jahre 1536,' in *Die Chroniken der Schwäbischen Städte: Augsburg*, Bd. 4. *Die Chroniken der deutschen Städte vom 14. bis ins 16. Jahrhundert*, Bd. 23, ed. Historische Kommission bei der Bayerischen Kommission der Wissenschaften. 1894. Göttingen: Vandenhoek & Ruprecht, 1966.

Strauss, Walter L., ed. *The German Single-Leaf Woodcut, 1550–1600: A Pictorial Catalogue*. New York: Abaris Books, 1975.

Wackernagel, Philipp, ed. *Martin Luthers Geistliche Lieder*. 1848. Hildesheim: Georg Olms Verlag, 1970.

Walder, Ernst, ed. *Religionsvergleiche des 16. Jahrhunderts*, I, Quellen zur Neueren Geschichte, Hft. 7. Bern: Verlag Herbert Lang & CIE, 1960.

Weller, Emil. *Die Lieder des Dreißigjährigen Krieges*. 1855. Hildesheim: Georg Olms Verlagsbuchhandlung, 1968.

Secondary Sources

Abray, Lorna Jane. *The People's Reformation: Magistrates, Clergy, and Commons in Strasbourg 1500–1598*. Oxford: Basil Blackwell, 1985.

Abray, Lorna Jane. 'Confession, Conscience and Honour: The Limits of Magisterial Tolerance in Sixteenth-Century Strassburg,' in *Tolerance and Intolerance in the European Reformation*, eds. Ole Peter Grell and Bob Scribner. Cambridge: Cambridge University Press, 1996.

Alcalá, Angel, 'Inquisitorial Control of Humanists and Writers,' in *The Spanish Inquisition and the Inquisitorial Mind*, ed. Angel Alcalá. Boulder: Social Science Monographs, 1987.

Allport, Gordon W. and Leo Postman. *The Psychology of Rumor*. New York: Henry Holt & Co., 1947.

Andersson, Christiane. 'The Censorship of Images in Nuremberg, 1521–1527: Art and Politics in the Reformation,' in *Dürer and his Culture*, eds Dagmar Eichberger and Charles Zika. Cambridge: Cambridge University Press, 1998.

Appold, Kenneth G. *Orthodoxie als Konsensbildung. Das theologische Disputationswesen an der Universität Wittenberg zwischen 1570–1710*. Tübingen: Mohr Siebeck, 2004.

Armon, Shifra. 'Ungilding Spain's Golden Age,' in *Tainted Greatness: Anti-Semitism and Cultural Heroes*, ed. Nancy Harrowitz. Philadelphia: Temple University Press, 1994.

Arnold, Martin. *Handwerker als theologische Schriftsteller: Studien zu Flugschriften der frühen Reformation (1523–1525)*. Göttingen: Vandenhoeck & Ruprecht, 1990.

Arroyo, C. M. 'The Inquisition and the Possibility of Great Baroque Literature,' in *The Spanish Inquisition and the Inquisitorial Mind*, ed. Angel Alcalá. Boulder: Social Science Monographs, 1987.

Asch, Ronald G. *The Thirty Years War: The Holy Roman Empire and Europe, 1618–1648*. New York: St. Martin's Press, 1997.

Baader, J. 'Preßmandate des Raths zu Nürnberg,' in *Anzeiger für Kunde der Deutschen Vorzeit* 8 (1861): 30–32.

Backus, Irena. 'The Disputations of Baden, 1526 and Berne, 1528: Neutralizing the Early Church,' in *Studies in Reformed Theology and History* 1(1) (1993): 1–130.

Baer, Wolfram and Hans Joachim Hecker, eds. *Die Jesuiten und ihre Schule St. Salvator in Augsburg, 1582*. Munich: Stadtarchiv Augsburg & Karl M. Lipp Verlag, 1982.

Balzer, Bernd. *Bürgerliche Reformationspropaganda: Die Flugschriften des Hans Sachs in den Jahren 1523–1525*. Stuttgart: J. B. Metzlersche Verlagsbuchhandlung, 1973.

Baring, G. 'Hans Denck und Thomas Müntzer in Nürnberg 1524,' in *Archiv für Reformationsgeschichte* 50(2) (1959): 145–81.

Barnes, Robin Bruce. *Prophecy and Gnosis: Apocalypticism in the Wake of the Lutheran Reformation*. Stanford: Stanford University Press, 1988.

Baufeld, Christa. *Kleines frühneuhochdeutsches Wörterbuch. Lexik aus Dichtung und Fachliteratur des Frühneuhochdeutschen*. Tübingen: Max Niemeyer Verlag, 1996.

Baylor, Michael G., ed. *The Radical Reformation*. Cambridge: Cambridge University Press, 1991.

Behringer, Wolfgang. 'Veränderung der Raum-Zeit-Relation. Zur Bedeutung des Zeitungs- und Nachrichtenwesens während der Zeit des Dreißigjährigen Krieges,' in *Zwischen Alltag und Katastrophe. Der Dreißigjährige Krieg aus der Nähe*, eds Benigna von Krusenstjern and Hans Medick. Göttingen: Vandenhoeck & Ruprecht, 1999.

Behringer, Wolfgang. *Im Zeichen des Merkur. Reichspost und Kommunikationsrevolution in der Frühen Neuzeit.* Göttingen: Vandenhoeck & Ruprecht, 2003.

Benzing, Josef. *Buchdruckerlexikon des 16. Jahrhunderts (Deutsches Sprachgebeit).* Frankfurt am Main: Vittorio Klostermann, 1952.

Benzing, Josef. 'Die Buchdrucker des 16. und 17. Jahrhunderts im deutschen Sprachgebiet,' in *Beiträge zum Buch- und Bibliothekswesen*, ed. Max Pauer. Bd. 12 (1982).

Benzing, Josef. 'Die deutschen Verleger des 16. und 17. Jahrhunderts: eine Neubearbeitung,' *Archiv für Geschichte des Buchwesens.* Bd. XVIII (1977).

Bergmann, Jörg R. *Discreet Indiscretions: The Social Organization of Gossip.* Hawthorne, NY: Aldine de Gruyter, 1993.

Bernstein, Eckhard. '"Auch ist zw dichten gar geferlich…" Literarische Zensur und Selbstzensur bei Hans Sachs,' in *Akten des VIII. Internationalen Germanisten-Kongresses, Tokyo 1990: Begegnung mit dem 'Fremden': Grenzen, Traditionen, Vergleiche*, 11 (1991): 15–23.

Beyer, Franz-Heinrich. *Eigenart und Wirkung des reformatorisch-polemischen Flugblatts im Zusammenhang der Publizistik der Reformationszeit.* Frankfurt am Main: Lang, 1994.

Bireley, Robert. 'The Origins of the "Pacis Compositio" (1629): A Text of Paul Laymann,' in *Archivum Historicum Sociatatis Jesu* 42 (1972): 106–27.

Bireley, Robert. *Religion and Politics in the Age of the Counterreformation: Emperor Ferdinand II, William Lamormaini, S.J., and the Formation of Imperial Policy.* Chapel Hill: University of North Carolina Press, 1981.

Birlinger, Anton, ed. *Schwäbisch-Augsburgisches Wörterbuch.* 1864. Wiesbaden: Dr. Martin Sändig oHG, 1968.

Blauert, Andreas. *Das Urfehdewesen im deutschen Südwesten im Spätmittelalter und in der frühen Neuzeit.* Tübingen: Bibliotheca Academica Verlag, 2000.

Blauert, Andreas and Gerd Schwerhoff, eds. *Mit den Waffen der Justiz: zur Kriminalitätsgeschichte des Spätmittelalters und der Frühen Neuzeit.* Frankfurt am Main: Fischer Taschenbuch Verlag, 1993.

Blaufuß, Dietrich. 'Das Verhältnis der Konfessionen in Augsburg 1555 bis 1648,' in *Jahrbuch des Vereins für Augsburger Bistumsgeschichte* 10 (1976).

Blendinger, Friedrich and Wolfgang Zorn, eds. *Augsburg: Geschichte in Bilddokumenten.* München: Verlag C.H. Beck, 1976.

Bogel, Else and Elger Blühm, eds. *Die deutschen Zeitungen des 17. Jahrhunderts.* Bd. 1. Bremen: Schünemann Universitätsverlag, 1971.

Bossert, Gustav. 'Zur Geschichte der Zensur in Augsburg 1538,' in *Beiträge zur bayerischen Kirchengeschichte* 15 (1909) 209–13.
Böttcher, Diethelm. 'Propaganda und öffentliche Meinung in protestantischen Deutschland, 1628–1636,' in *Archiv für Reformationsgeschichte* 44–5 (1953–54).
Bourdieu, Pierre. *Outline of a Theory of Practice*, trans. Richard Nice. Cambridge: Cambridge University Press, 1977.
Boyd, Stephen B. *Pilgram Marpeck: His Life and Social Theology*. Mainz: Verlag Philipp von Zabern, 1992.
Brady, Jr., Thomas A. *Ruling Class, Regime, and Reformation at Strasbourg, 1520–1555*. Leiden: Brill, 1978.
Brady, Jr., Thomas A. *Turning Swiss: Cities and Empire, 1450–1550*. Cambridge: Cambridge University Press, 1985.
Brady, Jr., Thomas A. *German Histories in the Age of the Reformations, 1400–1650*. New York: Cambridge University Press, 2009.
Braun, Placidus. *Geschichte des Kollegiums der Jesuiten in Augsburg*. Munich: Jakob Giel, 1822.
Brecht, Martin. 'Das Wormser Edikt in Süddeutschland,' in *Der Reichstag zu Worms von 1521: Reichspolitik und Luthersache*, ed. Fritz Reuter. Worms: Stadtarchiv, 1971.
Brecht, Martin. 'Die gemeinsame Politik der Reichsstädte und die Reformation,' in *Stadt und Kirche im 16. Jahrhundert*, ed. Bernd Moeller. Gütersloh: Gütersloher Verlagshaus Gerd Mohn, 1978.
Brednich, Rolf Wilhelm. 'Die Liedpublizistik im Flugblatt des 15. bis 17. Jahrhunderts,' Bd. I: Abhandlung, in *Bibliotheca Bibliographica Aureliana*, Bd. LV. Baden-Baden: Verlag Valentin Koerner, 1974.
Brednich, Rolf Wilhelm. 'Die Liedpublizistik im Flugblatt des 15. bis 17. Jahrhunderts,' Bd. II: Katalog der Liedflugblätter des 15. und 16. Jahrhunderts, in *Bibliotheca Bibliographica Aureliana*, Bd. LX. Baden-Baden: Verlag Valentin Koerner, 1975.
Breuer, Dieter. *Geschichte der literarischen Zensur in Deutschland*. Heidelberg: Quelle & Meyer, 1982.
Broadhead, P. J. 'Guildsmen, Religious Reform, and the Search for the Common Good: The Role of the Guilds in the Early Reformation in Augsburg,' *The Historical Journal* 39(3) (1996): 577–97.
Broadhead, Philip. 'Popular Pressure for Reform in Augsburg, 1524–1534,' in *The Urban Classes, the Nobility, and the Reformation: Studies on the Social History of the Reformation in England and Germany*, ed. Wolfgang J. Mommsen. Stuttgart: Klett-Cotta, 1979.
Broadhead, Philip. 'Politics and Expediency in the Augsburg Reformation,' in *Reformation Principle and Practice: Essays in Honour of Arthur Geoffrey Dickens*, ed. Peter Newman Brooks. London: Scolar Press, 1980.

Broadhead, Philip. *Internal Politics and Civic Society in Augsburg During the Era of the Early Reformation, 1518–1537.* Diss. Univ. of Kent, 1981.

Broadhead, Philip. '"One Heart and One Soul:" The Changing Nature of Public Worship in Augsburg, 1521–1548,' in *Continuity and Change in Christian Worship*, ed. R. N. Swanson. London: Boydell Press, 1999.

Brodrick, J. *Saint Peter Canisius, S.J., 1521–1597.* London: Sheed and Ward, 1938.

Brown, Christopher Boyd. *Singing the Gospel: Lutheran Hymns and the Success of the Reformation.* Cambridge, MA: Harvard University Press, 2005.

Brübach, Nils. *Die Reichsmessen von Frankfurt am Main, Leipzig und Braunschweig (14.–18. Jahrhundert).* Stuttgart: Franz Steiner Verlag, 1994.

Brückner, W. 'Die Gegenreformation im politischen Kampf um die Frankfurter Buchmessen: Die kaiserliche Zensur zwischen 1567 und 1619,' *Archiv für Frankfurts Geschichte und Kunst* 48 (1962): 67–86.

Brückner, W., ed. *Volkserzählung und Reformation. Ein Handbuch zur Tradierung und Funktion von Erzählstoffen und Erzählliteratur im Protestantismus.* Berlin, Erich Schmidt Verlag, 1974.

Brüning, Jochen and Friedrich Niewöhner. *Augsburg in der Frühen Neuzeit: Beiträge zu einem Forschungsprogramm.* Berlin: Akademie Verlag, 1995.

Brunner, Horst. 'Hans Sachs – Über die Schwierigkeiten literarischen Schaffens in der Reichsstadt Nürnberg,' in *Bedingungen und Probleme reichsstädtischer Literatur Hans Sachs zum 400. Todestag am 19. Januar 1976*, eds H. Brunner, G. Hirschmann and F. Schnelbögl. Nürnberg: Vereins für Geschichte der Stadt Nürnberg, 1976.

Brunner, Horst, Eva Klesatschke, Dieter Merzbacher, Johannes Rettelbach, Paul Sappler, Fieder Schanze, Burghart Wachinger, eds. *Repertorium der Sangsprüche und Meisterlieder des 12. bis 18. Jahrhunderts.* Tübingen: Maz Niemeyer Verlag, 1996.

Bubenheimer, U. 'Orthodoxie-Heterodoxie-Kryptoheterodoxie in der nachreformatorischen Zeit am Beispiel des Buchmarkts in Wittenberg, Halle und Tübingen,' in *700 Jahre Wittenberg: Stadt. Universität. Reformation*, ed. S. Oehming. Weimar: Verlag Hermann Böhlaus Nachfolger, 1995, 257–74.

Büchler, Volker. 'Die Zensur im frühneuzeitlichen Augsburg, 1515–1806,' in *Zeitschrift des Historischen Vereins für Schwaben* 84 (1991).

Buff, Adolf. 'Die ältesten Augsburger Zensuranordnungen,' in *Archiv für Geschichte der deutschen Buchhandels* VI (1881).

Burkhard, D. 'Repression und Prävention. Die Kirchliche Bücherzensur in Deutschland (16.–20. Jahrhundert)' in *Inquisition, Index, Zensur: Wissenskulturen der Neuzeit im Widerstreit*, ed. H. Wolf. Paderborn: Ferdinand Schöningh, 2001: 304–27.

Burkhardt, Johannes. *Der Dreißigjährige Krieg*. Frankfurt am Main: Suhrkamp Verlag, 1992.

Burkhardt, Johannes. *Das Reformationsjahrhundert. Deutsche Geschichte zwischen Medienrevolution und Institutionenbildung, 1517–1617*. Stuttgart: W. Kohlhammer, 2002.

Burkhardt, Johannes, and Stephanie Haberer, eds. *Das Friedenfest. Augsburg und die Entwicklung einer neuzeitlichen Toleranz-, Friedens- und Festkultur*. Berlin: Akademie Verlag, 2000.

Burnett, Amy Nelson. *Karlstadt and the Origins of the Eucharistic Controversy: A Study in the Circulation of Ideas*. Oxford: Oxford University Press, 2011.

Burschel, Peter. 'Das Heilige und die Gewalt. Zur frühneuzeitlichen Deutung von Massakern,' in *Archiv für Kulturgeschichte* 86(2) (2004): 341–68.

Burt, Richard. *The Administration of Aesthetics: Censorship, Political Criticism, and the Public Sphere*. Minneapolis: University of Minnesota Press, 1994.

Burt, Richard. '(Un)Censoring of Detail: The Fetish of Censorship in the Early Modern Past and the Postmodern Present,' *Censorship and Silencing: Practices of Cultural Regulation*, ed. Robert C. Post. Los Angeles: The Getty Research Institute for the History of Art and the Humanities, 1998.

Busch, Rüdiger. *Die Aufsichte über das Bücher- und Pressewesen in den Rheinbundstaaten Berg, Westfalen, und Frankfurt*. Karlsruhe: Verlag C. F. Müller, 1970.

Calhoun, Craig. *Habermas and the Public Sphere*. Cambridge, MA: The MIT Press, 1996.

Cavanagh, Dermont and Tim Kirk, eds. *Subversion and Scurrility: Popular Discourse in Europe from 1500 to the Present*. Aldershot: Ashgate Publishing Ltd., 2000.

Chartier, Roger. 'The Practical Impact of Writing,' in *A History of Private Life*. Vol. 3. Cambridge, MA: Harvard University Press, 1989.

Chartier, Roger. *A History of Private Life*. Vol. 3. Cambridge, MA: Harvard University Press, 1989.

Chrisman, Miriam Usher. *Lay Culture, Learned Culture: Books and Social Change in Strasbourg, 1480–1599*. New Haven: Yale University Press, 1982.

Chrisman, Miriam Usher. *Conflicting Visions of Reform: German Lay Propaganda Pamphlets, 1519–1530*. Atlantic Highlands, New Jersey: Humanities Press, 1996.

Clasen, Claus-Peter. *Die Augsburger Weber. Leistungen und Krisen um 1600*. Augsburg: H. Mühlberger, 1981.

Clemen, Otto. *Buchdruck und Buchhandel und die Lutherische Reformation*. Halle a.S.: Rudolf Haupt, 1904.

Clemen, Otto. *Die lutherische Reformation und der Buchdruck*. Schriften des Vereins für Reformationsgeschichte Jahrgang 57, Heft 1. Leipzig: M. Heinsius Nachfolger, 1939.

Close, Christopher W. *The Negotiated Reformation: Imperial Cities and the Politics of Urban Reform, 1525–1550*. New York: Cambridge University Press, 2009.

Corpis, Duane. 'Mapping the Boundaries of Confession: Space and Urban Religious Life in the Diocese of Augsburg, 1648–1750,' in *Sacred Space in Early Modern Europe*, eds W. Coster and Andrew Spicer. Cambridge: Cambridge University Press, 2005: 302–325.

Costa, G. 'Die Rechtseinrichtung der Zensur in der Reichsstadt Augsburg,' in *Zeitschrift des Historischen Verein für Schwaben und Neuburg* 42 (1916): 1–82

Cottret, Bernard. *1598: L'Edit de Nantes: pour en finir avec les guerres de religion*. Paris: Perrin, 1997.

Coy, Jason P. *Strangers and Misfits: Banishment, Social Control, and Authority in Early Modern Germany*. Leiden: Brill, 2008.

Coyne, G.V., Michael A Hoskin, and O. Pedersen, eds. *Gregorian Reform of the Calendar: Proceedings of the Vatican Conference to Commemorate its 400th Anniversary, 1582–1982*. Vatican City: Pontificia Academia Scientiarum Specola Vaticana, 1983.

Cressy, David. *Dangerous Talk: Scandalous, Seditious, and Treasonable Speech in Pre-Modern England*. Oxford: Oxford University Press, 2010.

Darnton, Robert. *The Literary Underground of the Old Regime*. Cambridge, Mass.: Harvard University Press, 1982.

Darnton, Robert. 'A Police Inspector Sorts His Files: The Anatomy of the Republic of Letters,' in *The Great Cat Massacre and Other Episodes in French Cultural History*. New York: Basic Books, 1984.

Darnton, Robert. *The Forbidden Best Sellers of Prerevolutionary France*. New York: W. W. Norton & Co., Inc., 1995.

Darnton, Robert. *Poetry and Police: Communication Networks in Eighteenth-Century Paris*. Cambridge, MA: Belknap Press, 2010.

David, Zdeněk V. 'Confessional Accommodation in Early Modern Bohemia: Shifting Relations Between Catholics and Utraquists,' *Conciliation and Confession: The Struggle for Unity in the Age of Reform, 1415–1648*, eds Howard P. Louthan and Randall C. Zachman. Notre Dame, Indiana: University of Notre Dame Press, 2004, pp. 173–4.

Davis, Natalie Zemon. 'Strikes and Salvation in Lyon,' in *Society and Culture in Early Modern France*. London: Duckworth, 1975.

Dear, Peter. 'From Truth to Disinterestedness in the Seventeenth Century,' in *Social Studies of Science* 22(4) (Nov. 1992): 619–31.

Dixon, C. Scott. 'Urban Order and Religious Coexistence in the German Imperial City: Augsburg and Donauwörth, 1548–1608,' in *Central European History* 40 (2007): 1–33.

Dollinger, Robert. 'Erhalt uns Herr, bei deinem Wort!' in *Zeitschrift für bayerische Kirchengeschichte* 29 (1960): 33–42.

Dooley, Brendan. '*Veritas Filia Temporis*: Experience and Belief in Early Modern Culture,' in *Journal of the History of Ideas* 60(3) (1999): 487–504.

Dresler, A. 'Der Augsburger Zeitungsdrucker Andreas Aperger,' in *Zeitungs-Verlag* 20 (May 18, 1929): 1007–8.

Dresler, A. 'Die Anfänge der Augsburger Presse und der Zeitungsdrucker Andreas Aperger,' *Zeitungswissenschaft* 5 (1930): 275–347.

Dülmen van, Richard. *Theatre of Horror: Crime and Punishment in Early Modern Germany*, trans. Elisabeth Neu. Cambridge: Polity Press, 1990.

Dürr, Alfred and Walther Killy, eds. *Das protestantische Kirchenlied im 16. und 17. Jahrhundert*. Wiesbaden: Wolfenbütteler Forschungen 31, 1986.

Edwards, Mark U., Jr. *Luther and the False Brethren*. Stanford: Stanford University Press, 1975.

Edwards, Mark U., Jr. *Printing, Propaganda, and Martin Luther*. Berkeley: University of California Press, 1994.

Ehrenpreis, Stefan. *Kaiserliche Gerichtsbarkeit und Konfessionskonflikt. Der Reichshofrat unter Rudolf II, 1576–1612*. Göttingen: Vandenhoeck & Ruprecht, 2006.

Eisenhardt, Ulrich. *Die kaiserliche Aufsicht über Buchdruck, Buchhandel und Presse in Heiligen Römischen Reich Deutscher Nation (1496–1806)*. Karlsruhe: Verlag C.F. Müller, 1970.

Eisenhardt, Ulrich. 'Staatliche und kirchliche Einflußnahmen auf den deutschen Buchhandel im 16. Jahrhundert,' in *Beiträge zur Geschichte des Buchwesens im konfessionellen Zeitalter*, eds Herbert G. Göpfert, Peter Vodosek, Erdmann Weyrauch, and Reinhard Wittmann. Wiesbaden: Otto Harrassowitz, 1985.

Eisenstein, Elizabeth L. *The Printing Press as an Agent of Change: Communications and Cultural Transformations in Early Modern Europe*. Cambridge: Cambridge University Press, 1979.

Elsas, M. J. *Umriss einer Geschichte der Preise und Löhne in Deutschland vom ausgehenden Mittelalter bis zum Beginn des neunzehnten Jahrhunderts*. Bd. I. Leiden: A.W. Sijthoff's Uitgeversmaatschappij, 1936.

Engelsing, Rolf. *Analphabetentum und Lektüre. Zur Sozialgeschichte des Lesens in Deutschland zwischen feudaler und industrieller Gesellschaft*. Stuttgart: J. B. Metzler, 1973.

Ennen, L. *Geschichte der Stadt Köln*. 5 vols. Cologne and Neuss, 1863–80.

Farge, Arlette. *Subversive Words: Public Opinion in Eighteenth-Century France*, trans. Rosemary Morris. University Park: The Pennsylvania State University Press, 1994.

Feather, John P. 'From Censorship to Copyright: Aspects of the Government's Role in the English Book Trade, 1695 to 1775,' in *Books and Society in History*, ed. Kenneth E. Carpenter. New York: R.R. Bowker Co., 1983.

Fischer, Heinz-Dietrich, ed. *Deutsche Kommunikationskontrolle des 15. bis 20. Jahrhunderts*. Munich: K.G. Saur, 1982.

Fischer, Hermann and Hermann Taigel, eds. *Schwäbisches Handwörterbuch*. Tübingen: H. Laupp'sche Buchhandlung/J. C. B. Mohr (Paul Siebeck), 1986.

Fisher, Alexander J. *Music and Religious Identity in Counter-Reformation Augsburg*. Aldershot: Ashgate, 2004.

Fitos, Stephan. *Zensur als Mißerfolg. Die Verbreitung indizierter deutscher Druckschriften in der zweiten Hälfte des 16. Jahrhunderts*. Frankfurt am Main: Peter Lang, 2000.

Flachmann, Holgar. *Martin Luther und das Buch: Eine historische Studie zur Bedeutung des Buches im Handeln und Denken des Reformators*. Tübingen: Mohr, 1996.

Flood, John L. 'Umstürzler in den Alpen: Bücher und Leser in Österreich im Zeitalter der Gegenreformation,' *Daphnis* Bd. 20(2) (1991): 231–63.

Fox, Adam, *Oral and Literate Culture in England, 1500–1700*. Oxford: Oxford University Press, 2000.

Foyster, Marc R. *The Counter-Reformation in the Villages: Religion and Reform in the Bishopric of Speyer, 1560–1720*. Ithaca: Cornell University Press, 1992.

François, Etienne. *Die unsichtbare Grenze: Protestanten und Katholiken in Augsburg 1648–1806*. Sigmaringen: Jan Thorbecke Verlag, 1991.

François, Etienne. 'Buchhandel und Buchgewerbe in Augsburg im 17. und 18. Jahrhundert,' in *Augsburg in der Frühen Neuzeit: Beiträge zu einem Forschungsprogramm*, eds. Jochen Brüning and Friedrich Niewöhner. Berlin: Akademie Verlag, 1995.

Franz, Gunther. *Bücherzensur und Irenik: Die theologische Zensur im Herzogtum Württemberg in der Konkurrenz von Universität und Regierung*. Tübingen: J. C. B. Mohr, 1977.

Freist, Dagmar. *Governed by Opinion: Politics, Religion and the Dynamics of Communication in Stuart London, 1637–1645*. London: Tauris Academic Studies, 1997.

Freund, Hilger. *Die Bücher-und Pressezensur im Kurfürstentum Mainz von 1486–1797*. Karlsruhe: Verlag C. F. Müller, 1971.

Friedman, Jerome. *The Battle of the Frogs and Fairford's Flies: Miracles and the Pulp Press in the English Revolution*. New York: St. Martin's Press, 1993.

Frisch, M. 'Zur Rechtsnatur des Augsburger Religionsfriedens,' in *Zeitschrift der Savigny-Stiftung für Rechtsgeschichte*. Kanonistische Abteilung 79 (1993): 448–58.

Fritz, F. *Ulmische Kirchengeschichte vom Interim bis zum dreißigjährigen Krieg (1548–1612)*. Stuttgart: Chr. Scheufele, 1934.

Fuchs, Konrad and Heribert Raab, eds. *Wörterbuch Geschichte*. München: Deutscher Taschenbuch Verlag, 1998.

Fudge, John D. *Commerce and Print in the Early Reformation*. Leiden: Brill, 2007.

Fulton, Elaine. *Catholic Belief and Survival in Late Sixteenth-Century Vienna: The Case of Georg Eder (1523–87)*. Aldershot: Ashgate, 2007.

Gantet, Claire. 'Die ambivalente Wahrnehmung des Friedens: Erwartung, Frucht und Spannungen in Augsburg um 1648,' in *Zwischen Alltag und Katastrophe. Der Dreißigjährige Kriege aus der Nähe*, eds Benigna von Krusenstjern and Hans Medick. Göttingen: Vandenhoeck & Ruprecht, 1999.

Gawthrop, R., and Gerald Strauss. 'Protestantism and Literacy in Early Modern Germany,' *Past and Present*, 104(1) (1984): 31–55.

Germanisches Nationalmuseum Nürnberg und die Evangelisch-Lutherische Kirche in Bayern, *Reformation in Nürnberg: Umbruch und Bewahrung*. Nürnberg: Verlag Medien & Kultur, 1979.

Gier, Helmut and Johannes Janota, eds. *Augsburger Buchdruck und Verlagswesen von den Anfängen bis zur Gegenwart*. Wiesbaden: Harrassowitz Verlag, 1997.

Giesecke, Michael. *Der Buchdruck in der frühen Neuzeit: eine historische Fallstudie über die Durchsetzung neuer Informations-und Kommunikationstechnologien*. Frankfurt am Main: Suhrkamp, 1991.

Gilmont, Jean-François, ed. *The Reformation and the Book*. Trans. Karin Maag. Aldershot: Ashgate Publishing Ltd, 1998.
Gingerich, Owen. 'The Civil Reform of the Gregorian Calendar,' in *Gregorian Reform of the Calendar: Proceedings of the Vatican Conference to Commemorate its 400th Anniversary, 1582–1982*. Vatican City: Pontificia Academia Scientiarum Specola Vaticana, 1983, 265–79.
Ginzburg, Carlo. *The Cheese and the Worms: The Cosmos of a Sixteenth-Century Miller*, trans. John Tedeschi and Anne C. Tedeschi. Baltimore: The Johns Hopkins University Press, 1992.
Göpfert, Herbert G. and Erdmann Weyrauch. *'Unmoralisch an sich…' Zensur im 18. und 19. Jahrhundert*. Wiesbaden: Otto Herrassowitz, 1988.
Göpfert, Herbert G., Peter Vodosek, Erdmann Weyrauch, Reinhard Wittmann. *Beiträge zur Geschichte des Buchwesens im konfessionellen Zeitalter*. Wiesbaden: Otto Harrassowitz, 1985.
Gößner, Andreas. *Weltliche Kirchenhoheit und reichsstädtische Reformation: die Augsburger Ratspolitik des 'milten und mitleren weges,' 1520–1534*. Berlin: Akademie Verlag, 1999.
Goldgar, Ann. 'The Absolutism of the Taste: Journalists as Censors in Eighteenth-Century Paris,' in *Censorship and the Control of Print in England and France, 1600–1910*, eds Robin Myers and Michael Harris. Winchester: St. Paul's Bibliographies, 1992.
Gotthard, Axel. *Der Augsburger Religionsfrieden*. Münster: Aschendorff Verlag, 2004.
Gottlieb, Gunter, Wolfram Baer, Josef Becker, Josef Bellot, Karl Filser, Pankraz Fried, Wolfgang Reinhard and Bernhard Schimmelpfennig, eds. *Geschichte der Stadt Augsburg von der Römerzeit bis zur Gegenwart*. Stuttgart: Konrad Theiss Verlag, 1984.
Gregory, Brad S. *Salvation at Stake: Christian Martyrdom in Early Modern Europe*. Cambridge: Harvard University Press, 1999.
Greiff, Ludwig. *Beiträge zur Geschichte der deutschen Schulen Augsburg*. Augsburg: J.N. Hartmann'schen Buchdruckerei, 1858.
Grell, Ole Peter and Bob Scribner, eds. *Tolerance and Intolerance in the European Reformation*. Cambridge: Cambridge University Press, 1996.
Grendler, Paul F. *The Roman Inquisition and the Venetian Press, 1540–1605*. Princeton: Princeton University Press, 1977.
Grendler, Paul F. *Culture and Censorship in Late Renaissance Italy and France*. London: Variorum Reprints, 1981.
Grendler, Paul F. 'Printing and Censorship,' in *The Cambridge History of Renaissance Philosophy*, eds. Charles B. Schmitt and Quentin Skinner. Cambridge: Cambridge University Press, 1988.

Griffin, Clive. *Journeymen-Printers, Heresy, and the Inquisition in Sixteenth-Century Spain*. Oxford: Oxford University Press, 2005.
Grimm, Harold J. *Lazarus Spengler: A Lay Leader of the Reformation*. Columbus: Ohio State University Press, 1978.
Grimm, Heinrich. 'Die Buchführer des deutschen Kulturbereichs und ihre Niederlassungsorte in der Zeitpanne 1490 bis um 1550,' *Archiv für Geschichte des Buchwesens*. Bd. VII (1967).
Grimm, Jacob and Wilhelm Grimm. *Deutsches Wörterbuch*. Leipzig: Verlag von S. Hirzel, 1935.
Grünsteudel, Günther, Günther Hägele, and Rudolf Frankenberger, eds. *Augsburger Stadtlexikon 2*. Augsburg: Perlach Verlag, 1998.
Guderian, Hans. *Die Täufer in Augsburg: Ihre Geschichte und ihr Erbe*. Pfaffenhofen: W. Ludwig Verlag, 1984.
Habermas, Jürgen. *The Structural Transformation of the Public Sphere: An Inquiry Into a Category of Bourgeois Society*, 1962, trans. Thomas Berger and Frederick Lawrence. Cambridge, Mass.: The MIT Press, 1995.
Hampe, Theodor. *Die fahrenden Leute in der deutschen Vergangenheit*. Jena: Eugen Diedrichs Verlag, 1924.
Hasse, Hans-Peter. 'Bücherzensur an der Universität Wittenberg im 16. Jahrhundert,' in *700 Jahre Wittenberg. Stadt, Universität, Reformation*. Weimar: Hermann Böhlaus Nachfolger, 1995.
Hasse, Hans-Peter. *Zensur theologischer Bücher in Kursachsen im Konfessionellen Zeitalter. Studien zur kursächsischen Literatur-und Religionspolitik in den Jahren 1569 bis 1575*. Leipzig: Evangelische Verlagsanstalt, 2000.
Heckel, Martin. 'Autonomia und Pacis Compositio: Der Augsburger Religionsfriede in der Deutung der Gegenreformation,' in *Zeitschrift der Savigny-Stiftung für Rechtsgeschichte*, Kanonistische Abteilung 76 (1959): 141–248.
Heckel, Martin. *Deutschland im konfessionellen Zeitalter*. Göttingen: Vandenhoeck & Ruprecht, 1983.
Heckel, Martin. 'Die Religionsprozesse der Reichskammergerichts im konfessionell gespaltenen Reichskirchenrecht,' in *Zeitschrift der Savigny-Stiftung für Rechtsgeschichte*, Kanonistische Abteilung 77 (1991): 283–350.
Heinritz, Reinhard. 'Politisches Musengespräch. Hans Sachs und die "Zensur" in der Reichsstadt Nürnberg,' *Archiv für Kulturgeschichte* 85 (2003): 493–507.
Heintzel, Alexander. *Propaganda im Zeitalter der Reformation: Persuasive Kommunikation im 16. Jahrhundert*. St. Augustin: Gardez Verlag, 1998.

Hemels, Joan. 'Pressezensur in Reformationszeitalter (1475–1648),' in *Deutsche Kommunikations-kontrolle des 15. bis. 20. Jahrhunderts*, ed. Heinz-Dietrich Fischer. Munich: K.G. Saur, 1982.
Hilgers, Joseph. *Der Index der Verbotenen Bücher*. Freiburg im Breisgau: Herdersche Verlagshandlung, 1904.
Hoffman, Carl A. 'Konfessionell motivierte und gewandelte Konflikte in der zweiten Hälfte des 16. Jahrhunderts – Versuch eines mentalitätsgeschichtlichen Ansatzes am Beispiel der bikonfessionellen Reichsstadt Augsburg,' in *Konfessionalisierung und Region*, eds Peer Frieß and Rolf Kießling. Konstanz: Universitätsverlag Konstanz GmbH, 1999.
Hoffman, Carl A. 'Strukturen und Quellen des Augsburger reichsstädtischen Strafgerichtswesens in der ersten Hälfte des 16. Jahrhunderts,' *Zeitschrift des Historischen Vereins für Schwaben*. 88 (1995): 57–108.
Hoffmann, Manfred, ed. *Toleranz und Reformation*. Gütersloh: Gütersloher Verlagshaus Gerd Mohn, 1979.
Holenstein, P. N. S. 'Geshwätzgeschichte(n): Ein kulturhistorisches Pläydoyer für die Rehabilitierung der unkontrollierten Rede,' in *Dynamik der Tradition*, ed. Richard van Dülmen. Frankfurt am Main: Fischer Taschenbuch Verlag (1992): 41–108.
Hopp, E. 'Zur Geschichte des Liedes "Erhalt uns Herr bei deinem Wort",' *Beiträge zur bayerischen Kirchengeschichte* 7 (1901): 79–87.
Horodowich, Elizabeth. *Language and Statecraft in Early Modern Venice*. Cambridge: Cambridge University Press, 2008.
Hoskin, Michael. 'The Reception of the Calendar by Other Churches,' in G. V. Coyne, Michael A Hoskin, and O. Pedersen, eds, *Gregorian Reform of the Calendar: Proceedings of the Vatican Conference to Commemorate its 400th Anniversary, 1582–1982*. Vatican City: Pontificia Academia Scientiarum Specola Vaticana, 1983, 255–65.
Houston, R.A. *Literacy in Early Modern Europe: Culture and Education, 1500–1800*. Harlow: Pearson Education Limited, 2002.
Hsia, R. Po-Chia. 'The Myth of the Commune: Recent Historiography on City and Reformation in Germany,' *Central European History*, 20 (3–4) (1987): 203–15.
Hsia, R. Po-Chia. *Social Discipline in the Reformation: Central Europe, 1550–1750*. London: Routledge, 1989.
Immenkötter, Herbert. 'Die katholische Kirche in Augsburg in der ersten Hälfte des 16. Jahrhunderts,' in *Die Augsburger Kirchenordnung von 1537 und ihr Umfeld*, ed. Reinhard Schwarz. Gütersloh: Gütersloher Verlagshaus-Gerd Mohn, 1988.
Iser, Wolfgang. 'Interaction Between Text and Reader,' in Susan K. Suleiman and Inge Crossman, eds, *The Reader in the Text: Essays on Audience and Interpretation*. Princeton, NJ: Princeton University Press, 1980.

Jegel, August. 'Altnürnberger Zensur vor allem des 16. Jahrhunderts,' in *Festschrift für Eugen Stollreither*, ed. Fritz Redenbacher. Erlangen: Universitätsbibliothek, 1950.

Jesse, Horst. *Die Geschichte der Evangelischen Kirche in Augsburg*. Pfaffenhofen: W. Ludwig Verlag, 1983.

Johns, Adrian. *The Nature of the Book: Print and Knowledge in the Making*. Chicago: University of Chicago Press, 1998.

Kalkoff, Paul. *Das Wormser Edikt und die Erlasse des Reichsregiments und einzelner Reichsfürsten*. München: R. Oldenbourg, 1917.

Kaltenbrunner, Ferdinand. 'Die Polemik über die Gregorianische Kalender-Reform,' in *Sitzungberichte der philosophisch-historischen Classe der kaiserlichen Akademie der Wissenschaften*. Bd. 87. Wien: In Commission bei Karl Gerold's Sohn, 1877.

Kaltenbrunner, Ferdinand. 'Der Augsburger Kalenderstreit,' in *Mitteilungen der Institut für österreichische Geschichtsforschung*. I (1880).

Kamen, Henry. *Inquisition and Society in Spain in the Sixteenth and Seventeenth Centuries*. London: Weidenfeld & Nicholson, 1985.

Kamen, Henry. *The Spanish Inquisition: A Historical Reassessment*. New Haven: Yale University Press, 1999.

Kaplan, Benjamin J., *Divided By Faith: Religious Conflict and the Practice of Toleration in Early Modern Europe*. Cambridge, MA: Harvard University Press, 2007.

Kapp, Friedrich. *Geschichte des deutschen Buchhandels bis in das siebzehnte Jahrhundert*, in Geschichte des deutschen Buchhandels. Band 1. Leipzig, 1886. Leipzig: Reprogr. Nachdruck, 1970.

Karant-Nunn, Susan C. 'What Was Preached in German Cities in the Early Years of the Reformation? *Wildwuchs* Versus Lutheran Unity,' *The Process of Change in Early Modern Europe: Essays in Honor of Miriam Usher Chrisman*, eds Phillip N. Bebb and Sherrin Marshall. Columbus: Ohio State University Press, 1988.

Kaufmann, Thomas. *Dreißigjähriger Krieg und Westfälischer Friede: Kirchengeschichtliche Studien zur lutherischen Konfessionskultur*. Tübingen: Mohr Siebeck, 1998.

Kaufmann, Thomas. *Das Ende der Reformation. Magdeburgs 'Herrgotts Kanzlei' (1548–1551/2)*. Tübingen: Mohr Siebeck, 2003.

Kießling, Rolf. *Bürgerliche Gesellschaft und Kirche in Augsburg im Spätmittelalter*. Augsburg: Mühlberger, 1971.

Kingdon, Robert M. *Myths About the St. Bartholomew's Day Massacres 1572–1576*. Cambridge, MA: Harvard University Press, 1988.

Kirmeier, Josef, Wolfgang Jahn, and Evamaria Brockhoff, eds. *"...wider Laster und Sünde." Augsburgs Weg in der Reformation*. Augsburg: DuMont, 1997.

Klaassen, Walter, Werner Packull, and John Rempel, eds. *Later Writings by Pilgram Marpeck and his Circle*. Vol. 1. Kitchener, Ontario: Pandora Press, 1999.

Knox, Ellis. L. 'The Lower Orders in Early Modern Augsburg,' *The Process of Change in Early Modern Augsburg: Essays in Honor of Miriam Usher Chrisman*, eds Phillip N. Bebb and Sherrin Marshall. Columbus: Ohio University Press, 1988.

Koch, Rainer, ed. *Brücke zwischen den Völkern – Zur Geschichte der Frankfurter Messe*. Bd. II. Frankfurt am Main: Union Druckerei und Verlag, 1991.

Köhler, Hans-Joachim, ed. *Flugschriften als Massenmedium der Reformationszeit*. Stuttgart: Klett-Cotta, 1981.

Köhler, Hans-Joachim. 'The *Flugschriften* and Their Importance in Religious Debate: A Quantitative Approach,' in '*Astrologi hallucinati*': *Stars and the End of the World in Luther's Time*, ed. Paola Zambelli. Berlin: de Gruyter, 1986.

Köhler, Walter. *Züricher Ehegericht und Genfer Konsistorium. Bd. II: Das Ehe-und Sittengericht in den süddeutschen Reichsstädten, dem Herzogtum Württemberg und in Genf*. Leipzig: Verlag von M. Heinsius Nachfolger, 1942.

Kolb, Robert. 'Mattheaus Judex's Condemnation of Princely Censorship of Theologians' Publications,' in *Luther's Heirs Define His Legacy: Studies on Lutheran Confessionalization*. Aldershot: Variorum, 1996.

Kolde, Theodore. 'Zum Prozeß des Johann Denk und der "drei gottlosen Maler" von Nürnberg,' in *Kirchengeschichtliche Studien* (Leipzig, 1888): 228–50.

Kolde, Theodore. 'Hans Denck und die gottlosen Maler von Nürnberg,' in *Beiträge zur bayerischen Kirchengeschichte* 8 (1902): 1–31.

Kraus, Jürgen. *Das Militärwesen der Reichsstadt Augsburg, 1548–1806*. Augsburg: Verlag Hieronymus Mühlberger, 1980.

Krusenstjern von, Benigna and Hans Medick, eds. *Zwischen Alltag und Katastrophe. Der Dreißigjährige Kriege aus der Nähe*. Göttingen: Vandenhoeck & Ruprecht, 1999.

Künast, Hans-Jörg. 'Augsburg als Knotenpunkt des deutschen und europäischen Buchhandels (1480–1550),' in *Augsburg in der Frühen Neuzeit: Beiträge zu einem Forschungsprogramm*, eds Jochen Brüning and Friedrich Niewöhner. Berlin: Akademie Verlag, 1995.

Künast, Hans-Jörg. '*Getruckt zu Augspurg.*' *Buchdruck und Buchhandel in Augsburg zwischen 1468 und 1555*. Tübingen: Max Niemeyer Verlag, 1997.

Laeven, A. H. 'The Frankfurt and Leipzig Book Fairs and the History of the Dutch Book Trade in the 17th and 16th Centuries,' *Le Magasin de l'univers: the Dutch Republic as the Centre of the European Book Trade*, eds C. Berkvens-Stevelinck, H. Bots, P. G. Hoftijzer, and O. S. Lankhorst. Leiden: E. J. Brill, 1992.

Langbein, John H. *Torture and the Law of Proof: Europe and England in the Ancien Régime*. Chicago: University of Chicago Press, 1977.

Leppin, Volker. *Antichrist und Jüngster Tag: Das Profil apokalyptischer Flugschriftenpublizistik im deutschen Luthertum 1548–1618*. Heidelberg: Gütersloher Verlagshaus, 1999.

Liedl, Eugen. *Gerichtsverfassung und Zivilprozess der Freien Reichsstadt Augsburg*. Augsburg: Hans Rösler Verlag, 1958.

Loetz, Francisca. *Mit Gott handeln. Von den Zürcher Gotteslästerern der Frühen Neuzeit zu einer Kulturgeschichte des Religiösen*. Göttingen: Vandenhoeck & Ruprecht, 2002.

Louthan, Howard. *The Quest for Compromise: Peacemakers in Counter-Reformation Vienna*. Cambridge: Cambridge University Press, 1997.

Louthan, Howard P. and Randall C. Zachman, eds. *Conciliation and Confession: The Struggle for Unity in the Age of Reform, 1415–1648*. Notre Dame, Indiana: University of Notre Dame Press, 2004.

Lutz, Heinrich. *Conrad Peutinger. Beiträge zu einer Politischen Biographie*. Augsburg: Verlag die Brigg, 1958.

Mäkinen, V., ed. *Lutheran Reformation and the Law*. Leiden: Brill, 2006.

Maier, Hans. *Die ältere deutsche Staats- und Verwaltungslehre*. Munich: C. H. Beck'sche Verlagsbuchhandlung, 1980.

Mandrou, Robert. *De la culture populaire aux 17e et 18e siecles: La Bibliotheque bleue de Troyes*. Paris: Stock, 1975.

Matheson. Peter. 'Breaking the Silence: Women, Censorship, and the Reformation,' *Sixteenth Century Journal* 37(1) (1996): 97–109.

Matheson, Peter. *The Rhetoric of the Reformation*. London: T & T Clark International, 1998.

Medick, Hans. 'Orte und Praktiken religiöser Gewalt im Dreißigjährigen Krieg: Konfessionelle Unterschiede und ihre Wahrnehmung im Spiegel von Selbstzeugnissen,' in *Religion und Gewalt: Konflikte, Rituale, Deutungen (1500–1800)*, eds K. von Greyerz and K. Siebenhüner. Göttingen: Vandenhoeck & Ruprecht, (2006): 367–82.

Merry, Sally Engle. 'Rethinking Gossip and Scandal,' in *Toward a General Theory of Social Control*, Vol. 1, ed. Donald Black. New York: Academic Press, 1984.

Meyer, Christian. 'Zur Geschichte der Wiedertäufer in Oberschwaben,' in *Zeitschrift des historischen Vereins für Schwaben und Neuberg* 1 (1874): 207–53.

Midelfort, H. C. Erik. *A History of Madness in Sixteenth-Century Germany*. Stanford, CA: Stanford University Press, 1999.
Moeller, Bernd. *Stadt und Kirche im 16. Jahrhundert*. Gütersloh: Gütersloher Verlagshaus Gerd Mohn, 1978.
Moeller, Bernd. 'Stadt und Buch: Bemerkungen zur Struktur der reformatorischen Bewegung in Deutschland,' in *The Urban Classes, the Nobility, and the Reformation: Studies on the Social History of the Reformation in England and Germany*, ed. Wolfgang J. Mommsen. Stuttgart: Klett-Cotta, 1979.
Moeller, Bernd. 'Imperial Cities and the Reformation,' in *Imperial Cities and the Reformation: Three Essays*, ed. and trans. H. C. Erik Midelfort and Mark U. Edwards, Jr. Durham, N.C.: Labyrinth Press, 1982.
Moore, R. I. *The Formation of a Persecuting Society*. Oxford; Basil Blackwell, 1987.
Moxey, Keith. *Peasants, Warriors, and Wives: Popular Imagery in the Reformation*. Chicago: University of Chicago Press, 1989.
Muckel, Viktor. *Die Entwicklung der Zensur in Köln*. Diss. Jur. Köln. Würzburg: 1932.
Müller, Arnd. 'Zensurpolitik der Reichsstadt Nürnberg,' *Mitteilungen des Vereins für Geschichte der Stadt Nürnberg* 49 (1959): 66–170.
Nauck, Ernst Theodor. 'Dr. Sigmund Grimm, Arzt und Buchdrucker zu Augsburg,' *Zeitschrift des Historischen Vereins für Schwaben*, 59/60 (1969): 311–19.
Naujoks, Eberhard. 'Vorstufen der Parität in der Verfassungsgeschichte der schwäbischen Reichsstädte (1555–1648). Das Beispiel Augsburgs,' in *Burgerschaft und Kirche*, ed. Jürgen Sydow. Sigmaringen: Jan Thorbecke Verlag, 1980.
Nelson, Eric. 'The Jesuit Legend: Superstition and Myth-Making,' in *Religion and Superstition in Reformation Europe*, eds. Helen Parish and William G. Naphy. Manchester: Manchester University Press, 2002.
Neumann, Helmut. *Staatliche Bücherzensur und Aufsicht in Bayern von der Reformation bis zum Ausgang des 17. Jahrhunderts*. Studien und Quellen zur Geschichte des deutschen Verfassungsrechts 9. Heidelberg: G.F. Müller Juristischer Verlag, 1977.
Oelke, Harry. *Die Konfessionsbildung des 16. Jahrhunderts im Spiegel illustrierter Flugblätter*. Berlin: Walter De Gruyter, 1992.
Oestreich, Gerhard. *Geist und Gestalt des frühmodernen Staates: Ausgewählte Aufsätze*. Berlin: Duncker & Humbolt, 1969.
Oestreich, Gerhard. *Strukturprobleme der frühen Neuzeit: Ausgewählte Aufsätze*. Berlin: Duncker & Humbolt, 1980.
Oettinger, Rebecca Wagner. *Music as Propaganda in the German Reformation*. Aldershot: Ashgate, 2001.

Olson, Oliver K. 'Theology of Revolution: Magdeburg 1550–1551' in *Sixteenth Century Journal* 3 (1972), pp. 69–70.
Ong, Walter J. *Orality and Literacy: The Technologizing of the Word.* New York: Routledge; 1982.
Oswald, Julius and Peter Rummel, eds. *Petrus Canisius – Reformer der Kirche. Festschrift zum 400. Todestag des zweiten Apostels Deutschlands.* Augsburg: Sankt Ulrich Verlag, 1996.
Overell, M.A. 'The Exploitation of Francesco Spiera,' in *Sixteenth Century Journal* 26(3) (Autumn 1995): 619–37.
Ozment, Steven. 'Pamphlet Literature of the German Reformation,' *Reformation Europe: A Guide to Research*, ed. Steven Ozment. St. Louis: Center for Reformation Research, 1982.
Paas, Martha White. *Population Change, Labor Supply, and Agriculture in Augsburg.* New York: Arno, 1981.
Packull, Werner O. 'Pilgram Marpeck: *Uncovering the Babylonian Whore* and Other Anonymous Anabaptist Tracts,' *The Mennonite Quarterly Review* 67(3) (1993): 351–5.
Packull, Werner O. Packull. *Mysticism and the Early South German-Austrian Anabaptist Movement 1525-1531.* Scottsdale, PA: Herald Press, 1977; reprint, Eugene, OR: Wipf and Stock Publishers, 2008.
Panzer, Marita A. *Sozialer Protest in Suddeutschen Reichsstadten 1485 bis 1525: Anhand der Fallstudien Regensburg, Augsburg und Frankfurt am Main.* Munich: Kommissionsverlag UNI-Druck, 1982.
Parker, Geoffrey, ed. *The Thirty Years' War*, 2nd edn. London: Routledge, 1997.
Patterson, Annabel. *Censorship and Interpretation: The Conditions of Writing and Reading in Early Modern England.* Madison, WI: University of Wisconsin Press, 1991.
Pettegree, Andrew. 'Books, Pamphlets, and Polemic,' in *The Reformation World*, ed. Andrew Pettegree. London: Routledge, 2000.
Pettegree, Andrew. *Reformation and the Culture of Persuasion.* Cambridge: Cambridge University Press, 2005.
Pfeiffer, Gerhard. 'Der Augsburger Religionsfrieden und die Reichsstädte,' in *Zeitschrift des Historischen Vereins für Schwaben* 61(1955): 214–321.
Pinto Crespo, Virgilio. 'Thought Control in Spain,' in *Inquisition and Society in Early Modern Europe*, ed. Stephen Haliczer. Totowa: Barnes & Noble Books, 1987.
Pinto Crespo, Virgilio, 'Censorship: A System of Control and an Instrument of Action,' in *The Spanish Inquisition and the Inquisitorial Mind*, ed. Angel Alcalá. Boulder: Social Science Monographs, 1987.

Poole, Robert. '"Give Us Our Eleven Days!": Calendar Reform in Eighteenth-Century England,' in *Past and Present* 149 (Nov. 1995): 95–139.

Poole, Robert. *Time's Alteration: Calendar Reform in Early Modern England*. London: UCL Press, 1998.

Preuß, Hans. *Die Vorstellungen vom Antichrist im späteren Mittelalter, bei Luther und in der konfessionellen Polemik*. Leipzig: J.C. Hinrichs, 1906.

Putnam, George Haven. *The Censorship of the Church of Rome and Its Influence Upon the Production and Distribution of Literature: A Study of the History of the Prohibitory & Expurgatory Indexes, Together With Some Consideration of the Effects of Protestant Censorship and of Censorship by the State*. New York: Benjamin Bloom, 1906.

Racaut, Luc. *Hatred in Print: Catholic Propaganda and Protestant Identity During the French Wars of Religion*. Aldershot: Ashgate, 2002.

Radlkofer, Max. 'Die volkstümliche und besonders dichterische Litteratur zum Augsburger Kalenderstreit,' in *Beitrage zur bayerischen Kirchengeschichte* 7 (1901).

Radlkofer, Max. *Die schriftstellerische Tätigkeit der Augsburger Volksschullehrer im Jahrhundert der Reformation*. Augsburg: Verlag der Schwäbischen Schulausstellung, 1903.

Rafetseder, Hermann. *Bücherverbrennungen: die öffentliche Hinrichtung von Schriften im historischen Wandel*. Wien: Böhlau Verlag, 1988.

Raymond, Joad. *The Invention of the Newspaper*. Oxford: Oxford University Press, 1996.

Rein, Nathan. *The Chancery of God: Protestant Print, Polemic and Propaganda against the Empire, Magdeburg 1546–1551*. Aldershot: Ashgate, 2008.

Reinhard, Wolfgang. 'Zwang zur Konfessionalisierung? Prolegomena zu einer Theorie des konfessionellen Zeitalters,' *Zeitschrift für Historische Forschung* 10 (1983): 257–77.

Reinhard, Wolfgang, ed. *Augsburger Eliten des 16. Jahrhunderts: Prosopographie wirtschaftlicher und politischer Führungsgruppen, 1500–1620*. Berlin: Akademie Verlag GmbH, 1996.

Reusch, Franz Heinrich. *Der Index der verbotenen Bücher*. 1883. Aalen: Scientia Verlag, 1967.

Rittgers, Ronald. *The Reformation of the Keys: Confession, Conscience, and Authority in Sixteenth-Century Germany*. Cambridge, MA: Harvard University Press, 2004.

Roeck, Bernd. *Eine Stadt in Krieg und Frieden: Studien zur Geschichte der Reichsstadt Augsburg zwischen Kalenderstreit und Parität*. Göttingen: Vanderhoeck & Ruprecht, 1989.

Rogge, Jörg. *Für den Gemeinen Nutzen: Politisches Handeln und Politikverständnis von Rat und Bürgerschaft in Augsburg im Spätmittelalter*. Tübingen: Max Niemeyer Verlag, 1996.
Roper, Lyndal. *The Holy Household: Women and Morals in Reformation Augsburg*. Oxford: Clarendon Press, 1989.
Roper, Lyndal. 'Tokens of Affection: The Meanings of Love in Sixteenth-Century Germany,' in *Dürer and his Culture*, ed. Dagmar Eichberger and Charles Zika. Cambridge: Cambridge University Press, 1998.
Roth, Friedrich. *Die Einführung der Reformation in Nürnberg 1517-1528*. Würzburg: A Stuber, 1885.
Roth, Friedrich. 'Wer war Haug Marschalck genannt Zoller von Augsburg?' in *Beiträge zur bayerischen Kirchengeschichte* 6 (1900): 229–234.
Roth, Friedrich. 'Zur Geschichte der Wiedertäufer in Oberschwaben, II' in *Zeitschrift des Historischen Vereins für Schwaben und Neuburg* 27 (1900).
Roth, Friedrich. 'Zur Geschichte der Wiedertäufer in Oberschwaben, III' in *Zeitschrift des Historischen Vereins für Schwaben und Neuburg* 28 (1901).
Roth, Friedrich. *Augsburgs Reformationsgeschichte*. Munich: Theodor Ackermann, 1907.
Roth, Friedrich. 'Zur Lebensgeschichte des Augsburger Formschneiders David Danecker u. seines Freundes, des Dicters Martin Schrot; ihr anonym herausgegebenes "Schmachbuch" *Von Erschrocklichen Zustörung unnd Niderlag deß gantzen Bapstumbs*,' in *Archiv für Reformationsgeschichte* 9 (1912): 189–230.
Rublack, Hans-Christoph. 'Martin Luther and the Urban Social Experience,' in *The Sixteenth Century Journal*. 16(1) (1985).
Rublack, Hans-Christoph. 'Augsburger Predigt im Zeitalter der lutherischen Orthodoxie,' in *Die Augsburger Kirchenordnung von 1537 und ihr Umfeld*, ed. Reinhard Schwarz. Gütersloh: Gütersloher Verlagshaus-Gerd Mohn, 1988.
Rublack, Hans-Christoph. 'The Song of Contz Anahans: Communication and Revolt in Nördlingen, 1525,' in *The German People and the Reformation*, ed. R. Po-Chia-Hsia. Ithaca: Cornell University Press, 1988, 102–120.
Ruthmann, Bernhard. *Die Religionsprozesse am Reichskammergericht (1555–1648)*. Köln: Böhlau Verlag, 1996.
Rummel, Peter. 'Kirchliches Leben in der Reichsstadt Augsburg vom ausgehenden Mittelalter bis 1537,' *Historisches Jahrbuch* 108(2) (1988): 359–78.
Russell, Paul A. *Lay Theology in the Reformation: Popular Pamphleteers in Southwest Germany, 1521–1525*. Cambridge: Cambridge University Press, 1986.

Rystad, Göran. *Kriegsnachrichten und Propaganda während des Dreissigjährigen Krieges: Die Schlacht bei Nördlingen in den gelichzeitigen gedruckten Kriegsberichten*. Lund: C W K Gleerup, 1960.

Sachße, Christoph and Florian Tennstedt, eds. *Soziale Sicherheit und soziale Disziplinierung*. Frankfurt am Main, 1986.

Safley, Thomas Max. *Charity and Economy in the Orphanages of Early Modern Augsburg*. Atlantic Highlands, New Jersey: Humanities Press, 1997.

Schelle-Wolff, Carola. *Zwischen Erwartung und Aufruhr: Die Flugschrift „Von der newen wandlung eynes Christlichen lebens" und der Nürnberger Drucker Hans Hergot*. Frankfurt am Main: Peter Lang, 1996.

Schild, W. 'Formen von Disziplinierung und (Straf-)Rechtsverständis,' *Disziplinierung im Alltag des Mittelalters und der Frühen Neuzeit*. Wien: der Österreichischen Akademie der Wissenschaften, 1999, 9–25.

Schiller, Lotte. *Das gegenseitiger Verhältnis der Konfessionen in Augsburg in Zeitalter der Gegenreformation*. Diss. München/Augsburg, 1933.

Schilling, Heinz. *Konfessionskonflikt und Staatsbildung: eine Fallstudie über das Verhältnis von religiösem und sozialem Wandel in der Frühneuzeit am Beispiel der Grafschaft Lippe*. Gütersloh: Gütersloher Verlaghaus Mohn, 1981.

Schilling, Heinz. 'The Reformation and the Rise of the Early Modern State,' in *Luther and the Modern State in Germany*, ed. James D. Tracy. Kirksville, Missouri: The Sixteenth Century Journal Publishers, Inc., 1986.

Schilling, Heinz. 'History of Crime or History of Sin? – Some Reflections on the Social History of Early Modern Church Discipline,' in *Politics and Society in Reformation Europe: Essays for Sir Geoffrey Elton on his Sixty-Fifth Birthday*, ed. E. I. Kouri and Tom Scott. London: Macmillian Press, 1987.

Schilling, Heinz and Heribert Smolinsky, eds. *Der Augsburger Religionsfrieden 1555*. Münster: Aschendorff, 2007.

Schmid, Hans-Dieter. *Täufertum und Obrigkeit in Nürnberg*. Nürnberg: Stadtarchiv Nürnberg, 1972.

Schmidt, Günther. *Libelli Famosi. Zur Bedeutung der Schmähschriften, Scheltbriefe, Schandgemälde und Pasquille in der deutschen Rechtsgeschichte*. Diss., Universität Köln, 1985.

Schmidt, Heinrich Richard. 'Sozialdisziplinierung? Ein Plädoyer für das Ende des Etatismus in der Konfessionalisierungsforschung,' in *Historische Zeitschrift* 265 (1997): 639–82.

Schmidt, Heinrich Richard. *Dorf and Religion. Reformierte Sittenzucht in Berner Landgemeinden der Frühen Neuzeit*. Stuttgart: Fischer, 1995.

Schmidt, Josef. *Lestern, lesen und lesen hören. Kommunikationsstudien zur deutschen Prosasatire der Reformationszeit*. Bern: Peter Lang, 1977.
Schmitt, Elmar and Bernhard Appenzeller, 'Die Ulmer Bücher und Zeitungszensur,' in *Balthasar Kühn. Buchdruckerei und Verlag Kühn, Ulm 1637–1736*. Weißenhorn: Anton H. Konrad Verlag, 1992.
Schnabel, Hildegard. 'Zur historischen Beurteilung der Flugschriftenhändler in der Zeit der frühen Reformation und des Bauernkrieges,' *Wissenschaftliche Zeitschrift der Humboldt-Universität zu Berlin, Gesellschafts-und Sprachwissenschaftliche Reihe* 14 (1965).
Schnell, Fritz. *Zur Geschichte der Augsburger Meistersingerschule*. Augsburg: Verlag Die Brigg, 1958.
Schottenloher, Karl. 'Beschlagnahmte Druckschriften aus der Frühzeit der Reformation,' *Zeitschrift für Bücherfreunde* N.F. 8 (1917): 305–21.
Schottenloher, Karl. 'Der Augsburger Winkeldrucker Hans Gegler. Ein Beitrag zur Schwenckfeld-Bibliographie,' *Gutenberg-Jahrbuch* 14 (1939): 233–42.
Schottenloher, Karl. *Philip Ulhart, ein Augsburger Winkeldrucker und Helfershelfer der Schwärmer und Wiedertäufer, 1523–1529*. Nieuwkoop: B. De Graaf, 1967.
Schottenloher, Karl. 'Silvan Otmar in Augsburg, der Drucker des Schwäbischen Bundes, 1519–1535,' *Gutenberg-Jahrbuch* 15 (1940): 281–96.
Schulze, Winfried. 'Gerhard Oestreich's Begriff Sozialdisciplinierung in der frühen Neuzeit,' *Zeitschrift für historische Forschung* 14 (1987): 265–302.
Schulze, Winfried. 'Concordia, Discordia, Tolerantia. Deutsche Politik im Konfessionellen Zeitalter,' *Neue Studien zur frühneuzeitlichen Reichsgeschichte*, ed. J. Kunisch. Berlin: Duncker & Humblot, 1987: 43–79.
Schulze, Winfried. 'Konfessionalisierung als Paradigma zur Erforschung des konfessionellen Zeitalters,' in *Drei Konfessionen in einer Region. Beiträge zur Geschichte im Herzogtum Berg vom 16. bis zum 18. Jahrhundert*, eds. Burkhard Dietz and Stefan Ehrenpreis. Cologne: Rheinland-Verlag, 1999.
Schuster, Britt-Marie. *Die Verstandlichkeit von frühreformatorischen Flugschriften: Eine Studie zu kommunikationswirksamen Faktoren der Textgestaltung*. Hildesheim: Georg Olms Verlag, 2001.
Schwedt, Hermann H. 'Der römische Index der verbotenen Bücher,' *Historisches Jahrbuchs* 107(2) (1987): 296–314.
Schwerhoff, Gerd. *Zungen wie Schwerter: Blasphemie in alteuropäischen Gesellschaften 1200–1650*. Konstanz: UVK Verlagsgesellschaft, 2005.

Scott, J. C. *Domination and the Arts of Resistance. Hidden Transcripts.* New Haven: Yale University Press, 1990.

Scribner, Bob. 'Is a History of Popular Culture Possible?,' *History of European Ideas* 10(2) (1989): 175–91.

Scribner, Bob. 'Preconditions of Tolerance and Intolerance in Sixteenth-Century Germany,' in *Tolerance and Intolerance in the European Reformation*, eds Ole Peter Grell and Bob Scribner. Cambridge: Cambridge University Press, 1996.

Scribner, R. W., *For the Sake of Simple Folk: Popular Propaganda for the German Reformation.* Cambridge: Cambridge University Press, 1981.

Scribner, R. W. 'Why Was There No Reformation in Cologne?,' in *Popular Culture and Popular Movements in Reformation Germany.* London: Hambledon Press, 1987.

Scribner, R. W. 'Oral Culture and the Transmission of Reformation Ideas,' in *The Transmission of Ideas in the Lutheran Reformation*, ed. Helga Robinson-Hammerstein. Dublin: Irish Academic Press, 1989.

Scribner, Robert W., 'Flugblatt und Analphabetentum. Wie kam der gemeine Mann zu reformatorischen Ideen?,' in *Flugschriften als Massenmedium der Reformationszeit*, ed. Hans-Joachim Köhler. Stuttgart: Klett-Cotta, 1981.

Scribner, Robert W. 'Sozialkontrolle und die Möglichkeit einer städtischen Reformation,' in *Stadt und Kirche im 16. Jahrhundert*, ed. Bernd Moeller. Gütersloh: Gütersloher Verlagshaus Gerd Mohn, 1978.

Scribner, R. W. and C. Scott Dixon, *The German Reformation*, 2nd ed. Basingstoke: Palgrave Macmillan, 2003.

Seebaß, Gottfried. 'The Reformation in Nuremberg,' in *The Social History of the Reformation*, ed. Lawrence P. Buck and Jonathan W. Zophy. Columbus: Ohio State University Press, 1972.

Seebaß, Gottfried. 'The Importance of the Imperial City of Nuremberg in the Reformation,' *Humanism and Reform: The Church in Europe, England, and Scotland, 1400–1643*, ed. James Kirk. Oxford: Blackwell Publishers, 1991.

Seebaß, Gottfried. 'Der Prozeß gegen den Täuferführer Hans Hut in Augsburg 1527,' in *Ketzerverfolgung im 16. und 17. Jahrhundert*, ed. Silvana Seidel Menchi. Wiesbaden: Otto Harrassowitz, 1992.

Seebaß, Gottfried. *Müntzer's Erbe: Werk, Leben und Theologie des Hans Hut.* Güthersloh: Gütersloher Verlagshaus, 2002.

Shagan, Ethan. *Popular Politics and the English Reformation.* Cambridge: Cambridge University Press, 2003.

Shapin, Steven. *A Social History of Truth: Civility and Science in Seventeenth-Century England.* Chicago: The University of Chicago Press, 1994.

Shell, Alison. *Oral Culture and Catholicism in Early Modern England.* Cambridge: Cambridge University Press, 2007.

Shibutani, Tamotsu. *Improvised News: A Sociological Study of Rumor.* Indianapolis: Bobbs-Merrill, 1966.

Shuger, Debora. 'Civility and Censorship in Early Modern England,' in *Censorship and Silencing: Practices of Cultural Regulation*, ed. Robert C. Post. Los Angeles: The Getty Research Institute for the History of Art and the Humanities, 1998.

Shuger, Debora. *Censorship and Cultural Sensibility: The Regulation of Language in Tudor-Stuart England.* Philadelphia: The University of Pennsylvania Press, 2006.

Sieh-Burens, Katarina. *Oligarchie, Konfession und Politik im 16. Jahrhundert: zur sozialen Verflechtung der Augsburger Bürgermeister und Stadtpfleger 1518–1618.* München: Verlag Ernst Vögel, 1986.

Simon, Gerhard. 'Täufer aus Schwaben, Täufer in Schwaben. Eine süddeutsche Region im Schnittpunkt der Täuferbewegung des 16. Jahrhunderts,' *Konfessionalisierung und Region*, ed. Peer Frieß and Rolf Kießling. Konstanz: Universisätsverlag Konstanz, GmbH, 1999.

Sirges, Thomas and Ingeborg Müller. *Zensur in Marburg, 1538–1832: Eine lokalgeschichtliche Studie zum Bücher- und Pressewesen.* Marburger Stadtschriften zur Geschichte und Kultur 12. Marburg: Presseamt der Stadt, 1984.

Smith, Anthony. 'The Long Road to Objectivity and Back Again: The Kinds of Truth We Get in Journalism,' in *Newspaper History: From the Seventeenth Century to the Present Day*, eds George Boyce, James Curren, and Pauline Wingate. London: Constable, 1978.

Soergel, Philip M. *Wonderous in His Saints: Counter-Reformation Propaganda in Bavaria.* Berkeley: University of California Press, 1993.

Sommerville, C. John. *The News Revolution: Cultural Dynamics of Daily Information.* Oxford: Oxford University Press, 1996.

Spalding, Keith, ed. *An Historical Dictionary of German Figurative Usage.* Oxford: Blackwell Publishers, 1991.

Spicker-Beck. *Räuber, Mordbrenner, Umschweifendes Gesind. Zur Kriminalität im 16. Jarhundert.* Freiburg im Breisgau: Rombach GmbH Druck-und Verlagshaus, 1995.

Spierenburg, Pieter. *The Prison Experience: Disciplinary Institutions and their Inmates in Early Modern Europe.* New Brunswick, New Jersey: Rutgers University Press, 1991.

Sporhan-Krempel, Lore. *Nürnberg als Nachrichtenzentrum zwischen 1400 und 1700.* Nürnberg: Vereins für Geschichte der Stadt Nürnberg, 1968.

Steinmetz, David C. *Reformers in the Wings: From Geiler von Kayserberg to Theodore Beza.* 2nd Ed. Oxford: Oxford University Press, 2001.

Steuer, Peter. *Die Außenverflechtung der Augsburger Oligarchie von 1500–1620: Studien zur sozialen Verflechtung der politischen Führungsschicht der Reichsstadt Augsburg*. Augsburg: AV-Verlag, 1988.
Stieve, F. 'Zur Geschichte des Augsburger Kalenderstreites und des Reichstages von 1594,' *Zeitschrift des Historischen Verein für Schwaben und Neuburg* 7 (1880).
Strauss, Gerald. *Nuremberg in the Sixteenth Century: City Politics and Life Between Middle Ages and Modern Times*. Bloomington: Indiana University Press, 1976.
Strauss, Gerald. *Luther's House of Learning: Indoctrination of the Young in the German Reformation*. Baltimore: The Johns Hopkins University Press, 1978.
Stuart, Kathy. *Defiled Trades and Social Outcasts: Honor and Ritual Pollution in Early Modern Germany*. Cambridge: Cambridge University Press, 1999.
Sutter Fichtner, Paula. *Emperor Maximilian II*. New Haven: Yale University Press, 2001.
Tarnói, László. *Verbotene Lieder und Ihre Varienten auf Fliegenden Blättern um 1800*. Budapest: Druckerei der Loránd-Eötvös Universität Budapest, 1983.
Tedeschi, John. *The Prosecution of Heresy: Collected Studies on the Inquisition in Early Modern Italy*. Binghampton: Medieval and Renaissance Texts and Studies, 1991.
Thompson, W. D. J. Cargill. *The Political Thought of Martin Luther*. Brighton, Sussex: Harvester Press, 1984.
Tlusty, B. Ann. *Bacchus and Civic Order: The Culture of Drink in Early Modern Germany*. Charlottesville: University Press of Virginia, 2001.
Tlusty, B. Ann, *The Martial Ethic in Early Modern Germany: Civic Duty and the Right of Arms*. NY: Palgrave Macmillan, 2011.
Tortarolo, E. 'Censorship and the Conception of the Public in Late Eighteenth-Century Germany: Or, are Censorship and Public Opinion Mutually Exclusive?' *Shifting the Boundaries: Transformation of the Languages of Public and Private in the Eighteenth Century*, eds D. Castiglione and L. Sharpe. Exeter: University of Exeter Press, 1995. 131–50.
Tüchle, Hermann. 'Der Augsburger Religionsfriede: Neue Ordnung oder Kampfpause,' *Zeitschrift des Historischen Vereins für Schwaben* 61 (1955).
Tyler, J. Jeffery. *Lord of the Sacred City: The* Episcopus Exclusus *in Late Medieval and Early Modern Germany*. Leiden: Brill, 1999.
Vogler, Günther. *Nürnberg, 1524/25. Studien zur Geschichte der reformatorischen und sozialen Bewegung in der Reichstadt*. Berlin: VEB Deutscher Verlag der Wissenschaften, 1982.

Vogler, Günther, 'Imperial City Nuremberg, 1524–1525: The Reform Movement in Transition,' in *The German People and the Reformation*, ed. R. Po-Chia Hsia. Ithaca: Cornell University Press, 1988.

von Greyerz, Kaspar and K. Siebenhüner, eds. *Religion und Gewalt: Konflikte, Rituale, Deutungen (1500–1800)*. Göttingen: Vandenhoeck & Ruprecht, 2006.

von Greyerz, Kaspar, M. Jakubowski-Tiessen, T. Kaufmann and H. Lehmann, eds. *Interkonfessionalität-Transkonfessionalität-binnenkonfessionelle Pluralität. Neue Forschungen zur Konfessionalisierungsthese*. Gütersloh: Gütersloher Verlagshaus, 2003.

von Stetten, Paul. *Geschichte der Heil. Röm. Reichs Freyen Stadt Augspurg, aus Bewährten Jahr-Büchern und Tüchtigen Urkunden gezogen, und an das Licht gegeben durch Paul von Stetten*. Frankfurt & Leipzig: Merz-und Mayerischen Buchhandlung, 1743.

Walton, Charles, *Policing Public Opinion in the French Revolution: The Culture of Calumny and the Problem of Free Speech*. Oxford: Oxford University Press, 2009.

Ward, Stephen J. A., *The Invention of Journalism Ethics: The Path to Objectivity and Beyond*. Montreal: McGill-Queen's University Press, 2004.

Warmbrunn, Paul. *Zwei Konfessionen in einer Stadt: das Zusammenleben von Katholiken und Protestanten in den paritätischen Reichsstädten Augsburg, Biberach, Ravensburg und Dinklesbühl von 1548 bis 1648*. Weisbaden: F. Steiner, 1983

Watt, Tessa. *Cheap Print and Popular Piety, 1550–1640*. Cambridge: Cambridge University Press, 1991.

Wedgwood, C. V. *The Thirty Years War*. Garden City, New York: Anchor Books, 1961.

Weller, Emil. *Die falschen und fingierten Druckorte*. Hildesheim: G. Olms, 1960.

Weller, Emil. *Lexicon pseudonymorum. Wörterbuch der Pseudonymen aller Zeiten und Völker; oder, Verzeichnis jener Autoren, die sich falschen Namen bedienten*. 1886. Hildesheim: G. Olms, 1963.

Wendland, Henning. 'Martin Luther – seine Buchdrucker und Verleger,' *Beiträge zur Geschichte des Buchwesens im konfessionellen Zeitalter*, ed. Herbert G. Göpfert, Peter Vodosek, Erdmann Weyrauch, and Reinhard Wittmann. Wiesbaden: Otto Harrassowitz, 1985.

Wettges, Wolfram. *Reformation und Propaganda: Studien zur Kommunikation des Aufruhrs in süddeutschen Reichsstädten*. Klett-Cotta: Stuttgart, 1978.

Whitford, David Mark. *Tyranny and Resistance: The Magdeburg Confession and the Lutheran Tradition*. St. Louis: Concordia Publishing House, 2001.

Wiedemann, Hans. *Augsburger Pfarrerbuch. Die evangelischen Geistlichen der Reichsstadt Augsburg, 1524–1806*. Nürnberg: Verein für bayerische Kirchengeschichte, 1962.
Williams, George Huntston. *The Radical Reformation*, 3rd ed. Kirksville, MO: Truman State University Press, 2000.
Wilson, Peter H. 'Still a Monstrosity? Some Reflections on Early Modern German Statehood,' in *The Historical Journal* 49 (2006): 565–76.
Wilson, Peter H. *The Thirty Years' War: Europe's Tragedy*. Cambridge, MA: Harvard University Press, 2009.
Wolfhart, K. 'Caspar Schwenckfeld und Bonifacius Wolfhart in Augsburg,' *Beiträge zur bayerischen Kirchengeschichte*, 7 (1901): 145–61.
Wüst, Wolfgang. 'Censur und Censurkollegien im frühmodernen Konfessionsstaat,' in *Augsburger Buchdruck und Verlagswesen von den Anfängen bis zur Gegenwart*, ed. Helmut Gier and Johannes Janota. Wiesbaden: Harrassowitz Verlag, 1997.
Wüst, Wolfgang. *Censur als Stütze von Staat und Kirche in der Frühmoderne: Augsburg, Bayern, Kurmainz und Württemberg in Vergleich*. Munich: Verlag Ernst Vögel, 1998.
Wüst, Wolfgang. 'Konfession, Kanzel und Kontroverse in einer paritätischen Reichsstadt. Augsburg 1555–1805,' *Zeitschrift des Historischen Vereins für Schwaben*. 91(1998): 115–143.
Wüst, Wolfgang. 'Konfessionalisierung und Censur in oberdeutschen Reichsstädten,' in *Konfessionalisierung und Region*, eds Peer Frieß and Rolf Kießling. Konstanz: Universisätsverlag Konstanz, GmbH, 1999.
Wüst, Wolfgang, ed. *Die gute Policey im Reichskreis*, Bd. 3: *Der Bayerische Reichskreis und die Oberpfalz: Zur frühmodernen Normensetzung in den Kernregionen des Alten Reiches*. Berlin: Akademie Verlag, 2004.
Wüst, Wolfgang, Georg Kreuzer, and Nicola Shümann, eds. *Der Augsburger Religionsfriede 1555. Ein Epochenerignis und seine regionale Verankerung*. Augsburg: Wißner, 2005.
Zaret, David. *Origins of Democratic Culture: Printing, Petitions, and the Public Sphere in Early-Modern England*. Princeton, N.J.: Princeton University Press, 2000.
Zeeden, Ernst Walter. *Konfessionsbildung: Studien zur Reformation, Gegenreformation und katholischen Reform*. Stuttgart: Klett-Cotta, 1985.
Zelinsky Hanson, Michele. *Religious Identity in an Early Reformation Community: Augsburg, 1517 to 1555*. Leiden: Brill, 2009.
Ziggelaar, August. 'The Papal Bull of 1582 Promulgating a Reform of the Calendar,' in G. V. Coyne, Michael A Hoskin, and O. Pedersen, eds, *Gregorian Reform of the Calendar: Proceedings of the Vatican Conference to Commemorate its 400th Anniversary, 1582–1982*. Vatican City: Pontificia Academia Scientiarum Specola Vaticana, 1983.

Zoepfl, Friedrich. *Das Bistum Augsburg und seine Bischöfe im Reformationsjahrhundert*. Bd. II. München: Schnell & Schneider, 1969.

Zorn, Wolfgang. *Augsburg: Geschichte einer deutschen Stadt*. Augsburg: Hieronymus Mühlberger Verlag, 1972.

Zschelletzschky, Herbert. *Die "drei gottlosen Maler" von Nürnberg. Sebald Beham, Barthel Beham und Georg Pencz: Historische Grundlagen und ikonologische Probleme ihrer Graphik zu Reformations- und Bauernkriegszeit*. Leipzig: Seemann, 1975.

Index

adaptation of texts, 8, 72–3, 85–6
Adler, Caspar, 79, 80
Adolphus, Gustavus, King of Sweden, 217, 220
Adrian VI, Pope, 73
Agricola, Johann, 70, 96
Alber, Matthäus, 70
Albrecht V, Duke of Bavaria, 58
Amman, Hans, 174
Anabaptists, 2 n13, 49, 51, 68, 92–5, 96
anonymous prints, 43–4, 73
Antichrist, 115–16, 139, 142
Aperger, Andreas, 218–19
Augsburg, 23, 25, 27, 32, 36, 43–4
    Anabaptist movement in, 94–5, 96
    booksellers in, 40–41, 42, 98–9, 172–8, 212–16
    and boycott of new clergy, 179–83
    Calendar Conflict in, 148–58, 168, 169–70, 172, 174–5, 183
    Capuchins in, 138–44
    censorship in, 1–3, 4, 17, 27, 33, 46, 51, 60–61
        during Calendar Conflict, 148–58, 168, 169–70, 183
        during Interim, 100–107
        in wake of Müller riot, 158–78, 183
        under Peace of Augsburg, 37–40, 115, 120–44, 145–6, 148–63, 198
        under Peace of Westphalia, 221–5
        following prohibition of Lutheranism, 190–216
        during Reformation, 68–75, 87, 97–100, 107–8
        of songs/singing, 29–30, 102–3, 106–7, 132–3, 138–44, 163–74, 190, 194–212
        during "Swedish Time", 216–21
        during Thirty Years' War, 186–7, 190–221
    communal influence in, 78–87
    confessional make-up of, 101, 120, 126, 130, 221
    and Edict of Restitution, 185, 198–201
    and its exiled clergy, 163–9 *passim*, 176–8, 179
    and Interim, 101–7, 120
    Jesuits in, 125–7, 129–31, 132–4, 164, 169, 197, 218
    and Leonberger Accord, 220–21
    Lutheranism outlawed in, 185, 198–216
    and Müller riot and its aftermath, 155–84
    and Peace of Augsburg, 119, 120–44, 145–6, 148–63, 184
    and Peace of Westphalia, 221–5
    protests in, 74, 78–87, 104, 148, 155–63, 183
    reform enacted in, 96–100, 120
    and Regensburg, 195–6
    and "Swedish Time", 216–21
    and Thirty Years' War, 185–7, 190–221
    and Ulm, 163–9, 173–4, 177–8, 179, 180, 196
    and Vocation Conflict, 158–63, 170, 183
Augsburg, Diet of (1530; 1548; 1551; 1555; 1559), 51, 100, 104, 138
Augsburg, Peace of (1555), 52, 53, 57, 110–11, 144–6, 183, 184, 221–5 *passim*
    censorship under, 110–44, 145–6, 148–63, 198, 221

Augsburg Confession, 175
  accepted in Augsburg, 97, 99
  "Altered Augsburg Confession"
    (*Confessio Augustana Variata*),
    116
  Apology for, 116
  and Peace of Augsburg, 109, 111,
    112, 115–17, 120, 182–3
Augsburg Interim (1548), *see* Interim
Austria, 42

Baden, Disputation of (1526), 92
Bader, Leonhart, 101
Bair, Hans, 137
Bamberg, 168
Banishment, 47–9
Baum, Bernhard, 201
Bavaria
  adoption of Gregorian calendar in,
    148
  censorship in, 4, 16, 17, 57, 58–9,
    168
Beham, Barthel, 91
Beham, Sebald, 91
Bentele, Jacob, 141–2, 143–4
bi-confessional cities
  and Calendar Conflict, 148–58
  and Müller riot and its aftermath,
    155–78, 179–83
  and Peace of Augsburg, 119–44,
    145–6, 147–63, 221–5 *passim*
  under Peace of Westphalia, 221–5
  and "Swedish Time", 216–21
  and Thirty Years' War, 185–7,
    190–201
Biberach, 120 n42
Bohemia, 186–7, 190, 192, 197
Bökh, Michael, 211 n117
Book of Concord, 116, 148
book prices, 31–2
booksellers, 35–7, 40–43, 66, 98–9,
    172–8, 212–16, 228–9
Borst, Anna, 171–2
Bosshart, Rudolph, 161–2
Bourdieu, Pierre, 18
Brandenburg, 56
Bucer, Martin, 103

Burtenbach, Johann Georg, 177

Cajetan, Thomas, Cardinal, 64, 68
Calendar Conflict (*Kalenderstreit*),
    117, 147–58, 168, 169–70,
    172, 174–5, 183
Calvinism, 11, 54, 182, 199
Campeggio, Lorenzo, Cardinal, 67
Canisius, Peter, 58, 125–6
Capuchins, 138–44
Catholicism, 9–10, 11–12
  and Calendar Conflict, 148–58,
    183
  during Interim, 100–107
  and Müller riot and its aftermath,
    155–78, 182, 183
  under Peace of Augsburg, 110–19,
    120–46, 147–63, 184
  under Peace of Westphalia, 221–5
  during Reformation, 63–100
    passim, 228
  during "Swedish Time", 216–21
  during Thirty Years' War, 185–7,
    190–221 *passim*
  and Vocation Conflict, 158–63,
    170, 183
Catholic cities/areas
  censorship in, 4, 9–10, 36, 57–61,
    78
censorship
  in cities, 25–7, 61–2, 64, 227–30
  enforcement of, 45–50, 62
  of oral culture, 27–30
  of print, 32–5
  of singing, 28–30
  of ideas, 6, 23, 27
  psychological consequences of, 10
  reasons for, 2–3
Charles V, Emperor, 74, 100, 102,
    104, 107, 114, 116, 120, 126,
    160
Cologne, 25, 32, 119
  censorship in, 33, 57, 60
  and ecclesiastical jurisdiction, 60
  print trade in, 25, 35–6, 57
communal values, influence of, 9, 20,
    78–87, 182

confessionalization, 6, 8–9, 114, 138–9, 229–30
Constitutio Criminalis Carolina, 48 n92, 51
conversion, 130–31
Cramer, Melchior, 136, 211–12
credibility in print, 187–201
Cristell family, 178

Danecker, David, 37–40
Daniel, Maximilian, 129–30
Darnton, Robert, 18
Davis, Natalie Zemon, 36
defamation, 2, 25–6, 51, 110–11, 121, 145, 218–19, 223
Denck, Hans, 91–2, 93, 94
Diesenhofer, Hans, 165–6
Diesenhofer, Leonhart, 165–6
Diez, Hans Christof, 203
Dilbaum, Samuel, 173
Dinklesbühl, 120 n42, 168
Dirr, Michael, 206
Dolmann, Jakob, 65
Donauwörth, 120 n42
Dugo, Johannes, 98, 99
Dürer, Albrecht, 91

Eberhart, Johannes, 140–41, 143–4
Eck, Johann, 58, 69, 92 n167
Eder, Georg, 112–13
Edict of Restitution (1629), 185, 198–201
Edwards, Mark, 8, 72
Eherer, Sixt, 142–3
Ehinger, Elias, 181
Eisele, Peter, 153
Eisenhardt, Ulrich, 16, 53
Eisenkramer, Wolf, 175–6, 180
Eisenstein, Elizabeth, 7
Elchinger, Hans, 98–9, 106–7
enforcement of censorship, 9
    in cities, 26, 28–30, 33–5, 37–50, 62
    and ecclesiastical jurisdiction, 59–61
    punishment, 48–50
    and territorial jurisdiction, 57–9

Enlightenment, 17–19
Erasmus, 85
Erhard, Jacob, 121–4, 131
Exsurge Domine (1520), 67–8, 69

Faust, Johann, 66
Feather, John, 19
Ferdinand II, Archduke of Austria, 42, 67, 154
Ferdinand II, Emperor, 114–18, 186, 187, 198, 217
Fersen, Hans, 128–9
Finck, Lenhart, 66
Fischer, Georg, 74–5, 157
Fischer, Marx, 102–3
France, 18
Frankfurt, 111, 173, 175, 189
    book fair in, 38, 40, 47, 53, 54, 77, 173–4
    censorship in, 34, 47, 53–5
Frankfurt, Diet of (1577), 111
Frankfurt Book Commission, 53–4
Frederick V, Elector Palatine, 54, 186
freedom of expression, 13–15, 17–18, 227
Frenkin, Catharina, 101
Friedrich, Johann, Duke of Württemberg, 114, 117, 118
Frosch, Johann, 79, 80, 96
Fugger, Hans, 159
Fugger, Hans Jacob, 99
Fugger, Jacob, 68, 159
Fugger, Marcus, 138 n115
Fugger, Marx, 137
Fugger, Octavius, 153–4
Fugger, Ottheinrich, 220
Fugger family, 68, 96, 137, 138, 143

Gallmeyer, Hans, 194–6
Geiger, Hans, 179–80
Geslerin, Magdalena, 127
Ginzburg, Carlo, 8
Glaser, Martin, 65
Glatz, Christof, 205–10, 211, 212
Göbel, Johann Conrad, 212–15
Goppolt, Veit, 127
gossip, 27–8, 78–82, 84–7, 179–83

Graf, Georg, 128–9
Great Britain, 19
Gregorian calendar, 147–8 *see also*
    Calendar Conflict
Gregory XIII, Pope, 147, 154
Greiffenberger, Hans, 90, 91
Guldenmund, Hans, 76–7

Habermas, Jürgen, 17–18
Haderdey, Simon, 134–6
Hafner, Melchior, 179
Hain, Balthasar, 202–3
Hainhofer family, 178
Hamburg, 189
Hasse, Hans-Peter, 17
Haßler, Hans, 187
Hätzer, Ludwig, 94
Heigele, Martin, 157
Helblingin, Margaret, 173
Herbst, Jacob, 180
Herbst, Matthaeus, 177, 180
Hergot, Hans, 49, 88, 90
Hermann, Michael, 173, 174
Hertzog, Caspar, 125–6
Herwart, Hans, 159, 177
Hesse, 57–8
Hieber, Leonhart, 2–3
Hilgers, Joseph, 12
Hirschmann, Claus, 80–81
Höltzel, Hieronymus, 89, 90
Holy Roman Empire
    censorship in, 15–17, 24, 61–2
        enforcement of, 56–7, 62
        laws, 50–57, 61–2
        under Peace of Augsburg,
            110–19, 145
        territorial jurisdiction and,
            57–9
    and Gregorian calendar, 147–8,
        149
    literacy in, 31
    and Thirty Years' War, 186–93
Honold, Hans, 160–61
Hörmann, Christof, 178
Hörmann, Johann, 215
Hötsch, Jacob, 132–3
Hüber, Caspar, 122–4, 131

Hüber, Mang, 181
Hundertkass, Sebastian, 29–30
Hunnius, Aegidius, 176–7
Hurter, Regina, 166–7, 168
Hut, Hans, 49, 88–9, 90, 91, 93, 94,
    95
Hypodemander, Peter, 167

iconoclasm, 82–3
ideas, censorship of, 6, 23, 27
Ilsung, Christof, 164
Ilsung, Hans Felix, 218, 219
Imhof, Hieronymus, 178
Imperial Aulic Council (*Reichshofrat*),
    50, 55
Imperial Cameral Court
    (*Reichskammergericht*), 50, 51,
    52, 55, 117, 149, 152, 154
imperial cities, 4–5, 25, 35–6, 46–7,
    50, 64, 100–101, 119–20, 228
Imperial Police Ordinance (1548),
    51–2, 56
Imperial Police Ordinance (1577), 53
Index of Prohibited Books, 9–10, 11,
    12, 58, 59–60
informants, 45–6
institutions, social and legal, influence
    of, 8, 24, 26
Interim, 100–101
    censorship in, 101–7
Italy, 9–10

Jesuits, 12, 54, 55, 58, 164, 169, 190,
    192, 197, 210, 218
    under Peace of Augsburg, 113,
        115, 118, 125–7, 129–31,
        132–4, 150–52, 160, 161
Johns, Adrian, 8, 72

Kant, Immanuel, 17
Kapp, Friedrich, 15
Kappel, Second Peace of (1531), 110
Karg, Joseph, 177
Karg, Michael, 164
Karlstadt, Andreas, 76, 89–90, 91,
    92, 93
Kaufbeuren, 120 n42

Keller, Michael, 87, 96
Kern, Thomas, 195
Kling, Balthasar, 179–80
Knöpflin, Hans, 142–3
Knöringen, Heinrich von, 198
Köhler, Hans-Joachim, 32
Koler, Casper, 137
Kraffter family, 178
Krebs, Caspar, 140–41
Kretz, Mathias, 96
Krug, Anton, 173, 176–7, 179
Künast, Hans-Jörg, 99, 100

Langenmantel, Eitelhans, 44, 94
Lecherer, Christof, 134–6
legal institutions, influence of, 8, 13–14, 24, 26
Leipzig, 36, 49, 71, 103
Leipzig Interim, 103
Leo X, Pope, 67, 69
Leonberger Accord, 220–21
Leutkirch, 120 n42
libels, 56, 114, 165
licenses, 53, 72
literacy, 5–6, 31, 83
Loher, Hans, 180–81
Losch, Jonas, 164–5, 166, 167, 168, 169
Ludwig, Duke of Württemberg, 157
Luther, Martin, 7, 63, 64, 76, 79, 85, 87, 116, 117
    and censorship, 11, 12, 14, 57, 64
    censorship of, 50, 57, 58, 65, 69–73
Lutheran cities/areas
    censorship in, 4, 54–5, 56, 76–8, 87–95, 97–100
Lutheranism, 11
    and Calendar Conflict, 148–58, 183
    during Interim, 100–107
    and Müller riot and its aftermath, 155–83
    under Peace of Augsburg, 110–19, 120–46, 147–63, 182–3, 184
    under Peace of Westphalia, 221–5
    during Reformation, 63–100, 107–8
    during "Swedish Time", 216–21
    during Thirty Years' War, 185–7, 190–221
    and Vocation Conflict, 158–63, 170, 183

Magdeburg, 102, 104
Magdeburg Confession (1550), 102
Mainz, 16, 17
Mair, Gideon, 152–3
Mair, Lucas, 174
Mair, Ludwig, 143
manuscripts, 30–31, 44–5, 144, 164–6, 205–12
Marburg, 57–8
Marschalck, Haug, 85, 86
Martin, Jacob, 181–2
Matthias, Emperor, 186
Maximilian, Elector, 59
Maximilian II, Emperor, 113
Meges, Thomas, 134–6
Mehlführer, Gabriel, 213–15
Meiderlin, Peter, 213
Meistersinger, 28–9, 76, 202
Melanchthon, Philipp, 11, 103, 116
Merzen, Endris, 178
Meyer, Hans (Gallmeyer), 194–6
Moeller, Bernd, 4, 64
Morhart, Johann Gottlieb, 212–13
Moritz, Elector, 56, 104
Mülhausen, 87–8
Müller, Georg, 155–7, 158–78 *passim*, 180
Müller, Ingeborg, 16
Müller, Sigmund, 174
Müller, Ulrich, 166
Müller riot and its aftermath, 155–78, 179–83
Munich, 59
Müntzer, Thomas, 76, 87–90, 91, 94
Musculus, Wolfgang, 98
Mylius, Georg, 155 n33

Nachtigall, Hans, 96
Nantes, Edict of (1598), 110
Nass, Georg, 82–3
Nausea, Friedrich, 58

Neumann, Helmut, 16, 58
news reporting, 187–201
news-sheets (*Zeitungen*), 188–94
Nicolai, Philipp, 54
Nideraur, Hans, 42
Nieschel, Christoph, 137–8
Nördlingen, 218, 220
Nuremberg, 25, 27, 32, 100, 119, 173, 174
   Anabaptist movement in, 92–4
   booksellers in, 43, 66
   censorship in, 4, 33, 44, 46, 49, 51
      under Peace of Augsburg, 115, 117
      during Reformation, 64–8, 75–8, 87–95, 107–8
      of singing, 8–9
   reform enacted in, 75–6
Nuremberg, Diet of (1524), 51, 65
Nussfelder, Bartolome, 83–5

Obermeyer, Christof, 206
Oecolampadius, Johann, 70, 92
Oleus, Michael Ulrich, 218–19
oral culture
   censorship of, 27–30
   transmission to/from print, 5, 27, 32, 78–87, 108, 201, 229
Osiander, Andreas, 65, 76–8, 87
Österreicher, Jeremias, 214–16
Othmar, Silvan, 70–73

Pantier, Daniel, 201–2
Passau, Peace of, 53
Peasants' War, 87–8, 94
Pencz, Georg, 91
Peter, Christof, 137–8
Pettegree, Andrew, 7, 32
Peutinger, Conrad, 68, 75, 209
Pfeiffer, Heinrich, 87–8
Pfundt, Ulrich, 203
Philip of Hesse, 57
Pilsen, siege of, 190, 192–3
placards, 46, 134–6, 149–50, 153, 165–6
Platner, Hans, 91

policing, 43, 45–50, 53, 59, 199, 228–9
popular values, influence of, 9, 78–87
Prague, Second Defenestration of (1618), 186–7
preaching, 63, 65, 74–5, 78–81, 83–7, 97–8, 120–21, 158
Priess, Sabine, 171–2
Princes' War, 106
print
   censorship of, 32–5
   impact on the Reformation, 4–9, 24
   transmission to/from oral culture, 5, 27, 32, 78–87, 108, 201, 229
print trade, 35–7, 105–7, 228–9
   regulation of, 34–5, 37–40, 43–5, 73, 103, 193–4, 205
privacy, 27–8
privileges, 54, 55, 56, 58, 113
Protestant cities/areas
   censorship in, 4, 10–12, 16–17, 50, 56, 57, 58, 61, 64, 87–95, 97–100
Protestantism, 10–12, 64
   and Calendar Conflict, 148–58, 183
   during Interim, 100–107
   and Müller riot and its aftermath, 155–83
   under Peace of Augsburg, 110–19, 120–46, 147–63, 182–3, 184
   under Peace of Westphalia, 221–5
   during Reformation, 63–100, 107–8, 228
   during "Swedish Time", 216–21
   during Thirty Years' War, 185–7, 190–221
   and Vocation Conflict, 158–63, 170, 183
psychological consequences of censorship, 10
punishment, 48–50
Purtenbach, Leonhart, 98
Pusch, Sebolten, 66
Putnam, George Haven, 11–12

Ramminger, Narciss, 102–3
Ravensburg, 120 n42
reading, 7, 8, 10, 31, 32, 72–3, 82–3, 203–5
Reformation, 63–100, 107–8, 227–30
    impact of print on, 4–9, 24
Reformed Church, *see* Calvinism
Regensburg, 44, 195–6
Rehlinger, Anton Christoph, 155
Rehlinger, Bernhard, 205
Rehlinger, Mattheus, 178
Reinhardt, Martin, 89
religious coexistence, 109–10, 119–46
Rem, Wilhelm, 68–9, 70, 74
Rembold, Philip Jacob, 128–9
reprinting, 8, 43, 70–73, 103
Reuchlin, Johannes, 50
Reusch, Franz Heinrich, 11
Rhegius, Urban, 70, 87, 92 n165, 96
Richsner, Utz, 85–6
Rimmele, Johann, 212–13
Rimmele, Johann (Jr), 213
riots, 84, 137, 155–7, 160–62
Rogel, Hans, 102
Roman Congregation of the Index, 11
Rudolf II, Emperor, 149, 158
rumor, 27–8, 78–82, 84, 86–7, 108, 126–9, 139–44, 150–54, 161–3, 197–201

Sachs, Hans, 76–8
Sangel, Michael, 142–3
Saxony, 17, 56, 57
Schädlin, Abraham, 171 n99
Schedle, Abraham, 165, 169–71, 174
Schick, Gregory, 179
Schilling, Johannes, 79–80, 84–5
Schilling, Sixt, 1, 3
Schleupner, Dominicus, 65, 88
Schloher, Georg, 168–9
Schmalkald Articles, 116
Schmalkaldic League, 97, 99, 100
Schmalkaldic War, 103, 120, 126, 220
Schmalzer, Hans, 203–5
Schneider, Anthony, 173
Schrot, Martin, 173
Schueler, Thomas, 203

Schuerl, Christoph, 67
Schuester, Hans, 142
Schultes, Hans, 140, 141, 173, 174–5
Schumann, Peter, 167–8
Schwemmer, Hans, 153–4
Schwenckfeld, Caspar, 1–3, 182
Scott, James, 28
Scribner, Robert, 31, 36
self-censorship, 10, 19, 26, 62, 71–2, 228–9
Sender, Clemens, 79, 83
Shugar, Debora, 110
Sirges, Thomas, 16
Sixtus IV, Pope, 46
smuggling, 41, 43, 175–6, 212–16
social control, 179–83
social disciplining, 6–7, 8–9, 229–30
social institutions, influence of, 8, 13–14, 24, 26
songs/singing, 28–30, 102–3, 106–7, 132–3, 138–44, 163–74, 190, 194–212
Spain, 9–10
Spanish Inquisition, 9–10
Speiser, Johann, 79
Spengler, Lazarus, 67–8, 93
Speyer, 51, 52–3, 65, 111
Speyer, Diet of (1529; 1570), 51, 52, 111
Spiritualists, 68, 91
St Bartholomew's Day Massacre (1572), 154
Stadion, Christoph von, Bishop, 69
Stengel, Endress, 66
Stenglin, Antony, 214–16
Stenglin, Lucas, 153–4
Stenglin, Mattheus, 178
Stier, Aaron, 165
Strasbourg, 25, 32, 177, 189
    censorship in, 34, 115
    and ecclesiastical jurisdiction, 60
Stuttgart, 115
Suarez, Francisco, 55

Thirty Years' War, 118, 145, 160, 184
    effect of, 186–220
    end of, 220–21
    outbreak of, 186–7

Thum, Friedrich, 104–5
Thumm, Theodor, 114–18
torture, 48
Tradel, Georg, 155
Trier, 168

Ulhart, Johann Anthony, 168 n88
Ulhart, Philip, 1, 3
Ulm, 120 n42
   and Augsburg, 163–9, 173–4,
     177–8, 179, 180
   censorship in, 115, 117, 163–4,
     168
   and Interim, 100
Ulmer, Nicodemus, 54–5
Unsinn, Bernhart, 1–3

violence, 26, 45, 136–7, 153
Vocation Conflict, 158–63, 170, 183
Vogel, Wolfgang, 49, 93–4
Voit von Berg, Hans, 199

Waldburg, Otto Truchseß von, 125
Weißenhorn, Alexander, 98, 99
Weiss, Hans, 124–5
Weiss, Matthaus, 202–3
Weiss family, 178
Weissier, Augustin, 153
Welser, Anton Felix, 159
Welser, Matthäus, 130 n75

Welser family, 130 n75, 143
Westermair, Hans, 98
Westphalia, Peace of (1648), 53, 160,
   184, 221–5
Wiblingen, Marx von, 90
Wickhaus, Hans, 202
Widenmann, Hans, 177
Widenmann, Christof, 152–3
Wild, Johann, 58
Wilhelm, Count of Öttingen, 158
Wilhelm, Duke of Bavaria, 158
Willer, Georg, 40–41, 42, 177
Windbusch, Hans, 136, 211
Wisperger, Erasmus, 90
Wöhrle, Josia, 173–4
Wolfenbüttel, 189
Worms, Diet of (1521; 1535), 51, 69
Worms, Edict of, 50–51, 52, 65, 70,
   71
Wunderer, Tobias, 141
Württemberg, 17, 114–18
Würzburg, 168
Wüst, Wolfgang, 17

Zeehen von Deibach, Hans Wolf,
   218–19
Zimmermann, Ludwig, 132–3, 137
Zobin, Berhard, 177
Zollinger, Barbara, 173
Zwingli, Ulrich, 68, 79, 85, 87, 92, 93

St Andrews Studies in Reformation History

Editorial Board: Bruce Gordon, Yale Divinity School, USA,
Andrew Pettegree, Bridget Heal and Roger Mason,
St Andrews Reformation Studies Institute,
Amy Nelson Burnett, University of Nebraska at Lincoln,
Euan Cameron, Union Theological Seminary, New York,
Kaspar von Greyerz, University of Basel and
Alec Ryrie, Durham University

The Shaping of a Community: The Rise and Reformation of the English Parish c. 1400–1560
Beat Kümin

Seminary or University? The Genevan Academy and Reformed Higher Education, 1560–1620
Karin Maag

Marian Protestantism: Six Studies
Andrew Pettegree

Protestant History and Identity in Sixteenth-Century Europe
(2 volumes) edited by Bruce Gordon

Antifraternalism and Anticlericalism in the German Reformation: Johann Eberlin von Günzburg and the Campaign against the Friars
Geoffrey Dipple

Reformations Old and New: Essays on the Socio-Economic Impact of Religious Change c. 1470–1630
edited by Beat Kümin

Piety and the People: Religious Printing in French, 1511–1551
Francis M. Higman

The Reformation in Eastern and Central Europe
edited by Karin Maag

John Foxe and the English Reformation
edited by David Loades

The Reformation and the Book
Jean-François Gilmont, edited and translated by Karin Maag

The Magnificent Ride: The First Reformation in Hussite Bohemia
Thomas A. Fudge

Kepler's Tübingen: Stimulus to a Theological Mathematics
Charlotte Methuen

'Practical Divinity': The Works and Life of Revd Richard Greenham
Kenneth L. Parker and Eric J. Carlson

Belief and Practice in Reformation England: A Tribute to Patrick Collinson by his Students
edited by Susan Wabuda and Caroline Litzenberger

Frontiers of the Reformation: Dissidence and Orthodoxy in Sixteenth-Century Europe
Auke Jelsma

The Jacobean Kirk, 1567–1625: Sovereignty, Polity and Liturgy
Alan R. MacDonald

John Knox and the British Reformations
edited by Roger A. Mason

The Education of a Christian Society: Humanism and the Reformation in Britain and the Netherlands
edited by N. Scott Amos, Andrew Pettegree and Henk van Nierop

Tudor Histories of the English Reformations, 1530–83
Thomas Betteridge

Poor Relief and Protestantism: The Evolution of Social Welfare in Sixteenth-Century Emden
Timothy G. Fehler

Radical Reformation Studies: Essays presented to James M. Stayer
edited by Werner O. Packull and Geoffrey L. Dipple

Clerical Marriage and the English Reformation: Precedent Policy and Practice
Helen L. Parish

Penitence in the Age of Reformations
edited by Katharine Jackson Lualdi and Anne T. Thayer

The Faith and Fortunes of France's Huguenots, 1600–85
Philip Benedict

Christianity and Community in the West: Essays for John Bossy
edited by Simon Ditchfield

Reformation, Politics and Polemics: The Growth of Protestantism in East Anglian Market Towns, 1500–1610
John Craig

The Sixteenth-Century French Religious Book
edited by Andrew Pettegree, Paul Nelles and Philip Conner

Music as Propaganda in the German Reformation
Rebecca Wagner Oettinger

John Foxe and his World
edited by Christopher Highley and John N. King

Confessional Identity in East-Central Europe
edited by Maria Crăciun, Ovidiu Ghitta and Graeme Murdock

*The Bible in the Renaissance:
Essays on Biblical Commentary and Translation
in the Fifteenth and Sixteenth Centuries*
edited by Richard Griffiths

*Obedient Heretics: Mennonite Identities in Lutheran Hamburg
and Altona during the Confessional Age*
Michael D. Driedger

*The Construction of Martyrdom in the
English Catholic Community, 1535–1603*
Anne Dillon

Baptism and Spiritual Kinship in Early Modern England
Will Coster

Usury, Interest and the Reformation
Eric Kerridge

*The Correspondence of Reginald Pole:
1. A Calendar, 1518–1546: Beginnings to Legate of Viterbo*
Thomas F. Mayer

Self-Defence and Religious Strife in Early Modern Europe:
England and Germany, 1530–1680
Robert von Friedeburg

Hatred in Print: Catholic Propaganda and Protestant Identity
during the French Wars of Religion
Luc Racaut

Penitence, Preaching and the Coming of the Reformation
Anne T. Thayer

Huguenot Heartland:
Montauban and Southern French Calvinism
during the French Wars of Religion
Philip Conner

Charity and Lay Piety in Reformation London, 1500–1620
Claire S. Schen

The British Union: A Critical Edition and Translation of
David Hume of Godscroft's De Unione Insulae Britannicae
edited by Paul J. McGinnis and Arthur H. Williamson

Reforming the Scottish Church:
John Winram (c. 1492–1582) and the Example of Fife
Linda J. Dunbar

Cultures of Communication from Reformation to Enlightenment:
Constructing Publics in the Early Modern German Lands
James Van Horn Melton

Sebastian Castellio, 1515-1563:
Humanist and Defender of Religious Toleration in a Confessional Age
Hans R. Guggisberg, translated and edited by Bruce Gordon

The Front-Runner of the Catholic Reformation:
The Life and Works of Johann von Staupitz
Franz Posset

The Correspondence of Reginald Pole:
Volume 2. A Calendar, 1547–1554: A Power in Rome
Thomas F. Mayer

William of Orange and the Revolt of the Netherlands, 1572–1584
K.W. Swart, translated by J.C. Grayson

The Italian Reformers and the Zurich Church, c.1540–1620
Mark Taplin

William Cecil and Episcopacy, 1559–1577
Brett Usher

A Dialogue on the Law of Kingship among the Scots
A Critical Edition and Translation of George Buchanan's
De Jure Regni Apud Scotos Dialogus
Roger A. Mason and Martin S. Smith

Music and Religious Identity in Counter-Reformation Augsburg,
1580–1630
Alexander J. Fisher

The Correspondence of Reginald Pole
Volume 3. A Calendar, 1555–1558: Restoring the English Church
Thomas F. Mayer

Women, Sex and Marriage in Early Modern Venice
Daniela Hacke

Infant Baptism in Reformation Geneva
The Shaping of a Community, 1536–1564
Karen E. Spierling

Moderate Voices in the European Reformation
edited by Luc Racaut and Alec Ryrie

Piety and Family in Early Modern Europe
Essays in Honour of Steven Ozment
edited by Marc R. Forster and Benjamin J. Kaplan

Religious Identities in Henry VIII's England
Peter Marshall

Adaptations of Calvinism in Reformation Europe
Essays in Honour of Brian G. Armstrong
edited by Mack P. Holt

John Jewel and the English National Church
The Dilemmas of an Erastian Reformer
Gary W. Jenkins

Catholic Activism in South-West France, 1540–1570
Kevin Gould

Idols in the Age of Art
Objects, Devotions and the Early Modern World
edited by Michael W. Cole and Rebecca E. Zorach

Local Politics in the French Wars of Religion
The Towns of Champagne, the Duc de Guise, and the Catholic League,
1560–95
Mark W. Konnert

Enforcing Reformation in Ireland and Scotland, 1550–1700
edited by Elizabethanne Boran and Crawford Gribben

Philip Melanchthon and the English Reformation
John Schofield

Reforming the Art of Dying
The ars moriendi *in the German Reformation (1519–1528)*
Austra Reinis

Restoring Christ's Church
John a Lasco and the Forma ac ratio
Michael S. Springer

Catholic Belief and Survival in Late Sixteenth-Century Vienna
The Case of Georg Eder (1523–87)
Elaine Fulton

From Judaism to Calvinism
The Life and Writings of Immanuel Tremellius (c.1510–1580)
Kenneth Austin

The Cosmographia *of Sebastian Münster*
Describing the World in the Reformation
Matthew McLean

Defending Royal Supremacy and Discerning God's Will in Tudor
England
Daniel Eppley

Adaptations of Calvinism in Reformation Europe
Essays in Honour of Brian G. Armstrong
Edited by Mack P. Holt

The Monarchical Republic of Early Modern England
Essays in Response to Patrick Collinson
Edited by John F. McDiarmid

Johann Sleidan and the Protestant Vision of History
Alexandra Kess

The Correspondence of Reginald Pole
Volume 4 A Biographical Companion: The British Isles
Thomas F. Mayer and Courtney B. Walters

Irena Backus
Life Writing in Reformation Europe
Irena Backus

Patents, Pictures and Patronage
John Day and the Tudor Book Trade
Elizabeth Evenden

The Chancery of God
Protestant Print, Polemic and Propaganda against the Empire,
Magdeburg 1546–1551
Nathan Rein

The Impact of the European Reformation
Princes, Clergy and People
Edited by Bridget Heal and Ole Peter Grell

Patents, Pictures and Patronage
John Day and the Tudor Book Trade
Elizabeth Evenden

The Reformation in Rhyme
Sternhold, Hopkins and the English Metrical Psalter, 1547–1603
Beth Quitslund

Defining Community in Early Modern Europe
Edited by Michael J. Halvorson and Karen E. Spierling

Humanism and the Reform of Sacred Music in Early Modern England
John Merbecke the Orator and The Booke of Common Praier Noted
(1550)
Hyun-Ah Kim

The Idol in the Age of Art
Objects, Devotions and the Early Modern World
Edited by Michael W. Cole and Rebecca Zorach

Literature and the Scottish Reformation
Edited by Crawford Gribben and David George Mullan

Protestantism, Poetry and Protest
The Vernacular Writings of Antoine de Chandieu (c. 1534–1591)
S.K. Barker

Humanism and Protestantism in Early Modern English Education
Ian Green

Living with Religious Diversity in Early-Modern Europe
Edited by C. Scott Dixon, Dagmar Freist and Mark Greengrass

The Curse of Ham in the Early Modern Era
The Bible and the Justifications for Slavery
David M. Whitford

Dealings with God
From Blasphemers in Early Modern Zurich to a Cultural History of Religiousness
Francisca Loetz

Magistrates, Madonnas and Miracles
The Counter Reformation in the Upper Palatinate
Trevor Johnson

Narratives of the Religious Self in Early-Modern Scotland
David George Mullan

Church Music and Protestantism in Post-Reformation England
Discourses, Sites and Identities
Jonathan Willis

Reforming the Scottish Parish
The Reformation in Fife, 1560–1640
John McCallum

Commonwealth and the English Reformation
Protestantism and the Politics of Religious Change
in the Gloucester Vale, 1483–1560
Ben Lowe

Heinrich Heshusius and the Polemics of Early Lutheran Orthodoxy
Confessional Conflict and Jewish-Christian Relations in
North Germany, 1556–1597
Michael J. Halvorson

Humanism and Calvinism
Andrew Melville and the Universities of Scotland, 1560–1625
Steven J. Reid

The Senses and the English Reformation
Matthew Milner

Early French Reform
The Theology and Spirituality of Guillaume Farel
Jason Zuidema and Theodore Van Raalte

Catholic and Protestant Translations of the Imitatio Christi, *1425–1650*
From Late Medieval Classic to Early Modern Bestseller
Maximilian von Habsburg

Getting Along?
Religious Identities and Confessional Relations in Early Modern England
– Essays in Honour of Professor W.J. Sheils
Edited by Nadine Lewycky and Adam Morton

From Priest's Whore to Pastor's Wife
Clerical Marriage and the Process of Reform
in the Early German Reformation
Marjorie Elizabeth Plummer

George Buchanan
Political Thought in Early Modern Britain and Europe
Edited by Caroline Erskine and Roger A. Mason